Christian Petzold: Interviews

Conversations with Filmmakers Series
Gerald Peary, General Editor

CHRISTIAN PETZOLD
INTERVIEWS

Edited by Marco Abel, Aylin Bademsoy,
and Jaimey Fisher

University Press of Mississippi / Jackson

The University Press of Mississippi is the scholarly publishing agency of the Mississippi Institutions of Higher Learning: Alcorn State University, Delta State University, Jackson State University, Mississippi State University, Mississippi University for Women, Mississippi Valley State University, University of Mississippi, and University of Southern Mississippi.

www.upress.state.ms.us

The University Press of Mississippi is a member of the Association of University Presses.

Any discriminatory or derogatory language or hate speech regarding race, ethnicity, religion, sex, gender, class, national origin, age, or disability that has been retained or appears in elided form is in no way an endorsement of the use of such language outside a scholarly context.

Copyright © 2023 by University Press of Mississippi
All rights reserved
Manufactured in the United States of America

First printing 2023
∞

Library of Congress Cataloging-in-Publication Data

Names: Abel, Marco, editor. | Bademsoy, Aylin, editor. | Fisher, Jaimey, editor.
Title: Christian Petzold : interviews / Marco Abel, Aylin Bademsoy, Jaimey Fisher.
Other titles: Conversations with filmmakers series.
Description: Jackson : University Press of Mississippi, 2023. | Series: Conversations with filmmakers series | Includes bibliographical references and index.
Identifiers: LCCN 2023002340 (print) | LCCN 2023002341 (ebook) | ISBN 9781496846105 (hardback) | ISBN 9781496846112 (trade paperback) | ISBN 9781496846129 (epub) | ISBN 9781496846136 (epub) | ISBN 9781496846143 (pdf) | ISBN 9781496846150 (pdf)
Subjects: LCSH: Petzold, Christian, 1960—Interviews. | Petzold, Christian, 1960—Criticism and interpretation. | Motion picture producers and directors—Germany—Interviews. | Motion pictures—Germany—History and criticism.
Classification: LCC PN1998.3.P467 A5 2023 (print) | LCC PN1998.3.P467 (ebook) | DDC 791.4302/33092—dc23/eng/20230331
LC record available at https://lccn.loc.gov/2023002340
LC ebook record available at https://lccn.loc.gov/2023002341

British Library Cataloging-in-Publication Data available

Contents

Introduction   ix

Chronology   xvii

Filmography   xxi

Three to Two a Potential Hit: A Conversation with Christian Petzold   3
    Stefan Ertl and Rainer Knepperges / 1995

In the Hinterland of Nihilism   11
    Ulrich Kriest / 2001

The *Flying Dutchman*: An Interview with Christian Petzold   20
    Jörg-Uwe Albig and Christoph Gurk / 2001

How the Politburo Made the Circumstances in German Film Dance   27
    Michael Althen and Bert Rebhandl / 2002

The Music Has to Sell Itself   34
    Christian Buss / 2002

Dead Man, What Now? A Frontrunner for the Television Prize—
Christian Petzold between Andersen and *Vertigo*   37
    Rainer Gansera / 2002

"This Typical FRG-Generation"   40
    Claudia Lenssen / 2003

The Cinema as an Experimental Setup: A Workshop Conversation
with Director Christian Petzold   42
    Stefan Reinecke / 2003

Interview: Christian Petzold   46
　　Nicolas Wackerbarth and Christoph Hochhäusler / 2003

"A Novel No Longer Holds Us Together Today"   54
　　Rüdiger Suchsland / 2004

To Listen with Closed Eyes   61
　　Cristina Nord / 2005

Stories of Ghosts   64
　　Tim Stüttgen / 2005

Carnival of Souls: Plot or World—A Conversation with Christian Petzold   70
　　Susan Vahabzadeh and Fritz Göttler / 2005

"The Cinema of Identification Gets on My Nerves": An Interview with Christian Petzold   73
　　Marco Abel / 2006/2007

Emigrating from Brandenburg   93
　　Ralf Schenk / 2007

"You Don't Want to Fall in Love"   96
　　Lars-Olaf Beier and Moritz von Uslar / 2007

How Many Drilling Holes Exist?   101
　　Alexander Reich / 2007

"The Car Is a Rich Location"   107
　　Cristina Nord / 2009

"Poverty Films Well? I Don't Like This"   111
　　Katja Nicodemus and Christof Siemes / 2009

"Nothing Is Innocent Anymore"   117
　　Denis Demmerle / 2009

"It's Risky Business"   121
　　Holger Kreitling / 2011

An Interview with Christian Petzold   127
     Jaimey Fisher / 2011

"I Wanted for the GDR to Have Colors"   144
     Cristina Nord / 2012

"Our Identity Defines Itself through Work"   147
     Wenke Husmann / 2012

"What Lunatics There Were!"   151
     Stefan Schirmer and Martin Machowecz / 2013

Interview with Christian Petzold about *Phoenix*   158
     Peter Osteried / 2014

"Uuuuuh, This Won't Only Be Pleasant"   163
     Norbert Thomma and Christiane Peitz / 2014

To Truly See: Christian Petzold at the dffb   169
     Volker Pantenburg and Michael Baute / 2015

The Cinema Is a Warehouse of Memory: A Conversation among Christian Petzold, Robert Fischer, and Jaimey Fisher   181
     Robert Fischer and Jaimey Fisher / 2016

"A Space in Which We Are at Home": Interview with Christian Petzold   196
     Ilka Brombach / 2017

"Escape Is the Normal Condition"   223
     Christiane Peitz / 2018

"The Cigarette Was a Respite in Life"   228
     Carolin Ströbele / 2018

Lives in Transit: An Interview with Christian Petzold   232
     Richard Porton / 2019

"I Write in a Condition of Complete Mental Derangement"   240
     Andreas Busche / 2020

"As If We Were Dreaming It": Christian Petzold's *Undine*   244
    James Lattimer / 2020

Key Resources   253

Index   255

Introduction

"I was an intellectual, so any form of playing innocent would have meant lying to myself. . . . I had no choice but to make films by reflecting on them." So states Christian Petzold in a 2006/2007 talk with Marco Abel while describing his relationship with his teachers Harun Farocki and Hartmut Bitomsky at the German Film and Television Academy or dffb (Deutsche Film- und Fernsehakademie Berlin). In what was at the time the first interview published in English with the esteemed German filmmaker, Petzold is offering a precise image to consider for his working method and philosophy. It is not viable for him merely to take "the camera into [his] hands and [start] shooting what [is] there." Rather, the only way that he can access reality cinematically is by factoring in the processes of mediation that are part of the very reality that he seeks to render sensible. For Petzold, in other words, filming the world is necessarily always a process of reflecting on the political economy of filmmaking—a reflective process that, in turn, needs to manifest itself in the film's texture. This reflective process of self-conscious mediation, however, diverges from contemporary peers in world cinema like Michael Haneke or film-modernist forebears such as Jean-Luc Godard or the duo Jean-Marie Straub and Danièle Huillet in ways that are discussed herein.

It is rare for any artist to proclaim that they are an "intellectual," indeed, to *identify* as an intellectual. In Germany, film critics have not infrequently complained about the *Verkopftheit* (overly cerebral nature) of both Petzold's films and those of the so-called Berlin School, the group of contemporary filmmakers with which he is indelibly associated and that includes Angela Schanelec, Thomas Arslan, Christoph Hochhäusler, Benjamin Heisenberg, Maren Ade, Ulrich Köhler, Valeska Grisebach, and Henner Winckler. Petzold has explained that even as a budding filmmaker "this romantic idea of filmmaking was not available to [him]" because of his biography—specifically, the fact that he "had acquired a graduate degree," and not from a film school. He earned his master's in modern German literary studies at the Free University Berlin. Petzold wrote a thesis on Rolf Dieter Brinkmann, a key figure in the West German pop literature movement. But at the same time he began to think, seriously and continuously, about switching to a career in filmmaking.

German film critics' problems with the Berlin School speaks volumes about the poor state of affairs that characterizes much of German film culture rather than about the quality and characteristics of Petzold's oeuvre. To this moment, Petzold has completed seventeen feature-length films (eight made for the big screen, nine for German TV) in a quarter of a century (1995–2020). His ouevre is arguably the most robust and influential of any German filmmaker since the country's unification in 1990. One of the most idiosyncratic aspects of this work is how in film after film he is trying to get closer to squaring a self-conscious circle: to make genre films in "the cemetery of genre cinema," as he puts it in the interview with Abel. He wants to "reconstruct" genre via a kind of "archeology" of it, without parodying what came before, as he has said in his interview with Fisher herein. His work aims to provide his viewers with the distinct pleasures filmmaking can instill without allowing the comforts of a cinema of identification. Such cinema "gets on [his] nerves" (Abel), not only because he considers it ideologically dubious but also because it is based on a reductivist notion of pleasure. Put differently, criticizing his films as too intellectual misses the fact that this intellectualization of the cinema is the vehicle by which Petzold's films bring a range of affective pleasures that far exceeds the simplistic works for which German film culture generally provides.

Petzold, then, is not at all opposed to making narrative cinema that induces pleasure in the viewer—i.e., a cinema that accepts and affirms that scopophilia is a legitimate aspect of any given viewer's complex desiring economy. Petzold is not trying to destroy such familiar pleasures but rather to render pleasure otherwise: to induce delight differently, to confront viewers with different possibilities of experiencing pleasure. We purposefully appropriate key phrases from Laura Mulvey's landmark essay on the male gaze because Mulvey proffers her influential analysis of Hollywood cinema's economy of (male) desire by drawing on the work of that master of suspense whose films time and again mobilize the male gaze to unsettling effects: Alfred Hitchcock, a filmmaker who has impacted Petzold perhaps more than any other director, as the interviews in this volume reveal. A voracious explorer of film history since his youth in the small West German town of Haan, Petzold seemingly cannot *not* refer to Hitchcock for more than a few interviews at a time. Indeed, one of the most notable aspects of how Petzold engages his interlocutors' questions is that he almost inevitably discusses aspects of his films with detailed reference to directors whose works have marked him, ranging from F. W. Murnau and Helmut Käutner to Michael Cimino and John Carpenter. He is also greatly influenced by his teachers, Harun Farocki and Hartmut Bitomsky, with whom he studied at the dffb between 1989 and 1994 and on whose films he often assisted.

There are other directors and films that are important to Petzold, and perusing the interviews in this volume affords readers the opportunity to observe how Petzold's career unfolds as an ongoing conversation with his many favorites, whether with Edgar G. Ulmer, whose *Detour* (1945) impacted the early TV film *Cuba Libre*; with Kathryn Bigelow and Sidney Lumet, whose *Near Dark* (1987) and *Running on Empty* (1988), respectively, influenced *The State I Am In*; with Herk Harvey, whose *Carnival of Souls* (1962) serves as a plot skeleton of sorts for *Yella*; or with the various adaptations of *The Postman Always Rings Twice* that inform Petzold's own take on the story in *Jerichow*. Finally, there are such all-time classics as Michael Curtiz's *Casablanca* (1942), important for *Transit*, and, of course, always Hitchcock, including, at least, *The 39 Steps* (1935), *Rear Window* (1954), *Vertigo* (1958), *Marnie* (1964), and *Torn Curtain* (1966).

Petzold's penchant of talking *through other films* about his own—a habit we witness in virtually all interviews included herein—can be understood, we submit, as a proof of his conviction that it is impossible for him to make films in an unmediated fashion. Just as he feels compelled to execute the praxis of filmmaking by filming "through" other films, so he seems unable to talk for long about his work without "detouring" through other directors' films. Or perhaps more precisely put, habitually positioning himself in conversation with other films is the most direct way in which Petzold can discuss his films: not doing so would result in nothing less than the promulgation of the romantic (and bourgeois) illusion of the (white male) genius artist whose art is the result of little more than intuitive expression grounded in the mysteries of one's precious (and privileged) self. Petzold, as readers of this volume will be able to ascertain, has no truck with such an individualized and individualizing view of art—one, it must be said, that is not only deeply romantic but also inescapably expressive of the cultural logic of neoliberalism, a regime of power the specific German evolution of which Petzold's films have trenchantly observed from his early student films on, and which constitutes one of the key discussion topics throughout the interviews assembled in this volume.

Petzold's work is also engaged with another textual ensemble, one further affirming the aforementioned intellectual mediation: his films manifest a wide range of other references, from US crime fiction to classics of German literature to the history of the visual arts (e.g., de Chirico, Paul Klee, Gerhard Richter) and even to sports (his love for the cinema is matched by his love for soccer). He is also familiar with, among others, the philosophical ideas of Walter Benjamin, Gilles Deleuze, Antonio Negri, and Étienne Balibar. On the one hand, Petzold has distanced himself from Deleuzian film philosophy in solving problems cinematically (see Abel), although, on the other, he turns repeatedly to a figure like Benjamin, who haunts both *Phoenix* and *Transit* (see the Richard Porton interview).

Petzold is very clear: his films are extended and considered collaborations, be it with his former teachers and mentors, with fellow filmmakers, or with his actors such as his recurring lead, Nina Hoss (who has starred in six of his films to date), or with Julia Hummer, Benno Fürmann, Paula Beer, Franz Rogowski, or Matthias Brandt. He has repeatedly credited Eleonore Weisgerber, who appeared in his first feature-length TV film *Pilotinnen*, for teaching him how to interact with actors (see the Ilka Brombach interview). Several interviews reveal how Petzold prepares his productions by watching and discussing a range of films with his actors and longtime collaborators, such as his cinematographer Hans Fromm. These are chosen for showing what cinema can depict beyond narrative—for example, space and atmosphere. Petzold screens these films to initiate a conversation about the *texture* of the world they seek to generate—a world that often ends up being characterized by a *Schwebezustand*, a state of abeyance, of in-betweenness, of ghostliness, to use terms that permeate the assembled interviews.

Ghostlike aspects haunt much of Petzold's work. His characters are frequently stuck in a present not allowing them to move on. The past has a powerful purchase on them, a phenomenon that, in toto, cinematically allegorizes the state of contemporary Germany. In fact, one of the most important ghost-forms, rather than -figures, might be the nation itself in the age of globalizing neoliberalism. Petzold considers the cinema's engagement with national discourse important, even as such discourses grow increasingly tenuous, even spectral. In Petzold's hands such images of the ghost intensify historical mediations of cinema itself: one of Petzold's favorite motifs, appearing in multiple interviews, is that films should show twenty years later just how we live now—a perspective underscoring a different, here temporal mediation in the work.

In this ghostly historical context, his biography—the details of which come increasingly into focus over the chronological course of interviews—becomes relevant. A child of parents who left East Germany before the Berlin Wall was built in 1961, Petzold had long avoided talking in detail about his personal relationship to crucial aspects of twentieth-century German history: its wars of death and destruction as well as postwar displacement and division. As is clear in the conversations around *Transit*, he considers himself a kind of refugee from points East. It is well known that Petzold for the longest time refused, and even polemically argued against, making historical films—i.e., films about and set in eras of German history, even if his films are always thinking history and historicity. In the 2010s, Petzold developed a new disposition towards producing films that were set other than in the present. It was with *Barbara*, *Phoenix*, and *Transit* that Petzold belatedly turned to the terrible German history of violence—in the form of the secret police in East Germany, the Holocaust, and the Nazis' occupation of France.

Why had Petzold so purposefully avoided the very events that have dominated the German public sphere since the late 1960s? For a dedicated student of such engaged filmmakers as Farocki and Bitomsky, one would anticipate an allegiance to that generation of student rebels and revolutionaries (the so-called 68-ers). However, it seems Petzold needed German *cinema* to develop in a discomfiting way to propel a radical change in his filmmaking. In opposition to German global blockbusters such as Oliver Hirschbiegel's *Downfall* (2004) and Florian Henckel von Donnersmarck's *The Lives of Others* (2006), as well as to their too-welcoming receptions, Petzold suspended his self-imposed moratorium on making films about German history. He directed *Barbara* as a rejoinder to Donnersmarck's depiction of life behind the Wall in East Germany, and *Phoenix* as a corrective to German cinema turning non-Jewish Germans into Hitler's "victims" as in *Downfall*. As for *Transit*, it is as an important cinematic intervention in the German discourse on immigration after Chancellor Angela Merkel's much debated decision to admit large numbers of refugees in the summer of 2015. Petzold ingeniously links in *Transit* the fascist past to present circumstances, revealing the continuity between them. This diagnostic insight flies in the face of a present in which many Germans feel over(t)ly proud of themselves for having (allegedly) successfully engaged in *Vergangenheitsbewältigung* (coming to terms with/mastering the country's past crimes), which, in turn, authorizes not a few Germans to assume once again the position of Europe's schoolmaster (dispensing moral[izing] lessons to others, as it infamously did in the euro crisis starting in late 2009). In this context, the reader of the following interviews can easily imagine Petzold taking recourse to (East-) German playwright Heiner Müller's biting declaration that "ten Germans are dumber than five Germans"—a pronouncement Petzold quotes herein in a different context (see the Beier and von Uslar interview).

Petzold's belatedness to deal with the big historical events in Germany's history has also to do with his being born in 1960. He was too late coming to filmmaking to be faced with the material conditions that enabled his mentors Farocki and Bitomsky, and also Rainer Werner Fassbinder or, across the Rhine, Godard, to make political films the way they did. By the time Petzold enrolled at the dffb in the late 1980s, the utopias that had energized people in the late 1960s had by and large not come to fruition. The radical film experiments of that time period, too, ultimately fell on fallow ground, with those famous Brechtian aesthetic strategies not leading to a palpable reeducation of viewers (especially not of those who were not already sympathetic towards the lessons those films sought to convey). Perhaps closest to home, Petzold had yet to come to terms with his personal history as someone who was disconnected or only intermittently connected to his family's East German lineage—a genealogical connection the working-through of which took him time, perhaps precisely because he could manage to do so only in mediated fashion *through* the complex debates, ongoing to this day, both about how unification came about and was managed and about what the value of East Germany's legacy is for post-unification Germany.

The many mediations above include the production conditions for Petzold's work, a fourth mode of mediation (after film history, literature/philosophy, and the collaborations that yield the finished films) that is a leitmotif in many of these interviews. Petzold is unusually reflective about the production conditions surrounding his filmmaking and his own relation to them, from the dffb through his early television work to the theatrical films and then, interestingly in the 2010s, back to periodic TV work between acclaimed feature films. For example, it was highly unusual for a film director at such a late, and still ascendant, point in their career to turn to the TV-funded and -exhibited collaboration that Petzold undertook with Christoph Hochhäusler and Dominik Graf, two of Germany's best-known directors: Hochhäusler is usually categorized as another Berlin School director and is the founding editor of its most influential associated journal, *Revolver*, while Graf, a generation older, is generally regarded as one of Germany's best genre directors. Their collaboration, entitled *Dreileben*, comprises a set of three films, with each directing one, based on the same crime. The directors developed this project after engaging in an extensive email exchange among the three of them, mostly focusing on contemporary film aesthetics and especially on genre. Set in a fictional contemporary town in the winter-resort region of Thuringia (in the former East Germany), *Dreileben*'s three films overlap in their narrative basis and then in one or two telling moments but diverge in revealing ways in terms of style. A study in the three auteurist directors' signature styles, *Dreileben* ended up on public television (on ARD's "das Erste" [the first station]) because, in the German film and television landscape, only public television could and would provide the financial and institutional basis with which such a collaboration, even among well-known and successful filmmakers, could be realized.

In the interviews herein, Petzold details his work making nine feature films for German television. Germany's public television stations—especially the "first" and "second" stations ("das Erste" [first] of ARD and then ZDF, respectively)—play much greater roles in the cultural and political public spheres than public stations do in the US. As their names indicate, they occupy the first two positions on the national spectrum of broadcast channels—perhaps less important now, but a considerable advantage for decades—and they are generously funded, along with radio and the cultural Arte stations (among others), through a tax levied on every German household. The amount of this tax is still a source of constant debate in Germany, not least because of what ends up being the approximately 8 billion euro in federal subsidies for public broadcasting (for comparison, PBS's total subsides are in the vicinity of $500 million—and this in the US, a country with a population about four times as large as Germany's). One example of the importance of public TV and televisual culture in Germany was, in our preparation of this volume, the challenge of translating the recurring term *Redakteur/*

Redakteurin (the latter for those identifying as female): the term comes up both as Petzold was first building his career while still in film school in a memorable anecdote about a crucial early meeting with such figures (see the Brombach interview) and during his later turn back to television (see the Fischer and Fisher interview). Dictionaries would usually translate *Redakteur/Redakteurin* as "editor," but here we settled on "commissioning producer," though even that phrase cannot quite capture the influence such figures have in postwar German culture.

A mixed-bag fact of life for most directors in Germany, such commissioning producers enjoy probably more power than even the most successful commercial film producers in the US, as they apportion considerable public funds for film subsidies while also offering/impacting exhibition nationally (even internationally in the case of Arte) in prime timeslots (or not) on those stations. The most famous example of the historical influence of such forms is probably the "Das kleine Fernsehspiel" ("The Little TV Play") of ZDF, which helped build the early careers of celebrated directors Fassbinder, Fatih Akin, and even Jim Jarmusch. With ZDF and Arte support, for instance, Petzold himself has made films that, we think, rank among his most accomplished, like the too-little-seen *Toter Mann* and *Wolfsburg* (like all of his TV films, never released in the US and difficult to find with subtitles). Similarly crucial and difficult to convey in brief translation is the cultural space occupied by German TV's longest-running drama *Tatort* (*Crime Scene*), the beloved crime series made by ARD that premiered in 1970, with a parallel, competitor series *Polizeiruf 110* (*Police Call 110*), first in East Germany and then on ARD after unification. There have been over 1,100 episodes of *Tatort* and some 400 of *Polizeiruf 110*, many of which feature Germany's most famous and best-liked film and television stars and directors (e.g., Götz George, Eva Mattes, Devid Striesow). Since 2015, Petzold has made three such detective episodes for *Polizeiruf 110*, which are discussed in detail herein (see the Fischer and Fisher interview). Petzold's love of these genre crime shows, and of the potential for varying them, comes out in these interviews, as do his perhaps confusing references to the timeslots of 8:00 or 8:15 p.m. for such broadcasts (see the Reich, Kreitling, and Brombach interviews). This talk of timeslots manifests an awareness of television production one is unlikely to hear cited from analogous US directors—at least in the prestreaming era, which is currently remaking this relationship of cinema to television worldwide.

Whether with film or television, Petzold's penchant for close collaboration is the embodiment of a belief that he cannot just hold the camera at reality and shoot. He time and again enters dialogues—whether with his actors; with fellow filmmakers; with the generic conventions of genre television; with his regular team including producers, editor, cinematographer, and costume designer; and most often in the past, with his closest friend, mentor, and former teacher, the late Harun Farocki, who for two decades served as Petzold's script advisor—as a means of deferring any tendency he might (unconsciously) harbor towards inadvertently giving in to a more romantic attitude towards filmmaking. It is as though the only way for Petzold to deal with the historical fact of having come too late—for a left politics and aesthetics as it was codified and practiced by a previous generation that was still able to affirm a sense of utopian possibility—is by *intensifying*, each time anew, this affective experience of belatedness: having come too late, he has to defer further by creating conditions for dialogue, for conversations, for interactive, collective thinking (with past and present interlocutors), only the practicing of which makes the shooting of his films possible for him.

And today? Can we say that his interviewers are also collaborators in his process of filmmaking? He has given literally hundreds of interviews, many of which are characterized by his astonishing eloquence, wit, and erudition. In response to virtually any question he is able to produce answers in the form of fully developed, thought-provoking, and print-ready *paragraphs*. An astonishing ability that can be understood as one important part of his film-production method. Thirty-five interviews with Petzold are collected for this volume, thirty of which are made available in English for the first time. We thank the publications in which these interviews first appeared for granting permission to reprint; the University of California, Davis's College of Letters and Sciences and Office of Research and the College of Arts and Sciences at the University of Nebraska–Lincoln for financially supporting this publication; and our editor, Emily Snyder Bandy, and her staff at the University Press of Mississippi for their support. Last but not least, we thank Christian Petzold for both his films and the time he has granted us editors over the years, sitting down for extensive interviews and remaining always responsive to new questions whenever we have approached him.

MA
AB
JF

Chronology

1960   Born September 14 in Hilden, Germany.
1979   Graduates from high school in Haan.
1979–81 Does his civil service by working in a small film club of the local YMCA.
1981–89 Moves to West Berlin and studies German literature [*Germanistik*] and theater at the Free University in Berlin. Graduates with a master's thesis on Rolf Dieter Brinkmann.
1988–94 Studies at the Deutschen Film- und Fernsehakademie Berlin (dffb). Takes seminars with Harun Farocki, Hartmut Bitomsky, and Helmut Färber, among others. Meets fellow future Berlin School directors Thomas Arslan and Angela Schanelec. The three occasionally work on each others' short films. Also collaborates with his future wife, Aysun Bademsoy, with whom he has two children. Makes several short films and graduates with *Pilots* (1995).
1996   *Cuba Libre* premieres on January 25 at the Max-Ophüls-Preis film festival in Saarbrücken. Receives the festival's *Förderpreis*, awarded to support new filmmakers.
1998   *The Sex Thief* premieres on January 30 at the Max-Ophüls-Preis film festival in Saarbrücken.
2000   *The State I Am In*, Petzold's first film made for the big screen, premieres on September 1 at the Venice International Film Festival.
2001   *The State I Am In* receives the German Film Prize in gold (for best feature). In the same year, it also receives the Hessian Film Prize and the Prize of the German Film Critics (der deutschen Filmkritik) for best feature, while Bettina Böhler wins the same prize for editing the film. *Something to Remind Me* premieres on October 26 at the Hof International Film Days. This made-for-TV film marks Petzold's first collaboration with actor Nina Hoss.
2002   *Something to Remind Me* receives prize for best television film from the Deutschen Akademie der darstellenden Künste (German Academy of Representational Arts) as well as the German Television Prize.
2003   Receives the Adolph-Grimme prize, Germany's most prestigious prize for TV productions, for *Something to Remind Me* (together with

	Nina Hoss, Hans Fromm, and Sven Pippig). Petzold's next made-for-TV film, *Wolfsburg*, premieres in the Panorama section of the Berlin International Film Festival (Berlinale) on February 11 and receives the FIPRESCI award (award of the international film critics).
2004	Receives the DEFA foundation's prize for the purpose of supporting German film art.
2005	Receives the Adolf-Grimme prize in gold for *Wolfsburg* (together with Nina Hoss and Benno Fürmann). *Ghosts* premieres in the Berlinale Competition on February 11. Receives the prize of the German Film Critics (best feature).
2007	*Yella* premieres in the Berlinale Competition on February 14. Receives the Prize of the German Film Critics (best feature) as well as for cinematography (Hans Fromm) for *Yella*. Nina Hoss receives the Silver Bear (and in 2008 the German film prize). Together with *The State I Am In* and *Ghosts*, *Yella* is part of what Petzold calls his "Ghost Trilogy."
2008	*Jerichow* premieres at the Venice International Film Festival on August 28. Receives the Prize of the German Film Critics (best feature) for *Jerichow*.
2009	Receives the Film Prize of the City of Hof. Directs his first (and to date only) theater play, Arthur Schnitzler's *The Lonely Way*, at the Deutsches Theater Berlin. Nina Hoss plays the lead. The play premieres on March 14.
2011	*Beats Being Dead* premieres together with the other two films comprising the *Dreileben*-project (the other two are Graf's *Don't Follow Me Around* and Hochhäusler's *One Minute of Darkness*) in the Berlinale's Forum section on February 16, 2011. The three films approach from different perspectives the same crime that took place in a fictional location in Thuringia called "Dreileben."
	Together with Graf and Hochhäusler, Petzold receives the German Film Prize for their collaborative project in the category of "Special Accomplishment Fiction."
2012	His first film set in the past (specifically, in the GDR of 1980), *Barbara* premieres in the Berlinale's Competition and receives a Silver Bear for best direction. The film is also awarded the German Film Prize in Silver for best feature, as well as the Prize of the German Film Critics (best feature). Bettina Böhler also wins the Prize of the German Film Critics for her editing of *Barbara*. Together with Graf and Hochhäusler, he also receives the Grimme-award "Spezial" for *Dreileben*.
2013	Receives the Helmut-Käutner-Preis, awarded for his intellectual acumen and his knack for compelling stories that make him an heir to

	Käutner, director of *Under the Bridges* (1945/46), one of Petzold's favorite films. Travels to New York City to attend the Museum of Modern Art's Retrospective of the films of the Berlin School.
2014	*Phoenix* premieres in September at the Toronto International Film Festival. It is Petzold's sixth and, to date, most recent collaboration with Nina Hoss. Receives the FIPRESCI award at the San Sebastian film festival. Working on the film's script is Petzold's last collaboration with his erstwhile teacher and longtime mentor, collaborator, and friend, Harun Farocki, who dies June 30, 2014.
2015	*Circles* premieres on June 28. This is Petzold's first of three contributions to the long-running German television series *Polizeiruf 110*.
2016	Receives a German television award for crime films for directing *Circles*. *Wolves*, his second contribution to *Polizeiruf 110*, premieres on June 25 at the Munich Film Festival. Focus of a full retrospective in the "Hommage" series at the Munich Film Festival.
2017	The Centre Pompidou honors Petzold and Farocki with a retrospective starting November 23 (ending January 14, 2018). For this purpose, Petzold collaborates with Hochhäusler on *Où en êtes-vous, Christian Petzold?* In *Where Do You Stand Today, Christian Petzold?*, Petzold and Hochhäusler analyze a sequence of Alfred Hitchcock's *The Wrong Man*. With this free-form short film, Petzold pays tribute to the spirit and methods of Harun Farocki.
2018	*Transit* premieres in the Berlinale's Competition on February 21. It concludes another trilogy, which Petzold calls "Love in Times of Oppressive Systems," of which *Barbara* and *Phoenix* are part of as well. *Transit* is an official selection at the film festivals in New York, Toronto, Chicago, and Sydney. The Lincoln Center in New York honors Petzold with "The State We Are In," a complete retrospective of his work to date. Petzold receives the Julius-Campe award for his "Service to German Literature [Verdienste um die deutsche Literatur]" with specific reference to the film *Transit*. Also receives the Bayerische Film Award for the script of *Transit* and is honored at the Neiße Film Festival for his filmic oeuvre. *Tatorte*, his third contribution to *Polizeiruf 110*, premieres on German television on December 16. Inducted into the Academy of Motion Picture Arts and Sciences.
2020	*Undine* premieres in the Berlinale's Competition on February 23 and receives the FIPRESCI award. The film is the first of another planned trilogy, which concerns itself with German Romanticism and especially the motive of elemental spirits. Petzold receives the Schiller-Prize of the City of Mannheim.

2021   Receives the Order of Merit [*Verdienstorden*] of the Federal Republic of Germany, which is Germany's only federal decoration and is awarded for special achievements in political, economic, cultural, intellectual, or honorary fields.

2023   *Roter Himmel* [*Red Sky*], the second entry in his trilogy concerning German Romanticism, premieres in the Berlinale's Competition. Plans to shoot a film based on a Georges Simenon novel.

Filmography

MISSION (1987)
Director: **Christian Petzold**, Frank Seeger
Screenplay: **Christian Petzold**, Frank Seeger
Camera: **Christian Petzold**
Editing: **Christian Petzold**
Cast: Frank Seeger

WEIBER (WOMEN, 1989)
Director: **Christian Petzold**
Screenplay: **Christian Petzold**
Production Company: Deutsche Film- und Fernsehakademie Berlin (dffb)
Camera: **Christian Petzold**
Editing: **Christian Petzold**, Christian Frosch
Sound: Stefan Pethke
Music: Beasts of Bourbon (DE)
Cast: Markus Wacker, Guido Petzold
14 minutes

SÜDEN (SOUTH, 1989/1990)
Director: **Christian Petzold**
Production Company: Deutsche Film- und Fernsehakademie Berlin (dffb)
Camera: **Christian Petzold**
Editing: **Christian Petzold**
Sound: **Christian Petzold**
Music: Sexteto Electronico Moderno
10 minutes

OSTWÄRTS (EASTWARDS, 1990/1991)
Director: **Christian Petzold**
Production Company: Deutsche Film- und Fernsehakademie Berlin (dffb)
Camera: Thomas Arslan, Jan Ralske, **Christian Petzold**

Editing: **Christian Petzold**
Sound: Stephan Pethke, Thomas Arslan
23 minutes

DAS WARME GELD (THE WARM MONEY, 1992)
Director: **Christian Petzold**
Screenplay: **Christian Petzold**, with Harun Farocki
Production Company: Deutsche Film- und Fernsehakademie Berlin (dffb)
Camera: Bernd Löhr
Editing: Aysun Bademsoy, with Bettina Böhler
Sound: Jan Ralske
Music: Markus Meyer-Grützmann
Cast: Manuela Brandenstein (Vera), Martina Maurer (Heike), Ulrich Ströhle (boss), Mark Schlichter (assistant cook), Sabahat Bademsoy (server), Halit M. Bademsoy (man at bar), Andreas Hosang (doctor), Kim Kübler (girl by the pool), Christiane Columbus (Medical Technical Assistant), Elke Naters (Medical Technical Assistant), Jörg Jettenberger (vacationer in Greece), Eva Maria Hammel (bar keeper), Stefan Gertzen (pursuer)
30 minutes

ABZÜGE (DEDUCTIONS, 1994)
Director: **Christian Petzold**
Production Company: Deutsche Film- und Fernsehakademie Berlin (dffb)

PILOTINNEN (PILOTS, 1995)
Director: **Christian Petzold**
Screenplay: **Christian Petzold**
Producer: Michael Weber and Florian Koerner von Gustorf
Production Companies: Schramm Film Koerner & Weber (Berlin), coproduced by Deutsche Film- und Fernsehakademie Berlin (dffb), by order of Zweites Deutsches Fensehen (ZDF) (Mainz)
Camera: Hans Fromm
Editing: Monika Kappel-Smith
Sound: Heino Herrenbrück
Music: Georges Delerue
Cast: Eleonore Weisgerber (Karin), Nadeshda Brennicke (Sophie), Udo Schenk (Juniorchef), Barbara Frey (Christine), Michael Tietz (Dieter), Ronny Tanner (short police officer), Wolfgang Hahn (tall police officer), Inge-Carolin Gremm (salesperson at supermarket), Kim Kübler (young cosmetician), Imke Barnstedt (older cosmetician), Hans Klima (first ambushed policeman), Rüdiger Tuchel

(second ambushed policeman), Michael Brennicke (sales rep "Dynamic"), Jörg Friedrich (sales rep "Self Defense"), Klaus Rätsch (dispatcher), Marie Bondeele (perfumer), Gilles Papelian (Michel), Peter Zarth (man at airport)
72 minutes

CUBA LIBRE (1996)
Director: **Christian Petzold**
Screenplay: **Christian Petzold**
Producer: Florian Koerner von Gustorf, Horst Knechtl
Production Companies: Cine Images Horst Knechtl (Munich), Schramm Film Koerner & Weber (Berlin), by order of Zweites Deutsches Fernsehen (ZDF) (Mainz)
Camera: Hans Fromm
Editing: Bettina Böhler
Sound: Heino Herrenbrück
Music: Stefan Will
Cast: Richy Müller (Tom), Catherine Flemming (Tina), Wolfram Berger (Jimmy), Raoul Schneider (Caddy), Anette Guther (salesperson), Gilles Papelian (innkeeper), Eleonore Weisgerber (not specified), Christoph Krix (guard), Mark Schlichter (commuter), Matthias Viehoff (medical doctor), Marquard Bohm (man from the beauty farm), Andrea Brose (girl at bistro), Wilfried Gronau (homeless man), Jörg Friedrich (homeless man)
93 minutes

DIE BEISCHLAFDIEBIN (THE SEX THIEF, 1998)
Director: **Christian Petzold**
Screenplay: **Christian Petzold** (Harun Farocki)
Producer: Florian Koerner von Gustorf, Omar Jawal
Production Companies: Schramm Film Koerner & Weber, by order of Zweites Deutsches Fernsehen (ZDF) (Mainz)
Camera: Hans Fromm
Editing: Bettina Böhler
Sound: Martin Ehlers, Heino Herrenbrück
Music: Stefan Will
Cast: Constanze Engelbrecht (Petra), Nele Mueller-Stöfen (Franziska), Wolfram Berger (the thief), Richy Müller (police officer), Nadeshda Brennicke (waitress), Andrea Brose (Miriam), Jörg Friedrich (first human resource manager), Tilo Nest (second human resource manager), Karl-Heinz Knaup (third human resource manager), Christoph Krix (man in bar), Bernd Tauber (Geldbote)
86 minutes

DIE INNERE SICHERHEIT (THE STATE I AM IN, 2000)
Director: **Christian Petzold**
Screenplay: **Christian Petzold**, Harun Farocki
Producer: Florian Koerner von Gustorf, Michael Weber
Production Companies: Schramm Film Koerner & Weber (Berlin), coproduced by Hessischer Rundfunk HR (Frankfurt am Main), Arte G.E.I.E. (Straßburg)
Camera: Hans Fromm
Editing: Bettina Böhler
Sound: Heino Herrenbrück
Music: Stefan Will
Cast: Julia Hummer (Jeanne), Barbara Auer (Clara), Richy Müller (Hans), Bilge Bingül (Heinrich), Rogério Jaques (man at beach bar), Maria João (concierge), Vasco Machado (police officer), Noberto Paula (man at train station), Bernd Tauber (Achim), Katharina Schüttler (Paulina), Günther Maria Halmer (Klaus), Inka Löwendorf (girl in school), Manfred Möck (teacher), Marc Sönnichsen (Heinrich's friend), Ingrid Dohse (restaurant manager), Henriette Heinze (hitchhiker)
105 minutes

TOTER MANN (SOMETHING TO REMIND ME, 2001)
Director: **Christian Petzold**
Screenplay: **Christian Petzold**, Jean-Baptiste Filleau
Producer: Bettina Reiz
Production Companies: teamWorx Filmproduktion (Berlin & Munich), in collaboration with Arte G.E.I.E. (Straßburg)
Camera: Hans Fromm
Editing: Bettina Böhler
Sound: Andreas Mücke-Niesytka
Music: Stefan Will
Cast: Nina Hoss (Leyla), André M. Hennicke (Thomas), Sven Pippig (Blum), Heinrich Schmieder (Richard), Kathrin Angerer (Sophie), Henning Peker (Ott), Michael Gerber (agent), Franziska Troegner (Peggy), Johannes Hitzblech (Seifert), Hilmar Baumann (janitor), Rainer Laupichler (police officer), Ingeborg Schilling (mother), Larissa Rimkus (child), Kai Schuhmann (waiter)
88 minutes

WOLFSBURG (2003)
Director: **Christian Petzold**
Screenplay: **Christian Petzold**

Producer: Florian Koerner von Gustorf, Michael Weber
Production Companies: teamWorx Produktion für Kino und Fernsehen GmbH (Berlin), coproduction with Arte Deutschland TV GmbH (Baden-Baden)
Camera: Hans Fromm
Editing: Bettina Böhler
Sound: Andreas Mücke-Niesytka
Music: Stefan Will
Cast: Benno Fürmann (Phillip Wagner), Nina Hoss (Laura Reiser), Astrid Meyerfeldt (Vera), Antje Westermann (Katja), Stephan Kampwirth (Klaus), Matthias Matschke (Scholz), Soraya Gomaa (Françoise), Martin Müseler (Paul Reiser), Anna Priese (Antonia), Florian Panzner (police officer), André Szymanski (new sales rep), Peter Kurth (Oliver), Simone von Zglinicki (nurse), Sven Pippig (scrap dealer), Margarita Broich (psychologist), Claudia Geisler (young mother), Andreas Petri (young father), Fritz Roth (mechanic at scrap yard), Thorsten Mischweis (security guard), Michael Poth (mechanic at car dealership)
90 minutes

GESPESNTER (GHOSTS, 2005)
Director: **Christian Petzold**
Screenplay: **Christian Petzold**
Producer: Florian Koerner von Gustorf, Michael Weber
Production Companies: Schramm Film Koerner & Weber (Berlin), coproduced by Les Films des Tournelles (Paris), Bayerischer Rundfunk (BR)/Arte (Munich), Arte France Cinéma (Paris)
Camera: Hans Fromm
Editing: Bettina Böhler
Sound: Andreas Mücke-Niesytka
Music: Stefan Will, Marco Dreckkötter
Cast: Julia Hummer (Nina), Sabine Timoteo (Toni), Marianne Basler (Françoise), Aurélien Recoing (Pierre), Benno Fürmann (Oliver), Anna Schudt (Kai), Claudia Geisler (director of youth shelter), Philipp Hauß (Mathias), Victoria Trauttmansdorff (Mathias's mother), Peter Kurth (foreman), Annika Blendl (agent), Rosa Enskat (nurse)
85 minutes

YELLA (2007)
Director: **Christian Petzold**
Screenplay: **Christian Petzold**
Producer: Florian Koerner von Gustorf, Michael Weber

Production Companies: Schramm Film Koerner & Weber (Berlin), coproduced with Zweites Deutsches Fernsehen (ZDF) (Mainz) and Arte Deutschland GmbH (Baden-Baden)
Camera: Hans Fromm
Editing: Bettina Böhler
Sound: Andreas Mücke-Niesytka
Music: Stefan Will
Cast: Nina Hoss (Yella), Devid Striesow (Philipp), Hinnerk Schönemann (Ben), Burghart Klaußner (Dr. Gunthen), Barbara Auer (Barbara Gunthen), Christian Redl (Yella's father), Selin Barbara Petzold (Dr. Gunthen's daughter), Wanja Mues (Sprenger), Michael Wittenborn (Schmitt-Ott), Martin Brambach (Dr. Fritz), Joachim Nimtz (Prietzel), Peter Benedict (Friedrich's lawyer), Ian Norval (receptionist), Peter Knaack (liquidator), Thomas Giese (cashier)
88 minutes

JERICHOW (2008)
Director: **Christian Petzold**
Screenplay: **Christian Petzold**
Producer: Florian Koerner von Gustorf, Michael Weber
Production Companies: Schramm Film Koerner & Weber (Berlin), coproduced with Bayerischer Rundfunk (BR) (Munich) and Arte Deutschland TV GmbH (Baden-Baden)
Camera: Hans Fromm
Editing: Bettina Böhler
Sound: Andreas Mücke-Niesytka, Martin Ehlers
Music: Stefan Will
Cast: Benno Fürmann (Thomas), Nina Hoss (Laura), Hilmi Sözer (Ali), André M. Hennicke (Leon), Claudia Geisler (administrator), Marie Gruber (cashier), Knut Berger (police officer)
92 minutes

ETWAS BESSERES ALS DEN TOD (BEATS BEING DEAD, 2011)
Director: **Christian Petzold**
Screenplay: **Christian Petzold**
Producer: Florian Koerner von Gustorf, Michael Weber
Production Companies: Schramm Film Koerner & Weber (Berlin), by order of Bayerischer Rundfunk (BR) (Munich)
Camera: Hans Fromm
Editing: Bettina Böhler
Sound: Andreas Mücke-Niesytka

Music: Stefan Will
Cast: Jacob Matschenz (Johannes) Luna Mijović (Ana), Vijessna Ferkic (Sarah Dreier), Rainer Bock (Dr. Dreier), Konstantin Frolov (Maik), Florian Bartholomäi (Philipp), Stefan Kurt (escapee Frank Molesch), Kirsten Block (medical doctor), Deniz Petzold (Edin), Evelyn Gundlach (Verwahrloste Frau), Kristof Gerega (civil service provider), Thomas Fränzel (male nurse), Eberhard Kirchberg (Kreil)
88 minutes

BARBARA (2012)
Director: **Christian Petzold**
Screenplay: **Christian Petzold**
Producer: Florian Koerner von Gustorf
Production Companies: Schramm Film Koerner & Weber (Berlin), in association with Zweites Deutsches Fernsehen (ZDF) (Mainz)
Camera: Hans Fromm
Editing: Bettina Böhler
Sound: Andreas Mücke-Niesytka
Music: Stefan Will
Cast: Nina Hoss (Barbara), Ronald Zehrfeld (André), Rainer Bock (Klaus), Mark Waschke (Jörg), Jasna Fritzi Bauer (Stella), Rosa Enskat (building superintedent Bungert), Christina Hecke (assistant doctor), Claudia Geisler-Bading (ward nurse Schlösser), Peter Weiss (medical student), Carolin Haupt (medical student), Deniz Petzold (Angelo), Peer-Uwe Teska (waiter), Elisabeth Lehmann (waitress), Peter Benedict (Gerhard), Thomas Neumann (retiree at car), Anette Daugart (colleague Schütz), Thomas Bading (piano tuner), Susanne Bormann (Steffi), Jannik Schürmann (Mario), Alicia von Rittberg (Angie), Selin Barbara Petzold (Maria), Jean Paschel (colleague Schütz), Christoph Krix (André's neighbor), Kirsten Block (Friedl Schütz), Irene Rindje (Friedl's sister)
108 minutes

PHOENIX (2014)
Director: **Christian Petzold**
Screenplay: **Christian Petzold**, with Harun Farocki
Producer: Florian Koerner von Gustorf, Michael Weber
Production Companies: Schramm Film Koerner & Weber (Berlin), in coproduction with Bayerischer Rundfunk (BR) (Munich) and Westdeutscher Rundfunk (WDR) (Cologne)
Camera: Hans Fromm
Editing: Bettina Böhler
Sound: Andreas Mücke-Niesytka

Music: Stefan Will
Cast: Nina Hoss (Nelly), Ronald Zehrfeld (Johnny), Nina Kunzendorf (Lene), Michael Maertens (doctor), Daniela Holtz (Sigrid), Imogen Kogge (Elizabeth), Nikola Kastner (young woman), Sofia Exss (cigarette girl), Valerie Koch (dancer), Eva Bay (dancer), Uwe Preuss (club owner), Trystan Pütter (soldier at the bridge), Felix Römer (violin player), Jeff Burrell (soldier at the club), Max Hopp (the man), Megan Gay (colleague central office), Kirsten Block (proprietor), Frank Seppeler (Alfred), Kathrin Wehlisch (Monika), Michael Wenninger (Walther), Claudia Geisler-Bading (Frederike)
98 minutes

KREISE (CIRCLES, 2015)
Director: **Christian Petzold**
Screenplay: **Christian Petzold**
Producer: Claussen & Putz Filmproduktion
Production Companies: Claussen + Wöbke + Putz Filmproduktion GmbH (Munich), by order of Bayerischer Rundfunk (BR) (Munich)
Camera: Hans Fromm
Editing: Bettina Böhler
Sound: Peter Preuß
Cast: Matthias Brandt (detective Hanns von Meuffels), Barbara Auer (Constanze), Justus von Dohnányi (Peter), Luise Heyer (Nadja), Daniel Stäßer (Jan), Jan Messutat (operations manager Schrader), Sascha Alexander Geršak (production manage Eberl), Annette Paulmann (Karin), Robert Besta (Czech police officer), Adam Markiewicz (Jiri)
90 minutes

WÖLFE (WOLVES, 2016)
Director: **Christian Petzold**
Screenplay: **Christian Petzold**
Producer: Jakob Claussen, Uli Putz
Production Companies: Claussen + Putz Filmproduktion GmbH (Munich), by order of Bayerischer Rundfunk (BR) (Munich)
Camera: Hans Fromm
Editing: Bettina Böhler
Sound: Peter Preuß, Kristofer Harris
Music: Stefan Will
Cast: Matthias Brandt (detective Hanns von Meuffels), Barbara Auer (Constanze), Sebastian Hülk (Dr. Biesinger), Michael Witte (operations manager Schrader), Anna Unterberger (Kristina), Ercan Durmaz (Mehmet Özhan), Rainer Egger

(pathologist Dr. Bruns), Jasna Fritzi Bauer (maid Anna), Teresa Weißbach (proprietor), Oliver Bürgin (BND employee)
120 minutes

OÙ EN ÊTES-VOUS, CHRISTIAN PETZOLD? (WHERE DO YOU STAND TODAY, CHRISTIAN PETZOLD?, 2017)
Director: **Christian Petzold**
Screenplay: **Christian Petzold**
Production Companies: Centre Pompidou, Schramm Film Koerner & Weber, with support from Arte France Cinéma
Camera: Hans Fromm
Editing: Hans Fromm
Sound: Hans Fromm
Cast: **Christian Petzold**, Christoph Hochhäusler
23 minutes

TRANSIT (2018)
Director: **Christian Petzold**
Screenplay: **Christian Petzold**
Producer: Florian Koerner von Gustorf, Michael Weber, with coproducer Antonin Dedet
Production Companies: Schramm Film Koerner & Weber (Berlin), in coproduction with Neon Productions (Marseille), Arte G.E.I.E. (Straßburg), Zweites Deutsches Fernsehen (ZDF) (Mainz), Arte France Cinéma (Paris)
Camera: Hans Fromm
Editing: Bettina Böhler
Sound: Andreas Mücke-Niesytka
Music: Stefan Will
Cast: Franz Rogowski (Georg), Paula Beer (Marie), Godehard Giese (Doctor Richard), Lilien Batman (Driss), Maryam Zaree (Melissa), Barbara Auer (woman with two dogs), Matthias Brandt (bar tender/narrator), Sebastian Hülk (Paul), Emilie de Preissac (hotel owner Paris), Antoine Oppenheim (George), Ronald Kukulies (Heinz), Alex Brendemühl (Mexican consul), Justus von Dohnányi (chaplain), Trystan Pütter (US consul), Agnes Regolo (secretary at Mexican council), Gregoire Mansaingeon (shipowner), Elisa Volsin (Claire), Jean-Jérôme Esposito (detective Marseille)
102 minutes

TATORTE (CRIME SCENES, 2018)
Director: **Christian Petzold**
Screenplay: **Christian Petzold**
Producer: Jakob Claussen, Uli Pütz
Production Companies: Claussen + Pütz Filmproduktion GmbH (Munich), by order of Bayerischer Rundfunk (BR) (Munich)
Camera: Hans Fromm
Editing: Bettina Böhler
Sound: Peter Preuß
Music: Samuel Barber, Adagio for Strings
Cast: Matthias Brandt (detective Hanns von Meuffels), Barbara Auer (Constanze), Maryam Zaree (Nadja), Bettina Mittendorfer (therapist), Aurelia Schikarski (Jasmina), Stephan Zinner (Jochen), Max Philip Koch (LKA-student Leon), Anna Drexler (LKA-student Jessica), Wiebke Puls (Mrs. Kapellmann), Sascha Maaz (Mr. Kapellmann), Michael Witte (Schrader), Till Firit (doctor), Gabriele Kastner (Mrs. Wegner), Anna Maria Sturm (Anna)
90 minutes

UNDINE (2020)
Director: **Christian Petzold**
Screenplay: **Christian Petzold**
Producer: Florian Koerner von Gustorf, Michael Weber
Production Companies: Schramm Film Koerner & Weber (Berlin), in coproduction with Les Films du Losange (Paris), together with Zweites Deutsches Fernsehen (ZDF) / Arte (Mainz), Arte France Cinéma (Paris), Canal + (Paris), Ciné (Paris)
Camera: Hans Fromm
Editing: Bettina Böhler
Sound: Andreas Mücke-Niesytka
Cast: Paula Beer (Undine), Franz Rogowski (Christoph), Maryam Zaree (Monika), Jacob Matschenz (Johannes), Anne Rattee-Polle (Anna), Rafael Stachowiak (Jochen), Julia Franz Richter (Nora), Gloria Endres de Oliveira (Antonia), José Barros (Miguel), Enno Trebs (waiter), Carla Becker (woman in work clothes)
90 minutes

Christian Petzold: Interviews

Three to Two a Potential Hit: A Conversation with Christian Petzold

Stefan Ertl and Rainer Knepperges / 1995

From "Drei zu zwei hitverdächtig: Ein Gespräch mit Christian Petzold," *Filmwärts* (1995): 73–76. Reprinted by permission. Translated by Aylin Bademsoy.

Stefan Ertl and Rainer Knepperges: Do you know the new short film by Eddi Herzog, *Eine Schürze aus Speck*?
Christian Petzold: Is that the sauna film?
Ertl and Knepperges: Yes, it is wonderful.
Petzold: No, unfortunately, I haven't seen it yet. A week ago, Eddi and I had to showcase our films to some officials from the employment office. They want to integrate the Art and Film Academies into the great "data freeway"; the dffb and the WDR as quasi-rest areas. And then they look for people at the film academy who can talk, and Eddi Herzog is one of them, as am I. So, we sat in front of these officials from the employment office, and they were such culture enthusiasts—apparently they have a lot of time. They seemed like longtime unemployed candidates from Helmut Lange's TV show *Kennen Sie Kino?* [*Do You Know Film?*] They were familiar with every film and even knew the names of the camera assistants. Then Eddi recounted that he came from the village, and his parents, whose hardware store he did not want to take over, met other parents at a hardware association meeting, who had the same problem with their son. And this son—it turns out—was [Frank] Castorf, the theater director. And his parents did not even know that he was famous with his "little" theater in Berlin.
Ertl and Knepperges: By the way, Eddi slipped us your old short films.
Petzold: Oh, you are well prepared, you studied my record.
Ertl and Knepperges: In *Women*, you literally wallow in the peculiar tristesse of the 1970s, the "Minidom"-site (the Miniaturwelt Minidom amusement park) in black-and-white. But you will probably say that you like that.

Petzold: Yes, here I have to think carefully, so that the romantic in me doesn't surface. But first of all, that's where I grew up. A line from a politician of the Social Democratic Party from the 1960s: "Each citizen should be able to reach a highway in five minutes!" This sentence stripped down the whole country tremendously. And when you are fifteen, it's hard to survive a Sunday afternoon between Dusseldorf and Leverkusen without a driver's license. But when you are eighteen you can cruise through the city, look at girls at the bus stop, and in the case of Haan, which has two highway on-ramps, you can speed over the highway and drive through the same city again, and do it all day long. But, when you are fifteen, at the most you can spit from the bridge and talk about Nastassja Kinski. At seventeen, I read Rolf Dieter Brinkmann for the first time and loved that he was not searching for uniqueness but discovered something in the trodden-down, the worn-down, and the effects of nonsensical transportation policies. As with Berlin, these places were filled with memories, but when one returns in order to shoot there, they are completely empty. And then in *Women*, I did the camerawork myself and failed totally. For example, one cannot even really see the trailer shop. That would have been one of the typical images of this area: the man who sits with his coffee machine in the trailer and waits for two Dutch people to stop by once a week to take a look at a camper. But I doubt that with these images I wanted to say, "You destroyed the whole world, you pigs." I just want to let stories take place in such areas, and hence the stories have to be suitable. *Pilots* chronicles commercial travelers who go after their work and don't search for "themselves." One has to dodge the romance trap.

Ertl and Knepperges: Hence two women as heroines? Because of the distance?

Petzold: That too can be dangerous, because of male fantasies, figments from the jack-off room. But the figure of the cosmetic sales representative did not come from nowhere. When my father was unemployed, my mother tried to become the district manager of Avon. And at the time Avon representatives came to see her. Many women without families, who always wanted something "better" and, just like in a film with Elke Sommer from the 1960s, waited for the big chance in their own cars behind their sunglasses. When I worked for [Hartmut] Bitomsky, he told me similar stories of representatives. He bought a mini-house close to Magdeburg in order to live there "like a Frenchman" on the weekends; which also meant to dine in "Zum goldenen Hirsch."[1] Of course, he refused the Hitler salute upon entrance, as it is customary there, but at some point he noticed a cosmetics sales representative, who sat there, dressed up fabulously, with a cell phone, who got stranded there passing through; and Bitomsky recounted how amazing it was to watch this woman's telepathic defense forces against the women-less male

---

1. A frequently used name for rather old-fashioned restaurants serving German-style meat-and-potato dishes and often associated with provincialism and a narrow-minded attitude towards non-locals.

brood. And then when I researched it myself, on behalf of [Harun] Farocki for a documentary on sales reps, and spent some nights in some hotels, I encountered such a woman as well, a sales rep for Merz Spezial Dragees, who studied French and was chased madly by men. At the latest, then, I was fascinated by the figure of the sales rep, which is not "fabricated," but is on the "verge," doesn't belong to anyone, me included, when I narrate her in the film. Would you like a cigarette?

Ertl and Knepperges: I've got my own—peppermint cigarettes.

Petzold: KOOL? Because of Willeford?

Ertl and Knepperges: Bingo. [Hoke Moseley, protagonist of some late novels of Charles Willeford, smokes the menthol brand KOOL.]

Petzold: I have to admit, his last two books—*Miami Love* and *Playboys in Miami*—[are] brilliant literature. *Pilots* is well received by female television commissioning producers; they especially like the film. Yesterday I proposed to a commissioning producer to make films of these two Willeford stories, as sort of a "supplement" to *Husbands* by Cassavetes. In Willeford, men are not married anymore, as they would've been in the 1960s; instead, they go to airport hotels for lonely stewardesses. Very modern appearances with brutal intelligence. . . . When in *Playboys in Miami*, one lets his buddy analyze the . . .

Ertl and Knepperges: Content of the purse of his girlfriend, and he writes him an assessment.

Petzold: Because this buddy understands psychology as well as cosmetics, he knows: this lipstick means she wants to be younger than she is; that hair color means if you really want to know whether her pubes are red, check her armpit hair. But when I told her of this assessment, the TV commissioning producer was, I think, shocked. Nevertheless, that's what I'd like to do after my next project. Next in line is something I already received script sponsorship for: a road movie on the axis Berlin-Leverkusen-Knokke. It's called *Cuba Libre*. Actually, they want to go to Cuba, but they only make it as far as Knokke.

Ertl and Knepperges: Knokke . . . That's the noble one among Belgian beach resorts. I was dumped by my girlfriend there because I refused to eat in an expensive restaurant.

Petzold: She despised you for that? I think that's right, actually. My girlfriend is exactly like that. What about her? Is she still there in Knokke?

Ertl and Knepperges: No, she's now working for an advertising agency in Dusseldorf.

Petzold: Yes, that sucks. To work for an advertising agency in order to be able to eat in Knokke, that's the pits. No—but in the off-season, Knokke looks like the beginning of [Jean-Pierre] Melville's *A Cop*. Only the banks are still open. Those beach resorts are like Märklin model railways, as if a nine-year-old came up with them.

Ertl and Knepperges: Whereas in Leverkusen it's always off-season.

Petzold: It's never high season there, not even early season.

Ertl and Knepperges: Everything belongs to the factories there, the rabbit breeder associations, art galleries, stamp clubs, stores, and everyone receives a newspaper for free, it's called "Bayer direkt."[2]

Petzold: Not far from Leverkusen, in Langenfeld, there's a psychiatric clinic. And so it happens that when you sit at the Spanish restaurant in Leverkusen near the underground garage, you see a lunatic who walks glaringly across the deserted pedestrian street. That is Leverkusen. I absolutely have to shoot there again, also because of the Rhine.

Ertl and Knepperges: The most impressive and odd picture in *Pilots* is the tiled basement entrance, this plain gateway to hell, with the sign: Cosmetician, Consultation hours by arrangement. Does that really exist?

Petzold: No, but I wanted to find something that looks very clean but still grimy. It took me a while to find this tiled corner typical of the Lower Rhineland.

Ertl and Knepperges: The sign is made up?

Petzold: Yes. First it was Cosmetician Hans-Hubert Vogts, but then luckily I changed my mind.[3] The film is overall twelve minutes shorter than planned, because in the end I cut all the gags. Actually, it should be a tragedy.

Ertl and Knepperges: Tragic as in Willeford, where everyone makes plans, great plans, but nothing works out.

Petzold: Each plan that counters the complex fabric of life with simplification has to fail. Hoke Moseley's two overalls in—perhaps this is his best—*Sideswipe*, where this gangster forges a family around himself: a woman with a battered face, an abstract painter from Haiti, and then an old man who painted side strips on car bodies on the assembly line by hand, since due to the finest irregularities it appears more dynamic than if it were painted mechanically. As he masters the line, he is one step ahead of the abstract painter. That is the terrific thing about American crime novels, that they are vessels of everyday knowledge. Something that Max Goldt provides in Germany and, before World War II, Siegfried Kracauer. Not many in this country can do that.

Ertl and Knepperges: Wasn't it lucky that you encountered Bitomsky and Farocki through the dffb?

Petzold: When I did my civil service in Haan at the YMCA, three days at the film club, two days open house for problem children, they had a *Filmkritik* subscription. And that was the best journal I've ever read. In such a small city,

---

2. The city of Leverkusen is headquarters of pharmaceutical giant Bayer.
3. Vogts was a famous German soccer star playing for Petzold's favorite team, Borussia Mönchengladbach, which is from the Lower Rhineland region.

you build your own world, and Bitomsky and Farocki were the kings there and especially interesting as "hostile brothers"—like Adidas and Puma. One of them John Ford contemplation romantic and the other James Joyce modernity montage. As if you had to choose between the two of them. And then I met Farocki in Berlin playing soccer, he was also playing in Wilmersdorf at the time. The work with both of them at the academy came later.

Ertl and Knepperges: But they are not really enemies. They stopped doing collaborative films especially because you can't live off of halved paychecks.

Petzold: I think it's good that they make movies separately. The highway in Farocki's *Wie man sieht* isn't the same as in Bitomsky's *Reichsautobahn*. But it is as if they would correspond through different approaches, through their films.

Ertl and Knepperges: Bitomsky is now in the USA.

Petzold: As the dean of CAL-ARTS in Los Angeles. [. . .] But I thought his last movie before he moved over there, *Imaginäre Architektur*, on Hans Scharoun, was so great. That was a powerful farewell.

Ertl and Knepperges: Absolutely.

Petzold: That he dared to play with the tricks, invigorated the rooms with threefold lighting.

Ertl and Knepperges: And he dares to show how hard it is to film the multiple potential vantage points in a Scharoun-house. He masterfully stages the failure to exhibit. And he also, again, accentuates his own presence, after there were such stupid restrictions by the ARD on his film on the UFA.[4]

Petzold: He is the deftest narrator in the world anyway. I believe, by the way, that above all it was music that lured him to the USA, a record such as "Highwaymen" with Willie Nelson, Kris Kristofferson . . .

Ertl and Knepperges: Johnny Cash and Waylon Jennings.

Petzold: But now he wrote to me that nobody over there knows this record. That's the sad truth.

Ertl and Knepperges: Let's talk about the music in your films. In the short film *The Warm Money*, there are three songs, which are more than just background music. One of them is Udo Jürgens's "Griechischer Wein" ["Greek Wine"].

Petzold: That's not meant to be "funny" by any means. This film was actually supposed to play only during the time frame of happy hour. Only two kinds of people go to happy hour: 1) cheapskates, and 2) people who come from work and want to experience this "happy hour" before they go home, who play one tearjerker after another on the jukebox, who have drinks for half price in the Dusseldorfer Erlebnisbahnhof and who then, when Udo Jürgens sings, feel like foreigners in their own country. The music is there in place of drama.

---

4. ARD is one of the two German television networks, the other being ZDF.

Ertl and Knepperges: *The Warm Money* is like a preliminary draft of *Pilots*: a woman has more reasons to become a criminal than a man, as she at some point hears the clock ticking and is afraid of running out of time. That's a tremendously vital motivation, and it hasn't been—as far as I know—used by anyone so far, except by you now . . .

Petzold: Life is certainly harder for women. When I presented the film at the dffb, students got upset about the women not going to the unemployment office. Whereupon Farocki said, "A sheriff wouldn't go to a social welfare office either." And while these film students asked why those women didn't look for a job, the people from the unemployment office knew the answer immediately: "Difficult to place." And then there is this critique that at the beginning the film lingers for too long on the work routine. On the contrary, I think I should've elaborated more on that—in order to clarify how elemental it is that the criminal fantasy of the two was limited to their field of work.

Ertl and Knepperges: It is very convincing in *Pilots* that the women are very dramatically marginalized and that the audience is very familiar with this margin—not from other films but because your film precisely defines the lives of the heroines.

Petzold: When we were looking for the hotels in the film, I initially wanted to find one like the ones I envisaged, with rotten wood panels and flickering neon lights outside where an elevated railway passes one centimeter from the window. Bullshit. Of course, hotels today look very different: pastel colors, with cable TV. But one has to manage that: narrate his story in an all-too-discernible world.

Ertl and Knepperges: It is part of the realism in *Pilots* that the women don't become friends right away, but at most . . .

Petzold: Companions. Friends—I couldn't have done that. The circumstances have to effectuate the rapprochement from outside. The handcuffs between man and woman in [Alfred] Hitchcock are also still the best reason to fall in love with each other.

Ertl and Knepperges: For that very reason, the heroic gesture at the end is convincing and touching. The protagonists are amazing.

Petzold: When I drove with my Opel Kadett from theater to theater, from one agency to the other—what you call "casting"—I had to pay a high price for not having watched any early evening series for ten years. Fortunately, I had seen Eleonore Weisgerber in a Chabrol film, and then I thought she was very intelligent . . . which I rely on, because I cannot stand to shoot someone who doesn't know what to do there. Weisgerber, who has the Prussian ability to not let on anything, needed a counterpart whose every impulse is visible in their face. And then one night, I met Nadeshda Brennicke in Berlin. She lived in a jeep with her dog, her clothes on hangers in the jeep. There, I knew that no matter if she was good or bad in [Peter Timm's] *Manta—Der Film* she was the right one for my movie.

Ertl and Knepperges: The clothes hung in the car, as well as some other things in *Pilots*, evoke [Michael] Cimino's *Thunderbolt and Lightfoot*.

Petzold: True. I just noticed that now, but it's true: Eleonore Weisgerber is the Clint Eastwood of the German association of cosmeticians and Nadeshda Brennicke . . .

Ertl and Knepperges: Soft like the young Jeff Bridges.

Petzold: He is still totally soft there, and that's what I really liked about Nadeshda Brennicke. She was *Bravo* "girl of the year" twice and knows exactly how closely she has to look past the camera. This mixture of innocence and tricks, I thought, wasn't bad. I depended on the facial effects due to the spatial narrowness of the car and the hotel room—as well as that they understood their roles straightaway. There wasn't any psychological acting direction or shit like that. We only spoke about the gesture, the duration, and the pause, and not about: "Where do I come from?" or "Where do I want to go?" If they began to do drama school shit there, I'd have bunked. Actors only want to perform as skinheads nowadays. If you say: "I'll make a film with ninety-nine skinheads," they'll act for free, because then they can do method acting and knock over tables.

Ertl and Knepperges: A pitfall in writing a screenplay is the dialogue. They are at times too "funny," in my opinion.

Petzold: True. When I cut, I took in such cases always the "most tired" takes, where they didn't feel like reciting the text anymore. I am just happy that I managed to fit the whole embezzlement, job loss, and pregnancy story in so few sentences, but that also forced me to leave out a few important sentences, which really hurts now.

Ertl and Knepperges: When it comes to the plausibility of speech, one is much more patient in foreign-language films. And the synchronization in its falsity is strangely pleasant to us.

Petzold: As the dubbing actors have the microphone right in front of their lips, any emphasis miraculously disappears. American films walk a tightrope over a net consisting of thousands of fictions, of a thousand well-known sentences. In German films, one is immediately embarrassed by each wrong emphasis. Even in a brilliant film like [Rudolf Thome's] *Red Sun* there are such awkward moments, but Marquard Bohm . . .

Ertl and Knepperges: He was, most recently, also fantastic in *Turn Down the Music* by Thomas Arslan.

Petzold: Even if he has only four sentences, he is always good. Perhaps because he always alludes to the staging a bit. With him you never feel like he tried hard to get an A from the director.

Ertl and Knepperges: Do you have any idea what happened to Werner Enke? (The protagonist of all films by May Spils, *Go for It, Baby, No Pawing, Darling,* and three more, all produced till the early eighties.) He also had the same quality.

Petzold: I might be wrong, but I remember having read that he owns a beverage superstore. I wouldn't be surprised; soccer players open a Lotto-Toto kiosk and former actors from Munich open a beverage store.

Ertl and Knepperges: Enke was even able to write his own texts but still speak them in a very disinterested manner.

Petzold: These Munich films, also the ones by Klaus Lemke, were a real enrichment . . . When my parents allowed me to watch *Rocker* on TV, when I was thirteen, it was an introduction to another world, it was the dark corner of an amusement park. In one hundred years, one will be able to reconstruct the FRG based on Lemke's TV films—and the soccer style of Borussia Mönchengladbach. I really believe that. Lemke, Thome, and [Wim] Wenders are now far removed from these beginnings and surely long to return there.

Ertl and Knepperges: There is this self-pity. Wenders says that in Germany soccer, politics, and cinema are treated unjustly, that he can't make films there anymore.

Petzold: Perhaps he is a little bit right too, because after the World Cup everyone knew how we could've won the world cup, just like Germany's film critics write as if they knew how to make better films. Even though the people from the Nouvelle Vague made similar claims, they justified it intellectually and made it a political matter. Today, it is sufficient for a critic to say that he did not like a film. This development comes from the town newspapers, on which Farocki wrote something in 1978.

Ertl and Knepperges: He thanked the post office for not permitting parasites to start a feuilleton in the phone book. You collaborated with Farocki on the screenplays of *The Warm Money* and *Pilots*.

Petzold: We sat at the open-air pool and recited the women's dialogues. Farocki was, so to speak, my script adviser—a script adviser [*Dramaturg*] with little interest in the script's structure and more interest in what we talked about before, the everyday knowledge in crime novels.

Ertl and Knepperges: Doesn't he, just like Bitomsky, really want to make another fiction film?

Petzold: Definitely. I notice this in the enthusiasm with which he contributes to my stories. But I think he has the aspiration to make something really modern, and he thinks that my stuff is too old-fashioned.

In the Hinterland of Nihilism

Ulrich Kriest / 2001

From "Im Hinterland des Nihilismus," *film-dienst* (March 2001): 10–14. Reprinted by permission. Translated by Marco Abel and Jaimey Fisher.

Ulrich Kriest: There was a time when a film about terrorism was considered such a tricky subject that one essentially could only do things wrong: depending on one's perspective, such films would be deemed too supportive of the state, apolitical, or too insider-ish. In the 1990s, films repeatedly used the topic in order to work through other concerns. The "old" politics ended up via the "RAF phantom" on respectable Grimme-prize television. How does *The State I Am In* relate to this?

Christian Petzold: When I started thinking about *The State I Am In* at the beginning of the 1990s, the film did not seem to have a neighborhood. As an aesthetic phenomenon, terrorism was dead as a doornail. When the film was finished, there was [Volker] Schlöndorff and state television by [Heinrich] Breloer, and suddenly one believed that the world would somehow care about this. That's when I said to myself: "When the Americans use the Mafia in order to create Greek tragedies, then we can certainly use the RAF [Red Army Faction], the political underground, as a stage." For me this topic was not a hot potato. Most people do not even know about it; it is rather forgotten, even though remnants, memories, of this episode can be found everywhere. It is also not the case that people throw their hands up in horror and you don't get any money when you say "RAF." The first funds for the film I received from the state. Later on, however, I received some strange suggestions from the television people: the story was so beautiful, they said, that I should erase the references to the RAF and replace them with the real-estate speculator Schneider. After all, he had to hide as well. This would have destroyed the entire project, for Schneider is a petit bourgeois, and I am concerned with very different people.[1]

---

1. Utz Jürgen Schneider, a German real-estate tycoon, went bankrupt in 1994 and was arrested in 1995 for credit card fraud and forgery. After several years in prison, he was released on probation in 1999.

UK: There's also this film by Sidney Lumet with River Phoenix . . .

CP: *Running on Empty*. I've seen it. There's a parallel, namely, that people who live clandestinely are on the run as a family cell. But the film ultimately works through an age-old American topic. In the USA, one is not required to register with the police when moving to a new town, so that one can live secretly, without anyone knowing, anywhere in the country. In my film, the family lives an entirely ghostly existence. They don't even exist.

UK: The press materials state: "When ghosts desire to become human, they are always protagonists of a tragedy." When watching the film, I had to think of Kathryn Bigelow's *Near Dark*, especially with regard to the scene that takes place at the German-French border. It's early morning. The girl is by the banks of the Rhine and regards the German flag. And then, in the background, the door opens of this coffin- and tank-like white Volvo, and the parents, pale like vampires, get out and embrace her.

CP: I didn't want to be too obvious, but the film is shot through with these kinds of images. We also always show how the doors of this Volvo open. This Faraday cage is extremely important for the family. The border crossing by Strasbourg fits this, but also the scene with this lawyer who doesn't help them. They disappear in this dark forest like apparitions. Or how one morning the mother suddenly appears next to her daughter in the forest—we wanted to highlight the ghostly, the bodyless. To return to *Running on Empty*: there is not really an ending for a vampire film, other than that at some time death delivers the ghosts. In later vampire films, they suffer and beg to die so that they finally can come to rest. This aspect is also in my film. The daughter almost betrays her family so that at long last this endless drifting stops.

UK: The protagonists don't talk about politics. One can watch the film, pretend to be ignorant, and for a long time one wouldn't know what the deal is with this family. In a way, this is a political statement as well, no?

CP: When you make films here in Germany, you are surrounded by a large number of advisors with regard to script, the script's approach, or development. You meet and discuss. All suggestions always pushed in this direction: "Please incorporate dialogue scenes in which the political background is represented! Is it not possible for the daughter to say to her parents: 'Why did you kill this GI in Frankfurt back in the day?'" This really got on my nerves. When a family has managed to stay together for fifteen years under such conditions, then it has recourse to an inner discipline that's incredible. They don't talk about things from 1965, 1973, or 1977. And they also don't talk to the viewer. I'm interested to image the reality, this physical presence of the family—and not a theater group that blabbers pedagogical stuff.

UK: It would indeed have been awful had the family watched the news and Richy Müller grumbles: "Damn it, this fucking system!"

CP: Exactly! When researching, one of course encounters the "political speech" of [Andreas] Baader, the cadaver-obedience [*Kadaver-Gehorsam*] of Stammheim.[2] Using this kind of language in the script would have been catastrophic, utterly unbelievable. As I imagine it, these people lost their idea fifteen years ago; they are surrounded by historical silence, having fallen out of history. For years, they've been living withdrawn, with their backs to society. It is this complex family dynamic that the film is about. This has to be absolutely realistic: we observe a family and its economy of guilt and its sign-like existence.

UK: Against this, the accusation generally is that in this way the resistance is retrospectively depoliticized, incapacitated, one more time, specifically from the perspective of the victors.

CP: Personally, I feel that the family in *The State I Am In* is highly political. Everything they produce among each other every evening at the table and in their conversations is political—micropolitics: how can I maintain this cell (the family) and lead it through the world without being a power-seeker? This family would not have lasted for fifteen years if it were to repress, if it were uncommunicative, if it were not transparent. It would have been destroyed after two or three years. This is highly political, only that here micropolitics is being negotiated instead of continuing to have discussions about the military-industrial complex.

UK: This certainly seems more interesting than to leaf through Stefan Aust one more time to know how "it really was." Eighty-five percent of German films about the topic terrorism are de facto literature adaptations of his *Baader-Meinhof-Komplex*.

CP: For the last ten years, every cover story of the *Spiegel*, *Focus*, or *Stern* has served as the basis for a film. As soon as one reads about a new flu-virus, *Die Todesgrippe von Köln* is on TV. It's not that using Aust is bad, but to get an idea of what "underground" is would mean engaging with books like [Joseph] Conrad's *The Secret Agent* or [Fyodor] Dostoevsky's *The House of the Dead*.

UK: There are the old stories. "I don't have anything to do anymore with this shit," says the lawyer who doesn't want to help. "History lesson," says Richy Müller, when he gives his daughter the now worthless bank notes he retrieved from a depot in the ground. Is your film also a history lesson?

CP: In school, I majored in history, but I didn't learn anything about the world there. Afterwards I swore to myself that I would never give history lessons.

---

2. Stammheim, near Stuttgart, was the location of the high-security prison in which the members of the RAF were imprisoned in the 1970s—and where several of them died.

UK: But there's a film called *History Lessons*.

CP: Yes, by [Jean-Marie] Straub [and Danièle Huillet]. That's more like it. If you give a history lesson, then you should make films so that when seeing them in twenty or thirty years from now one knows how we lived, loved, and traveled today.

UK: It's possible that this comes from somewhere else, but I was impressed by the soundtrack of *The State I Am In*. One could hear the forest, the wind at the beach in Portugal, and Lisbon as a city.

CP: I discussed this with the sound engineer. I wanted that one can hear the wind traversing the meadows by the Elbe when the girl leaves the villa early in the morning and walks across the bridge. I believe that films should be more sensuous, not in the sense of adding some random stuff from the archive but of being able to feel that it is the present world through which the girl moves, in other words: that which her parents are lacking. They don't have a present; they feed themselves from the past and talk about things in the future. But the girl regards the present world, goes to schools, and falls in love.

UK: I'm reminded of the films by Rudolf Thome: this documentary moment in each fiction film that also always documents the presence of the actors' work.

CP: Recently I read a text by Jean-Louis Comolli. He writes that the greatest moment in a documentary is when it becomes fictional. When one pans with a person and this pan then congeals into a fiction. In turn, the greatest moments in fiction films are the ones that become documentary, when that which is not staged manifests itself in the narrative.[3] Of course, this requires the right kind of production circumstances. One has to shoot for much longer than one is usually approved for in Germany.

UK: What made sense to me as subtext is the line, "She's walking away," in Tim Hardin's song, "(How Can We) Hang on to a Dream." The daughter starts to live her own life, and the parents feel that something is getting out of control.

CP: The song poses a question, not a demand, as the frequently used abbreviated version of the title suggests. This is much more tragic. In the film, all those things happen that also happen in normal families. The daughter falls in love, severs her ties with her parents. One argues about clothes and pocket money. But, in the context of the family's very specific existential conditions, all this daily nonsense is charged to a higher degree. Suddenly, it's about really big things such as trust, openness—one can say: politics. Stealing clothes in order to dive into normality means for the daughter becoming human, whereas for the parents it might very well mean death. The resulting tension holds together not only the family but also the film.

---

3. Jean-Louis Comolli, "Detour by the Direct," in Christopher Williams, *Realism and the Cinema: A Reader* (London: Routledge, 1980), 225–43.

UK: The life in underground appears utterly unglamorous. At one time the daughter accuses her parents: "Too much conformity also renders you suspect!" When she is forced to wear the tracksuit from the used clothing collection, the film represents this as the worst thing one can possibly imagine. A really painful moment, connected with this glamorous term "underground." The daughter's friend doesn't understand the term either, for the relevant history is long gone. The enemy of the state as star, Baader and his BMWs: this is no longer communicable. For this scene, in which Jeanne has to put on this Aldi tracksuit, a director would have gotten a beating in the 1970s, no?

CP: I'm sure! It was really hard to find these clothes. To depict poverty in cinema is incredibly difficult. Everything looks great in a film. You cannot represent poverty; you have to produce it. It took weeks to find these "nonclothes," this incredible ugliness of the nylon tracksuit. The protagonists wear clothes that one associates with people whom human traffickers smuggle at night across the border from the Czech Republic to Austria. Horrible leather jackets or silky sweatpants—I think this is today the only thing that one can recognize as "misery" in an image.

UK: Let's talk about a script structure of compression. Two scenes in the film immediately fascinated me. First the idea with the holiday acquaintance: the boy invents a dream biography, and the film shows completely "realistically" an "imaginary" tour through the villa. Here, various stories are being told simultaneously, from which the film's narrative logic benefits multiple times: the interiors are already known, when the family arrives at the villa, and the boy's presence is plausible. This device also shows how strong the girl's desires are. It works like a sponge for the boy's desires, which is why the place looks like how he thinks it looks like.

CP: Yes! When I was fourteen or fifteen, I saw a film by Juan Buñuel, *The Woman with the Red Boots*. It's about a girl in puberty whose desire is so strong that her fantasies are able to impact the course of the world. When writing the script, Harun Farocki and I thought: there's a girl that desires reality so strongly—and there's a boy who dreams of a normal life—she desires it so strongly that the normal life, when she arrives there, is exactly as she imagined it. But, simultaneously, what the boy told her is a lie, because he himself, as an orphan, desires the normality into which he narrates himself. Thus, in the film we are at places that are the fantasy of two lovers.

UK: And the boy creates his fantasy at the expense of his mother who committed suicide in a swimming pool . . .

CP: I did my civil service with youth, including a lot of orphans, in form of a drop-in shelter. What was brutal was that especially boys always had two fantasies; in reality, they are children of kings, abandoned but of better blood.

They glorified their parents but simultaneously sent them into horrible deaths—I recalled this when writing. That's how the boy imagines his wonderful lineage: big house, incredibly rich, but then he has his mother find her death in the symbol of wealth, the pool. This is really important to me, that these secondary figures are also charged with fictional energy and do not merely serve as stooges. They have their own stories of suffering—if the film would change its perspective it could also continue to narrate their stories. When the boy says that he did not complete an apprenticeship as heating engineer and that there is floor heating in this house, then it is possible for him to have participated in installing it. We left such traces in the story.

UK: The second scene is the "suspense scene" at the intersection in the industrial area, when the black cars arrive from all directions, making it appear as if they are about to catch the family. Richy Müller gets out of the car, raises his hands above his head, the traffic lights all switch to green, and he stands there like a deer in headlights with his tail between his legs. This is terrible, but it's also terribly funny.

CP: This scene looks simple, but it took two days to shoot because the shooting logistic was complicated. I figured that one has to experience for once in a film what paranoia is. For paranoia is not just endangering but also welding together. A nonverbal communication, a program transpires: state of emergency—push the daughter down, I get out and distract them from the bullets. The second thought was: when one takes seriously the term "internal security" [the literal translation of the film's German title, *Die innere Sicherheit*], then this concept referring to the state contains a moment of physical hygiene. A body fights the viruses that are attacking it. My idea was that the family drives in a white car like an invading virus on autobahns and streets, and the black cars that position themselves around them are like antibodies that eliminate the virus. That's why there are those long shots that show the movements of the white and black cars—a molecular image. Eventually the black cars were supposed to encircle the Volvo and eliminate it by throwing it out of the blood stream, which is indeed what happens at the end.

UK: With regard to the black cars, when at the end the arrest occurs, the situation is comparatively unambiguous: they eliminate them completely professionally.

CP: Yes, even though the film is over before the actual ending. The girl tells the boy: "I'll stay with you." He betrays the parents in order to cut off their way back, in order to save her (for himself). Then she disappears again. When we then see the Volvo driving on an empty street, the film could have ended with this shot. At the time, the commissioning producer said: "They will no longer arrive anywhere." We added the action in order to give the film a real ending.

UK: Is this redemption?

CP: It's a redemption that isn't one. This is why the film ends on a close-up of Jeanne, who in a way is being birthed here by the state, which is why she has this slime from the accident in her face. Like a kind of birth slime. In this moment she's all alone, surrounded by an infinite emptiness. You can hear only what one could hear on location that morning. The parents have disappeared, and there is no one who puts a blanket around her, a preferred image for concluding films.

UK: Julia Hummer reminded me of Linda Manz in *Out of the Blue*....

CP: When I saw her during casting, I also thought of Linda Manz. I also mentioned it to her, but she did not know her. She only started watching films a year or two ago. But the character that Dennis Hopper found with this end-of-the-1970s girl has indeed a lot to do with Julia.

UK: She has this grumpiness and reluctance in the way she moves. She also looks rather unique.

CP: I love it. Today, everyone is talking about cloning, but this casting has proven to me that this has long become reality. These young actors that agencies offer up all have the same body and haircuts—all these youth from preprimetime TV series. In contrast, Julia is able to tell stories through the way she walks and how she dangles her arms. This is why I filmed so many walking moments with her. Fifteen-year-olds have a way of communicating their resistance against, or even disgust for, the world through their body, but her face is incredibly concentrated and alert. Julia identified with her role in such a way that I was almost afraid. In the scene when her mother slaps her and lays claim to it later in the kitchen ("Other children who are beaten by their parents at least can escape from home: I can't!")—when she says this, she suddenly ages, as if the slap in the face had turned her into an adult. What transpires on her face at this moment is fascinating.

UK: One of your films is called *The Sex Thief*. One immediately is reminded of Alexander Kluge, something that happens regularly with your films: like with an experimental setup, the stories can be condensed into three or four sentences, but then it pivots, and one discovers another dialectic. And the films exhibit parabolic structures, but they are realized in a very realistic, "truthful" manner. This mixture appears to me as rather "Kluge-esque."

CP: Strange, for I just read my way through *Chronicle of Feelings* and the two Vorwerk 8 volumes. I have really been influenced by Kluge ever since I read *Case Histories* towards the end of the 1970s. In it, I found something that revealed ruptures in this awful German townhouse normality and made horrible tragedies visible behind it. The "sex thief" is a Kluge motif, but it also has to do with my great admiration for Georges Simenon. In *Intimate Memoirs*, he compared the sex thief with a regular prostitute. The prostitute sells her body.

The sex thief considers herself something better because she doesn't sleep with men and instead merely seduces them and then knocks them out with knockout drops. My film is about the fact that the sex thief must sell much more of herself, for she has to seduce. In seducing, she reveals her intelligence, her dreams, and desires. Compared to a prostitute, she doesn't sell her body but her soul. This certainly has something to do with Kluge.

UK: In Kluge's works, a specific worldview is inscribed, a coldness of the gaze, combined with a specific humor. I find both in your films as well [and] also in Farocki's *Betrayed*, which is the film of his that's the closest to yours.

CP: I think Farocki is heavily influenced by Kluge. So is Bitomsky. When I visited him in Los Angeles, his only request was for me to bring *Chronicle of Feelings*! By the way: the first sentence of Bitomsky in *Das Kino und der Tod* was the first thing I said every morning during shooting, as a sort of calendar slogan of the day: "Our film takes place in the hinterland of nihilism." On set, everyone always said: "Yes, yes, yes."

UK: How does your collaboration with Farocki work?

CP: I've been collaborating with Harun for years; this goes so smoothly that I do not even try to think about why it is so easy to work with him. I'm a bit afraid that too much reflecting about this lightness might rob us of its secret. At the end, when one knows how it works, one can no longer work together, and all that remains is to write textbooks, give seminars about script writing, or becomes a city chronicler—a kind of Syd Field of Sebnitz.[4] When I got to know Harun and we worked for the first time on a story, he mentioned Hitchcock's *39 Steps*. What he liked about it was that two people fall in love, but through the police rather than at first sight. Handcuffed together, they have to arrange and organize their escape—and that's how their love comes about. This is always something that's in the stories that Harun and I develop. People who are forced to do certain things. Love is not the starting point but the consequence. Work. Things that once were part of the protagonists' repertoire—the strategies of seduction in *The Sex Thief*, the sales strategies in *Pilots*—are being transformed by the protagonists. Strategies of seduction become strategies in job interviews. In *The State I Am In*, a strategy that seems to be the last possibility in a police cross-examination becomes a defense strategy in a conversation between two lovers.

UK: In 2000, films such as [Michael Mann's] *The Insider*, [Romuald Karmakar's] *Manila*, [Wong Kar-Wai's] *In the Mood for Love*, [Lars von Trier's] *Dancer in the Dark*, or [Oskar Roehler's] *No Place to Go* had theatrical releases—all films without worn-out videoclip mannerisms and with a palpable effort to closely

---

4. Sebnitz is a small, remote town in Saxony, near the German-Czech border.

observe the behavior of people. Would you locate *The State I Am In* as part of this trend of a "new seriousness"?

CP: Alexander Kluge's book *Bestandsaufnahme: Utopie Film* includes a "list of the un-filmed" that Claudia Lenssen put together. Somewhere it more or less says: as long as such films aren't filmed we do not perceive our country. We've had the Berlin Republic for ten years, life changes daily, yet the films don't tell stories about it. Cinema is no longer the place that interrogates one's own society. But this is exactly what Kluge manages to do with *Chronicle of Feelings*. I believe this tendency towards seriousness has already existed for years. When I studied at the dffb, there was a group that was annoyed by the fact that one no longer does proper research. It wanted to get away from this nonsense coming from Munich, from these rucola-salad apartments and the jobs the protagonists have, where nothing has anything to do with reality.[5] Where our patchwork biographies, stories of migrants, don't even take place. At the time, Thomas Arslan or Angela Schanelec were part of this group. I think many of the films that one can take seriously emerged from these discussions, which correspond everywhere in the world. After all, we can't just leave the world to these twenty-three-year-olds with their DV-cameras. In these new editing suites, only nineteen-year-olds with piercings and tattoos run around, who are able to operate software but don't know how to cut because they lack any kind of experience with life and art.

---

5. Petzold is referring here to the difference between the more intellectually minded dffb and the more commercially oriented film academy in Munich.

The *Flying Dutchman*: An Interview with Christian Petzold

Jörg-Uwe Albig and Christoph Gurk / 2001

From "Der fliegende Holländer: Ein Interview mit Christian Petzold," *Texte zur Kunst*, no. 43 (September 2001): 43–53. Reprinted by permission. Translated by Aylin Bademsoy.

Texte zur Kunst: *The State I Am In* was released in a moment that you couldn't have predicted. The debate around the Sponti-movement past of Joschka Fischer and 1968 brought unexpected success to your film. But didn't it also affect its reception negatively?

Christian Petzold: When I received calls from the distributor saying that 5,000 people went to watch the film because of this discussion, and when the champagne corks popped, I wasn't quite happy. That for me was a week of real crisis. The film cannot deliver any answers to this discussion. Regardless, as the person behind this film, I was invited to all kinds of events. I rejected these invitations, as I didn't want to go to a talk show as an RAF specialist. I was afraid that this would draw my film into an abyss, because the discussion was extremely primitive. Terms whose origins and biographical entanglement nobody remembered kept reappearing for two to three weeks. Those are knee-jerk movements that go from the Bundestag to *Sabine Christiansen*, and then it's over again. In the end, the discussion did not really harm the film. I feel more like the questions remained and no answers were delivered. Since Red-Green [the coalition between the SPD and the Green Party] and the Berlin Republic, it seems impossible to catch up with all that's unresolved, that hasn't been worked through, that keeps springing up.

Texte zur Kunst: What was the impetus for this film?

Petzold: The primary metaphor that I had in mind was a sentence from Hans Blumenberg's book *Shipwreck with Spectator*: "If ships that function like conceptual apparatuses run aground, is it possible to build something viable out of the wreckage swimming, floating around?" How can the left survive after such a bestial breakdown? When Harun Farocki and I began to work on the screenplay, we concluded at some point that this raft of wreckage was the nuclear family. In Kreuzberg, where I live, you can observe this quite well. Here, left collectives retreated to nuclear family cells with a burrow to hibernate.

Texte zur Kunst: For the raft that's floating in your film, though, there is no land in sight.

Petzold: In Klaus Theweleit, there is a reference to the autobiographies of Georg K. Glaser and Franz Jung and the notion of *Geschichtsstille* [standstill of history], which plays a role in them. After the storm, when the ship is capsized and shatters on the cliffs, silence unfurls. Leftists like Glaser and Jung suddenly realized that history and society didn't need them anymore. Only after this moment did they think of having the occasion to write their autobiographies. Jung describes how he managed a match factory close to Moscow, how the relations of production and love are intertwined. And suddenly this man is nothing but a specter, a ghost.

Texte zur Kunst: In your film, nature sounds are often more forceful than human voices.

Petzold: In some American comics by artists such as Daniel Clowes or Adrian Tomine, you can find a similar moment, where figures drop out. There, sensual impressions suddenly become extremely powerful before the total crash happens. In *The State I Am In*, the daughter lives in the present, while the parents move between the past and the future. All of a sudden, the daughter smells, tastes, senses. Perhaps the parents enabled their daughter through their defeat. During the production, together with the cinematographer and the sound engineer, I was always careful to shoot at localities where the wind is visible and audible. The places in between were important to us, for example the path right before you reach the city, a house on the outskirts, or the highway service station next to the highway, a highway hotel.

Texte zur Kunst: There is no history between people and their environment anymore.

Petzold: The fact that I was making an auteur film seemed to me at times almost as ghostly as the situation of the protagonists in the film. At one point, it swirled through my mind that the right-wingers always have caves, for example Hans-Jürgen Syberberg, who in documenta X showed vaults with Hitler and Wagner figures in them. The leftists who were in the underground, members of the RAF, had on the contrary only their flash photographs taken by speed traps. This difference—the transparent phantom-like left versus the earthy, heavy, mythical right—preoccupied us for a while.

Texte zur Kunst: Is the car not a cave as well?

Petzold: I think the car has the same impact on the structure of the family as the dinner table does. Both appear in the film. The left isn't loved anymore.

We thought that it was like the *Flying Dutchman*, who has to wander the seas forever. Just that we chose, instead of the sea, the highway as the stage, as it represents a crucial aspect of the surveillance system's computer search. The police infringement at the end of the film is practically some sort of proof for the left of the state's love, which shows them that they still have an identity. Only the girl, who is in the present, has a chance. If she can leave a memory trace somewhere, through a kiss, a touch, can inscribe herself into the bodily memory, then she will exit the track. That is why she betrays her parents.

Texte zur Kunst: She, together with the audience, is also the final authority in front of which her parents must justify their life.

Petzold: They have explained themselves for fifteen years and reached the highest form of transparency. For the whole film, we watch these parents legitimating themselves. They explain their domestic transgressions, which would be totally ridiculous in a normal life, but which in such an exceptional situation can lead to the collapse of the whole organism. It interested me how the protagonists tried to survive in their economy of family and guilt. The parents begat their daughter consciously as an attempt to liberate themselves from the moment of *Geschichtsstille*. One perceives the world one more time through their own child. Everything that we learned has to be revised in communication with the child. In puberty, usually the cellular existence ends. The last scene of the film is some sort of a cell division, the birth of the daughter as a social being. She is thrown out of the car, which lies on its roof in the background. She is totally alone on the field. And then the film ends.

Texte zur Kunst: Is this family a mere construction, or is there a model for it in the history of the RAF?

Petzold: I had the image of the family in mind for a long time. I wanted to focus on a group and not on an individual. With the figure of the daughter, I created a fictional instance, from whose perspective the group can be described in the first place. Only after the film did I find out that Hans-Joachim Klein also had two daughters while he was in the underground. He wanted to turn himself in, but before that he wanted to spend three months with his kids. Since 1975, he had lived half-hidden in France as a farmhand on a farm and wasn't politically active at all anymore. In all his *Spiegel* interviews, he talks about love, the smells, and the wine. He just wanted to live a normal life. The kids were an attempt to find some grounding in the present.

Texte zur Kunst: In the prison letters of the RAF, one can read how the prisoners melt together into one body. Any deviation, just like the girl in *The State I Am In*, has to be punished as a threat to the entire body.

Petzold: The RAF had *Moby-Dick* as their guide. The members gave themselves artist names based on this novel, and Andreas Baader was, of course, Ahab.

They liked the image of the white whale as the leviathan, the humongous, bloated state as the monster, and the organized cell, the ship's crew, fighting against it. That's why the book comes up in the film and also, of course, because it's among my favorite books. At the beginning, in the first fifteen pages, the first-person narrator recounts why humans gravitate so much to the water. That the water consoles one and that it's something that outlives the human. At the end there's a great image: everything sinks, the narrator hangs onto the coffin of the harpooner and survives. That's a wonderful metaphor for the narrator, who is never really involved but then derives strength from the dead in order to tell his story.

Texte zur Kunst: Your film also begins with the sea, before the storyline shifts to the highway, the concrete river. But the highway is still a street, and the street as a political arena got lost in the seventies. Is the escape to the highway an attempt to reclaim the streets?

Petzold: The highway is closely linked to the title of the film, *The State I Am In*. It has something absolutely hygienic: a girl who wants to grow up, and a state that, through its physical hygiene, also wants to grow up. I had the image in mind that the body of the FRG was infected by a virus. The highways are the veins of the body. And therefore the white Volvo roves about like a pathogenic particle. The cars of the BKA [*Bundeskriminalamt*, Federal Criminal Police Office] are like the white blood cells that surround and eliminate the pathogen.

Texte zur Kunst: The street plays an important role in the German auteur film, for example in Wim Wenders's *Im Lauf der Zeit* [*Kings of the Road*, 1976]. The time of the RAF also coincides with the German *Autorenfilm* [auteur cinema]. Did the inventory of expression of this genre have an impact on your film?

Petzold: Don't forget that 80 percent of what the auteur cinema produced was crap. But three or four films of Wenders, for example *Summer in the City* [1971] or *Alice in den Städten* [*Alice in the Cities*, 1974], are infused with tremendous melancholy. The imminent destruction of the cinema is also thematized there already. From this melancholy arises a very peculiar engagement with Germany by someone who basically has only American records but suddenly begins to discover John Ford landscapes within the German borders. Wenders produces images that do not sell themselves but observe, register, and identify deserts—psychical and moral ones. With the loss of the *Autorenkino* [auteur cinema], a form of engagement with our conditions got lost too.

Texte zur Kunst: Are the flat images your film presents a play with TV aesthetics, which cofinanced your film?

Petzold: You cannot differentiate between cinema and TV on the basis of the depth of images. That would imply that *Citizen Kane* [Orson Welles, 1941] is the best film because it has depth, but it merely resembles the darkest nineteenth century. *Rote Sonne* [*Red Sun*, 1969] by Rudolf Thome, in contrast, plays only against colored walls; it's flat as hell. We wanted to show specters, bodies that are almost transparent. That's why the film is set always in the light and practically never at night. Every scene takes place in front of a window. Even the house in which the family hides is made of glass. That's one of the three thousand Reemtsma villas, which you can find everywhere. That one was bought by a South African art collector who didn't consider that he cannot hang pictures in a house of glass. In front of this background, the figures should be visible-invisible. They are everywhere, but nobody looks at them: the vampire-theme—to not really be on earth anymore. That's why there are platitudes in this film.

Texte zur Kunst: So, if anything, you actually tried to avoid TV aesthetics?

Petzold: In the seventies until the beginnings of the eighties, film criticism fulminated tremendously against the TV language. "Shot/reverse shot" was already considered smut. I don't agree with that. Worse is that TV doesn't know its audience, or rather that it made it disappear. The images address an unrespected, measured audience, and that's why they have to turn tricks, to mean something. The TV movie creates only images to which you can respond with "yes" or "no." If one wants to show that an actress like Katja Flint plays a rich woman, then there is a close-up of her putting on her Gucci shoes. TV, which shoots everything on 35 mm or 16:9, imitates a cinema, which luckily doesn't exist anymore. A cinema that employs fantastic music, insane opening credits, and incredible establishing shots at the beginning, and then ends up at the same setting. In Deleuze, it's called the "terror of the medium close-up [*Terror der Halbtotalen.*]" The face of the person speaking has to be always visible, the exchange value of the actor's face has to be exhibited because it costs so much. *The State I Am In* was from the beginning conceptualized against this mindset. We showed people often from behind, and we never filmed the car rides through the windshield, because that's an absolute TV image.

Texte zur Kunst: Was it a problem to produce the film with the help of TV?

Petzold: When we recognized that we, with the exception of some small state institutions, wouldn't get any money, TV became a big must. Especially smart commissioning producers told me that the topic was dead for the FRG since Gerhard Richter's Stammheim paintings. I told this person that this seemed to be the first time in history that a topic was settled by art. TV stations have an immense power today. The commissioning producers, of course not all, live in terraced houses, read *Spiegel* and *Stern*, experience every day a tremendous pressure to hit their numbers, and see the audience only virtually. They think everything that's being discussed at the moment must definitely be in a film.

Texte zur Kunst: Doesn't TV have the advantage of being able to react quickly?

Petzold: I believe that TV never discovered or experienced anything despite being so quick. TV is always just where other cameras have already been. It is a place where the presence is digested like in gastric acid. The cinema, in contrast, accomplishes a quite different memory work. Michelangelo Antonioni had never in his life listened to pop music, and in the sixties, with *Blow-up* [1966], he shot a film that perfectly captured the situation in London at that time. Cinema films have a different form of production relations, which are slow. They expose themselves differently to the space. That's why reality is much more likely to entangle itself there.

Texte zur Kunst: *Deutschland im Herbst* [*Germany in Autumn*, 1978] by Alexander Kluge, Volker Schlöndorff, and others was also a snapshot.

Petzold: The only contribution worth seeing in *Germany in Autumn* is the one by Rainer Werner Fassbinder, where he almost documentary-like snorts his cocaine and yells at his mother because she was in favor of the RAF prisoners being executed in Stammheim. That's an incredibly amazing document. There you hear the FRG the last time before Helmut Kohl took over. After that the atmospheric space was shut down.

Texte zur Kunst: Fassbinder, so to speak, lets the film run through his own body. Is that an option with which one can work today?

Petzold: Klaus Theweleit demands this authenticity with respect to the completely destroyed imageries and relations in the Federal Republic. The counterstrategy, for him, consists in making a film deploying one's own life. Then one lands eventually, like Rainald Goetz did back then, in Klagenfurt and tries to convince the jury members with a razor blade. Even though I am a big fan of Goetz in other respects, I totally disagree with that. What I thought was interesting about Fassbinder's contribution wasn't the authentic moment, since the scene is also fiction at the same time. Fassbinder shows in a historical moment that he is not capable of thinking of Douglas Sirk, of dismantling something in a magnificent title such as *Liebe ist kälter als der Tod* [*Love Is Colder Than Death*, 1969]. There are moments in life in which one cannot write love letters, cannot manage to produce a form, and doesn't have time. That he confronts that moment, in which everything glides out of his hands as an artist and author—I didn't find that authentic in the sense of a cult of a genius or figure of an artist, which absorbs the reality.

Texte zur Kunst: He only shows that what happens in the film affects him too. How is *The State I Am In* related to you?

Petzold: The girl in the film is approximately my age at the end of the seventies when I lived in a small West German town between Wuppertal and Dusseldorf. She also walks similar paths. The pedestrian zone, the record shop: these are all places that I rediscovered as motifs. Back then, in this small city, I felt like the state, in search of the RAF, had arrived in this little town too. The town became uneasy, the teachers became anxious, and I liked that. Suddenly each highway exit was loaded with meaning and fiction. The miserable housing project at the highway looked then exactly like the conspirative apartments from the *Tagesschau*. Such memories are perhaps reflected in a few images, but it is not a biographical film. We are trying to move away from the autobiographical, authentic, and to reach a much higher form of veracity.

Texte zur Kunst: How did you perceive the political events back then?

Petzold: My parents were Helmut Schmidt fans. They both thought that he personally pushed the flood out of Hamburg. For Schmidt, the RAF was like the SS, and my parents absolutely agreed with that. For them, they were pigs who turned their back on the bourgeois middle in which everything is negotiable. My parents had this basic anxiety that this, whether it's coming from the left or right, would always lead to fascism in Germany. And this fear of my parents was one of the most beautiful feelings in the seventies. The TV didn't unite the family in a semicircle anymore but split them in separate splinters, and impassioned discussions took place.

Texte zur Kunst: Did the media images of 1977 awaken your interest?

Petzold: No, that started for me with the Alfred Hitchcock retrospective in the cinematheque in Cologne. That was during the German Autumn, but it represented a completely different world. *North by Northwest* [1959] led me directly to the New Wave. This form of stylization, design, elegance—that all did not exist in the political sphere at all. The parents wanted to normalize everything, to not attract any attention. These fantastic suits, ska music, which they were completely at odds with, were much better than the RAF. When it came to the RAF, my father could still argue in terms of Schmidt. But when you sat there in a suit and smoked a menthol cigarette, he didn't have a terminology available to confront that.

Texte zur Kunst: Did the aesthetics later flip over to politics?

Petzold: When I frequently visited a friend in Italy, the first time was in 1979, I came into contact with the German *Verfassungsschutz* [Office for the Protection of the Constitution]. It was noted that I went to Italy seven times in a year. My friend wrote for the periodical *Il Manifesto*. That was a tough group, some of them were in prison. They listened to punk and discussed the control societies by Deleuze. I had no idea at all, but they politicized me quite a bit. Talking Heads and RAF, that was approximately at the same time. Disintegrated political groups, no utopias, incredibly good new music. That was all a part of it. And the question of how you can produce. That you had to be against the status quo but couldn't offer an alternative. And that it wasn't actually that bad not being able to offer one.

How the Politburo Made the Circumstances in German Film Dance

Michael Althen and Bert Rebhandl / 2002

From "Wie das Politbüro die Verhältnisse im deutschen Film zum Tanzen brachte: Die Filmemacher Christian Petzold und Harun Farocki erzählen, was passiert, wenn sich deutsche Regisseure in einer Kneipe treffen" (How the Politburo Made the Circumstances in German Film Dance: Filmmakers Christian Petzold and Harun Farocki Talk about What Happens When German Directors Meet at a Bar), *Frankfurter Allgemeine Zeitung*, May 23, 2002. © Frankfurter Allgemeine Zeitung. All rights reserved. Provided by Frankfurter Allgemeine Archiv. Reprinted by permission. Translated by Marco Abel and Jaimey Fisher.

Michael Althen and Bert Rebhandl: At the Berlinale in February, German film made a strong showing. And independent of how the German directors fared, one could tell how strong their desire was to finally appear again as a group or at least to declare solidarity with each other. How strong is your desire to find common ground?

Christian Petzold: The Export Union organizes these trips for German directors to Los Angeles, Rome, Paris, London, and Vladivostok, where one gets together but actually does not speak much with each other. Some time ago, however, I was in Kreuzberg in a restaurant and had an embarrassing moment. This was the first day after the film festival in Hof, where *Something to Remind Me* premiered. I went to this restaurant because it has a lot of newspapers for its guests. I wanted to read what they were writing about my film. When I returned from the newspaper rack with a stack of daily papers, I saw in the corner Tom Tykwer and Romuald Karmakar having lunch together. They saw me with my stack of newspapers and of course immediately knew what was going on. I apologized to them for this image I presented. But they said that they would do this every day. Then we sat there for two hours, and that is when I realized that something like commonality exists: that one doesn't talk about money, but that one simply talks about, for example, how it is when as a director one reads, say, a novel and when one begins to feel the pressure to exploit it—that was quite interesting. Yes, one wishes, like in this book by [François] Truffaut about Hitchcock, that this affirmative interest in the work of another is there. Only rarely do I have the experience that I'm impressed and enthusiastic about a German director and also want to express this in words and sentences. This happened to me only once, when I saw Dominik Graf's *Deine besten Jahre*. I wrote him a letter, and two days later I received one back. So, this desire to communicate with another certainly exists. When I buy a CD and see what musicians are assembled there and exchange their experiences, then I think that this is the only way that something can emerge. And in our politburo group, we sometimes have this to some extent.

Harun Farocki: When I watch films by Thomas Arslan or Angela Schanelec, I do think that all of them and their films are somehow in contact with each other, and this is what culture in the broadest sense is.

Althen and Rebhandl: Do they also belong to the Berlin group, which you call "politburo"?

Farocki: Yes. The group consists of Thomas Arslan, Michael Baute, Ludger Blanke, Michel Freericks, Stefan Pethke, Angela Schanelec. Some of them write, some make films, some do both.

Petzold: Exactly. These are basically people who were at the dffb in the 1980s. There was a seminar and . . .

Farocki: From 1985, I gave one or two seminars per year, called "Film Analysis." We watched a film at the editing table, and sometimes this took just one day, sometimes four. In the following six, seven years, a group came together—as in soccer, some left, others joined, but it was always a team with its own game. (Alas, it was also a men's group.) I've already taught at many places, but only here did this result in lasting collaborations. I worked on every film Christian has made since, and I also collaborated with Ludger Blanke and Stefan Pethke on films. With others there's an exchange of ideas, not just about film. And this relationship is quite undogmatic, different from how it was in the past when I was at the film academy and there was a strong tendency to form fractions.

Petzold: When, in 1989, I was in my first year at the academy, we also tried to represent ourselves in such a fraction; we gave ourselves an identity and beat up on each other. But this quickly collapsed. Hartmut Bitomsky was the other teacher who gave seminars. On his films we also served as assistants or worked the camera, etc. I was not even at the academy but was already a guest. Back then, the theater institute still existed: 500 students, one monitor. The topic was Hitchcock, and one tried to read *Vertigo* with the help of Erich Fromm's *The Art of Loving*. This was quite tough. Compared to this, the dffb was, of course, a research laboratory. The first film in the first seminar I took was William Friedkin's *To Live and Die in L.A.* I was totally depressed when the seminar was over.

We watched scene by scene at the editing table. And once a day or every other day, we also watched the entire film projected, sometimes also just one scene. We discussed one shot setup at a time—organization and architecture of a film. What was fantastic was that the film never lost its secret as a result of the analysis. On the contrary: it became ever more multilayered. I remember we discussed a [Roberto] Rossellini film . . .

Farocki: Yes, this was *Fear* . . .

Petzold: There was a family scene in the yard. Everyone is embracing, and the camera keeps circling around them, and then a student stands up and says: "This is family harmony." But when you look closely at these movements, you see that the camera movement rather describes a prison around Ingrid Bergman. This was fantastic.

Farocki: Film analysis—to really focus on the film itself—was for me a program. In the 1960s, ideology critique dominated due to the overall politicizing; Adorno was the model, and it only got worse. It was like in school: there was no doubt about how an interpretation had to be done. The interpretation basically accused the work of not having said right away what it thought to have conclusively established. I really wanted to insist that cinema contains possibilities that can be detected in a detailed analysis. Just like Barthes claimed that Balzac was not a realist of the nineteenth century but a predecessor of modernism, in essence an avant-gardist. At the time, I tried to ignore content as much as possible, just as when one listens to Bach one listens to the music and not for a message. But today I think about this differently: I no longer object to a critique of the story as long as it is smart enough to enrich rather than to impoverish the film or at least the reader. Serge Daney is someone with whom I can imagine growing up. To admit that film is not just about the cineastic.

Petzold: But the effect of the seminars was that at some time one got the feeling that the films are self-sufficient. During the first few seminar days, there were always some people who interpreted each shot setup as if it prostituted itself and they were the customers. And after one delved ever more into the architecture, one saw what states of abeyance and relations of tension existed; one saw both that even though the construction is so beautiful there were still secrets and that the film itself sufficed—one gained an entirely different access to the film. This was something that deeply influenced me.

Althen and Rebhandl: When we return to the New German film, back then there was a romantic fraction and one that was more political or ideological. And one can say that both failed, if one excluded Alexander Kluge. In the early 1990s, did you have the feeling that it was necessary to start anew with something? Was there an explicit attempt to figure out where one could actually start again?

Petzold: For me it was like this: one also goes to the film academy to make films. I initially wanted this as well, but during the first three years, I did not produce anything. I merely watched, and together with the people around me, I quickly acquired the reputation of a loser within the academy, whereas others already went to eat with commissioning producers and did not have to pay for their meals. During these three years, I realized that I was really empty, or becoming empty, and that perhaps it would be best to have no tradition at all. Or to have that tradition be the 1960s and 1970s, which we would really need to read and see anew—and the same with the B-movie tradition, to which we should reestablish contact. Then, in the early 1990s, I wrote for the first time something like a script. I was also always afraid of actors because one was surrounded by the dumbest acting one could imagine. Towards the end, the *Autorenfilm* [auteur cinema] recruited its actors only from the ensemble of the Schaubühne theater [in Berlin]. There was nothing left to discover. That was how I justified to myself a bit why I was not interested at all in working with actors. This changed only when I made my first film.

Farocki: Christian, I think that your, or our, work entails a lot of the *Cahiers* tradition, and this would be different under different circumstances. You can find film academies where this is no longer the case. I don't even want to complain about this, but this is a fact. I think that there are different nuances. So, it was not zero.

Petzold: But in one seminar we had, for example, two films: [Jean-Luc Godard's] *First Name: Carmen* and [Francis Ford Coppola's] *Rumble Fish*. And that was the first time when I saw my own life situation and position reflected in the so-called contemporary cinema. It was then that I noticed that we are surrounded by old stuff—including old discourses—to which we can no longer relate but with which we still have to grapple. I always had to laugh how Matt Dillon says: "Man, what the fuck do the Greeks have to do with anything?" And Mickey Rourke is really the guy who, in the old myths, is the ancient one who is still hanging around.

Althen and Rebhandl: In *The State I Am In*, it is the mythos of the RAF, in which the parents are trapped, while the daughter, Jeanne—and the film—wants to get beyond it.

Petzold: Yes, that's correct. At some time, I have to retrieve all of this from my computer, the different ideas we had during writing the script. We had an intense phase when I was in America with Harun; we kept cutting everything out of the script that extended the myth, the legend, of the RAF. At the beginning, there were still scenes with the Federal Criminal Police and interrogation scenes. For those, I always imagine people in long trench coats who smoke.

Farocki: [Claude] Chabrol. We discussed him at the academy as well.

Petzold: Right, we discussed him in the seminar, too. That's when I realized how little interest I have in parasitical situations—that one essentially first creates a myth in order to stick to it, as a kind of host, and to then suck this host dry once more before throwing it on the street. Peter Handke's *Falsche Bewegung*, the basis for Wenders's *The Wrong Move*, was really important for me. This is also a story about someone who travels through West Germany and essentially creates a myth one more time. He is looking for father figures in order to work things through, but they no longer exist. Even the Nazi beats himself up on a daily basis and doesn't need the young person anymore who tells him: you dirty Nazi. This was similar to the situation regarding *The State I Am In*: I was interested in the RAF myth precisely because it no longer was one. In the middle of the 1990s, the RAF had disbanded for about the nineteenth time, so this news was nothing sensational anymore. And this is exactly what interests me, when things finally disappear for good and perhaps develop one last time some nobility in their failure.

Farocki: When one asks why we are still debating about 1968 to begin with, I think the answer is quite banal: no one has managed to establish anything else since. Simply because the things afterwards were so weak, it keeps coming back and shines through. I think this is not even such a big historical thing. Also, at the beginning of the 1970s, when the small Marxist worldview had started to run its course, I still frequently went to Klaus Heinrich, where we learned one sentence: no remythification.[1] That was the most important thing. And I think this is still valid. It's certainly OK to violate or correct and take back some modernist principles, but to remythify, to relinquish the project of the Enlightenment by creating new myths: that's completely off the mark.

Althen and Rebhandl: And why did you need a new group with whom to talk about film? What was missing in the conversation about film or in the consensus of the film critics?

Farocki: Perhaps like I just said: that with the film magazine *Filmkritik*, we tried for too long to somehow save this pure doctrine. We ended up in this defensive position. For we did not conquer the *Filmkritik*; rather, no one of the generation around Helmut Färber and Frieda Grafe wanted to continue running it.[2] Experience also teaches that one does something like this only until one has found one's career. After that, such a magazine no longer works. Because we managed to postpone our settlement, we ended up starting when we were thirty and were still at it when we were forty-five. But this group did not manage to make a

---

1. Heinrich was a well-known philosopher of religion and was a cofounder of the Free University Berlin.
2. *Filmkritik* was the most important West German film journal. Grafe and Färber both wrote for it, as did Farocki, who eventually became its editor (1974–1984).

real connection with the new developments. We not only misjudged Fassbinder, but we did not even attend to him; we ignored him only because we were politically irritated by how he was discussed and how he was co-opted. But it sounds so fundamental when I say I now need a new group. I always need people when I find myself in a film crisis.

Althen and Rebhandl: *Something to Remind Me* is a kind of pulp [*Kolportage*] story as one finds it in the local section of a newspaper. One could think of Fritz Lang films, which are also always a bit too constructed and become plausible only in their mise-en-scène. Is this form perhaps better off today on television?

Petzold: Initially, I thought that way about *Something to Remind Me*. Truffaut once said that one should make a big film and immediately after that a small one. This is all humbug, calendar wisdom, but perhaps there's something to it. I had the feeling that when one has made a film like *The State I Am In* people immediately want another film from you. And I liked the conditions that television provided: exactly eighty-six minutes, no worries about getting financing, only a few people who participate and want to have a say, a very small loyal team that protects you, so that you could almost make a B-movie that—as I saw it—would have no reality at all in the cinema. If you were to approach a film subvention body, they would demand that you add something to the film, something personal, another height for a fall [*Fallhöhe*], a star or whatever, so that the film will get the boost of cinema. I wanted to avoid this discussion. As I had already shot the film and saw the first edited sequences, I was quite sorry that I had not insisted a bit more aggressively to turn this into a cinema film after all—that is, to organize financing that would keep the film from being screened on TV for two years and that would lend it its own film identity.

Althen and Rebhandl: Harun Farocki, your work with Christian Petzold on scripts is merely one aspect of your production. What role do you play with documentary films in the context of "German cinema," or do you play in your own league because your films are often happily co-opted by the fine arts?

Farocki: I'm still a modernist at heart, but I can pursue this with my own production only at a low level. And then there is the sphere where this is possible, as with Straub or Godard or Rossellini, where it's necessary to experience an entirely different conception. And then there is this constraint that the story-film has: that you cannot include everything in it and that you would have to create an entirely different form. Right now, I am working on putting something together about intelligent weapons and machines. It's quite difficult to get one's hands on images, which is why I have to find an entirely different form. . . . This is an altogether different activity. I compare this with the Nouvelle Histoire and its difficulties to even get rid of the concept of the king, to transcend it in the description of historical events. We invent heroes in order to narrate the mechanism of the events, for it exceeds that what we know about dynasties.

Petzold: On the way here, I read an old issue of the *Filmkritik*, and you write that in the end, soccer culture is in all likelihood stronger than film culture. You offer the example that in the 1960s soccer was about to be destroyed by defensive strategies, and suddenly there's a game like in 1972 that is completely self-sufficient, where a team plays beyond itself but in a way that is still highly disciplined.[3] And then you write that you thought that this would also occur in the cinema. You wrote this. When I was on the way here, I noticed that there is not a single cinema on the entire boulevard Unter den Linden, that the film festival takes place in public spaces that are owned by private investors, and I believe that cinema really needs a public, everyday space. And, when you have an entire boulevard here that is completely owned by insurance firms and banks, then it is difficult to even make films. For which places? Where do the people glide into and out of the cinema? This is not even discussed in the so-called German cinema, that places are being lost, that there are no longer distributors. There's permanent talk about authors and heights for falls, but the entire macropolitical context that surrounds the cinema is being dismantled.

---

3. This is likely a reference to West Germany's famous 3–1 victory against England in the quarter final of the European championship. The 1972 team, which came into its own with this game, is generally considered (West) Germany's best-ever team.

The Music Has to Sell Itself

Christian Buss / 2002

From "Die Musik muss anschaffen gehen," *taz*, May 28, 2002. Reprinted by permission. Translated by Marco Abel and Jaimey Fisher.

Christian Buss: Last year you received the German Film Prize for *The State I Am In*—together with producer Florian Körner von Gustorf, who plays in the band Mutter. An almost unknown director and the drummer of the most radical German underground band bag the most coveted prize of the German film industry.

Christian Petzold: Truth be told, we did not believe that we would win. We certainly also got lucky, for our film received a lot of attention as a result of the Fischer debate that was going on at the time.[1] But then I was not able to really celebrate, as I started shooting *Something to Remind Me* immediately after the award presentation. That filmmaking could be an everyday matter was a new experience for me. You normally have to wait around with your scripts for five years in producers' offices before you are allowed to realize them. Fortunately, I had initiated two new projects even before I completed *The State I Am In*: contract work for television, without the usual subvention processes involved. I was horrified by the prospect of once again having to deal for years with the financing of a film. That's why I wanted to follow up with two B-movies. Noir films that no longer have a home in the cinema. Together with the same ensemble I used for *Something to Remind Me* I will soon shoot another film for the ZDF.

CB: Was the decision to work for television also influenced by the production difficulties you encountered for *The State I Am In*? During preproduction, the distributor went belly up.

CP: I'm not sure whether this was not also a matter of lack of courage on my part. In any case, I found the idea of making two films for TV very attractive.

---

1. Joschka Fischer, member of the Green Party and then Germany's foreign minister, was at the time in the news for his militant activities in the 1970s as an active participant in the left-wing extra-parliamentary opposition in West Germany.

Everything was taken care of. We had twenty-eight days of shooting and a budget of 2 million DM.² Besides, I was always interested in crime stories. I did not want to make such a lonely film as *The State I Am In*, for which you could not find any kindred spirit productions of neighbors around here.

CB: Are the high-ratings-producing *Tatorte* on TV not neighbors that are a bit too loud? Does television really offer a neighborhood for such a quiet crime drama such as *Something to Remind Me*?³

CP: Well, I sure hope this neighborhood won't end in disaster.

CB: In any case, *Something to Remind Me* offers quite a challenge for the prime-time viewer. The use of pop songs alone radically breaks with the consuming habits of the viewers; it's not every day that a man and a woman play records for each other.

CP: *Something to Remind Me* is also a love film. By playing records, they lay themselves bare for each other. I did not want to dictate the rhythm with extra-diegetic music but rather derive it from the scene itself. In general, the musical choices are horrific on German television. There, music has to turn tricks. Songs are being downloaded from a data bank in order to call forth specific feelings in a viewer. Sometimes television productions remind me of breakfast rooms in hotels, where one is permanently being blasted with music. Speaking of: I have a friend who toured with Kraftwerk through the US as a roadie. When he was with them in an elevator to get to the fifteenth floor, horrible Muzak came out of the speakers. One of the musicians cut the wires with a nail clipper. I basically wanted to repeat this deed for television.

CB: Even when you use music only sparsely, it often inscribes itself via detours into your films. When you worked on *The State I Am In*, you once said that you constantly listened to Blumfeld's *Old Nobody* record, which is about the encroachment of the private into politics—just as in your film at the time.

CP: Later on, I had a strange experience with Blumfeld. When I was a child, my parents always played me Hanns Dieter Hüsch's "Abendlied." Eventually, I knew it by heart. When preparing for the shoot of *Something to Remind Me*, I listened to it with Nina Hoss, and then the Blumfeld record was suddenly released, which included just this song as well. I was totally shocked. I realized how synchronized [*gleichgeschaltet*] people are who were similarly socialized. We proceeded to listen to this song time and again with the other actors.⁴ In general, we listened to a lot of music. The male protagonist in my film is part of this lonely group of men around forty with a large record collection. They put a record on, stare out the

---

2. Deutschmark.
3. *Tatort*, which premiered in 1970, is the longest running (crime) series on German television.
4. Petzold would end up memorably using the song in *Transit*.

window, and then go on a trip like pilots. Their emotional world comprises all the same songs from the cassette tapes they put together, which does not make their feelings any less real.

CB: You seem to trust music more than words. For there is not much dialogue in *Something to Remind Me*.

CP: That's what I like in westerns: the characters don't speak a lot. In [Anthony Mann's] *Winchester '73*, for example, James Stewart, together with his companion, is looking for years for his brother, whom he hates. At some time at the campfire, he is asked: "We've now been riding for ten years together. Are we friends?" James Stewart says, "Yes." Then the conversation is over. This has nothing to do with an artificial laconism. For here, two people create a real relationship with each other. This is different from most TV productions, where, notwithstanding endless dialogues, the social situation of a character is never explained from within the character. One gets the impression that TV has a kind of social office, where former kindergarten teachers put together the biographies of the characters. Whereas it is crucial to approach one's characters with respect, whether they are good or bad.

CB: German TV frequently has recourse to a strange sense of revenge. In the *Tatort* "Bestien," for example, the detectives make evidence disappear in order to protect a mother who kills the murderer of her daughter. And in the Grimme-Prize-winning "Tanz mit dem Teufel," which like your film was produced by teamWorx, simple schemes of revenge are exercised. Is it not possible to seriously engage the perpetrator?

CP: When working on *Something to Remind Me*, I dealt a lot with research about victims, including with the "Weißen Ring." As soon as a perpetrator is on trial, the representatives of these revenge-oriented clubs ask why one even bothers caring for him [sic]. But the perpetrator is a member of society, which is why we should be interested in the motives for his actions. It is true that dealing with the victim doesn't lead to results. For it is part of the role of the victim to be subjected to the absolute arbitrariness of the perpetrator. As horrible as this sounds, we do not learn anything about the character of crime from the victim. We must take evil seriously.

CB: Notwithstanding the metaphysical heaviness, the first half of *Something to Remind Me* is defined by a peculiar lightness. The characters hover through Stuttgart's polished-up architecture. The sun is shining, but there are hardly any people. Why?

CP: Imagine two lovers meet in this café where we are sitting right now, to have their first rendezvous. All conversations and faces would be pushed into the background; the couple would disappear in a bubble. For this physical sensation I tried to find images—not in the romantic but in the modern sense. We really do not need another love movie in which a German metropolis looks like Paris.

Dead Man, What Now? A Frontrunner for the Television Prize—Christian Petzold between Andersen and *Vertigo*

Rainer Gansera / 2002

From "Toter Mann, was nun? Ein Favorit beim Fernsehpreis—Christian Petzold zwischen Andersen und Vertigo," *Süddeutsche Zeitung*, October 2, 2002. Reprinted by permission. Translated by Marco Abel and Jaimey Fisher.

Rainer Gansera: *Something to Remind Me* is expected to receive several television awards. What is your newest project?

Christian Petzold: The next film for the big screen we are making is called *Ghosts*, with Julia Hummer (who was in *The State I Am In*). Before that I made a television film with the same team, producer, and TV producers as for *Something to Remind Me*. Nina Hoss and Sven Pippig are in it again. The film is called *Wolfsburg*. It takes place in the city of Wolfsburg and is about a car dealer who commits a hit-and-run after he hits a child. Subsequently, he cannot find his way back into his daily routines. The child's mother is thrown off track as well. For a brief moment, the two adults manage to build an arch, a connection, that allows them to live. But this arch collapses. When I saw Tom Tykwer's *Heaven*, I understood what my film is really about: how can you become free of guilt in a world without religious foundations? *Heaven* thinks love can get you there; I don't think so.

RG: Redemption through love is the guiding star in many of Tykwer's films.

CP: In the films that impressed me, love does terrible things. Even when there's a kiss at the end, a happy end, I always feel that the final embrace is the result of tiredness and exhaustion.

RG: What, then, is this arch of connection that your protagonists build?

CP: When I studied German literature, I discovered in one of Kleist's diary entries a part that I really liked. In it, Kleist is on a walk: sweating, he runs out of the city but suddenly comes to a stop underneath an archway in a city wall.

He looks up and sees these stones that all support each other. The archway is the result of the fact that all these stones actually want to fall down. This is a terrific metaphor for how people might possibly escape fate, disaster. At least for a brief moment. Many of the films I like are based on such an archway architecture. Everything is bound for destruction, but things are propped up one final time.

RG: Many scenes in *Something to Remind Me* take place near water: at the beginning, a woman steps out of a public indoor swimming pool.

CP: I wanted for the film to be permeated by a water imagery. I had purchased for my daughter Andersen's fables, and we read the story of the Little Mermaid. When Nina Hoss emerges from the water in the first scene, it is supposed to appear as if she now arrives on Earth and wants to love. And if she is properly loved she is allowed to stay; if not, she has to return. Part of the play with water imagery is also a small homage to [Helmut] Käutner's *Under the Bridges*.

RG: You've described *Something to Remind Me* also as a film noir. . . .

CP: In Germany, film noir was largely received as a camp phenomenon: men in trench coats, women in front of blinds. I wanted to make a film noir that is bright, that doesn't play in a studio world, and that nevertheless contains such metaphors: the mysterious woman emerging from the water; the man who rises as if from the dead in order to feel once more.

RG: Would it be incorrect if at times one felt reminded of *Vertigo*?

CP: Not at all. A film like *Vertigo* is deep inside me. It was with Hitchcock that I first started to really take an interest in cinema. Today, with Hitchcock, I am sometimes put off by the myth of his craftmanship, this narrow-minded [*spießig*] translation of an idea into an image. But then I see once again one of his films and am deeply impressed by the intelligence, the marvelous lack of interest in method acting and other nonsense. Recently I saw *Torn Curtain*, where Paul Newman runs through a museum in East Berlin in order to get rid of pursuers. He traverses the rooms, looks around. And then one of these magic Hitchcock moments occurs: the film does not continue to follow Newman, lets him go, and cuts back to a full shot of a room that he had already traversed. In the distance, one still hears his footsteps echoing in this empty room, and for a moment one doesn't know whether it's really his steps or the steps of a pursuer, who may just be a figment of Newman's imagination. The chase scenes in *Vertigo* with James Stewart and Kim Novak left a deep mark on me, and even on my bodily memory, with their somnambulistic slowness.

RG: The settings in *Something to Remind Me* look like cursed locations where love cannot possibly stand a chance.

CP: I always feel that love requires the boulevard, public space, open meeting places. Since my childhood I have been experiencing the increasing disappearance of public space; it barely exists anymore. When scouting for locations in

Stuttgart, I once again became aware of this: public space is dominated by banks and trust companies. Then they build restaurants nearby that pretend to be public space, but in reality they have the character of shopping malls. How can one possibly fall in love in such spaces? How can one look into each other's eyes? These are questions in which I'm interested. I'd like to find appropriate images for them.

RG: In German cinema, some are currently trying to create closeness to reality in the form of cinéma direct or Dogme 95.

CP: Frieda Grafe once wrote that cinéma direct, which appeared like a burst of fresh air at the start of the 1960s, aged amazingly fast. These films, like today's Dogme films, pretend to feel the pulse of life but are in actuality considerably more artificial and mannered than films by [Vincente] Minnelli. I'm not interested at all in such agitated, pseudo-spontaneous films shot with shaky cameras. I'm interested in situations that have something to do with aftershocks: something is deposited and becomes sediment. For this you need a slowness, without which form cannot emerge.

"This Typical FRG-Generation"

Claudia Lenssen / 2003

From "'Diese typische BRD-Generation,'" *taz*, February 13, 2003. Reprinted by permission. Translated by Marco Abel and Jaimey Fisher.

Claudia Lenssen: In *Something to Remind Me*, Nina Hoss hides a secret that is only revealed at the end of the film. In *Wolfsburg*, we know from the start that Benno Fürmann remains silent about his guilt. Is playing with suspense your *Leitmotiv*?

Christian Petzold: I wrote *Wolfsburg* first. But because the ZDF had at the time a film by Max Färberböck on the topic of hit-and-run in the works, I developed *Something to Remind Me* as an alternative and shot it first. I now see how the two films correspond with each other, not just because Nina Hoss stars in both of them. In *Wolfsburg* I intended for it to be clear from the start what the crime is and who did it. It's a catastrophe film that does not sketch a clichéd normality and then introduces the catastrophe as a cathartic shock. Such John Does would not have interested me.

CL: Why, then, a different kind of catastrophe film?

CP: It's about the fault lines with which people continue to live. The time before nevertheless plays a part because it introduces a discourse about love. In the car, Benno Fürmann's character is on the phone with his wife. Shortly thereafter he runs over a child and commits a hit-and-run. Each time it's about neglect.

CL: Did you already have this view of the story when writing it?

CP: No, only during editing did I understand that in principle we are sacrificing a child in order to tell the story about a new couple. The child's mother struck me as if her entire life had focused on him. By virtue of the fact that the script sacrifices the son, she can start anew. Nina Hoss realized during rehearsals that from that moment on, she is getting younger. The maturity of this woman was also a hardening that resulted from her being alone. When she then drives in the car with Fürmann and changes her clothes on the backseat, she is suddenly eighteen again. I found such moments more interesting.

CL: How do you prepare for the shoot?

CP: I look for films that resonate. For *Wolfsburg*, I chose films with men and women in cars. In Walter Hill's *The Driver*, for example, a man is completely reduced to driving and listening to country music, until a woman looks into the car and upsets his life. Part of Benno Fürmann's story in *Wolfsburg* is that as an eternal son—he talks about his parents—he climbed the ladder from car mechanic to sales manager at a car dealership and thinks that everything belongs to him. He and his wife [Antje Westermann] are part of this typical FRG-generation. They live in a wonderful bungalow, which belongs to her and is a complete fetish, just like the dealership, which her brother inherited.

CL: But nothing is right in this marriage.

CP: Like everyone who is used to theater and rehearsals, Antje Westermann asked the right questions of her character: how do I wear a dress, how do I traverse the bungalow as a child of parents who were social climbers? She walks through the bungalow as if through the piles of presents after Christmas. The husband is hers as well.

CL: Her husband lives in the car, not at home?

CP: Yes, we tried to work with Fürmann's physical charisma by almost always shooting real driving situations. We flowed with him through traffic in Wolfsburg. It was important to me that the moments of confession, desperation, atonement, and tenderness all take place in the car. The car as pressure chamber. In it, he fights with his wife, later practices his confession, and his love for Nina Hoss also emerges while driving together. The end also has to unfold in the car.

CL: Why *Wolfsburg*? Could the film not also have been titled "Oldenburg" or "Lowlands"?

CP: I've been familiar with Wolfsburg since my assistantship for Hartmut Bitomsky's film about the Volkswagen factory. The car city is the center. I'd say that everything that is not the factory is included in my film. In no other city did I find the history of Germany to be so compressed at the periphery. If VW is in trouble, Germany is in trouble. The person who has been put in charge of fighting German unemployment is the VW manager [Peter] Hartz. The traces of the Nazis are everywhere in Wolfsburg. At the same time, it is a location of incredible modernity and productivity, at least with regard to the streamlining production.

CL: But the city is not even in the film. What we see is life in the car.

CP: In the first shot, one sees a wide field and in the background four chimneys of the VW factory. This determines the space. The factory is always somehow palpable. I did not want to make a portrait of the city, but to narrate my personal experience of West German history as a history of urban sprawl.

The Cinema as an Experimental Setup: A Workshop Conversation with Director Christian Petzold

Stefan Reinecke / 2003

From "Das Kino als Versuchsanordnung: Ein Werkstattgespräch mit dem Regisseur Christian Petzold," *epd film* (October 2003). Reprinted by permission. Translated by Marco Abel and Jaimey Fisher.

Stefan Reinecke: *Wolfsburg* is about both a man who kills a child in a hit-and-run and how this accident changes his life. *Something to Remind Me* is about a crime in the past that a woman seeks to avenge. Why are you so interested in the question of guilt?

Christian Petzold: I am less interested in guilt itself than the work it takes to overcome guilt. What is involved is a kind of economy: society, the law, an individual has been wounded, and through movement it is being sutured again. I am not interested in metaphysical guilt but in showing the work of atonement.

SR: *Wolfsburg* poses a question not unlike the one Dominik Graf asks in his *A Map of the Heart*: how are existential experiences possible in the middle-class working milieu [*Angestelltenmilieu*] in which we live and in which everything is orderly? And what happens when this order breaks down? In *Wolfsburg*, it appears as if the car salesman Phillip [Benno Fürmann] comes alive only through this incident.

CP: It was important to me to narrate a catastrophe but to avoid the usual script structure. A traditional story would spin a tale of a more or less caricatured normality, followed by a flood or earthquake, and then the revelation that the prostitute, from whom you'd least expect it, actually has a heart of gold. That is: normality, catastrophe, catharsis—I wasn't interested in this. This is why the catastrophe occurs right at the start. I wanted to show how someone who thinks he is secure reacts. He drives home to his bungalow, he puts the car keys where he's been putting them for a long time, but in the apartment is already a foreign body. Life already begins to drop him.

SR: The bungalow is quite neat, everything has its spot—dignified, tasteful. The apartment of Laura [Nina Hoss], the mother or the dead boy, looks different, less neat, more normal. We see IKEA furniture that one has at home as well. It happens only rarely in cinema that one sees things one owns oneself.

CP: It is difficult for actors to play if it looks like in their own homes, when the telephone book is fully scribbled, etc. For many, this is too personal. When I'm scouting for locations, I don't want those that enrich the image and add production value. I try to find locations in which the actors are not just in the foreground and the locations setting but in which there is an exchange between the two.

SR: Why Wolfsburg and not another city that would be understood as a symbol for provincialism?

CP: Because I don't know of another city in which the history of the Federal Republic can be found in such compressed manner on its periphery: the traces of the Nazis, modernity, and at the center the Volkswagen factory. I wanted to show a specific German form of being for which the bungalow and the car dealership are characteristic. I grew up in such a suburb that exists in Wolfsburg as well. With clean yards, the living room with Danish furniture and later in the style of the Bauhaus. This is the attempt to create clarity and order. This is how this bungalow was supposed to appear as well, completely without expensive, noble designer lamps but, recognizably, with the attempt to live hedonistically, with one's individual freedom. It is this into which guilt erupts.

SR: When one states it this way it sounds like Lars von Trier.

CP: No. That's too moralizing for me. I engage morality but don't want to make moralizing films.

SR: Even more important than rooms is the car. Almost everything that's essential happens there or is initiated there. At the moment when Phillip, the car salesman, loses his job and is walking, he almost looks naked.

CP: In a western, this is the scene in which the hero loses his horse. He then has to carry the saddle, just as Phillip carries his suitcase in this scene. I watched a lot of car commercials for this film. A Mercedes advertisement showing a man in Cairo was especially characteristic. It's hot, people are crowding him, they don't have the polite distance we are used to here, they jostle and push. Then he gets into the car, everything falls silent, and a slogan appears: finally at home. That's the idea of life in the Federal Republic: to create a life sphere that does no longer have anything to do with the complex public sphere.

SR: The car is an armor?

CP: As of a few years ago, there are more and more extras in cars: odor filters, pollen filters, CD changer, navigation system, hands-free device. The car is turning into a completely individualized living space. It separates the driver from the exterior: inside an I, outside a film. That's what *Wolfsburg* is about: a man who opens the car door and has to recognize that the windshield isn't a screen and the soundtrack from his CD player isn't reality.

SR: There's only one scene in *Wolfsburg* with music. At the end, during the lovemaking scene at the Baltic Sea, when the fiasco is already a fait accompli. Why?

CP: In my view, German TV uses music as a simplistic attempt to trigger emotions. I thought that if this story were a Greek tragedy then the gods would appear in this scene. It's the point at which others have to bring the story to an end. The music doesn't humanize the scene; it transforms it.

SR: At the end the car salesman dies—perhaps. He looks into the camera and says, "Highway 248, Bad Salzungen." The last words of a car salesman: it contains a hint of satire. I think Fassbinder once said about Chabrol that he looks at his characters like a scientist at insects. This harsh perspective exists in *Wolfsburg* as well. The film is a melodrama, but cold.

CP: The film is like a physical experiment. It creates a distance. In Germany, we are surrounded by films that force us to identify, that sell themselves in order to solicit empathy from the viewer. I don't like this. One can characterize *Wolfsburg* as cold, but then one also has to characterize every western or thriller of the seventies as cold. Even a film such as [Sydney Pollack's] *Three Days of the Condor*, with Robert Redford, shows in a very distanced manner the movement of a man who is falling out of a system. Even the love story between Redford and Faye Dunaway looks as if a physicist were observing what results from this attempt at love and in so doing briefly turns the heater on. But it is especially these distanced films that enable a more complex form of empathy than the therapeutic empathy that most German films produce.

SR: Did you think of Hitchcock's *Vertigo* when creating the scene in which Nina Hoss falls into the river and is being saved by Benno Fürmann?

CP: Well, I basically always think of *Vertigo* [*laughs*]. The river is the Mittellandkanal. That's the reason why the Nazis built Wolfsburg there, precisely because it's located at this convenient transportation path. This channel divides Wolfsburg into a production sphere on the one hand and a living and shopping sphere on the other. And she enters the water at this border. That was my idea, even if one cannot recognize this.

SR: Harun Farocki worked on your scripts. You have worked with Hartmut Bitomsky. Do you have role models?

CP: Yes. When I was eighteen, nineteen years old, I went to the cinema almost every evening. That's when I discovered the *Filmkritik*, the film journal for which Farocki and Bitomsky wrote. I was impressed because the journal posed questions about the images and thereby started to structure my cinephilic chaos. Later I took seminars with them at the dffb, which are still something like highlights in my life. This has sharpened how I look.

SR: Bitomsky directed the documentary *Der VW-Komplex*, which shows what is missing in *Wolfsburg*: the VW factory. Were you influenced by Bitomsky's film?

CP: Of course. I worked as his assistant in Wolfsburg when he shot the architecture film about Hans Scharoun [*Imaginäre Architektur*]. My entire team watched *Der VW-Komplex*. It has a scene I thought was important: Zählpunkt 8. That's where the car is finished and has to be assigned to dealers or car trains. It has to be moved for one hundred meters and filled with a liter of gas, and this unskilled job to drive the car for one hundred meters is handled by women. They walk back on foot. And they walk this distance as if on a catwalk—as if they wanted to extract some surplus from this undignified, unskilled labor. At this moment, Bitomsky uses music. This is what the actresses watched who had to play workers or service providers. How do you walk in the supermarket at a moment when you don't have to do anything?

SR: The aesthetic calling card of *The State I Am In*, *Something to Remind Me*, and *Wolfsburg* is the reduced use of music, of the actors' emoting, the dispensation of many techniques associated with psychological realism. The stories are about the classic big topics of melodramas—love and death—but they use small, reduced means.

CP: This is why Stefan Raab is terrible and Helge Schneider good. Because Raab can only caricature melodramatic feelings, whereas Helge Schneider is capable of excavating the sadness and sentiment from a popular song [*Schlager*] that's buried in it.[1] Melodramas contain material that one has to work on properly. That's what I try to do.

---

1. Both men are well-known German entertainers.

Interview: Christian Petzold

Nicolas Wackerbarth and Christoph Hochhäusler / 2003

From "Interview: Christian Petzold," *Revolver*, no. 10 (2003): 41–62. Reprinted by permission. Translated by Marco Abel and Jaimey Fisher.

Nicolas Wackerbarth and Christoph Hochhäusler: How do you get going on a film?

Christian Petzold: For the last three or four films, in the beginning, there was a small scene that didn't have anything to do with the plot or story. With *Wolfsburg*, it was the scene of a woman who goes to a coffee machine in a hospital and pushes the button . . . And then just leaves. A man watches her. In the next thirty seconds—the machine says "brewed in thirty seconds"—she goes to the window and looks out. And then she walks away. The man goes to where she has been standing and sees that the window still has her breath on it, because she was crying. When her breath has almost faded, the coffee machine suddenly sounds: the coffee is ready. The man takes the coffee cup. The woman comes back and says, "That is my coffee."

That was all that I wrote. Then I sent it to Harun Farocki, with whom I always write. He either says "interesting" or nothing at all. If nothing at all comes back, I know that I have to send him something else. Otherwise, we go for a walk and think about what could have happened before and after this scene.

Wackerbarth and Hochhäusler: This is a kind of playful process?

Petzold: Yeah, a bit like spinning a yarn. The story [in *Wolfsburg*], with the hit-and-run accident and car dealership . . . those are all things that came later. The "original scene" was the one in the hospital, and I always try to shoot that scene as the first one. And with that, on the first day of shooting, I remember all over again how it all started.

Wackerbarth and Hochhäusler: The window with her breath on it does not appear in the final cut.

Petzold: I tried it with artificial breath in the frame's foreground . . . and that looked like shit [*laughs*]. For me, the scene was about a voyeur watching grief. Thus, it is someone who nourishes himself with her tears, with her breath on the window. The coffee machine gives a unit of time without any particular symbolic meaning. Someone like him, a salesman who is leading a very nouveau life, suddenly experiences a depth to his life through the suffering of another, and that brings him out of his regular rhythm. That is really the basic motor driving the whole story forward, and that is already readable in the scene. That probably sounds much cleverer now than it was in reality, but that's the way it was, more or less.

Wackerbarth and Hochhäusler: I assume that you did not write five "original scenes" for five films, rather that there was much more material than that. How do you decide on which scenes you want to keep working?

Petzold: I would say that it decides itself. In Patricia Highsmith's book *Suspense*, there are two things that I think about a lot. She writes that you can sleep as long as you want, but that you should get up immediately as soon as you wake up. And that when you notice on page 122 of a book that there's not much happening, you should throw it out. And I believe in that, too. I have often experienced that the potential that the "original scene" seems to promise is just never realized. Funnily enough, this scene can appear once again in a different context, but you can't be too narcissistic about it.

Wackerbarth and Hochhäusler: What was the point of departure for *The State I Am In*?

Petzold: I started with the family scenes. The whole RAF story came later, although, if I'm honest, it was already in there, too. Yes, it was a very normal family, almost stereotypical, father, mother, child . . .

Wackerbarth and Hochhäusler: And a Volvo . . .

Petzold: That came later. But I knew that it had to be something Swedish, the car that a teacher would have. They are in a hotel room, and then they check out, looking around each other weirdly. The hotel is empty, in the background a tray falls to the ground, and then they get into the car and drive to an intersection. At the intersection, the traffic light isn't working, and suddenly a whole bunch of cars pull up around them. But then that dissolves, and the family drives on. That was basically the scene that I had in my head. That was already at the end of the 1980s.

Wackerbarth and Hochhäusler: But is there much work on story construction after these impressionistic beginnings?

Petzold: Well, my work method has a lot to do with American short stories I read when I was sixteen or seventeen. Very precisely written scenes that contain a lot of the world in their very selectivity. Dennis Johnson or Rainald Goetz's *Deconspiration*. There are scenes . . . a door behind which you see a DJ who is sorting albums, suddenly he cries, a girl goes by. I search for scenes with a strange charge that I then basically build into a house with Harun Farocki on our walks.

Wackerbarth and Hochhäusler: But you do not adapt existing stories?

Petzold: No. I'm not so interested in plots. I am more interested in how you go from one charged scene to the next. There's of course some kind of plot thinking behind that, but, from the perspective of *Something to Remind Me* and *Wolfsburg*, in which everything more or less works, I often established at the editing table that the plot is not really worked through. There's a kind of grammar to film narrative with which I often have failed and for which I really only found a solution with the help of my editor Bettina Böhler. These mistakes, of course, reveal, unintentionally, my own interests, which are clearly not in the plot.

Wackerbarth and Hochhäusler: Why is there even a plot? Why does there have to be one? You could decide, in the tradition of modern narration, to arrange just some very precise moments. Does one sacrifice a valuable precision for plot?

Petzold: I find that as soon as there's a plot, a narrative, there are also certain laws. And films are all about either laws or criminals who break laws. You can apply that to plot. There must be a law, and you have to rub up against this law. That's what it's about. That's really necessary for me and for my work. There are, of course, other things, but when you look at the films of Antonioni, for example, then there's also a very clear narrative structure. Nonetheless, the ensemble in his work or in the film and its structure has to leave the plot behind all the time, even to return to it at some point. Through this, you reach a kind of abeyance [*Schwebezustand*], which I find really great.

Wackerbarth and Hochhäusler: It occurs to me that all your films are full of coincidences. What does coincidence mean for you?

Petzold: That just means, in a narrative, that the people who have led a very exact life are suddenly pulled out of this kind of self-control and have to leave it behind. That's when this world of coincidence hits them. But I do not feel that the structures of a story are coincidental.

When people or figures in a film are charged with something, whether it is love, revenge, or escape, there's immediately a kind of paranoia, a selective perception—you refer everything to this. But it also has something to do with cinema. A lover interprets every look according to his [*sic*] passion. All the others around them know that she does not love him. This kind of perception automatically produces a kind of coincidence or condensation in cinema with which I don't have any kind of issue. I just don't like any forced coincidences that the commissioning producers or the audience numbers dictate or that comes from a kind of arbitrariness of the creator. It has to have a kind of fundamental dynamic to help the coincidence to its correct conclusion.

Wackerbarth and Hochhäusler: What kind of role can coincidence have in the shooting process? Your films seem incredibly controlled.

Petzold: Yes, sometimes it rains, and it really wasn't planned. No, the shooting of my films is extremely controlled, I have to admit. I like it when everybody knows what it's about and then they have some freedom. It is, for example, almost always the case that the dialogue I wrote is cut in half by the actors. We dropped a ton of dialogue for *Wolfsburg*. We sit for three or four weeks with the script, agree among ourselves about the scene, and talk about the locations. Then we travel to the locations, taking our bikes or on foot, and check it out. And in that way, a thousand planned shots vanish into thin air. For example, the question comes up of how one can shoot a garage, parking lot, parking garage. And then we think about it, photograph the locations, and put those together. The actors also get this material. In a regular film production, they get this material on the day of the shoot, when they're actually there on site, and so they really can't develop a relationship to the spaces—not least because frequently the place is already completely distorted by the lighting and technical apparatus.

For *Wolfsburg*, we shot in a villa that was built in the beginning of the 1960s by the architect Alvar Aalto with money from Volkswagen. And before all of our film stuff lands there, beams for light, etc.—before the place itself disappears—I made sure we all sat there together, had a coffee, and thought about what kind of space that is. We looked at how Aalto designed the entrance and the tables and the glass-pane view of the books and albums. There is a music library with a milk bar, so an attempt at a social place and thus a real counter-design to the city of Wolfsburg.[1] One has to experience this so that one can work appropriately with space. In this way, the actors and I have a bodily memory of a place. That is interesting to me because then we know how we can shoot there.

Wackerbarth and Hochhäusler: The mature actor is really at the middle of it.... You share the scene setup, the space, the background of the character. You show films as preparation.

Petzold: That really has to do with the difference between theater and film. We like to pretend with film that it's just like playing a theater scene: you speak with the actors about the arrangement in space, about psychology, about whatever—but the camera is treated as if it's just a recording instrument. Most actors are just really intelligent in terms of what the camera does. They go to the cinema all the time and understand what a camera does and build on what they've seen in films.

With the preparations for *Wolfsburg*, I spoke with Benno Fürmann, and he said, "that all has to come from the gut." That seems so anti-intellectual. Then, with

---

1. Petzold seems to be referring to Wolfsburg's reputation as an industrial city that exists primarily as a manufacturing site for Volkswagen and the contrasting impulse to establish community-friendly venues.

him, I watched *The Driver* by Walter Hill and *Two-Lane Blacktop* by Monte Hellman, as both concern how you drive a car. The performance by Ryan O'Neal [in *The Driver*] impressed Benno. It's not so much about watching films with a certain theme, but rather the physical forms. For those purposes, American cinema really delivers good material—because it's essentially more physical.

Because the character that Benno plays in *Wolfsburg* is not loaded up with psychology—it never becomes clear where he's from—his body needs a story. Similar to the original scene for the whole film [see above—eds.], there are keys for the character that lie in bodily memory. I wrote a story: in the 1970s, a great many workers were able to climb professionally into the skilled laborer stratum through training and education. That means that those workers left their class behind. A townhouse becomes possible, trips across the Atlantic, or learning a foreign language. All that was new for these workers. At the same time that they left their old class behind, they did not arrive in a new one. This thought preoccupied me with the character of Benno. I wrote a biography that had to do with his own personal actor biography. He had made this TV series *Und tschüss!*, in which he played a gas station attendant. In a sense, this gas station attendant managed to become [in *Wolfsburg*] the sales chief in an auto dealership, to marry the sister of the boss, to jump a class. And, basically, the film narrates how he once again falls out of this class.

Wackerbarth and Hochhäusler: But how can you assure that this abstract information can become bodily? How should you play a worker who has made it into a new class?

Petzold: That isn't what I want. It should not be translated into the performance, that would be terrible. "Play a social climber!" You just end up with a caricature. No, that is information that the actor gets a grip on six, seven weeks before the shooting. That all works together—the biography, the films. Then, at some point, they deliver that NSU Ro 80 [a car that plays a crucial role in *Wolfsburg*], a car that not many people have had the chance to drive in real life. Benno immediately took it and disappeared with it for a while as he wanted to get used to driving it. That was his reaction to it. This kind of acting really pleases me.

Wackerbarth and Hochhäusler: At the Berlin Film festival in 2003, a woman in the audience asked you about *Wolfsburg*. She said, "Such terrible things happen in the film, why don't the characters react more emotionally?" And you said in response that you do not want that actors sell themselves.

Petzold: Yes, that's true. When an actor gives everything and screams, they are awarded a Federal Film Prize [*Bundesfilmpreis*]—same when they play someone with a disability, in the German form of method acting. I believe that extreme expressions produce only clichés. Therefore, I don't say "play it coldly" but rather "play it turned away." If something is done to someone because the plot demands it, the actor does not have to perform for the viewer exactly what they learned in acting school. I can do without the surplus value of real tears or, craft-wise, a first-class screaming fit.

Wackerbarth and Hochhäusler: I also suspect that art films are developing an anti-conventionality, so to say. Wherever Hollywood films would go, art films would never.

Petzold: That's not right. The Hollywood of the present is probably at the end anyway, but when you look back at the cinema of the 1970s, you would say that the actors of Don Siegel, for example, or in the films of New Hollywood don't peddle their wares or sell themselves. All the wonderful films are actually quite reserved and cold. Not in the sense of a coldness of feeling, but rather in a figurative sense: the narrative position is cold. I find it simply indecent to do a push-in on someone who, in that moment, is screaming. Or if someone turns away, then to dolly around them [to see their faces].

But I want to turn this all positive: terror is really much greater in elision. That is not cold in a general sense, but it is—crudely said—more effective: in trash horror films, you see the monster for hours on end, but in very good horror films, you never see it.

Wackerbarth and Hochhäusler: You work a great deal with elisions. Would you say that you react to that which we all already know? We all see films every day, more or less consciously, and there are certain things that you can just narrate in a more efficient way because everyone knows where it is going.

Petzold: I don't know. I'm not interested in how someone pulls up before the house, undoes the seat belt, gets out, rings the doorbell, waits, a wink to the other detective, "hopefully she's still there . . ." And that way, sixty TV seconds pass by, but that doesn't interest me. I want to know how people leave a house. Much more is narrated in the leaving of a house, and one gives the viewer the chance to reconstruct the scene. The viewers can fill it in according to their own experiences in the level of detail that you could never manage narratively.

Wackerbarth and Hochhäusler: In *The Sex Thief*, you go from Agadir to Cologne, only showing the train compartment. That is a very beautiful shot: you see the rail bridge structure flashing by in the windows. That was then Cologne, but without any postcard shots.

Petzold: The establishing shot that explains the space is so popular because subsequently you can do what you want. That is really a 1950s grammar, but it is unfortunately still around. It would go like this: first a shot of the Cologne cathedral, then everything after that is completely interchangeable. You can shoot that in every terrible studio. You have to do that when you only have twenty-one shooting days and only one crime scene, because otherwise the whole thing will collapse. But when you have five or six more days available, you can think a little differently. Working without establishing shots of course means much more work, but it's worth it.

Wackerbarth and Hochhäusler: How interested are you in style? It seems that you have developed a certain method, one that is clearer from film to film. That what you just described is part of this aesthetic, the Petzold style, if you will. "This is how Petzold shows a man dying." There are certain situations that you have mastered in the style. And they can continue to be. Is that something that interests you?

Petzold: I try not to think about it too much, otherwise the bulb explodes.... I already control so many different areas.

Wackerbarth and Hochhäusler: Fear of too much control?

Petzold: Since I've been making films, I've been working with the same people. And because of that, because we have spoken so much with one another, certain things are just understood. It's always the same cameraman, Hans Fromm, the same designer, Kade Gruber, the same editor, Bettina Böhler, the same costume designers, Lisy Christl and Anette Gunther, the same sound people, Martin Ehlers, Andreas Mücke-Niesytka, and Heino Herrenbrück. This continuity really goes very far. And when I meet with, for example, Kade Gruber, we talk about the project, we watch films, etc. ... And then I leave him alone for a couple of weeks, and he builds something. And what he then brings I always find correct. We really have found a common language together.

For *Wolfsburg*, for instance, I sat there with Lisy Christl and agreed on a color palette based on the still lives of Giorgio Morandi that I had brought with me.

Wackerbarth and Hochhäusler: Why?

Petzold: What I really like about Morandi's still lives is their ordinariness, but nonetheless I never have the feeling this ordinariness belongs to me—it is always as if the pictures are looking at me. That moves on the edge of the esoteric, but it is really so. And when you really work through that, then it is also good for the actors because they can work that into their relationship. But, please, never this everyday realism! The can of ravioli on the table, no one can bear that.

Wackerbarth and Hochhäusler: Jacques Rivette said that one has to tremble before certain subjects. For example, you can't elegantly approach the ultimate things, death, etc. My feeling is that the confidence that your films radiate sometimes comes into conflict with their topics.

Petzold: I think that's a pretty petit bourgeois perspective on art. As if there are certain controlled areas and then other small corners where it really becomes dangerous... that sounds as if the controlled area is Stammheim and the others are the hidden pistols.[2]

---

2. Petzold is referring to the high-security prison in which many members of the RAF were imprisoned. One of their lawyers smuggled in a gun by concealing it in a book.

I do not have any pictures in my head. I find it terrible when someone says, "I have an image in my head that I have to get out." The best images do not come from anybody's head, but rather from a collective. You cannot forget how important the production conditions are for the creative process. If you permanently have conflict, then you notice that in the film. I find that you can see in most films the production conditions. And we work in a focused manner, with apparent unity—if you want, a certain confidence—that during the shoot actually allows for an incredible amount of freedom. In the end, every setup I designed ends up being altered: there is no storyboard that was ever realized in the way I had imagined beforehand. When I come to the set, then the first two or three hours are collective work. Therefore, I need people who can contribute and not think within a hierarchical system.

Wackerbarth and Hochhäusler: Do you see a connection between your work and any particular socio-political hopes? Do you understand your films as political?

Petzold: No, because I think that means that one is leaving the level of film. There's a book by Peter Nau, *Critique of the Political Film*, which has the thesis that the medium itself is political, whether it depicts politics or not. That always made sense to me. Politics inscribe themselves in the very production conditions of a film. They don't have to appear directly in the narrative.

"A Novel No Longer Holds Us Together Today"

Rüdiger Suchsland / 2004

From "'Ein Roman hält uns heute nicht mehr zusammen,'" *Artechock.de*, March 11, 2004. Reprinted by permission. Translated by Marco Abel and Jaimey Fisher.

Rüdiger Suchsland: Your films appear as entirely singular in the German film landscape. You yourself belong to an in-between generation, in this perhaps most like Dominik Graf: too young for the New German Cinema of the 1970s, somewhat older than Oskar Roehler and Hans-Christian Schmid, and considerably too old for the young uninhibited such as Denis Gansel and Hans Weingartner as well as the young arthouse generation around Christoph Hochhäusler and Ulrich Köhler. Where do you see yourself?

Christian Petzold: This is a question of film references, of films that shaped us, that brought us to the cinema. For me, this is certainly the New Hollywood cinema, which is why the last Berlinale with its retrospective was fantastic for me. Then there are old police films that do not narrate in a psychological way and instead take seriously the city as a location; and there's of course French cinema. My friendly relationship with Dominik Graf has perhaps to do with the fact that we share preferences, and I simultaneously consider him someone who is similarly singular.

In a certain sense we are all auteurs. The industry makes television. This, too, is a laboratory that one could still understand with the help of auteurism. But in cinema, at least, every film is connected with the person of the director. German cinema suddenly has again films that render visible something and do not have their eyes on cable television. When they produced more films, I personally did not benefit from this; as a director I did not do any better then. But now, after the collapse, I also don't do any worse. This is the same situation for Christoph Hochhäusler and Ulrich Köhler. However, they had to get their first films made with the help of the French; they had distribution there before their films were shown in the theaters here.

What I am seeing in these new films is definitely better. But the craft is secondary to all this. Rolf Dieter Brinkmann once said: "Craft is like brushing teeth"—you learn it anyway.

RS: History is right now very much "in" in German cinema. Do you feel any connection to this type of cinema?

CP: The production companies apparently all have calendars in their offices in which they look out for anniversaries and upcoming dates: Auschwitz, June 17, soccer world cup 2006.[1] For that you can get money. But I don't even know how to film historical subject matters—a carriage or a Nazi film: I can't do this. I've also already received offers to make a soccer film.

RS: Could you describe your expectations for the inclusion of your film in the competition at the Berlinale?

CP: I am completely empty. We just finished the film. At that moment one is always easily nervous, for now the film no longer belongs to me but is public. It now belongs to the people who watch it—it's up to them whether they accept or reject it. I'm looking forward to this. In the competition, attention is, of course, especially intense. But I really am not worrying about any prizes.

The awarding of a prize always tries to lend the festival a narrative retroactively. The best-case scenario is when Cannes, with David Cronenberg as jury president, awards [the Dardenne brothers'] *Rosetta* the prize. Worst case scenario is when one sees that a handful of people are uninterested, and seven countries and three minorities have to be recognized. I hope that for this Berlinale the narrative is good—like with the last two when Michael Winterbottom and Fatih Akin won.

RS: Dieter Kosslick has, of course, his narrative, too. It's about the German cinema's new economic might and about cinema as event. Part of it is that Roland Emmerich, not exactly famous for artistic highlights but for elaborate mass cinema, is now going to be jury president. Not everyone likes this. What do you think about this?

CP: I neither can nor want to comment on this. If a jury is good, it always becomes independent.

RS: *Ghosts* is your first film that takes place in a big city. Was it a big difference from other locations to narrate the metropolis? In your film, Berlin almost looks like a small city or like mid-size cities such as Wolfsburg.

CP: If you look closely then this is indeed the case—in contrast to many other big cities. If you film Berlin, you have to film it differently. There is no sprawl

---

1. June 17 refers to the workers' uprising against the East German government in 1953.

in Berlin: the city doesn't have suburbs, and one doesn't need a car. Berlin has a number of centers, not just one big street where everyone goes shopping but in the evening is dead—I like this. In Georges Simenon's novels you can find this as well. His Paris is one of neighborhoods. There are people who have never left their arrondissement.

RS: The film begins and ends in a quite primordial, almost paradisical-seeming nature, even though it is only the park. Of all things, it is the metropolis that appears here very close to nature . . .

CP: My two French actors talked a lot about the smell of Berlin, the perfume of Berlin. They said that they had never been in a city that smells so much of nature. Berlin is not vertical like Hong Kong or Shanghai, but horizontal. It has an enormous number of parks, is incredibly green, and likely houses more animal species than any small town. Because here non-simultaneities, which in the countryside fall victim to monoculture, continue to exist also in nature, not just among people.

In the exposé, I called the character Julia Hummer plays the "forest girl." She is being pushed by another girl to go to the city in order to actualize herself there and find her own narrative.

The first intertitle in [F. W.] Murnau's *Nosferatu*—and in silent films intertitles are also shots—is called: "And when he had crossed the bridge, the phantoms came to meet him." I saw this for the first time when I was twelve, and it really impressed me. That was the initial idea for *Ghosts*. And with "bridge," "ghosts," I soon had an idea about a fairy-tale scenario at the Tiergarten: a lot of green, trees, behind the tree crowns the city, and from there is a girl, who is an orphan and to whom other traces of fairy tales stick. In the tales of the Brothers Grimm, there is an enormous number of children who are abandoned in a forest, and they live there, silent, with wolves, in trees, or in some enchanted cracks in the earth. And then they have to leave the forest.

This was the fictional basis that I had. And she meets another girl that is only city. Perhaps she wants to sell jewelry there, and at first one might think she's being raped.

RS: But she could also have come from the forest: she's got torn clothes, she's dirty, she's partially naked. . . .

CP: Exactly. But she's always pulled back into the city. When she's out and about with her new friend, she pulls her along. She always wants to go where the lights are. Marguerite Duras writes in her autobiography that for her Paris is a novel. She became a writer in order to become a character in this Paris novel: she wanted to write herself into it. For the character of Toni, Berlin is a casting call. There are thousands of lofts belonging to TV suppliers—and in there, casting calls take place without end. For whatever sort of shit.

RS: She wants to enter this world . . .

CP: ... just to obtain an identity. There's someone who cooks for you, dresses you—and you have an identity. Berlin no longer manufactures anything but is a media location.

RS: It's a stage!

CP: Yes. And that's where she's from. The forest girl meets the casting girl. And this relationship lasts because they want something from each other. The one uses the forest girl because she's got a certain kind of authenticity that opens the door for her ...

RS: ... and also in order to obtain a narrative. This happens then quite literally.

CP: Right. Toni has no memory; she erased everything. And the other is, in contrast, a diary. Nina is a past full of stories, and Toni is pure presence. The one wants to be present: at long last, she wants to be seen, to touch, to love; and the other wants to have a narrative that opens doors for her.

RS: And she wants to leave ...

CP: She wants to leave with it, yes. The original idea was to tell the story of these two girls. I developed it nine years ago; it was called "Chill Out" at one time. I was inspired by a story by Cesare Pavese in which two girls perish. And that's where the second story of the mother was added. Not as an auxiliary construction, but in order to clarify even more the girl's longing for the present.

RS: The mother, however, also has to satisfy her own memory, but in this she's a repeat offender. Recollection and repetition: these are the keywords. "Repetition is a memory turned towards the future," Robbe-Grillet wrote. In this sense. For she knows from the start that her effort to find her daughter will fail ...

CP: Exactly! She's like a junkie. But because film can, in my opinion, only film the present, which is why I don't make costume films—her memory cannot have any present. The present is the moment when mother and daughter are sitting in the hotel lobby, eating. They do not speak a single word. A bit of normality, familiarity. As if they just hadn't seen each other for a few weeks. They are present, and as a mother you relish in this. The presence of the child. She enjoys this moment, but she knows that it will be the last. And then her husband arrives.

To film such presence is important to me, not conversations about the past. The past is something that is always being imposed by the present. When, in the middle of the film, she explains herself to her alleged daughter, it is the opposite of a typical television drama in which mother and daughter meet at the beginning and then keep separating time and again. That's why I added Toni, so that she adds a present into the narrative about the past. She looks around and searches for something she can steal.

RS: The mother. ...

CP: I made the mother especially intelligent. She is intellectually superior to her husband. From the man's point of view, the woman whom he loved has died fifteen years ago together with the child. He cannot just pick her up; instead, he has to create some surplus value. She is not just victim but also perpetrator. I like this.

RS: In essence, ghosts are quite literally dead people who continue to live on. The one who talks about ghosts believes that the dead continue to live, that there is some form of life after death. Do ghosts have this connotation for you as well?

CP: For *The State I Am In*, we used the *Flying Dutchman* as the background myth. A figure who did not complete the process of dying—just like the RAF will not die all the way. This is why the RAF is ghostly, because it still appears to the living in some fashion, for the living are not really finished with it.

RS: These are the European ghosts: those who cannot die. Asian ghosts, in contrast, are those that are simply there . . . who sometimes say hello . . .

CP: But the European ones are always repressed material. In this case, there's a girl that was loved so much that she cannot die, that she remains in the mother's memories. And the mother even uses photos to calculate how the daughter would look today—in order to give the child a fictional present. And Nina, played by Julia Hummer, is such a person who has been calculated: she never lives properly, but she's not dead. But she wants to live. And that she manages only at the end.

RS: When watching the film, I spontaneously thought it was primarily Julia Hummer's story. After the film, someone said that there are essentially two stories that intersect only briefly. Later, I thought, "There are three women who, quite equally, react in quite different ways. Who have various ways to withdraw from the world, with dreams that are turned towards the past, the future, and the present."

CP: That's right. When I write a script, I always try to imagine, even for the least important characters, what other possibilities there could be for them. For this film, too, there is another possibility to keep narrating. I could focus on another character. For example, Benno Fürmann's character, a filmmaker who is married to a producer. One could turn their marriage into a feature film: where a man produces shit and really wants to do something else but lacks the strength to do so—but she loves in him something that she cannot have. That's how I conceptualized all characters.

RS: All of your films have in common that communication between people doesn't work, that it always goes awry. It works for brief moments, more through gestures, embracing each other, but not through talking. But in essence, the setup's circumstances are without communication, characterized by a depression that the people cannot quite shake.

CP: Today, this has to do with the fact that I do not believe that one can solve whatever problem dialogically.

RS: *Wolfsburg* also features two people who want something different from one another and somehow don't manage to come together.

CP: They don't even have a chance to talk with each other. They nevertheless develop a truthfulness through their gestures and looks and the manner in which they treat each other—even though everything is based on a lie.

It's the same in *Ghosts*. The relationship between the two girls: they don't have a common present, as each wants something else. But through gestures they start engaging with each other. This is a kind of economy of relationships: gestures, looks, how one walks together, whether one has the same rhythm, these kind of dancing movements—that is also a kind of dialogue. But this has been buried in cinema—not just in German cinema, but that's where it is especially noticeable because it is so dialogue-heavy. But I'm interested in this.

RS: For long stretches you completely do without dialogue. And your characters don't have that which one sees over and over again in, for example, Eric Rohmer's films: this everyday small talk. They don't necessarily say "hello" but right away something else . . .

CP: In Rohmer films, they mostly live in Paris [*sic*]. That itself is already a massive narrative. There's a secure, taken-for-granted cultural background that we do not know here. Not even in Berlin. While there's this longing for the "Berlin film," this conjuring of this old glamorous metropolis, this does not work anymore since the time of National Socialism. The longing is turned towards emptiness, is artificial. In Germany, people have to invent themselves anew; they cannot rely on any references, on old narratives that one can simply dial up. In France this is possible.

RS: Is it the cinema's job—in this case, the job of German cinema—to create such a frame of reference? So that perhaps in twenty years this film, *Ghosts*, forms a background in front of which another film can tell a story and enter a dialogue with it?

CP: Yes, exactly. At the film academy, Helmut Färber always used to say: "Good films show in twenty years why and how we lived twenty years ago." I agree. In a Klaus-Lemke film, you learn everything about the 1970s. Without the need for films to be documentary-like or having to film the latest *Spiegel*-series.

Until a few years ago, cinema could only tell stories about teenagers who escape, because it's such a nice movement. The idea of departure is deeply rooted in cinema. But with five million unemployed, people who are no longer needed, this desire has shifted. People want to remain quiet.

For me, departures that are modern are those that occur because it is important to depart but that do no longer have a utopia. I think this is already a real movement. In Truffaut's first film, the protagonist heads to the sea, but just in order to really breathe for once.

RS: Would you say *Ghosts* is a film about three or four people? Where the fourth would be the absent daughter?

CP: I don't think the absent daughter plays a terribly important role. At one point, I thought about it. I wanted the entire team to believe that this is the daughter. I said, "It's her, but this doesn't help us at all." This story is really so clear. There's a mother who is looking for her daughter, and there's a girl who is looking for her mother. In the past, one would have said, "This is mutually supportive." Here, the old narratives are no longer strong enough—all of this today is no longer strong enough. Today, a novel no longer holds us together. Or a story.

I gave the actors the ending of Flaubert's *Sentimental Education*. Two friends spend their entire lives together. And at the end, one says to the other: "The only beautiful moment in our lives was the one when we stole an apple and ate it together." That is so sad! And that's what was important to me: that this melancholia is in this film as well.

RS: But one can also understand the ending as liberation . . .

CP: Yes. She goes into the city. And she can no longer rely on her diary, nor on her projections and stories. This no longer helps her; such dreams no longer help her.

RS: How many takes do you actually need?

CP: Two, three at the most. Sometimes there are more complex scenes. For those, we practice and repeat more often. I have a fixed script, but it is always being cut down further. Dialogue falls by the wayside. The actors act, and I think that the rest can be cut.

RS: You rehearsed a lot . . .

CP: We rehearsed for a week in the hotel where we also shot. Everyone who is in the film was present during the first two days. That's when we discussed the script, watched excerpts from films that I found interesting. And then I rehearsed for two days only with the girls. And two days with the mother and the girls. Then we took walks to the shooting locations.

RS: Which films did you watch?

CP: Robert Bresson's *Mouchette* and Barbara Loden's *Wanda*—that's one of the most beautiful scenes I've ever seen. Those were the main ones. We watched them twice because here one can see models for the two girls. And Robert Siodmak and Billy Wilder's silent film *People on Sunday* was also very important. I once had the title "People in Summer" in my head.

RS: Do you have someone for whom you make films—a sort of addressee?

CP: No. It's a bit the case that it's Harun Farocki, who works with me on my scripts. I haven't told him this in this way, but the moment when he watches the first raw cut is for me one of the most important ones. For I don't "film" a script. But whether that which he and I discussed—the idea that touched us—is in the film, that's always an important moment. Otherwise, it won't exist.

To Listen with Closed Eyes

Cristina Nord / 2005

From "Mit geschlossenen Augen hören," *taz*, February 15, 2005. Reprinted by permission. Translated by Marco Abel and Jaimey Fisher.

Cristina Nord: Mr. Petzold, *Ghosts* has something to do with a tale by the Brothers Grimm called "The Shroud." How so?

Christian Petzold: Among the Grimm Brothers' tales there are many smaller ones that I did not even know. I have a three-volume set from Insel-Verlag, which I read to my daughter one after the other. I didn't know "The Shroud." I was devastated as I was reading it.

CN: Why?

CP: Because it's a brutal tale. It's about a mother who mourns so much for her dead child that it cannot ascend to heaven. This is why it returns from its grave to its mother's house—wearing a shroud, stained with the dirt of the grave—and says, "Your grief is so strong that I have to wander about as a ghost. Please stop mourning so that I can get to heaven." After three days, the mother is able to let go of her grief, and the child disappears. I had this tale in my head when I saw posters of missing children identikit pictures at post offices in Belgium and Northern France.

CN: Those were photos of children who had disappeared?

CP: Exactly. These were computer-generated composite sketches; they had to be ordered by the parents who had been missing their children for years. Perhaps the daughter would now be fifteen, seventeen, perhaps she's still alive, and, if she's still alive, then she would look like the image created by the computer. Parents' groups hung those posters up, not the police. And there's of course something in them that recalls the Brothers Grimms' tale: one cannot let go of a daughter who has disappeared.

CN: So, the character of Françoise, the mother, is searching for a ghost?

CP: Yes, she is looking for the materialization of one of these ghost photos. I imagined this more or less as follows: one sees this computer-generated photo, and the person imagined in it has socially not aged: she does not have life experiences. A girl in Berlin . . .

CN: Nina, the film's protagonist played by Julia Hummer . . .

CP: . . . has to give life to this computer-generated image. And what we see in the film is how she socializes herself, how she steps outside of her ghostly bubble, falls in love, and is led by another girl into the world.

CN: The fairy-tale impression is also created by the location. The Tiergarten appears in *Ghosts* like an enchanted forest.

CP: The Tiergarten area where we filmed used to belong to the GDR. It was a no man's land of the Warsaw Pact. For example, there were a circle of wagons that retreated there because the West German police was not able to enter this area. At these sites, the Tiergarten assumes an enchanted quality. Never properly landscaped, it's a bit wild. There are trails that were not designed by Lenné or some landscape architects. I always liked this. Moreover, when framing shots or when shooting its bridges and paths, we incorporated this romantic German material that exists in, for example, art galleries.

CN: You repeatedly use a shot of a front of trees. How the leaves rustle in the wind evokes Kracauer's desire for the redemption of external reality. On the other hand, I had the feeling that this emphasis of the physis results in a transcendence of external reality.

CP: We felt the same. In *Eureka*, a Japanese film by Shinji Aoyama, there is also this kind of wind. It did not just render visible the physical dimension, the anti-studio; it also infused the story with some breath, a metaphysical wind. I very much liked this. In *Blow-up*, the photographer walks through London. At one time, he opens a very small door, walks around a house, and then a large park opens itself up to him, and the wind is there. And instead of adding artificial wind noises, we recorded many original sounds in the Tiergarten. We tried to hear the location.

CN: How does one do this?

CP: During preproduction, you normally walk together with the cinematographer across the locations. I always insisted that the sound engineer, Andreas Mücke, joins as well. Sometimes we just stood there, with closed eyes—we must have looked like idiots—and listened. The Tiergarten has an acoustic that I have never perceived anywhere else in the world. The city is incredibly near and simultaneously so far away. And somehow cinema is something like it: very close yet so far away.

CN: In the film, what is the relationship of the Tiergarten to Potsdamer Platz?

CP: When I was at the Berlinale with *Wolfsburg*, I walked across the Tiergarten during the premiere. I'm always so nervous at premieres and am not able to stay in the audience because every cough totally unnerves me. So, I entered the

Tiergarten, stopped somewhere, smoked, turned around, and saw above the top of the trees Potsdamer Platz. Suddenly it was there like Angkor Wat. It didn't have anything of the city to it anymore. I thought of all the myths associated with Potsdamer Platz: the busiest place in the world, Weimar Republic, Liza Minnelli. And now Angkor Wat is here, as if the jungle almost tried to take over the place again. At the time we were in the middle of preparing *Ghosts*, and originally the film was supposed to take place at the Woltersdorfer lock, in the old UFA settings of [Joe May's] *The Indian Tomb*. But at this moment I thought, "It is so much more interesting here, so much more charged."

CN: With the film, one doesn't get a sense of the contemporary myths related to Potsdamer Platz—the hype of the new center of Berlin or the criticism thereof.

CP: One can make fun of Potsdamer Platz. One can say, like Harald Schmidt, it looks as if the Ceaușescus got money one more time before their untimely demise. But in a film one must not show off such a location; one should take it seriously. In this case, one is interested in the transitions and paths, not the place as a background.

CN: Since you mention the paths: it seems to me that walking plays a big role. We see especially Julia Hummer permanently walking.

CP: That's no coincidence. Béla Bálazs's *Visible Man* was one of the foundational film books for me, and in one of his film reviews he describes a Griffith film. A woman receives news that her son has drowned. Griffith does not show her reaction on her face, even though the actress, Lillian Gish, was a star and everyone wanted to see her. Instead, she turned around and walked away. There was no traveling shot yet, the camera was not able to follow and simply let her walk away. Bálazs is enthused by the view of Gish's back because, as he writes, at this moment the cinema begins. Because the viewer starts to project. I explained this to the actors during rehearsals. I do not want to enter into the psychology of the characters but follow them.

CN: In a film by Claire Denis something similar happens. It is the vampire film . . .

CP: *Trouble Every Day*. We watched it as part of our preparations.

CN: I'm thinking of the shot of the neck of the chamber maid.

CP: It's simply incredible. In many ways I find *Trouble Every Day* brilliant, but somehow Claire Denis lost control of it. I think that if you make a B-picture about mad scientists you have to take this seriously, and she doesn't do this.

CN: She simply feels so enthusiastic about bodies.

CP: Yes, but then this enthusiasm dissipates because it is not surrounded by enthusiasm for other things. Nevertheless, the film is one that one always likes to watch again. And this chamber maid. . . . Laurent Cantet did something similar in his film *Time Out*. That's how I discovered Aurélien Recoing.

Stories of Ghosts

Tim Stüttgen / 2005

From "Geschichten von Gespenstern," *Jungle World*, August 31, 2005. Reprinted by permission. Translated by Marco Abel and Jaimey Fisher.

Tim Stüttgen: Your new film is called *Ghosts*. It's a term that is in vogue in political and theoretical discourses. Derrida's *Specters of Marx* was hyped; in the new B-Books-Reader "Outside" there's talk of the "ghostliness of queer rooms." Do you see any connection between this and the title of your film?

Christian Petzold: *Ghosts* refers to a key intertitle of Murnau's *Nosferatu*, which the doctor reads on his way to Dracula's castle: "And when he had crossed the bridge, the phantoms came to meet him." As a viewer in the cinema, you find yourself in a dreamlike state. You are simultaneously physically present and absent—like you dream while lying in bed. There is of course a relationship. For my ghost films are not merely those kinds of films that are about the supernatural. The characters in a film are always in the process of losing their materiality, and they try to remain material. This is also the case with Jack Lemmon in Billy Wilder's *The Apartment*, as he lives a lonely life as a nobody in the mass machinery of a large-scale office and at home in front of a permanently running TV. Suddenly, this woman appears, Shirley MacLaine, who is also a ghostly projection. The ghostly slipping into interstices, the falling out of normality, is part of many films, and I always liked this.

TS: Nevertheless, choosing *Ghosts* as a title, which you had already considered for *The State I Am In*, isn't necessarily obvious, considering the story.

CP: I did not decide to make a film about ghosts; after I had written the story, I noticed that, if you followed the correct story and correct grammar, you would not necessarily think of the term "ghosts," that one may not immediately think of the term "ghosts" if you have the correct narrative with the correct grammar and are able to follow it. But this film is about something belated, something coming after the real story. Not in the sense of "post-history," which is not what I mean; but the stories are already told. A mother carries a trauma with her. A girl, who might be the daughter, invents stories about the future. And another girl invents stories with which she can sell herself. These stories are being told in this film, but the film itself is not this story. These are all aftershocks of narratives. This is why I realized that these are all ghosts, as echoes of stories that others already experienced and for which they lived.

TS: This state of abeyance lends the film a strange effect. When the credits rolled, I felt that the film had not even started yet. Everything has already happened, but only in the imagination or in the beginning stage.

CP: Yes, exactly. Perhaps it is for once correct to say: OK, one can no longer complete telling the stories because the identities, which a story that is completed still pretends to have, are in a crisis. Such a story, which works like a *Bildungsroman* where the protagonist has a problem, solves it, and at the end has advanced a step, is today perhaps no longer believable. Perhaps one simply has to dare, then, to affirm that a film is now merely exposition.

TS: Did you realize from the start that the film obviously works through questions of representation and narration, of how today one can even still tell stories?

CP: When one starts shooting, one no longer can be quite so smart or else the film implodes. This became quite clear in my conversations with Harun Farocki, who always worked on the script together with me, or with the actors. I never knew how the film would really end. I always deferred this with a certain trepidation and ultimately left this up to Julia Hummer. She really did the right thing. She has the photos in her hand that point to her possible origin and her trauma, and she throws them into the trashcan and walks into nothingness. This always makes me very sad when I watch the film. I myself am still so romantic that I hope everything will end well. But suddenly all these stories and the music, the city and nature, and everything making up such places that help you define yourself, help you to become sensual again, no longer respond.

I often thought of Truffaut's *400 Blows*. The final image always totally got to me. The homeless boy walks towards the sea, the camera circles around him, and for this moment he is happy. But he can't go on. He will never have this feeling of happiness again. That's the feeling with which you leave the film.

TS: You once characterized and criticized German cinema as two-dimensional, that actors always stand in front of the same backgrounds and recite their dialogue without being in concrete, historical locations with a concrete sense of their space and time. This is why you work differently with the actors: you invite them prior to shooting and give sociological lectures about the locations.

CP: I always liked doing this, but never so extreme as with this film. We spent a week at the Marriott hotel where much of the film takes place and watched films, read the script, and I told them everything from my work journal about *Nosferatu*, ghosts in cinema, etc. I also do this in order to make my work transparent, so that later I do not have to act like some director-god who harbors some mystical secrets.

TS: What kind of films does the team watch? Sabine Timoteo, for example, convincingly plays a young woman who is homeless, unemployed, but still driven by the desire not merely to survive but if at all possible also to become a star or starlet on TV.

CP: I don't use films that directly relate to my film but look for a fiction that, for instance, provides a relationship of fear for a character. The girl Toni is a character who is drifting, still young but already at the threshold of no longer being quite so young. A character who wants to enter this whole casting- and media-world—a new biopolitical world—but her biological clock is already ticking. She will no longer be able to really become part of this world. Perhaps she will be used by a director for a few days, and then she falls completely out of this world. And this final falling out of this world and then entering a state of drifting from which there is no escape—this is what impressed me so much about a film such as, for example, *Wanda* with Barbara Loden. In this film, the protagonist is also so exhausted. She is also a ghost, a living dead, an employed woman who has no longer places for herself and nothing left to do but pass the time. Just time, no place.

TS: How was shooting after these preparations?

CP: They were incredibly easygoing. Each day, we only shot for seven or eight hours. That way, everyone was able to return to their private social sphere. Everything was so relaxed, even though a lot was at stake.

TS: When I tell acquaintances about your new film, they reply: "Ah, two girls without home and a rich couple that is looking for a daughter—this sounds quite cliché and not very original."

CP: What I'm interested in is the perspective on a story, a displacement or difference. It's the same in westerns: these are actually always quite classical stories that can be summarized in two or three sentences, but it's about so much more. To get this right was my primary concern. I did not want to film the search of a bourgeois French woman, but rather to narrate from the point of view of a girl similar to institutionalized children who fantasize about their origins—otherwise life would not be bearable. To imagine that your parents simply threw you away or left you behind: that turns you into a nobody. And you don't have anyone who can offer you an identity. And while therapists in such an institution can more or less patch you up, they cannot replace your parents or provide a loving context. This often leads to the construction of Caspar-Hauser identities—in reality they are loved children who were abandoned in a forest only due to an intrigue.... As in a fairy tale: this happens quite frequently. Suddenly another girl appears who seduces this institutionalized girl so that she's being loved as well, and a woman appears who also provides her with an origin. Both are part of this story, but in the end this girl knows that neither of the two can help her. Neither realization of these dream worlds helps her. The only chance for her to no longer be a ghost is to step beyond these narratives.

TS: There's a special tension in the film. On the one hand, the characters seem to hover above their stories, constantly refusing offers to be written into them and to be given biographical significance; on the other hand, the film is photographed in a very naturalistic and concrete way.

CP: In this respect I was quite influenced by literature. It is sometimes great when one reads something like Rainald Goetz—everything is so concrete. He describes a morning after a party almost like a Nouveau Roman. Every cover of an LP that's on the floor, every spilled drink and cigarette butt on the floor is incredibly concrete, yet simultaneously as if in a still-life painting. It no longer belongs to you, it exists so much for itself. This is short-circuited, and you merely cross and observe but are no longer part of this world. I quite liked this moment.

This frequently happens in cinema as well. Recently, I watched John Ford's *My Darling Clementine*. A very concrete film: the people have very concrete preferences and desires. Then, one morning, Marshal Wyatt Earp [Henry Fonda] steps out of the hotel, and all the townspeople pass him by on their way to a dance. He is no longer really part of them. He sits down in his rocking chair, watches the people, and remains in a state of abeyance. He doesn't belong, yet simultaneously is nevertheless there. I always like in cinema this state of abeyance and this tension in the characters. I wanted this suspension in my film as well: is this now a fairy tale or concrete?

TS: Isn't *Ghosts* secretly also a western?

CP: Yes, it is a western. From the start I told the actors that we would make a western. At some time, I became conscious of this and thus had to react to it. Everyone always stands in open windows, just like in Ford films, where someone then steps outside and is outside. There, the world is basically like a desert. The characters always gallop restlessly from one location to the next, searching for something: everything is just a stopover. All of this is set to hardly any music but to a lot of nature sounds. Westerns always have a small ensemble and a small town surrounded by desert. You never know from what the people live. At the same time, it is all so concrete. The way they hold pistols and mount a horse is so physical.

TS: This is also interesting with regard to what's called political cinema: on the one hand, the way you tell your stories cannot be reduced to an unambiguous message; on the other hand, the people in your films are all very real. Almost all of them are workers who are lost or people who have lost their jobs.

CP: This relation between something mundane and something that is perhaps excessive, exaggerated, is what I'm interested in. This was already what motivated me when making a film about members of the RAF, because the RAF had merely become a ghostly figment and a myth in which Ulrike Meinhoff was always represented as the Virgin Mary. I was fascinated by what merely existed as aftershocks of specific events.

TS: What's your attitude towards the cinema's notion of politics at a time when every trivial film, whether [Mark Rothemund's] *Sophie Scholl—The Final Days*, [Wolfgang Becker's] *Good Bye, Lenin!*, or [Hannes Stöhr's] *Berlin Is in Germany*, is received as explicitly political?

CP: In terms of film history, I don't like watching political films. I do not like it when images are made for the sole purpose of translating an issue and which as a viewer you have to translate back. This is GDR-cinema where you hide metaphors to get past the censors, and the viewer is supposed to deconstruct them. This only rarely preserves richness and complexity. I sidestep this discussion with auxiliary constructions: you make films politically but not political films. But we are far removed from making films politically. The structures are complicated, and to make a film without money like a garage band makes a record is more often than not rather subculturally petit bourgeoise [*subkulturelles Kleinbürgertum*]. To shoot without money, a camera, and a team of six people—this is more the wish of commissioning producers who work in government structures ravaged by cost-cutting measures. Film is also commodity and money, and this conflict needs to be reflected in the films.

TS: You managed to wrest something away from the system. After it took you three years to finance *The State I Am In*, each subsequent film was successful.

CP: Yes, since then I cannot complain.

TS: Many talented filmmakers of your generation don't have the fortune to be supported at the right moment. Why is this? Does the system have room only for a few interesting filmmakers after all? Many interesting films barely manage to be screened for one week at an arthouse cinema in a big city.

CP: Wherever you go—to Italy, Spain, or Portugal—you notice that they all have the same problem. Cinema as a public space is disappearing. [A] multiplex is simply something different, a sales booth for mainstream cinema, with popcorn and a McDonald's, where the bags for children contain a *Shrek 2* figure. But that you walk through your own city, step out into the evening, and then come out of the theater and remain quiet for a bit after the film has finished—this no longer exists. That's the problem. I also do not believe that the DVD and home projection can replace all of this, even though I myself am also a DVD junkie. Of course, it's fun to watch a film with eight friends and a lot of beer. And yet this is not the same as "going to the movies."

TS: To what extent does a filmmaker have to cater to classic artist clichés? You once said you'd rather be a worker at an assembly line of an old American film factory than the great author whom you always have to play in European cinema.

CP: I truly would prefer it if I could bring my kids to school every morning and then simply go to work. I would prefer to make films that way. I don't like the artist pretensions of some actors, and I don't like this for myself either. I prefer simply working. I don't mean to put craft against art, but it's very important for me to be working consistently. Godard said that he would not want to fly with a pilot who enters a cockpit only every third year; I think the same is true for film directors.

Carnival of Souls: Plot or World— A Conversation with Christian Petzold

Susan Vahabzadeh and Fritz Göttler / 2005

From "Karneval der Seelen: Plot oder Welt—Ein Gespräch mit Christian Petzold," *Süddeutsche Zeitung*, September 15, 2005: 14. Reprinted by permission. Translated by Marco Abel and Jaimey Fisher.

Susan Vahabzadeh and Fritz Göttler: Your films concern themselves time and again with family, children, and parents. What role does the cinema play in your own family?

Christian Petzold: My daughter is nine, and each Friday we watch together a film on DVD. Her favorite film is François Truffaut's *The Wild Child*, and I did not influence her at all. I was super happy. For a week I ran around: "She loves *The Wild Child*." For this was a comedy. She had just entered third grade and had already several years of experience with the pressure of school. And there is a child who resists education—she died laughing.

Vahabzadeh and Göttler: Did she also see *Ghosts*?

Petzold: No, I had to tell her the story. She had a tiny part in it, but I ended up cutting it. This plunged her into a real crisis. The girls—Julia Hummer and Sabine Timoteo—walk through the city and cross the empty Potsdamer Platz, which was really empty: we did not cordon off anything. A few days earlier, I had checked it out and thought that something should happen in this emptiness, as in an Antonioni film, for then it appears even emptier: two girls, coming from school, their backpacks discarded, hula-hooping. I had Chirico in mind, his evening moods—but somehow it ended up looking too contrived, so I took the scene out.

Vahabzadeh and Göttler: Contrived: does this mean a surplus of consideration and staging? Is this an important criterium?

Petzold: Very important. It's OK for something to be contrived, but so that it still has soul in it. But when it just points to the author then I hate it. The construction must be such that it can then become independent. I do not like the *new writing* [in original] of the new American novels—five hundred pages, a lot of metaphors, the plot is quite elaborate. I always liked novels like Ross Thomas's, where people have to do small dirty jobs and carry with them a simple, dirty, small feeling.

Vahabzadeh and Göttler: Compared to previous Petzold films, *Ghosts* appears more relaxed, less strictly constructed. Previously there was always a certain kind of dramaturgy. Whereby, for example in *Wolfsburg*, one sometimes wished for an open ending—that the protagonists' love remains for a while and is not terminated by revenge right away....

Petzold: I had the same thought—whether one should not end with this moment of abeyance, of love, which they had to work towards and which is predicated on entirely false assumptions. Whether this might not have been the more anarchic ending. But in this film, I really struggled to let a child die. To write into the script a dying child: earlier, when I was twenty, I would have had no problems with it. I never understood when Hitchcock tells Truffaut he would never again send a boy through the city with a bomb that then even detonates; I never perceived this as the breaking of a taboo. This happened only once I had children myself. One becomes more cautious, more sensitive. And in the case of *Wolfsburg*, I thought that I had to bring this to an end, that I could not conclude on a happy ending.... As for the approach to the script: shortly before shooting I met Dominik Graf, and he said, "There's basically only portrait or plot." So, I told Harun Farocki, with whom I always write my scripts, "This time I do not want to do a plot. I want to narrate the world coming after some plot." "Yes," Harun said, "but this is difficult. For plot isn't just prison but also something with which one has to grapple." I had read many novels in which things have aftershocks, about later-born, those born too late, who no longer exist in a plot construction, but rather afterwards . . . the economic situation, the world of work is completely down the tubes, but identity depends on work. In the sixties and seventies, the grand narrative of the SPD [Germany's Social Democratic Party] existed, but they can no longer manage today's new narratives . . . all of this went through my mind. And Harun thought. "OK, but the plots that are no longer in the presence of the film have to be incredibly powerful."

Vahabzadeh and Göttler: How do the actors cope with such a plotless situation?

Petzold: We met for a full week and talked about the stories that are over before the film begins, as well as about Potsdamer Platz: this story is over too. All of this came together really well, and suddenly the characters had a present tense, the present tense of improvisation. I really don't like to check a scene right away on the monitor while one is still shooting. For the actors are building a room, and when the scene is over they fall into a void, for they don't have an audience, they don't know with whom to communicate. And then they see these dudes hunched behind the monitor. . . . bizarre. I think one can see this in today's films if they were shot in that manner. In those cases, the actors look as if they are making their way hand over hand along the text, as you do with a banister.

Vahabzadeh and Göttler: In contrast to this, your sets are characterized by considerable openness.

Petzold: The video-monitoring while shooting also means disenfranchising the cameraman. When three or four people are right behind the monitor and blather on about an image, judging it, then it loses all its secrets. And there's nothing left in it that manages to escape control. We shoot incredibly fast, just seven hours a day, and I need precise preparation of logistics. You can't tell actors: just do it. . . . They are not able to handle this, such a degree of improvisation. One would have to have four months of rehearsals, like Cassavetes, so that an ensemble can find its own voice.

Vahabzadeh and Göttler: Is *Ghosts* conceptualized as a genre film, a ghost film?

Petzold: My next film will be a real ghost film, a remake of [Herk Harvey's] *Carnival of Souls*, here in Germany and once again with Nina Hoss. It's always the same with ghost films: there's a story that is not yet fully processed, so there are ghosts. The question is: why is all of this happening? And when the story has been processed, then the ghosts can either go into the grave or become human again. I don't believe in this any longer. I don't believe any more that there is a story that materializes the ghostly in any way. But the longing for the continued existence of such a narrative I find really pronounced.

Vahabzadeh and Göttler: This seems to be somehow our fate . . .

Petzold: This is the modern, not an eternal, fate. When you watch city films, they all touch on the ghostly. . . . On cable TV, they screen these documentaries that demonstrate a real contempt for their subjects' humanity; they focus on people who haven't been able to pay their rent for half a year and who haven't been evicted. And then the TV camera is present. Godard once said that there are so many detective films because detectives are allowed to enter the private sphere. . . . Today, cable TV stations enter with nasty off-commentary into the apartments of those who can no longer cope with modern life. In the past, these would have been characters in films such as Sterling Hayden, who commits a final robbery at a racetrack and everyone tries to get their act together one final time. Ghosts have something seductive—to let oneself fall, to not play the game any longer. On TV, this doesn't come across as a documentary but as a disciplinary measure: if you want to get comfy in the hammock of social security and no longer want to participate, then we will show up and you will be evicted—you'll be ghosts. *Carnival of Souls* is about this: an unemployed woman who is looking for a new job but who doesn't realize that she's already dead.

"The Cinema of Identification Gets on My Nerves": An Interview with Christian Petzold

Marco Abel / 2006/2007

From *Cineaste* online 33, no. 3 (Summer 2008). Interview conducted in August 2006 and October 2007. Reprinted by permission.

Marco Abel: How did you develop an interest in film?

Christian Petzold: I grew up in Hilden, a small town that did not have any movie theaters, at a time when West Germany had only two or three TV channels. So, there were very few movies and images in my childhood. Towards the end of the 1970s, when I was still in high school, I began to drive to larger surrounding cities to watch films. My parents had given me the Hitchcock-Truffaut interview book. I was fascinated by the interview. So even without having seen Hitchcock's films, I already knew a lot about them based on these interviews. But I also recall two or three films I saw on TV. And then there was the Hitchcock retrospective at the Cinematheque inside the Wallraf-Richartz Museum, which is today the Museum Ludwig, located in Cologne, the largest city of the region where I grew up. I think I watched forty-one Hitchcock films! I was seventeen. Subsequently I saw a retrospective of Fritz Lang's films. And I also began attending a small film club in Solingen or Wuppertal, which was run by a homosexual who loved to show Murnau's *Tabu*. Tom Tykwer, who also grew up in the region, told me that he knew that guy as well, as he was in the same film club; he recalls also having seen *Tabu* there. So that's how it started.

As an adolescent, I did not have a narrative for the place where I lived. These suburbs—these German suburbs, which are quite different than American suburbs—lack a narrative. Germany did not have its neorealism, nor did we have an early Michelangelo Antonioni whose films talked about how a country builds itself, crumbles, and falls prey to an increasing individualism. I think out of a need for just such narratives, which I also failed to find in German literature, I began to become interested in the cinema, for I did find such narratives there.

Subsequently I discovered the films by Wim Wenders and Rainer Werner Fassbinder in which I found something that allowed me to see and explain my own world in a proper manner.

MA: Nevertheless, you initially decided to study German literature rather than film at the university. Only after you received a master's degree with a thesis on Rolf Dieter Brinkmann did you enroll at the dffb to study filmmaking. Why did you eventually decide to switch from literature to film?

CP: When I moved to Berlin to study literature, I already knew that I would eventually turn to film. But literature had the capacity to make the world complicated for me, which I liked quite a lot. It offered me the world in such a way that I enjoyed looking at it. I also felt that you couldn't make good films without also knowing something about life. Even today I maintain that no film school should admit students who are not at least twenty-six years old. Most film students are simply too young. You can tell this because most films continue to be about some teenagers struggling against their parents—which simply is a boring topic if it is told from the perspective of a young filmmaker. Nicholas Ray once told such stories much better than today's young directors. So, when I moved to Berlin I knew it was too early for me to make films. I nevertheless made a few short films [such as *Mission*, *Weiber*, and *Süden*] with my own money, but they were no good; something was simply missing in them. Perhaps humility. These films were merely sketches; they were small, arrogant movies. I did not like them one bit. So instead of making features I simply went to the movies all the time. I also audited classes at the film academy, while simultaneously studying literature. I worked then for four or five years in the theater before applying at the dffb towards the end of the 1980s, when I was twenty-seven years old.

MA: And when you seriously began to study filmmaking at the dffb . . .

CP: It was a shock! I thought that because I had studied literature—and I had also written a lot, short stories and such—it would be really easy for me to make narrative cinema. I thought I would write a script, cast some actors, get the production in order, and direct the film myself. But during the first year at the academy, I found out that I was not capable of doing this. We were three groups of six students each, but even with only six members we were a rather complex group. I was in a group with people such as Jan Ralske and Christian Frosch, with whom I am still in touch today. We watched a whole bunch of films and ceaselessly discussed them, so much so that my head was spinning. It was a permanent state of crisis for me. I had once experienced a similar state of crisis when I was still in high school, when I listened to new music toward the end of the 1970s: punk, New Wave, Talking Heads, etc. With this music everything was confused as well. And I experienced just such confusion at the dffb, too. Of course, I knew Robert Bresson, films by François Truffaut, etc., but at the moment when I tried to *make* films they were of no help to me! I was simply incapable of making a film. For more than two years, I did not make a film. I merely watched and thought about what I saw. I really went through a serious crisis—a crisis that affected the entire group. Eventually we thematized this crisis situation.

MA: Were Harun Farocki and Hartmut Bitomsky already your teachers then?

CP: Yes. But they don't help you get out of such a crisis: they *are* the crisis! [*Laughs*] But, no, this was great. They were the key to our development. We simply sat there and watched films; we were bombarded with a wealth of images, and I simply could not take a camera into my own hands. The standard myth of the young filmmaker who always says, "I took the camera into my hands and started shooting what was there" ... this romantic idea of filmmaking was not available for me. But, of course, this had to do with my biography: I had acquired a graduate degree, and I was an intellectual, so any form of playing innocent would have meant lying to myself. I had no choice but to make films by reflecting on them. Once I began assisting Bitomsky and Farocki on some of their productions [on the documentaries *Die UFA* and *Ein Tag im Leben des Endverbrauchers*, respectively], I gradually began to understand; and when I was allowed to work with them at the editing bay, that's when I really began to comprehend something.

MA: You were taught by filmmakers who cannot be said to make narrative cinema, yet your films qualify as narrative cinema. Was following Farocki and Bitomsky into the avant-garde or documentary tradition never really an option for you?

CP: Only briefly. During my time of crisis, I made two shorts, which were more or less "essay" films. But I quickly realized that I could not work that way. In this kind of filmmaking, the editing bay is like a desk; you essentially collect material to work on it later, in isolation. The loneliness of Jean-Luc Godard, Jean-Marie Straub, Farocki, and Bitomsky—which in many ways is self-imposed by them—that was not the kind of work environment I desired. I cannot work this way. I did this for five years as a literary scholar; I did not start making films to emulate this experience. But it should be noted that both Farocki and Bitomsky love narrative film. If you look closely at their films, you see that theirs are films that actually desire narrative cinema, while perhaps simultaneously being about the impossibility or crisis of narrative cinema. But I did not want to pursue their path. I still learned more about the art of narrative from them than from people who are so-called storytellers, who, however, do not interrogate themselves. I also learned more about American cinema from Godard films than by watching American films themselves.

MA: Since you received formal training at the dffb, I wonder whether you also had to take courses in film theory?

CP: Yes, some. But since I had already studied film theory when I still worked on literature, I had sworn to myself that I would never study this again! I don't think highly of film theory. I don't say this because I want to be revisionist about my intellectual biography. But the theories of Christian Metz, Pier Paolo Pasolini, or whomever else we studied simply did not grab me. I always thought that Roland Barthes was right when he argued that a film, an image, is not a sign. But, of course, we did study film theory at the academy, for you can't simply say, "Now I take the camera and shoot." In any case, you *have* to become theoretical at the very moment when you begin to edit. You constantly have to explain yourself as a director. You have actors whom you have to tell things. You can do this in a military style, where you do not allow objections, where you merely follow a certain grammar. But that's not how I work. I require more explanation: of myself, of others—I have to collectivize this process. For this reason alone, I was involved in film theory, but not in the sense that the great film theoreticians would have advanced my abilities to make films. They did advance me in other areas, however. Gilles Deleuze's books on cinema are brilliant as philosophy, but they are not something that helps me make films. And I do not expect this of them.

MA: Volker Schlöndorff argues that the crisis of German cinema in the 1990s—by which he primarily meant the yuppie comedies that Harvard film scholar Eric Rentschler labeled the German "cinema of consensus"—had to do with a general resistance among German directors against theory. In his opinion, the problem continues to be that German film academies do not offer enough theory for their students.

CP: I'm not sure about this. I don't think we will improve filmmaking in Germany by offering more film theory seminars. We were in need of instructors who could *think* cinema rather than divide it into neat, teachable categories. The latter approach began, and dominated film teaching, in the 1980s, and the German *Autorenkino* [auteur cinema] is at least partially to blame for this. They participated in this pigeonholing—art house over here, mainstream over there, non-stars vs. stars, etc.; those who participated in divvying up cinema this way were the death of cinema. And the cinema for which Schlöndorff stands was involved in this process because it began to focus on adapting great German literature. Hitchcock said that you couldn't film a great novel, only a bad one. I find myself agreeing with this, for cinema is not literature. But towards the end of the 1970s, all of a sudden everyone made films based on novels by Uwe Johnson or Thomas Mann, and this was the most boring and impoverished cinema imaginable. Thus, by the end of the 1980s, we had two kinds of cinema: the miserable cinema of literature and an escapist, lowbrow cinema, which *wanted* to be the opposite of this literary cinema. And before you knew it someone like Dominik Graf, for whose attempt at making intelligent genre films I have the utmost respect, found himself in an incredibly lonesome position.

MA: Your films have many genre elements that you take from crime stories, mysteries, even melodramas. Graf, who is a relentless proponent of genre cinema, publicly bemoans with great regularity the apparent inability of German directors to make good genre films. I don't know what he thinks of your films, but it's clear that your way of dealing with genre fundamentally differs from his.

CP: I feel closely related to Dominik, even though we most certainly work and think differently. I think that it does not make much sense to demand, as he does, genre cinema in Germany because genre cinema requires *genres*, something that already exists; you cannot artificially make it or revive it as a retro-event. German comedy of the late 1980s, early 1990s was genre cinema, and perhaps one should have responded back then; perhaps we should have worked through this occurrence, in this area, for we would have had neighbors: each film noir has a film that's similar, that has similar light or a similar situation. Of course, television has absorbed genre cinema, which is why you can't revive it in the cinema as a retro event. The traces of genre are like echoes. Graf loves English directors such as Mike Figgis and Nicolas Roeg who went to America out of love for Hollywood, which is genre cinema, to make one more time a genre film; he likes directors who want to revive and rediscover this genre one more time. Graf's Sisyphus work is to keep making a film here and there that reminds us of how wonderful streets used to look in cinema, of how great nights used to look, and of how awesome women looked. I am fascinated by this labor, in which he invests enormous, almost suicidal energy, because each of his films goes beyond well-established boundaries. I have the feeling that I make films in the cemetery of genre cinema, from the remainders that are still there for the taking.

MA: Of late there appears a revival of German cinema. Perhaps it's too early to call it a new golden age of German film, but the signs—I'm thinking here also of the so-called "Berlin School"—point towards something like a renaissance of filmmaking in Germany.

CP: Indeed, German cinema has become much more interesting of late. It has become really a very rich cinema, but cinema as such does not exist anymore. There are films, but there is no public for them. We have to face this without illusions; and you can't change it either. You cannot invent a film infrastructure with films, since this infrastructure is determined by television, which rules everything, certainly in Germany. The large trusts and monopolies homogenized everything; as a result, one makes films in niches. But if you dwell too long on this fact you go crazy. But if I consider that *Ghosts* had about 40,000 viewers, that's not encouraging. But it would have been presumptuous to believe that we would have reached more viewers in the theaters with this film. It's just the way it is.

MA: Certainly the fact that *Ghosts* is such an aesthetically reduced film would have made it illusory to assume it would attract a larger audience. I assume you were even surprised that *The State I Am In* managed to attract more than 100,000 theater viewers.

CP: Around 200,000 even. We were able to make some money with it! [*Laughs*] It did profit from the fact that at the time Germany witnessed another debate about the RAF.

MA: Your graduation film, *Pilots*, commences in Paris, with an image of the protagonist's hands. As we see them, she says, "At some time a place will belong to us." Then you cut to her driving in a car on the autobahn, and you set a reduced piano score to this scene. This is your very first scene in a narrative feature film. Two questions: Was the decision to begin this film in Paris a conscious gesture, a nod to the Nouvelle Vague, to the *cinéma des auteurs*? And, looking back, is it correct to see in this scene already somewhat of a paradigm for your films: the automobile landscape, the industrial environment, the gray-blue and green-blue colors, the piano score that is always extremely minimalist, etc.? Christoph Hochhäusler calls this aesthetic "technological lyricism."

CP: Yes, that's right. But Paris has less to do with the Nouvelle Vague than with the fact that the protagonist is a saleswoman for cosmetics. On every cosmetic bottle are the names of Paris, Milan, or London—and in one of these cities the film was supposed to begin. As well, I am interested in transitional spaces. Modern capitalism has created them. And cinema, like the car and the car radio, always existed to provide a mythos for these spaces: the solitariness of driving, road movies, all of these things derive from this. And in the 1950s these transitional spaces were rendered in hedonistic terms, with teenagers driving in Nicholas Ray's films: driving, drive-in movies, sex in cars, etc. And I thought, when I began the film, right now this mythos is in the process of dissolution: people are no longer on the road in order to find themselves but because they cannot find an exit, because there are no more cities. This is why the film starts in Paris, because its name is on the perfume bottle, which suggests Paris is still a city, which is where I want to go. The woman who keeps driving on the autobahn net desires a real city, and Paris is a real city, and the man with whom she is together is French, even though we never see him. This was the initial situation. And the path to get there, via a process of criminalization, that's always of interest to me: not in the sense that people have machine guns but that the everyday things that surround us can acquire criminal energy.

MA: What is interesting is that as a male director you chose to make a first film that is as much about female rivalry, friendship, and solidarity as it is about the early effects of globalization on reunified Germany.

CP: I wrote the story together with Harun Farocki. But the simplest explanation for the choice of subject matter is that women are foreign to me. Focusing on a female character prevents me from getting too biographical. Focusing on men driving on the autobahn would inevitably have something to do with me (search for self, etc.). When telling a story about women, the danger is, of course, that one desires them, that the storyteller desires his own characters, but I'm aware that I am not 100 percent neutral. Nevertheless, the choice of protagonists enabled me to assume greater distance to the narrative. I was able to see from a greater distance the mechanisms of dependence and exploitation that prevail: the men still own the companies, while the women have to work. The women want to be free, so there are no children: they immediately get rid of them if they don't function. I was able to film all of this from a point of greater distance than I would have been able to if the characters would have had too much of myself in them. The "cinema of identification" gets on my nerves, so I made a film that was not about identification, or, in any case, where the degree of identification is lower than usual. I wanted to see the world, not merely the subject (through whom one is invited to see the world in the traditional "cinema of identification").

MA: This strategy seems to be part of all your films: most of your primary protagonists are women, and even in films such as *Cuba Libre* and *Something to Remind Me* men are, at best, in positions equal to the female characters. In this respect your films almost seem to evoke the cinemas of Pedro Almodóvar or Douglas Sirk, that is, melodramas—films in which women have big roles.

CP: Exactly. These directors are also somewhat like fathers, as is Hitchcock.

MA: In your early films, many of the characters seem to share the desire to leave Germany. Do you share this dream without ever having realized it?

CP: That's true, although the direction of this dream then reverses itself in the more recent films. I think most great narratives are travel narratives in one form or another. In the final analysis, such narratives only pretend that people set out on a journey into the foreign. But in the end it's all a version of Homer's *Odyssey*: mostly, such narratives are about getting home. So, when my characters talk about some islands, Bora Bora [in *The Sex Thief*] or whatever, that's actually a synonym for finding one's place in life. The point is not even to get to know that which is foreign, or to cross some threshold; the point is to get back home, to find one's home. That's the subject matter for me. And Bora Bora merely represents something like a metaphysical home. But eventually I stopped with this: *The State I Am In* is about Germany, and from then on all of my films are about Germany, not about escaping it.

MA: Since the mid-to-late 1990s, a public debate has been going on about this very issue: that Germans are immobile, that the country is paralyzed (psychologically as well as materially and culturally), that we need change. It was hardly a coincidence that two of the last three German presidents, Roman Herzog (1994–99) and Horst Köhler (2004–10), respectively, delivered well-publicized and controversial speeches in which they explicitly admonished citizens to embrace neoliberal ideas of mobility. Given this context, it is interesting to see that you make films about mobility—transformation and change—at the very moment when such mobility is *absent* in the social reality of Germany.

CP: The entire neoliberal nonsense began in the 1980s. Even though the unification in 1990 momentarily covered over this, the political impetus was always to destroy all well-established social institutions. The polis, the public space, the common, all sexy terms such as the "lean state"—all of these were merely synonyms for the essential desire of neoliberals to destroy the political society. Like in the US. And in this context talk began to turn to the issue of flexibility; that's when a discourse appeared that turned against those people who were unable to move, who wanted a permanent home. At that time, I read novels by Georges Simenon, which are all about individuals who want to be modern but fail to accomplish this, for Simenon, like Anton Chekhov before him, believes that people are poorly prepared for modern life and always carry archaic remainders of another life. It is these people who are being pushed out of societies or are put in motion, but they do not even know where to go, where all of this is supposed to lead. They consequently end up in transitional spaces, transit zones where nothingness looms on one side and the impossibility of returning to what existed in the past on the other. These are the spaces that interest me.

MA: Normally, when films deal with mobility, they rely on a style made up of quick cuts, short takes, lots of action, and various clichés that somehow try to represent mobility or movement. Your films, however, treat the "mobility" in fundamentally different ways, for your films, stylistically speaking, are rather static. So, if your films can indeed be said to be about mobility, do you see yourself consciously resisting the impetus to "represent" mobility? Do you see yourself putting the concept of "representation" as such at stake?

CP: Indeed! When you're in an airplane and then get out, you suddenly notice an enormous mobility among businessmen and tourists, who get out their cell phones and run like crazy people to cabs, who slam doors as if they want to say, "We are mobile." But in the end, if you take a closer look, you notice how all airports look alike, that all airports have a Burberry store, a Rolex store, a Bulgari store, and everyone carries a two-liter bottle of water, everyone wears suits or leisure wear and sleeps with their heads on their carry-ons in some corner. So, on one hand there's an enormous mythologizing of mobility, which is shown with the help of quick cuts and cars in advertising; on the other hand, the more mobility is represented in films or is demanded by advertising the less it actually exists. Nothing is moving! This unmoving movement, this immobile mobility, I think, is something, a place, an uncanny place, that has emerged as a fundamental condition of life in the present: a new form of loneliness of the traveler. And this new loneliness has not even been researched. That's why those road movies get on my nerves in which some people want to see the ocean one more time, or which show handicapped people just before dying. That's eighteenth century, or the worst of the nineteenth!

I am interested in the mobile immobilities, the so-called transit zones, these no-places: that's where something modern is happening. And they expand in a metastatic way. Today I met a friend who told me that most recent horror films, with their scenes of torture and mercenary characters, take place in Eastern Europe, in CIS [Commonwealth of Independent States] countries. This is because the capitalist map has become so vast that everything is homogenized. There are but a few spots left where we can still imagine horror, an outside, but it is in this outside where horror occurs, where capitalism is in the process of intruding, where in three years it'll all be over, where cheap labor, low taxes, low cost of employment essentially are already destroying everything. That's why horror does not even come anymore from countries in Asia or Africa but rather from Kazakhstan, Georgia, the Ukraine, etc. This is quite fascinating. I think this has to do with the fact that today films are not really made by studios anymore but by humongous, publicly traded global corporations. And they know that they cause capital to deterritorialize the entire world, that they force the world to become ever more flexible, but also that they force the world into paralysis. That's why they have to push ever further to the margins, but soon no more margins exist. But they don't look inside, they don't analyze the inside—which is what I would love to do. I am not so much interested in the margins—Bora Bora, etc.; I am interested in the center, what happens there.

MA: The sensation of movement that your films set loose functions on the level of affect. Movement is rendered sensible as something intensive rather than extensive. In patiently lingering on an image, change becomes somehow sensible on an affective, haptic level. Your camera is not interested in looking beyond what is occurring. It's not a matter of depicting a drive to the ocean, which almost always tends to evoke transcendence, a utopian mobility *beyond* the here and now. Instead, your camera tries to inhere in the event, to give us the event and to push it to its limit, to the limit of what is visible, and thus to affect the moment of transformation that occurs from within, immanently, rather than from without, caused by a clearly delineable object-cause. It is these immanently produced moments that for me constitute in principle the opposite of the neoliberal version of mobility. You once said that we are still far away from making political films. But could we not say that your films are political precisely because your images put into question one of capitalism's most important aspects: that of mobility?

CP: Yes, I absolutely agree. I once talked with Christoph Hochhäusler for a long time about the question of political filmmaking. Both of us had read [Peter Nau's *Critique of the Political Film*] on the issue of political filmmaking. Nau explicitly demands that films have to be made politically. In our case, production circumstances for films are of course capitalist, which is why film has to reflect its own conditions of production. Each great filmmaker, be it Truffaut, Godard, or Fassbinder, has made films about making films—that is, they placed themselves and their conditions of production center stage. These are political films for me. I also believe that I think in some form politically about film, yet most of the time what is political about my films occurs to me mostly after the fact.

MA: Yours are not thesis-driven films.

CP: Exactly. Something happens in the telling; something emerges out of its complexity. When the film is done, I sometimes realize that there is a thought that I have not even finished thinking; even though it is somehow realized in the film, it was not there at the beginning. There are always a lot of philosophical texts that accompany the shooting process, but they are more something that I read to the actors, just as I play music, which leaves a mark on the shooting process. Sometimes all of this becomes a web that fits together, and at other times it has nothing at all to do with the final film.

MA: Your films are characterized by a certain aesthetic asceticism, or sternness. Do you have models for this?

CP: When I was eighteen, I saw John Carpenter's *Halloween*. That was a major filmic event for me, which left its mark on me to this day. It's a film with mental, subjective images, as well as objective ones, which alternate and thus create the sensation of horror. You never really know whether what you see is a look or a recording. And sometimes the one who looks suddenly steps into what appears as a point of view shot, thus appearing as an object, not subject, in front of the camera. This comes as a shock every time anew. I think this really formed me. Hitchcock does this frequently as well, so that you are never sure who the agent of the look is: is it Hitchcock, a narrator, or the character? And in Edward Hopper's late paintings, he stopped painting figures in borderline situations and instead painted the borderlines themselves, *as* look. I think that toward the end of his career Hopper painted like Yazujiro Ozu made films.

I always ask myself together with my cinematographer, Hans Fromm, when we have rehearsed a scene with the actors for a long time, *how* can we cinematically realize this scene? How can you film it? Who does the looking here? And what comes before, what after? I always try to forge a connection between the mental and the objective image. From this it's possible that something like an aesthetic style develops, and at times my figures are part of a spatial psychology, a spatial rhythm, whereas at other times they appear as if in a portrait. That is, sometimes it's the space that is being rendered as a portrait with people, at others it's the figures themselves who make up the classic portrait. This changes, depending on how the characters themselves feel. That is, sometimes they are beaten down by their environment, and sometimes the environment exists merely because of them.

MA: You just mentioned Hopper. Do you have other extra-cinematic models that conceptually influence you? For instance, in *The Sex Thief* a poster of Gerhard Richter's "Betty" hangs on a wall. And then there are a number of scenes that almost appear as if you restaged the German artist's seascape paintings such as the "Seascape" series or "Iceberg in Mist." I'm thinking here, for example, of various scenes in *Cuba Libre*, *The Sex Thief*, or *Wolfsburg*. In general, it seems that your images have a lot in common with Richter's blue-gray tones as well as his particular use of "focus" (which so often is just a bit "off").

CP: Yes, Richter has been a really important painter for me. He still is! I like that his paintings are simultaneously turned toward and away from the beholder. This relates to the issue of subjective vs. objective that I just discussed. American actors are superior to all others in the world because they *act*, that is, they are next to themselves while concurrently remaining identical to themselves. Look at Robert Duvall in [Coppola's] *Apocalypse Now*. He plays a dirty GI, and we see the pleasure he takes in acting, but simultaneously he also *is* this figure, he identifies with it. I like this simultaneous identification and stepping-out-of-himself a lot, which is something like an American way of Brechtian acting. I try to get this from my actors: I want them to give themselves totally over to the characters they play and simultaneously step outside of these figures.

MA: You once wrote that you would not be interested in making films about the German past because film, for you, is about the present. You quoted Truffaut on the problem of the sky in historical films, that for him the sky in an image always points to the present . . .

CP: That was in an essay I wrote on [George] Romero.

MA: In some sense, one might be able to read "Betty" (and many of Richter's paintings) with recourse to Walter Benjamin's angel of history: there is nothing but the present, yet the angel's gaze, *in* its radical presentness, directs us to history, to the question of the past.

CP: Yes, what I want to do with my films has a lot to do with this. Benjamin's "Theses on the Philosophy of History" was an important text for me during my time as a literary scholar.

MA: Earlier you mentioned Deleuze, his books on the cinema. Are you also familiar with his book on the Anglo-Irish painter Francis Bacon?

CP: No.

MA: Deleuze argues that for Bacon, in terms of his painterly practice, the canvas is initially full of images, which is why his first task is to abstract from this only apparently empty canvas all pictorial clichés. How does this work for you when you start a new film? Do you also face the problem that the cinema's projection surface, the screen, is a priori full of moving images? I am thinking, for instance, about your approach to locations, as in *Ghosts*, where at the beginning the camera almost crawls across the ground of some not-yet-specified forest—a forest that does not immediately announce itself to the viewer as the famous Tiergarten in Berlin. The film does not immediately provide viewers who know Berlin only from film and TV images with the "meaning" of the image. The film does not immediately announce that we're in Berlin by, say, showing an image of the city's TV tower or whatever other cliché-like images of Berlin you could have used. It seems almost as if you abstracted our stale ideas of Berlin from the screen in order to find, or invent, new possibilities for rendering this space visible.

CP: Yes, exactly. I would love to work in a studio. What would be of interest to me about working in a studio is the ability to go there at 9 a.m. and return home at 5 p.m., every day; that is, I would love to work in a more industrial manner. I also think that the cinema does not belong into museums. Hence, I don't think it should be something akin to a nineteenth-century artist cinema; rather, cinema ought to be serial in some form or fashion. I would love to work serially. Which is why I think that the images that are currently being produced in the US, their TV series, are the most interesting laboratories. What HBO does is fantastic. But this is not television. That is, people buy or rent the series on DVD and essentially watch them as if they were cinema. This is a new form of watching movies that is currently approaching us. You sit together and escape in some world: it's *ersatz* cinema. But I would be interested in such continuity of work in the cinema itself, in a studio, though the studio itself would be less interesting to me. I am not interested in being faced with empty rooms, which I then have to fill; rather, I have to find a point *in* a room, which is the present, from which to look out, and I need to find a second point that I relate to the first. I have to discover segments, fragments, that narrate the space at hand in a way that is larger than it would appear if I merely shot it in an establishing shot that shows everything at once.

MA: All of your films take place in real space, which is emphasized by the way you photograph these spaces. We can really sense the realness of your spaces, which seems a direct effect of the insisting gaze of your camera. André Bazin once affirmatively described "true realism" with recourse to what he identifies as Erich von Stroheim's operational filmmaking principle: "Look precisely at the world [and] *keep on* looking." This ongoing process of looking, this ceaseless staring, has something to do with duration, with enduring, with singularity, and with intensity; in this manner, your camera renders sensible the singularity of a space that, consequently, cannot be replaced with another space.

CP: Exactly. You have to behold the most everyday space until it looks back, until it becomes mysterious. This takes work: you have to select segments, and you have to manipulate space; each light is a manipulation of space. In Germany you have furniture stores that learned this only because of the success of IKEA. IKEA furniture looks ugly. But in their catalogue they are beautifully photographed: there's always a rising sun, there's always a diagonal sun light, a Hopper light that shines through the room. This light tells us that this room, the day, is only at its beginning: everything is still ahead of you, everything is free. But once you got IKEA furniture at home everything is over; that's when the long night begins! Every setting-into-light is an act of pushing something into the foreground while letting other things drift into the dark. So, one renders space colorful. This isn't merely a matter of representing the preexisting space along the lines of traditional realist aesthetics. But even though this is not representational realism everything of what you do to the room has to be derived from within the room itself, immanently, if you will. There are so many people who suddenly stare at something and thus *see* something—this staring means duration, and we have to insist upon doing this: you have to stare and find a second view, and then things begin to become mysterious and complex. Bad cinema merely provides us with things that we are asked to decode: one object means richness, another old age, yet another youth, etc. But to find youth *in* old age, or death *in* morning, as with IKEA's commercial images, that is of interest to me.

MA: What you're saying is that one stares and stares, and suddenly the object one stares at metamorphoses *in* your eye. This once again returns us to the issue of immanent transformation or movement, which is not being generated by some form of decoding operation or extensive force, but . . .

CP: This is what you said at the beginning about the cinema of mobility, with its rapid cuts, etc.: it does not need space anymore, as it almost exclusively appears to work with time.

MA: In your films, families assume an important role. You often talk about your interest in in-between spaces. And the families in your films often find themselves in such spaces and assume a ghost-like quality: the attempt at forging a home by the sales woman in *Pilots*; the failed attempt of the two protagonists in *Cuba Libre* to share a life together; Petra's desire to return to her family home and live with her sister in *The Sex Thief*; the ex-terrorists on the run with their teenage daughter in *The State I Am In*; the violent destruction of a family's togetherness in *Something to Remind Me*; the car accident in *Wolfsburg*, which destroys one family and momentarily seems to forge the potential for creating a new one; the orphaned children (and parents, if you will) in *Ghosts*; and most recently the undoing of family life as a result of devastating economic postunification circumstances in *Yella*. Where does your interest in this subject matter come from?

CP: My generation was taught by all these leftist teachers whose consciousness was shaped by the events of 1968. At that time the family was seen to be the smallest cell of the state, of fascist structures, that is, as the biggest piece of shit imaginable. It was the site where discipline and training were implemented. In this context, Deleuze's essay on control societies impressed me immensely when I began making films in the mid-nineties, just before Deleuze's death. Deleuze argues that the extra-familiar institutions that cropped up everywhere, those hedonistic communities, the patchwork families, the communes, and the shared apartment-living situations, which were established in direct opposition to the traditional father-mother-child neurosis—that these new forms, which were and are perceived as liberatory, actually embody the modern control society, that is, are modern forms of oppression that suddenly exert their force upon people. I was impressed by this insight, and subsequently I began to examine what happened to the traditional family. This family really does not exist anymore. It is being subvented by the state: couples now get money so that they produce children. But the desire to have children does not come out of desires immanent to couples' relationships anymore; the reproduction of society does not work anymore, which is why I took an interest in the family. This is quite pronounced in *The State I Am In*. But even in *Something to Remind Me*, we see a remnant of this family, and my new film, *Yella*, is also about this issue.

MA: In *The Sex Thief*, too, we find a rupture within the family: the two sisters permanently lie to each other. And the men, who barely show up but who are constantly being talked about and fall for Petra's criminal schemes, are desperately searching for something-something that they do not have at home but that they believe they *should* have. The film suggests this socio-psychic wasteland, this boredom—which might very well be merely a medially produced suggestion, a feeling instilled by advertising that tells people how their lives *should* be—is characteristic of life in the post-Wall era.

CP: I always like it when people play something, when they believe that they have to play the role of father or daughter, but then they lose control over the staging. Those are the best moments.

MA: One of the most fascinating moments in *The State I Am In* is that for the daughter, Jeanne [Julia Hummer], the idea of a normal family is almost something utopian, something positive, something that she does not partake of in her real life. It's a complete reversal from what her parents' generation believed, even though her terrorist parents decided to try out life with a child.

CP: What I liked about the film was that the terrorist family in the film *is* a model family. They negotiate problems and conflicts with their child in a totally open manner. Yet, there is also discipline and strictness, and the people Jeanne meets outside, they are mostly remainders, children of divorces, orphans, etc. who are lost and already destroyed before their life ever had a chance to begin. It is as if the people who ended up in the transit spaces of international terrorism wanted to maintain, like immigrants, something that really does not exist anymore.

MA: Your most recent film, *Yella*, also incorporates the notion of the "family," albeit more on the level of the film's subtext: her caring, loving relationship with her father, the absence of any trace of a mother, her marital breakdown. In Germany, and for a much longer time of course in the US, the institution of the family has fallen victim to capitalism's imperative for citizens to be mobile, individual, and workaholics; on the other hand, there is the family values discourse, which, it seems to me, is going through a renaissance in Germany these days.

CP: Indeed. This is the kind of contradictoriness that is in *Yella*. She sheds herself off everything; she makes herself lean, streamlined. She has no ballast. She carries remarkably little with her and lives in hotels, in transit zones. On the other hand, she is plagued by ghosts that are pursuing her—ghosts that come not only from outside but are *within* her and want to pin her down, to ground her. And communism—"A ghost is haunting Europe . . ."—all of this has something to do with this. Nina Hoss, who plays Yella, physically understood this right away. She could not even explain this, but she understood *physically* what Yella's turmoil is.

MA: Recently I found what I think is the first critical essay in English dealing with one of your films, in a volume on psychoanalytic readings of contemporary European films. It would appear that your most recent film, *Yella*, might also be of great interest to psychoanalytic film critics, given the importance of dreaming in this film. What is your relationship to psychoanalytic thought?

CP: When making *Yella*, I reread a good number of key texts. When I was a student I took a number of courses at the Free University in Berlin on the philosophy of religion, and in this context I also examined the relationship between Freud and Marx, which really interested me when conceiving of *Yella*. From the beginning, we premised the film on the notion of dream work, for the film is about a woman who works on her dreams, which is why I revisited some of the literature I had read as a student, including two of my favorite texts, Freud's *Civilization and Its Discontents* and Marx's essay "18th Brumaire of Louise Bonaparte." I am certain that we would have won a few revolutions if Marx and Freud were to have met!

MA: By now, most critics discussing your work talk about your "ghost trilogy," comprising of *The State I Am In*, *Ghosts*, and now *Yella*. Did you conceive from the start to make such a trilogy?

CP: Originally no. But during preproduction for *The State I Am In*, the concept of "ghosts" was very much present in my conversations with Harun. We almost worked one full year on the film, and during that period we often discussed the idea of people who have fallen out of history. The left has fallen out of history, too. In the autobiography of German communists in the 1930s, for instance, we frequently find that they feel not needed anymore: National Socialism is in power, Stalinism is not an alternative, so they end up in a no man's land. For instance, Georg K. Glaser, author of the autobiography *Geheimnis und Gewalt*, moves as a coppersmith to Paris in 1935, where he initially hid and eventually lived the rest of his life. He invented the concept of "the silence of history" for himself. He suddenly realizes, as if on a sailboat on the ocean, that there's no wind anymore: a ghostly atmosphere, where no one needs you anymore, where there is no drive left. Based on these conceptual issues I began to think whether it is not the case that the cinema does not always tell stories about ghosts anyway: stories of people who have fallen out of love, out of work processes, people for whom there is no use anymore. Through these reflections we ended up moving from *The State I Am In*, which concerns the political left and terrorism, to the girls in *Ghosts* who have no biography, no genealogy, and for whom the generalized labor process has no use, to, finally, *Yella*, which is a film about a woman who exists in a twilight zone between death and life.

MA: We already noted that you are not interested in making films about the [German] past. But it seems to me that one could argue that you are making films about the lingering *consequences* of the past in the present, as evidenced by the "ghost trilogy" but also *Cuba Libre*, *Something to Remind Me*, or *Wolfsburg*. Given that *Yella*'s obvious subtext is the German unification, I wonder how much this event played a role for your conception of the film?

CP: Initially I could not come up with any image for the reunification. Jean-Luc Godard once spoke at the dffb and told us that if he were to make a film about the German reunification then it would be a film about the loneliness of Germany. He would have Erich Honecker, the GDR's second to last chairman of the Council of State, drive in a car across the West German autobahns. This is pretty much as lonely as it gets! But initially I had no thoughts on this topic. I only began thinking about it when I started making films in the East, when I discovered the mythological location of so many German legends—the river landscapes, etc.—as a place abandoned by the women who used to live there. All the women gone: this was the first moment when I thought, this is movement, this is an image, and I can make a film about this! Then I watched Fritz Lang's *The Blue Gardenia*, for I was always curious about these women who, in the 1930s in the US, live together in large urban environments, working as phone operators or in department stores, who are nineteen, twenty years old, and who all came from the country, from Arizona, Texas, Montana, who now sit in bars and become protagonists in gangster stories, who are there to find millionaires. And I thought: where did all the girls from the former East Germany go? Which dreams do they have? What kind of fortune hunters are they? Then I read a lot about Irish women. And when you watch John Ford films, you notice how women always seem to sit in the front of stagecoaches. Of course, it is the men on whom the films focus—they fight, shoot, scream—but it is the women who are the real agents of movement. One always has the feeling that it is the women who leave because there is no place for them anymore, no riches, no one who can take care of them. And this was the starting point for *Yella*: we narrate the topic of the reunification as a story about a woman who is looking for fortune.

MA: You just referred to John Ford's westerns. Which role does the notion of genre play for *Yella*? The film takes some of its conceits from Herk Harvey's cult B-horror movie, *Carnival of Souls*, and Ambrose Bierce's much-anthologized short story "An Occurrence at Owl Creek Bridge." But it also has elements of Japanese horror/ghost stories. What, in your view, does the element of the "unreal," which you seem to take from these sources, add to *Yella* that the film otherwise would not have if it played exclusively on the level of "normal" reality?

CP: The infusion of the unreal into the real is of course also a crucial part of the German cultural tradition. For instance, a few weeks ago I watched together with my children Murnau's *Nosferatu* and *Phantom*. You can really sense how the German black romanticism of the nineteenth century suddenly takes place in the scripts of the 1920s. That such things happen has always something to do with the fact that a part of communal life, of the social, has been destroyed. Everything is being privatized; people are not being used anymore; they are left staggering about. This is already thematized in E. T. A. Hoffmann and Hugo von Hofmannsthal: a social class is in the process of dying, and like ghosts they relive their lives one more time. This interested me, but because this is so German, so close to me, I never had any real access to this idea, except through literature. In terms of cinema, I started relating to this issue only through American films—*Carnival of Souls*, [M. Night Shyamalan's] *The Sixth Sense*—which is capable of dealing with it much more naturally because it does have the very genres German cinema does not have. I simply enjoy the way American cinema deals with American mythologies: rather than poking fun at them, they continue working with them. In Germany, however, cinema stopped working with mythologies ever since the fascist period, when the Nazis appropriated German mythology. Which is why American cinema is something like a home for me in this respect.

MA: I once read an interview with, I believe, Japanese director Takashi Shimizu, who remade one of his Japanese horror films, *Ju-On* for the American market as *The Grudge*. Explaining the difference between these two versions of the same story, he argues that whereas for a Japanese audience he does not need to explain the supernatural aspect of the story because ghosts are a component of everyday life in Japanese culture, for an American audience he had to provide more "realistic" explanations precisely because the supernatural is not part of their daily culture.

CP: There is some truth to this. I think it has to do with the fact that in the US Christians have occupied mythologies. In Germany, like in Japan, ghosts connote phantoms, dark forests, uninhabitable nature, *Rübezahl* [a legendary spirit of the Sudeten mountains]. The country is full with such stories, and so is Japan. I think American cinema remade films such as *The Ring* [Gore Verbinski] and *Dark Water* [Walter Salles] because the US horror film, which used to be fantastic, was completely destroyed as a result of all these awful, ironic horror film parodies. This was a result of the ratings system: if you can laugh about monsters even fourteen-year-olds can go to see the film. Japanese films are much harder hitting, though. But through remakes such as *The Ring*, US cinema has found back to mythologies that are serious and heavy, and which are not Christian! I find this quite interesting as a social history of US cinema. But this has also something to do with capitalism—with the fact that people do not understand something essential anymore: that their houses have suddenly lost their value, that there are no securities anymore, that they are being forced into a terrifying independence. That is the moment, of course, when stories begin again; that we now see the reemergence of films about the civil war and the nineteenth century—Jesse James, etc.—that has a lot to do with this.

MA: To me, *Yella* is really one of the great films about capitalism in general and finance capitalism in particular. What makes this film so great is the way it takes seriously how this economic system really operates. The film shows, to me compellingly, how this latest stage of capitalism is much "lighter" than its predecessors, which were still characterized by "heavy" labor. And Yella has understood this, whereas her husband hasn't, which, presumably, is why his company went bankrupt. He still mourns for an earlier, "traditional" stage of capitalism (and, in a last-ditch effort to get his wife back, even promises her again to become what he thinks Yella wanted him to be all along: a regular blue-collar worker), whereas Yella immediately understands that the venture capital environment functions on the level of images, gestures, rumors, surfaces, attitudes, games, etc. Given how precise this film is with finding "proper" images for twenty-first-century capitalism, I wonder how you went about approaching the question of imaging venture capitalism?

CP: To start with, there was Harun Farocki's film *Nothing Ventured*. For three days, he filmed a venture capital negotiation like an ethnographer. Harun's premise was the insight that we do not even have any new images of capitalism yet. Sure, we have these airport boarding zones, where we see modern people with laptops, reading high-gloss magazines, wearing Rolexes and Burberry clothes. All this is only a surface, but we do not have images for how this new form of capitalism *operates*. We have books about it, but we do not find those images in films. In cinema, capitalism is still being imaged as Charles Chaplin did in *Modern*

Times. Because Harun approached his task ethnographically, rather than assuming a priori a denunciatory perspective, the film managed for the first time to render visible the flexible, modern people who are involved in these operations: we gain insights into their lust for victory (as this is now also described a bit in Naomi Klein's *Shock Doctrine: The Rise of Disaster Capitalism*) and where the cheekiness and posing of new "Chicago Boys" comes from. In *Yella*, each sentence of the negotiation is from Harun's film: none of this was invented, everything is based on real negotiations, including the vocabulary.

I think you can only make a film about someone who is concurrently young and old, light and heavy, who wants to flow with modern capitalism but also dreams of owning a house, and who wants to move about but also wants to be rooted. And this inner turmoil is probably why *Yella* is so successful. For I think its success here has to do with the audience understanding this conflict when they see it in the film. In Germany, they have been parroting neo-conservative ideology for the last ten, fifteen years: endless chatter about the lean state, the need for citizens to become independent, and the need to give up the belief that issues such as health, schooling, or prison are the responsibility of the state. The only task for the state now seems to be the executive, whose only job appears to be to regulate the field in favor of capitalism. So, the simultaneous occurrence of this lean, sexy language on one hand and the incredible impoverishment, destruction of wage labor, the total loss of security on the other leads to a remarkable regionalization of people. As well, in Germany we are now witnessing an uncanny return of racism: the now "useless" working class beats up asylum seekers, people from foreign countries, gays, etc. That is how you notice the contradictions of the system, which are precisely the contradictions of Yella.

MA: Earlier, you briefly touched on Nina Hoss's performance, for which she received the Best Actress award at the Berlin film festival in 2007. To bring this interview to a conclusion, could you talk about how you worked with the actors, especially Nina Hoss and Devid Striesow, who plays the venture capitalist, Philipp—that is, how you designed and developed their roles? For instance, how did you instruct Ms. Hoss to play Yella, a role that is very much ambiguous in terms of who she "is": a ghost, a real person, both, and which at what moment in time?

CP: Nina reminded me a week ago of an interesting story. Like Jean Renoir used to do, I stage "Italian rehearsals." That is, initially we merely read the text, coldly: I instruct the actors simply to read the text, to talk and think about it, but not to play right away. Then, during the first two days, I rehearsed without the main actors, that is, with everyone—those who participate in the negotiations, the one who plays Yella's father, etc.—but not Nina Hoss, Devid Striesow, and Hinnerk Schönemann [who plays Ben, Yella's soon-to-be ex-husband]. I simply wanted that at first the so-called supporting characters would not merely be supporting characters. I wanted for them as characters to obtain a certain "richness" of their own, especially since I was afraid that they—the capitalists, if you will—would otherwise be in danger of seeming ridiculous. Only then did I begin working with the three main actors. For three days, we essentially talked only about venture capitalism. After that we drove to Wittenberge [in former East Germany, the place Yella leaves to find her luck in Hanover, the host city of the World Expo 2000 in former West Germany] in order to take walks there. We strolled through this astonishingly beautiful landscape, which is, however, also characterized by many industrial ruins. We had our conversations about venture capitalism in our heads, as well as Harun's film. The actors even went to their tax accountants in order to observe their poses. That's how it was. [*Laughs*] So the actors had both: an impression of the beautiful landscape, where one simply gained the feeling that one ought to make a nineteenth-century movie, and an incredible quickness of mind necessary for taking over companies only to quickly sell them for profit. In other words, we did not really do much acting work in the traditional sense. Only later did I work with Nina and Devid on how to walk, how to look at and past each other, how one seizes up another person. But mainly our work oscillated between the two extremes of being in a mythical landscape and immersing us in the process of venture capital negotiations.

MA: Do you have already a sense of how many people have seen the film in Germany, where the reviews of the films have been overwhelmingly positive, with some, like Georg Seeßlen, calling the film a "masterpiece"?

CP: I stopped calling the distributor after the first couple of weeks. It's too embarrassing. But the film started its run with thirty copies, and I think it is enjoying a really good run. I think that it will eventually cross the 100,000 viewers mark, which for such a film in Germany is a really good number.

Emigrating from Brandenburg

Ralf Schenk / 2007

From "Auswandern aus Brandenburg," *Berliner Zeitung*, February 14, 2007. Reprinted by permission. Translated by Marco Abel and Jaimey Fisher.

Ralf Schenk: In your new film [*Yella*], which premieres this evening in the competition at the Berlinale, you tell the story of a young woman from Brandenburg who flees her marriage and is seeking her fortune in the West. This protagonist is called Yella. What is the origin of this name?

Christian Petzold: It is inspired by Wim Wenders's *Alice in the Cities*, which I saw when I was fourteen or fifteen. Back then, I was familiar with *Jaws*, but I did not know auteur films [*Autorenfilme*], and I wasn't interested in them either. I only went to see the film because I liked the music of CAN, which was on the soundtrack. Suddenly, however, I saw on screen the world in which I lived. This was for me a fascinating process that formed me. The eight-year-old Alice was played by a girl named Yella Rottländer. This child opened the senses; she was permanently in motion. In Arabic, "Jalla" means "move." And this is precisely the theme of my new film.

RS: Seven years ago, you made *Something to Remind Me* also with Nina Hoss. That film concerns a movement from West to East. Now you are narrating a trip in the opposite direction.

CP: Back then we shot in Wittenberge and discovered a city that was brutally liquidated by the Treuhand.[1] The sewing machine factory, which was once the largest in all the Warsaw Pact countries, had perhaps thirty jobs left. We looked at the Elbe as a sort of border, a river that one could cross to reach a new world. We invented Yella, who leaves this eastern world. She wants to dispense with ballast and experience lightness.

RS: Did you already have images in mind for how the West ought to look in your new film?

---

1. The controversial agency created in 1990 by the (soon-to-be-dissolved) East German government to sell East German state assets to private interests.

CP: I came up with those when reading Marc Augé's *Non-Places: An Introduction to Supermodernity*. In it, the French ethnologist narrates the morning of a businessman who takes a cab to the airport and in a traffic jam is confronted with social reality. Eventually he enters without any luggage the boarding zone, for Augé a non-place of modernity: shot through with light, big glass windows everywhere, a world of leather, Burberry, Rolex, glossy magazines, and advertisement for resort hotels in Dubai. Here this man is incredibly relieved. He's discarded ballast—not just his suitcase but also social reality. That's when I realized that in the film the Elbe could assume this function, the river as transition into the boarding area. My coauthor, Harun Farocki, and I wondered how we could narrate modern capitalism. In the past, capitalists were depicted as fat and with a top hat and cigar. In Harun's documentary *Nothing Ventured*, however, they look very different: they are dressed just right, listen to Mozart and Bach, stay at the best hotels, drive cars with navigation systems that whisper. At this moment I know where Yella wants to go.

RS: One of the literary sources that inspired you was Ambrose Bierce's story, "An Occurrence at Owl Creek Bridge." What did you find fascinating about it?

CP: The sliding out of the everyday and simultaneously the yearning to find one's back to normality. The desire to live a life that heretofore one didn't know. I love this short and very painful story from the American Civil War about being a stranger in one's own country. I found something similar in E. T. A. Hoffmann's novellas, in the German black romanticism. But for me *Yella* has also something to do with old ballads about emigration. When Van Morrison sings of Irish exiles, one senses an incredible feeling of homesickness. At the same time, these songs are an accusation of the old homeland that can no longer feed its population. Yella, too, leaves a country that cannot nourish her. She wants to find a place in the West, but she knows that it cannot offer her the kind of life she is really looking for. The conflict resulting from this constitutes the emotional tension of the film.

RS: What did Nina Hoss bring to this role?

CP: We both like the notion of "Italian practice" which Jean Renoir invented. This means that prior to shooting, one empties oneself out intellectually and emotionally, that one liberates oneself from all the reflections one had previously accumulated. From within this emptiness, one cautiously commences to formulate anew, to have ideas. In this respect Nina is incredibly radical. She cannot stand any meaningless gestures and chatter. Together, one has to find something that reveals the core of the tension. It was fascinating to observe how Nina and Devid Striesow liberated the script from all sentences that were no longer necessary.

RS: To set the mood for a new project, you like watching old films with your actors. Did you do this again this time around?

CP: Yes, for *Yella* I selected films in which women go on a journey. We watched Hitchcock's *Marnie* and Barbara Loden's *Wanda*. I had the sense that Nina took something especially from Wanda. Wanda is from a working-class background and did not have the possibility to hold the reins. Thirty years later, Yella believes that she does hold the reins. She tries to pull on these strings.

RS: In the film, Nina Hoss often walks straight as a pin; she appears like an antique statue.

CP: I love watching people as they work, people who try to keep their internal turmoil in check, who create a protective armor and embody a style. They have the feeling that the slightest relinquishing of tension and attention would lead to their collapse, indeed their death. A sort of model for Yella was also Franz Jung's *Torpedokäfer*. An insect/beetle starts, completes a near fatal flight of hundreds of meters, crashes, lies for days as if shattered on the ground, and then rebuilds himself for a new flight. This was Nina's concept for Yella: she shows a woman who is strong, but when the door of her hotel room closes behind her, she collapses.

RS: Yella dives into the world of financial transactions. She becomes the assistant of a venture capital manager and gets caught up in guilt. Isn't her story a moral one?

CP: A friend of mine said about Stanley Kubrick's films that they are always about upstarts. Protagonists who want to leave one socioeconomic class for another, but who never get comfortable in the latter. When I read this, I thought that this is my topic as well. I'm interested in people who try to get a grip on their lives and in so doing commit incredible mistakes. Perhaps my films aren't moralizing, but they are about people who try to climb up and in so doing no longer manage to merge their moral categories—solidarity and friendliness—with their next existences.

RS: When you developed *Yella*, German was synonymous with bad mood. Today, many talk about the end of the crisis.[2] Does the film therefore come too late?

CP: No. The evocation of a boom is the bull market of the feuilleton. I am sure that there are as many people as two years ago who are not doing well.

---

2. After the initial high of the country's unification in 1990, Germany subsequently struggled both economically and socially. The 2006 soccer World Cup in Germany, often referred to as a *Sommermärchen* [summer's fairy tale], is seen as a turning point in the country's overall mood, momentarily leading people to feel that the socioeconomic crisis that has been weighing on them might be over.

"You Don't Want to Fall in Love"

Lars-Olaf Beier and Moritz von Uslar / 2007

From "'Man will sich nicht verlieben,'" *Spiegel*, no. 37 (September 9, 2007): 186–90. Reprinted by permission. Translated by Marco Abel and Jaimey Fisher.

Lars-Olaf Beier and Moritz von Uslar: Mr. Petzold, your film *The State I Am In* was one of the most discussed German films of the last few years, but it had only 100,000 viewers. When is a film successful for you?

Christian Petzold: The numbers say very little. There is a discrepancy between those films with production costs of several millions, which therefore turn into an event, and those that I make. I can notice whether a film leaves a trace or whether it's basically dead in the second week of release.

Beier and von Uslar: Do you like having as many viewers as possible? Or is your attitude: better a small audience as long as it's one that reflects on the experience?

Petzold: Of course, I would like to have as many viewers as possible. But when making a film, it's not like I'm thinking about the market. I don't do previews or test screenings. You can tell if a film panders to its audience. And I can't stand to be taken by the hand in a film.

Beier and von Uslar: For your new film *Yella*, which is about a young woman who leaves her hometown of Wittenberge and falls in love in Hannover with a private equity manager, you picked a demanding topic that is difficult to get a handle on: modern capitalism.

Petzold: It's almost impossible to represent capitalism. So, I sat down with my coauthor, Harun Farocki, who directed the documentary *Nothing Ventured*, and we realized that we still have the clichéd images of capitalists in our heads—that is, cigar, potbelly, naked secretary kneeling under the desk, a Jekyll-and-Hyde existence with family at home and lover in St. Tropez: it's so terribly 1950s, this whole Willi-Heinrich [high-flying soap opera-y] world.

Beier and von Uslar: In your opinion, what does a modern capitalist look like?

Petzold: He [sic] might be Buddhist, listens to Mozart, and travels by high-speed train, while the regular prole is still speeding down the autobahn. It started about fifteen years ago that capitalists suddenly had a body, sensuality, and became sexy, which has to do with his purchasing power that is of interest to the advertising industry.

Beier and von Uslar: When did you last encounter modern capitalism in real life?

Petzold: Together with Nina Hoss, who plays Yella, I took the train to Hannover to shoot scenes. We were in first class. There, train conductors are required to wait on the customers—to bring them coffee, etc. The history of the German railway is that all employees are craftsmen, from conductor to train operator. And now a man approaches, about fifty years old, has worked for the railroad for thirty years, and asks as server in a conductor's uniform whether we want coffee. And one realizes, from how he says this, that this is not his language.

Beier and von Uslar: If you had to come up with an advertising slogan for *Yella*, what would it be?

Petzold: The distributor asked me this as well. I completely failed in the search for this sentence. In the film's trailer, you now see sequences from the film, followed by a question on two title cards: "How dangerous is it to dream . . . in the age of venture capital?"

Beier and von Uslar: Your new film takes place in the East German small town of Wittenberge and on the World Expo grounds in Hannover, a glassy, unreal area. Doesn't your films' lack of commercial success also have something to do with the fact that you do not allow your protagonists to have a home?

Petzold: But where would this home be? There's nowhere else where one feels as estranged as at home. Bob Dylan's "Wanted Man," the entire American country music, tells stories about coming home, but as a process and not as a feeling that one can simply call up. The American western, film noir, Melville films from France: they all are about the unfulfilled longing for a location where one can finally lie down.

Beier and von Uslar: In *Yella*, the heroine says goodbye to her father in front of a wooden wall near a dumpster.

Petzold: This was not gloominess; I hate films in which social sadness is celebrated. The man simply works by the dumpster. Yella leaves her town because it cannot nurture her either economically or emotionally. And then we see the river Elbe, and that's crucial: in Wittenberge, the Elbe is the park.

Beier and von Uslar: Are you purposefully trying to convey a different image of Germany?

Petzold: I'm not interested in a Danish film that pretends to be an American one. I'm interested in a Danish film that takes place in Denmark. German cinema has more force when it's not ashamed of taking place in Germany—or when it is so ashamed that it renders this shame its topic.

Beier and von Uslar: Shopping malls and supermarkets are "enchanted sites" for you. What kind of magic do you discover there?

Petzold: I grew up in such locations—in Haan, a small town in North Rhine Westphalia. This sprawling Federal Republic with thirteen-years-old kids who somehow hang around there between high rises and junction boxes—this was, for me, a reform school. You can load up any kind of crap with emotion, even a junction box that's there all by itself. You can even tell a love story set in the last taxpayer-funded shopping mall in the East, where there is nothing left but a cheap supermarket and a postal office. It's just that this story must not pretend as if it takes place in Paris' XVI arrondissement.

Beier and von Uslar: In general, are you afraid of love scenes?

Petzold: Do you mean love or sex?

Beier and von Uslar: A love scene.

Petzold: That's not something of which I'm afraid. I find them interesting. I want to film the production of love, the resistance therein, not the simple state of being in love. I don't like love scenes that announce: "Hey, they are in love." Everyone pretends that love is the best thing on earth. But, in reality, there's resistance, too, for you don't want to fall in love because you know the problems and uncertainty that come with it. I find it interesting to film this conflict.

Beier and von Uslar: Like all of your films, *Yella*, too, is ultimately quite dark. The ending is a bona fide punch in the viewer's gut. Simply put: is it not allowed to have a happy Petzold film?

Petzold: I actually think there are many happy moments in *Yella*. Perhaps it is a matter of what music one listens to: is this not all sad? Among the thousand films I'd take with me to a desert island are many comedies, but there's nothing sadder than a comedy.

Beier and von Uslar: Should the German film be tougher or meaner?

Petzold: Or more complicated. When I watch a film such as Helmut Käutner's *Under the Bridges*, which was produced during the war: how complicated is this ménage-à-trois? Friends, who desire the same woman, come into conflict with one other and end up risking their friendship. The film's structure has to be simple in order to narrate this complicated a relationship—I find this only rarely in German films. Most recently, I saw it in Valeska Grisebach's *Longing*—to me this is emotional cinema.

Beier and von Uslar: For some time now, German cinema has been successful once again. Last year it had a market share of 26 percent. Are you happy about this?

Petzold: Sure. When *The State I Am In* was released, the picture wasn't pretty. Even though Tom Tykwer's *The Princess and the Warrior* had just been released with a lot of promotion, one was mostly alone, which today is quite different. After all, you make films because there are other films.

Beier and von Uslar: Today it can't really be so lonesome for you. You are considered a figurehead of a movement of young German filmmakers known as "Berlin School," which is being closely watched especially outside of Germany. What's it all about?

Petzold: The term "school" signifies a loose connection of filmmakers. We all once studied at the German Film and Television Academy [dffb] in Berlin and then got to know those who studied in Hamburg and Munich. We talked about film at a time when we thought that there is no more cinema in Germany.

Beier and von Uslar: In France, there is also talk of a "Nouvelle Vague Allemande." Is the comparison to the French cinema of auteurs of the 1960s and 1970s justified?

Petzold: I don't think this is so wrong. The Berlin School is always accused of not having any economic, measurable successes. And yet, other than [Godard's] *Breathless*, the films of the French New Wave also did not make a lot of money.

Beier and von Uslar: The old chasm between auteurist films and mainstream cinema: does it still exist? By now, Tom Tykwer has made a film with Bernd Eichinger.

Petzold: I always thought this opposition was stupid. Eichinger is an author as well. He comes from the Munich film school, saw Wenders's films, and tried to make such films himself.

Beier and von Uslar: "To bring into sharper focus the foggy view of [Til] Schweiger, [Doris] Dörrie, and [Bernd] Eichinger": this used to be your motto. Does mainstream cinema no longer serve as a good bogeyman?

Petzold: No. One no longer has to engage with them. Of course, I still find it terrible that the big productions receive all the funding, to which TV helps itself from the film subvention system, usually for its two-parters in the most brutal manner.[1] As a result, smaller films such as *Longing* do not receive any funding for a year and a half, because the wallets are empty. When Truffaut and Godard really got going in the 1960s, their politics was: for all the money of a mainstream film, we can make ten films—films that meander here and there, loop around, are richer and more complex. This is still true today.

Beier and von Uslar: For the last three years, the newly founded German Film Academy awards the German film prize. What are your thoughts about it?

---

1. "Two-parters" refers to so-called *Amphibienfilme* that Petzold despises—films that are screened in a longer, multi-part version on TV after their initial theatrical release. Petzold dislikes such an approach to filmmaking because it allows the production logic (and aesthetic) of TV to infiltrate that of cinema.

Petzold: I am strictly opposed to it. The academy members receive DVDs of the nominated films, watch them at home, and then vote. This doesn't have anything to do with cinema. Cinema is a place to which one travels, in which one moves as if half-dreaming. After the film, one goes to a bar, to a river or the sea, and one talks about it. Heiner Müller said: "Ten Germans are dumber than five Germans." This is true for the academy as well.

Beier and von Uslar: Is the academy too provincial?

Petzold: Provincial, but as always in Germany, when it's provincial there are big carpets, limousines, cleavage down to the knees.

Beier and von Uslar: Bernd Eichinger was instrumental in the founding of the academy. Would you be able to have a conversation with him as artists?

Petzold: Of course. Eichinger still has the ambition to be a tycoon. He's still the Gatsby of German cinema. He wants to lift something; he wants to bring Technicolor to the drab city centers. I admire everyone who has some enthusiasm left; he just surrounds himself with an entourage that is, of course, lacking this.

Beier and von Uslar: A director such as Tom Tykwer has emancipated himself from film criticism through his collaboration with Eichinger for the mega production of *Perfume: The Story of a Murderer*—he's become untouchable. Do you have your emancipation still ahead of you?

Petzold: I'm not interested in the somewhat boring politics of adapting bestsellers. I agree with Hitchcock when he says that one can only adapt bad books.

Beier and von Uslar: Is it necessary for the filmmaker Petzold to liberate himself from the intellectual Petzold in order to make really great cinema?

Petzold: No. In principle, I agree with what Diedrich Diederichsen once said about Mark E. Smith, the singer of the Fall: the man had a brilliant idea in his life, that's enough. One has to intensify one's topic, to approach it time and again from different perspectives. Every director who says that he is not an intellectual is crazy. How can you possibly make a film otherwise? For you permanently have to explain yourself. This starts when looking for funding.

Beier and von Uslar: Film critics are getting impatient: when will it finally come—the big bang, the big Petzold film? Have you already made the film you really want to make?

Petzold: The film Martin Scorsese always wanted to make was *Gangs of New York*, and I'm sorry to say that I did not like that one at all. Since then, I believe that directors are better off not making the film that they really want to make. The big bang always means: I build myself a mausoleum. I penetrate the world, and then I can retire.

How Many Drilling Holes Exist?

Alexander Reich / 2007

From "'Wie viele Bohrlöcher gibt es?,'" *junge Welt*, September 13, 2007. Reprinted by permission. Translated by Marco Abel and Jaimey Fisher.

Alexander Reich: In *Yella*, the eponymous protagonist [played by Nina Hoss] flees from the east of Germany to West Germany. But she doesn't quite arrive in this world of venture capitalism, of empty hotels made of glass and steel. She seems to be rooted too deeply in this anachronistic East—in this natural world (water, meadows, forests) and human nature (physical closeness, family). Usually, I wouldn't touch the term "nature" with a ten-foot pole, but I was quite moved by this.

Christian Petzold: Fortune-seeker stories like this one have existed for thousands of years. And these fortune-seekers of the occidental capitalism always move towards the West. Our production was guided by the term "dream work." When the script was finished, I had to write about [Victor Fleming's] *The Wizard of Oz* and got out a Walker Evans's book, *Let Us Now Praise Famous Men*, which contains a lot of photographs. It documents the poverty, the complete destruction of US American farmers of the 1930s. It has photos of incredibly emaciated people. They were destroyed by banks—a really deep wound also in pop culture.

AR: Shot, bleeding to death, Sterling Hayden as bank robber in John Huston's *Asphalt Jungle* wants to return to his parents' farm from which he was expelled. He dies underneath a horse that they never should have sold and that is now owned by the bank. The horse nudges the dead body with its nose—and licks it. A brutal image.

CP: In *Wizard of Oz*, these small Evans farmers appear. They are the foundational materials of the system, but they are simultaneously the most exploited. The girl from the destroyed worker- and farmer-class imagines herself into this country, "somewhere over the rainbow," into the world of fables, also into that of cinema. But up there, in this Technicolor country, everything that she has experienced reappears as fairy-tale characters, including the serfs. She processes a terrible reality in this dream but falls back into reality. My daughter, who saw the film when she was seven years old, did not think of this as a happy end. This perfect world is quite porous and complicated.

AR: It's similar in *Yella*. Just that on top there are no witches but private equity people. Yella believes that happiness is where one wants a slimmed down government: to completely transform the German railway into a shareholder corporation, to privatize water, and to sell to poor Berliner sods stocks that they own anyway.

CP: When I graduated from high school in the early 1980s, studying business and administration was bullshit. Whoever wanted to study this could not find a girlfriend and was not going to be invited to anything at all. With the emergence of cable TV and the incredible expansion of advertisement, new groups of customers with a lot of purchasing power have to be developed. Suddenly they were told: you are cool, you are sexy. And ever since, they sit around everywhere, cross their legs, wear Rolex Submariners. Suddenly there's wellness and bodies and Buddhism and all this shit. Yella dreams herself into this world because she believes that she can find happiness [*Glück*, also good fortune] there.

AR: Isn't it the case that by now fewer people believe this?

CP: Right. But in the 1980s and 1990s there were few explanatory narratives. Neither cinema nor literature really understood them.

AR: Why does Yella actually leave the East?

CP: [Andrei Tarkovsky's] *Stalker*. And she wants to get to the place across the river, where it's easy, where things flow.

AR: But, in her dream of the West with its empty hotels and nice cars, she carries a lot of baggage because she is also attached to her father and loves the location that repels her.

CP: I listened to a lot of Van Morrison with Nina Hoss. The Irish of the nineteenth century starved on their island. It was economically destroyed. Today in New York, they celebrate on every Irish holiday the green of Irish meadows. This is the new in the old in which I am interested.

And this conflict is not an accident: on the one hand, people are supposed to be flexible and become shareholders, while, on the other, they are supposed to make sure that the government continues to exist and raise their children. They are crushed by this contradiction. And this contradiction doesn't just happen. It's politics.

AR: New to venture capitalism, Yella has absolutely no scruples and drives a family man and father to suicide with exaggerated demands.

CP: She does not navigate this private equity world any better than Leo Kirch, who bought the broadcasting rights to Formula One racing for 500 million euro from some English barristers. Her demands of this entrepreneur are sick. It's a bit like these people from Cuba in [Brian De Palma's] *Scarface* who think: I just off four or five people and am the boss. One has to make sure not to tighten the screws of oppression and exploitation too much.

AR: Ben [Hinnerk Schönemann], who as a petit bourgeois went bankrupt, harasses Yella with a seemingly simple solution. He wants to work as a plumber once more and offers Yella love in a more modest context.

CP: In all films on this topic that are shown on prime-time TV, the reformed man proposes at the end: let's simplify our lives, rent a modest apartment, and be contented with us. If we have children, we'll manage to find a public school that is not yet run down. Then they walk off into the sunset—and then the "heute journal" follows.[1] People are being deceived with this modest wish: a small bank account, small car, even if it is rusty. . . .

AR: Yella's new lover earns plenty with negotiating risky credit deals. Otherwise, this Wessi [Devid Striesow] doesn't have anything to offer.[2]

CP: He doesn't want anything from her. In the beginning, he pays her 1,000 euro in a parking lot, as if she'd given him a blow job instead of cracking the code of a balancing sheet. She wants to be respected by him because he does not constrain her. She savors this.

AR: After she's spent the night with him towards the end of the film, he approaches her several hours later at the Elbe to apologize for a tantrum he'd thrown. He doesn't say, "I love you," and the viewers know, yes, they are in love and the contract is valid. Rather, he asks, "Do you know how many industrial drill holes exist in the world?"

CP: That is his declaration of love. We must not stop. As people, we have to flow just like the flow of capital. If we want to slow down and become part of the community again, then everything is over. We have to be as fast as money.

AR: This declaration of love results in two people embracing by the banks of the river in an image that is not overly romantic. It's a bit askew. We've changed the side of the river, etc.

CP: He shows her a diary of sorts. It's filled with notations about a mechanical piece you can buy cheaply at any hardware store. He wants to sell these pieces for 300,000 euro per unit to oil companies.

AR: Use value and exchange value. One can keep pushing and go too far and get ever further removed from the real thing. . . .

CP: Yes. The difficulty is not to produce objects but commodities. In the film, all the objects about which there are negotiations and that were invented

---

1. A late-evening news magazine on ZDF, the second German public TV network.
2. "Wessi" is a derogatory term for people from former West Germany, similar to how "Ossie" is a derogatory term for those from former East Germany.

or constructed by German middle-class companies—I've taken all that from Harun Farocki's research materials for his film about private equity negotiations, including that with the drill pieces.

AR: Leaving aside the 8:15 p.m. prime-time issue we just discussed [i.e., 8:15 p.m. is prime time/just after the evening news]: is it really reprehensible if lovers renounce money? Is renunciation not an option to calm down, to take care of one's emotional life, to no longer have to panic after half an hour in which nothing has happened?

CP: When men approach women and say, let's just simplify everything, they want to purchase islands on which they want to live with the women. Essentially Islam. They want the situation to be so simplified that they dominate the woman. When Ben says, "I will become a plumber," we move into a small apartment—then this could go on, "You are at home and cook, I go to work." He would like to have back a kind of Märklin world.[3] Man goes to work; woman stays at home. These are the models of the CSU [Christian Social Union party of Germany]: when we have children, you will receive a care allowance so you can stay at home, so we won't have to put the children into kindergarten. What he has to offer as utopia is a return to the nineteenth century or a false idea thereof. And she sees through this. After all, she is a very modern woman. She's mobile. He tells her: our problems have nothing to do with me but result from your restlessness and desire to go everywhere. Why don't you come home?

AR: Is this connection necessary? Does it not merely apply to these characters?

CP: Isn't everything so complicated? Capital flows through the world; we as people aren't allowed to do the same. People are interned in Africa or wherever.

Now they once again talk about the need to get these locusts and capital flows under control.[4] The left begins, just like the right, to talk about a national economy. They try once again to create borders: we have to live for ourselves, be self-sufficient, because everything is so abstract. This is reactionary. That's not how we can get capital . . . that's not how we can defeat capitalism, because this is capitalism's own game, as it were. It incorporates these nineteenth-century romanticisms because it can cope really well with inequalities.

I read an old essay by Étienne Balibar: He says that the economies will become so incredibly abstract and removed from any form of narrative, poetry, and imagination that a counter-movement will emerge. Already in 1983 did Balibar construe the Taliban. The body, the total investment: I control my existence

---

3. Märklin refers to model railways that are popular with German children.
4. Petzold refers here to the so-called *Heuschreckendebatte* of 2005. The then-leader of the center-left Social Democratic Party, Franz Müntefering, likened the activities of anonymous investors to locust plagues.

because I get to determine when I will die. Something similar is part of the plumber's simplified model of living.

AR: Is it not also part of the game of capitalism to downplay the idea of a national economy? The percentage of the economy spent by the government has sunk to a bit over 45 percent. That decrease is a result of politics.[5]

CP: But what is it that they do around here? They globalize themselves. They have taken over this neoliberal shit.

AR: As national economists.

CP: This national economy merely exists now to help executives push through what they want. When there's a water main burst and I go check it out with my son, the workers from the Berlin utility observe that the city still owns 51 percent, but this is about to change.

I was in Turkey; Nestlé owns all of the water there. You can no longer drink it. That's why all of Turkey is covered in plastic bottles from Nestlé. People from the mountains have to buy water, and Nestlé doesn't take care of the garbage. That's the job of the state. And this version of privatizing, of neoliberalism plus national economy, is horrific.

AR: And yet, the national approach is all there is. One does not elect the UN.

CP: But that's where politics has to go. This is as much the fault of the German labor unions: it negotiated only national collective agreements, but they never took care of four million unemployed people. They did not talk about a society in which work is disappearing. And they did not internationalize themselves, as capital did. That's the really big mistake.

AR: Back to the film: the Ossis don't quite come across as Ossis in terms of their habits, including Hinnerk Schönemann's Ben.

CP: He grew up in the Prignitz.

AR: Biographies aren't necessarily relevant here. The one who plays the Wessi is also from the East. Schönemann is more a kind of snotty-nosed prole. He lacks roughness, directness.

CP: There's an image of the Ossi that I no longer agree with: the Ossi is someone who hangs out by the grilling station in Adidas slides [a type of sandal] and works on his car, a kind of camping sex vacationer, nudist, etc.—horrible.

During preproduction, I listened a lot to Hinnerk but also told many stories. They fixed up all streets in the East. Infrastructure is there. Large gas stations are everywhere. And there are a lot of Jeeps on the roads. I think that large parts of the East have America as their model. They want to be like in the US. Do you

---

5. Compared to the US economy, Germany's has historically had a greater share of governmental investment.

know how many of these Chevrolets Pickup trucks are driving around there? That's America: pickups, highways, gas stations, six packs, and BBQ.

Hinnerk Schönemann performed how people get out of their cars: hey, come on, Bruno, let's go. I'm interested in how it's really like there, not in this cliché of the Ossi as slow and homey—that is all too much for me. A caricature like the private equity agent on prime-time TV, with his hair gel, cool shirt from Van-Laack, terrific lover. He lacks a bit of romanticism, but the goal of the prime-time film is: if we also implant something romantic in him, then he's a good person. And that's not viable. That's not realistic or what have you.

AR: And at 10:15 p.m. comes the *American Psycho* [Mary Harron].

CP: Well, he started it all. With him, it was already game over.

AR: I did not notice until the credits that Kerl Fieser worked as a train courier.

CP: He isn't an actor. He played in the band, Mutter, just like Florian Koerner von Gustorf, the producer of *Yella*.

AR: Kerl Fieser was thrown out of the band in August 2006.

CP: Correct. And in the evenings he always came to our set and picked up the filmed material, the film rolls, sound and image, and took them back on the train. He loved this because it's simply beautiful, to travel all day through Germany by train. That's the train courier Kerl Fieser. Terrific name, in my opinion.[6]

---

6. Because in German, "fieser Kerl" means "nasty guy."

"The Car Is a Rich Location"

Cristina Nord / 2009

From "'Das Auto ist ein reicher Ort,'" *taz*, January 7, 2009. Reprinted by permission.
Translated by Marco Abel and Jaimey Fisher.

Cristina Nord: Mr. Petzold, what kind of car are you driving?
Christian Petzold: A Mercedes. The car is there to take occasional trips with the kids on the weekend. You generally don't need a car in Berlin. I drive 6,000 or 7,000 kilometers per year. That's nothing.
CN: I'm asking because cars play an important role in all of your films—and in *Jerichow* even more so than usually. What percent of the film was shot inside a car?
CP: Almost half. It was a shock for my cinematographer, Hans Fromm. When he read the script, he said, "This is really great, but all of this takes place in the car." And since we shoot while actually driving, rather than with the car on a trailer, the options for camera positions are limited. I really can't stand the woeful shot composition in which the camera looks from outside the windshield into the car, as if it were a stage. That doesn't have anything to do with car driving because one knows that they are not really driving the car, that the car just sits on a trailer with the camera fixed in the front while the car is being pulled. This quickly becomes theater.
CN: You prefer it when the camera observes the driver and passenger from the backseat.
CP: We discovered this position when shooting *The State I Am In*. This results in a profile view of the actor, slightly from the back, so that the world through which one is moving and the character are simultaneously in the image. I like this.
CN: You really shot every scene in the car while driving?
CP: Yes. This has something to do with language and its rhythm. As soon as you create a theatrical, undisturbed scenario, the actors speak in a way that I can't stand. But, when they really have to drive and are together, they manage to produce a unique conversational dynamic, one that really has something to do with their surroundings. For example, I cannot properly shoot in a studio

because I want that the actors get a feeling, have respect, for the location where we shoot, even if it is for a hotel or a meadow. The world must be visible for the actors, not necessarily so that it is represented in the image but so that it exists in the actors' perceptions.

CN: What was it about the location of the Prignitz that intrigued you?

CP: I started to take interest in this area when I shot *Something to Remind Me* there. I have never seen a country that aligns itself so much toward America. I always thought that in Wuppertal, Dusseldorf, Solingen, where I'm from in North Rhine Westphalia, we are the Los Angeles of the little guy. I felt quite comfortable in Los Angeles because it reminded me of the Ruhr Valley, of car driving, of the autobahn system. In *The Crying of Lot 49*, Thomas Pynchon describes this as a transistor radio when looked at from above. I always loved this. And when I got to the Prignitz, I thought, "This is Cormac McCarthy country . . ."

CN: . . . a US American writer who has written, among other novels, *All the Pretty Horses* and *No Country for Old Men*.

CP: When we shot *Yella* there, Hinnerk Schönemann, the actor who is from there, said that the script is right on the money with its sense that everyone is driving Range Rovers in this region. For everyone drives pickups or off-road vehicles, as if they were far north, at the border to Canada. I frequently am in Brandenburg, near Bad Saarow and Fürstenwalde, and there the towns of Philadelphia and Neu Boston are right next to each other. I always thought this has something to do with the fact that they wanted to get to America but managed to get only as far as Neu Boston.

CN: Is this correct?

CP: After the discovery of so-called America, there was a large colonizing movement away from Europe. The poor, the mercenaries, the serfs, all these destroyed, beaten-down existences—they suddenly had the possibility to escape, a promised land. Friedrich the Great stopped the escape by offering people something like job creation measures. He said, "Please don't go, for otherwise I no longer have vassals, but for staying you will receive a hamlet, a village."

CN: And this was called Neu Boston?

CP: Exactly. And the fact that many generations ago one really wanted to leave is still deeply inscribed into the country. Now the Wall has fallen, and all these names and pickups and the whole dream of America reappears, but it does so as if it had existed underneath a bell jar. For today neither America nor the car represent the myth of freedom and individualism. I really liked [Quentin] Tarantino's *Death Proof*; that the film was not successful surely has to do with the fact that the car is no longer a desiring- and dream-machine.

CN: This is an idea off of which the cinema of the 1970s fed in films such as [H. B. Halicki's] *Gone in 60 Seconds* or *Two-Land Blacktop*.

CP: And even then it was in the process of going extinct. For one final time the grandeur of the car manifested itself, just as objects at flea markets report of their beauty before they disappear in the attic forever. Ali's Range Rover, the driving in the Prignitz—today this doesn't get you very far.

CN: What, then, differentiates a dialogue scene between Ali and Thomas in the car from one that takes place in a room?

CP: In the past, when I traveled by carpooling, I often experienced that after 200 kilometers of driving one talked about the most private matters. One is isolated while driving in a car, like in a cage, one forms a tight-knit community. At the same time, one doesn't sit across facing each other, one doesn't look at each other. Looking away is the normal movement of the head, as a result of which facing each other becomes an event. The car is a rich location, just not for the camera. I like this, for I like all forms of restrictions.

CN: This supports my impression that from film to film you are becoming more economical. Why?

CP: Together with Harun Farocki, I have now written ten scripts. He is a fan of the superfluous. He always wants to be wasteful: here another secondary scene, here more explanation. In contrast, I am the Protestant in our relationship. I love ellipses as long as they are grounded in the story and aren't used for their own sake. When you watch TV, you are surrounded by images that no longer show anything. A documentary on public television about temp work is unable to show what temp work actually means. Instead, all we see are interviews with people at home.

CN: But images for temp work exits—the *Gurkenflieger* in *Jerichow* is a good example, this mixture of tractor and plane that is being used to harvest cucumbers.

CP: Yes, because the *Gurkenflieger* delivers an image. It represents one of the last forms of exploitation. A machine would cost much more money, and it is cheaper to have young Poles and Ukrainians lying on the machine. This narrates one more time what capitalism in its pure form used to be. But these machines are disappearing; the cucumbers are now being farmed in Turkey. When we were shooting, everyone was shocked, but not by the fact that this is even still possible in Germany, but by the fact that this thing looks like a plane. I thought of Hitchcock's *North by Northwest*. The people were students; during breaks they read or listened to classical music. This did not fit the images of exploitative labor that we had in our heads. While shooting, suddenly some low-flying aircrafts appeared and broke the sound barrier right above our heads. It made an incredible bang....

CN: ... that one can hear in the film, right?

CP: Yes—and one can see it on the faces as well. They look as if it was the fourteenth bang of the day. Apparently, this is an area where the German air force frequently breaks the sound barrier. This connection of the jet fighters, the *Gurkenflieger*, the soldiers, and the farmers triggered wild associations in me. Perhaps it was a bit crazy, but I thought, "Somehow the soldiers always manifest misery for the farmers." And these soldiers up there—I felt they purposefully broke the sonic barrier where the *Gurkenflieger* is. That way they show those on the ground: you aren't really pilots.

CN: What was the shooting of this scene like?

CP: I was afraid to shoot there because it is often uncomfortable when one invades such a location with one's makeup trailer and people who have showered. You quickly have an atmosphere in which one really should feel ashamed. But Benno actually participated for half a shift. The machines drive alongside the rows. When someone doesn't do a good job picking they will be fired. His ditch then needs to be harvested again. We paid a little bit of money, and one of the Poles was supposed to walk behind the machine in order to pick Benno's cucumbers. Benno said: "No way, no one walks behind me here." He worked hard and afterwards was really tired. Of course, he knew: the workers next to him know that he gets 2,000 euro per day, which is about 2.50 euro per cucumber, whereas the workers get 0.04 cents. Nevertheless, they could tell that he wanted to work.

"Poverty Films Well? I Don't Like This"

Katja Nicodemus and Christof Siemes / 2009

From "'Arm filmt gut? Das gefällt mir nicht,'" *Die Zeit*, January 8, 2009. Reprinted by permission. Translated by Marco Abel and Jaimey Fisher.

Katja Nicodemus and Christof Siemes: We want to talk with you about money. How does it determine your work?

Christian Petzold: For the *Autorenfilm* [auteur cinema], also known as low-budget film, there is always little money available. But it is precisely these films that have to pretend that they don't even care about money; they are responsible for feelings. And they have to pretend that feelings don't obey any economy. That is: poverty films well. I don't like this. And when a film has a sizable budget then it is supposed to show this as well: in the costumes, the set design. There's a scene in *The Simpsons* where the boss of General Motors asks Homer Simpson as the prototypical "simple man" to design a car for everybody. Homer can have as much money as he wants, and the result is the most disgusting of all cars: overloaded, without style, six horns, twenty-five bars, thirteen TVs . . . that's not a car but the fantasy of Powerball winners. This is what frequently happens to films with a budget of 15 million euro: they have to display their budget, which puts pressure on everyone at the set as well as the viewer. For they have to be watching in order to decode: wow, that's really expensive!

Nicodemus and Siemes: Would you like to have more money available for your films?

Petzold: I would use more money to have forty, fifty shooting days for once, in order to get to know the locations even more precisely, in order to succeed at creating a more complicated choreography. I always write dinners for just three people, but I'd like to stage an orgy. Not so that the people would be naked and throw around food, but so that the food would obtain an enormous sensuousness.

Nicodemus and Siemes: Would you be willing to compromise for this? How vulnerable to extortion are you when looking for funding for your films?

Petzold: I've been lucky commercially and artistically. Since I received the German Film Prize for *The State I Am In*, I always had enough funding for a new film. But one must not forget: my films are so cheap that they make a profit, albeit at the lowest level. All of my films cost 1.8 million euro. 100,000 viewers suffice to pay back all subvention funds. And that's what we do, unlike others, who have over 3 million viewers.

Nicodemus and Siemes: In *Jerichow*, money can be seen in almost every scene. Is this meant to reflect the conditions of your production?

Petzold: This should be in every film. Every Chabrol film communicates his desperate longing for his film to take place somewhere else: in America. But that's also the beauty of the Chabrol films: that the bourgeoisie itself, with its drinks and suburban women, has this yearning. It's an encounter between the Americanization of French life and Chabrol's yearning for American cinema.

Nicodemus and Siemes: Does this mean that you would have preferred to shoot *Jerichow*, which takes place in the western-like wide open spaces of East Germany, in America?

Petzold: The town of Jerichow itself has something about it that is American. These highways that traverse the East—you now only pass the towns by. Even though the town centers have now all been renovated, there is no longer any community. Our free-market economy has renovated these cities in order to transform them back into the bourgeois cities they used to be. Everything is repainted, but the bourgeois society has disappeared, and the market square is empty. The people are facing horrible loneliness and are pushed to the margin. At the outskirts, at the autobahn exits, you find the truck stops and shopping malls—and that's American. I therefore don't have to make American cinema in Germany: America is already here.

Nicodemus and Siemes: The landscape in *Jerichow*, as well as in your previous film, *Yella*, looks like a capitalist's nuclear testing site.

Petzold: I was intent on communicating isolation. The lonely house in the forest. The parking lots with snack bars. Jean Baudrillard once wrote about Disneyland just based on its parking lots. Disneyland itself shines brightly, but the parking lot area is gigantic and dreary—as if the entire world were a drive-in cinema, just without a screen. The East German malls look like that. Between the guardrail and grass block paver that what used to be the market square is left as a ruinous remainder.

Nicodemus and Siemes: *Jerichow* tells the story of a love triangle between Laura [Nina Hoss], her Turkish husband Ali [Hilmi Sözer], and Thomas [Benno Fürmann], who crashes their financially negotiated relationship. What function does money have for the three protagonists?

Petzold: Ali is the Turkish businessman, who saved his money to buy himself a spot in the society: a snack bar chain in East Germany, a nice house, and an exciting woman—who married him only because he assumed her financial debts. It's about the economizing of feelings and bodies. Like a child, Tom stashed the money he embezzled in a tin hidden in a tree house, even though we're talking about 40,000 euro! In so doing, he infantilizes himself: he wants to be twelve once more. Laura does something similar: she steals from her husband as if all she were doing is keeping the change from the shopping money. Like a child, she hides the money in a hole and speaks in a children's voice when she's found out. So here, too, money, debt, and age are infantilized. The idea was for the money to be a substance when it is imaged and a debt when it is not.

Nicodemus and Siemes: Does money lend itself to being filmed well?

Petzold: Yes, just like everything familiar from the everyday can be filmed well. All you have to do is to shoot it properly and thoughtfully. Just like in a Godard film when someone retrieves a money clip out of a pocket. Small bill in the front signifies: a modest man. Large bill in the front means: a show-off. In bad films, a suitcase is opened, and someone in the background says: wow!

Nicodemus and Siemes: How do you extract the relationship to money from two actors and their bodies?

Petzold: Nina Hoss had a coach. Around here this is generally considered as a no-go: manager training, brainwashing. In my other films, she plays a bit as if in exile, but this would not be the right approach here. So, we hired this woman who has also coached Tom Cruise. She worked for two weekends with Nina—and completely focused on "money and sex." She was not interested in anything else. I then said, "Hold on, there are other issues: Germany, wide open spaces, myths, forests!" But she completely took away my position and gave Nina an egocentric, ruthless point of view on her character: "I give my body, in exchange I receive money and security. How long can I endure this economization?" I loved this.

Nicodemus and Siemes: Benno Fürmann, too, has a different physicality than usually.

Petzold: I spoke with him a lot about sailors. His character, Thomas, is simply being washed up: shipwrecked with naked torso, he lies in the yard of his mother's house. And then he rises, like Robinson Crusoe on the island. Based on this sailor idea, Benno was also able to incorporate his character's silence and way of looking as a matter of course. This isn't a case of the "terribly communicative silence of German films," as Dominik Graf always calls it. This is the silence of people who, like Thomas, work as guards in Afghanistan, a terribly boring job. A wakeful tiredness.

Nicodemus and Siemes: The protagonists in all of your films talk so little anyway that at times one would like to yell at them so that they come out of their shell.

Petzold: The point, however, is not that people hide something but, rather, that they are being economized. The characters in *Jerichow* are no longer in the mood to explain themselves. That's in their past. I like people who don't have much time, who get impatient, and don't aim to take the viewer by the hand. The viewer has to deal with these characters and their complexity without me telling him: "I had a difficult childhood."

Nicodemus and Siemes: Do you compress the script further while shooting?

Petzold: Sure. In the morning after Laura and Thomas have slept with each other, Ali joins them. This scene originally consisted of four script pages. But now it is much crazier, the pressure is stronger, because not everything is talked about. Now the focus is on how the two men put their mugs down, how they light their cigarettes, how they appraise each other. This, too, is language.

Nicodemus and Siemes: How do you create the obsessive rhythm of such a film?

Petzold: After the lovemaking scene, Thomas has to walk to the bus stop. To act such a walk in a long shot is very difficult. In order to walk properly, the actor has to know much more than what he has to know for a dialogue line. Prior to walking, Benno, quietly and slightly embarrassed, asked me, "Did I come?" With this question it suddenly became crystal clear what they are all about: they do not come. And in the end, after they wake up after spending an entire night together, they want to kill. After waking up there's an emptiness. And they fill this emptiness with criminal energy. Prior to this, they have to wrestle their passion away with kisses and aborted sex scenes.

Nicodemus and Siemes: You once quoted Helmut Färber: "Good films show in twenty years why and how we lived twenty years ago." What will we learn in 2029 about Germany in 2009?

Petzold: If one thinks like that one has already lost. This sentence expresses a kind of responsibility for locations, the circumstances, the dreams in which one automatically finds oneself with cinema. Think, for example, of *Rosetta* by the Dardenne brothers: if in twenty years you want to find out something about the decline of wage labor then one has to watch this film. Any sociologist or historian will learn more from it than from any statistic.

Nicodemus and Siemes: One thing one can learn from your films already now: that at the beginning of the twenty-first century people drive a lot in their cars. And that the people are often more at home in their cars than in their apartments.

Petzold: I have a lot of perceptions from my childhood that have something to do with the backseat of my parents' car. Driving was always the aftershock of something else. Half asleep, one hears what an idiot Uncle Günter has become, or parents fighting with each other. The car turns into a pressure chamber. I do not love the car as a location at all. Car means stress. I am the only one who is not present when shooting—simply because there is no space for me in the car. My cinematographer hates the car as well, for in it there are only three available camera positions. And the actors hate it because they have to drive for four hours and can barely move. In such a reduced scenario every movement matters: When do I switch on the radio? How do I reach the blinker? How do I shift gears? How do I grab the steering wheel?

Nicodemus and Siemes: What car are you driving?

Petzold: Mercedes 200 C-class. The way it looks and is parked on the street, the car itself is aware that it no longer plays a significant role in my life. Sometimes I freak out, drive to the gas station, and clean it for hours—because I feel sorry for it. Then it is as if new—and still I pity it. I come from a suburb near Wuppertal, where the car was vital. One had to take driving lessons when one was seventeen so that one would definitely have one's license when one turns eighteen. But now the car matters to me only as an atavism, as something with which I once had fun.

Nicodemus and Siemes: Your films seem to have a nearly prophetic quality: *Wolfsburg* anticipated the crisis of the car industry; *Yella*, the madness of venture capitalism; *Jerichow*, the destruction of all relationships by capitalism. Do you feel unsettled to be right? Or are you proud about this?

Petzold: I always have the sense that I slightly missed the target. For the cinema does not discover these things; it just knows its way around dreams and repression really well. Better than any other medium. Here the collective unconscious finds images and sounds, here it is about people who crack due to the circumstances and who fight against it. For all the topics we now discuss—climate catastrophe, financial crisis—have really existed for thirty years. Anyone who has, in the last seven years, watched even ten minutes a week of *Sabine Christiansen* knows what kind of people are doing their lobbying work in Germany. Everyone who has their wits halfway about them surely knows that any return of more than 6 percent can only be criminal. Such productivity simply does not exist.

Nicodemus and Siemes: And the cinema always knew this.

Petzold: This is why I am so pissed off that older films, and so film history, are no longer broadcast on public television. I recently wrote something about film noir. These films are about corrupt societies, destructive passions, and death drives. And also about the lust for life, about the emerging capitalist selfishness. This simply has to be on TV! These are our dreams!

Nicodemus and Siemes: Currently, the opposite takes place on TV and in the cinema: a remythologizing, a reheating of big historical stories.

Petzold: Remythologizing makes profit and does not take much work. It replaces the confrontation with the present. This is also the misery of literature adaptations. In responses to the question why they film *Buddenbrooks*, they simply say: because it is an important book. When Truffaut adapted the story of the wild child, it contained the consideration: why am I doing this in France in 1969? We show how the institutions of enlightenment, which are being criticized today, were even formed: as a form of mastering wilderness. That is a stance! But if you simply use myths to ensure that a murmur goes through the crowd, then it won't even work by the second viewing because there's just nothing to it.

Nicodemus and Siemes: And the actors are wasted.

Petzold: Because for 300 days a year all they have to do is recite lines. Dominik Graf once spoke of an actress who listed thirty sentences that were in each of her last five films. First place: "We must talk with each other." That's enough: you immediately know in what direction that is heading.

Nicodemus and Siemes: Do the actors suffer from this themselves?

Petzold: Absolutely. Germany does not have stars. At the Bambi awards, Keanu Reeves receives the prize, and there's a standing ovation. As a German actor, you can go home. That would not happen in France. They would never treat their actors this way.

Nicodemus and Siemes: So, there is no culture that sustains the actors.

Petzold: Here we cheer for Jopi Heesters.

Nicodemus and Siemes: Can you afford the actors with whom you would love to work?

Petzold: Always.

Nicodemus and Siemes: Because they give you a discount?

Petzold: I was always astonished how much money they make. I earn much less. I once spoke with an actress about this, when the fees skyrocketed before the Kirch bankruptcy. She said, "But the Americans earn even more." I replied, "Half the world knows the American actors, you are not even known in Denmark." She did not talk to me the next day.

"Nothing Is Innocent Anymore"

Denis Demmerle / 2009

From "'Nichts ist mehr unschuldig,'" *Planet Interview*, January 9, 2009. Reprinted by permission. Translated by Marco Abel and Jaimey Fisher.

Denis Demmerle: In your new film *Jerichow*, Laura [Nina Hoss] says, "You cannot love without money." How loveless is our world in which more and more people have less and less money?

Christian Petzold: This sentence is more a reference to this *Pretty Woman*–cinema, which tells love stories about people from different classes and social levels and pretends as if love were capable of healing everything. The way Laura delivers the sentence and cries while doing so, she asserts based on her innermost experience: "This doesn't exist." People stay within their class when selecting their partners. Academics marry academics. In contrast, literature tells stories about how an academic gets to know a gypsy girl, which is complete humbug. This recognition is painful for Laura. She knows that this kind of romance [*Romantik*] doesn't help. Neither the cinema nor her.

DD: How difficult was it for Nina Hoss to deliver this sentence?

CP: Originally, I did not even want her to verbalize this sentence. But Nina is a very complete actress. When she spoke the sentence she cried so much that one couldn't understand it. As a result, she wanted to redeliver it so that it could be understood. I thought this was too theatrical. Only when editing did I notice that we needed it after all.

DD: Is the belonging to a social class of which you speak responsible for the protagonists' mistrust of other people?

CP: What I really like about the three is that they are unified by the longing to be eighteen once more. They hide their money at playgrounds and say things like, "Go pack your things and come with me." This is seventeen-year-old-like, á la "we jump on a moped and drive to the sea." They dream of a time when the world with all its possibilities was still open to them. But they live in a world in which all doors are closed. This tension permeates the film. And their mistrust contains a longing for deception. They long for longing but know that at the end what matters is money.

DD: This is especially pronounced in the figure of Ali [Hilmi Sözer], whose mistrust verges on being paranoid, yet is always confirmed in his negative assumptions. Is this a message of the film: "Don't trust anyone"?

CP: This is what's so fantastic about paranoids: that through their selective way of perceiving things, they end up seeing what they want to see. The film plays with this. In the film, it is as if Ali's paranoia, his imagination, is what causes the two to get together in the first place. This is essentially what happens. In the picnic scene, he basically puts the couple together that later kills him.

DD: In the context of this film, you talk about "islands" on which people create a home for themselves. Ali actually managed to successfully build his own island. Is it part of being human that we permanently put this island on the line and even destroy it ourselves?

CP: The problem is that this island isn't society. For his island he is the architect and creator. He has his house, wife, job . . . but that's not how life is. There are always external influences. As soon as a person comes from outside onto the island, like Friday comes onto Robinson's, the structure immediately collapses. These built existences are not capable of surviving. They are laboratory experiments. In *Jerichow*, it is this island state that comes in contact with another.

DD: Is this why the film fits into the East German nirvana?

CP: I thought of this story there, back when we shot *Yella* in this region. I saw the town sign "Jerichow," and I like the region a lot, the Americanness of it. Or better: the completed dream of America there. The malls, the gas stations, the car dealerships. All of the dreams appear so far away. Nothing is innocent anymore.

DD: Which is fitting for today.

CP: Absolutely. One could feel this. I then remembered James Cain's *The Postman Always Rings Twice* and talked with Nina about it. This conversation generated her character. I then developed the story with Harun Farocki.

DD: You frequently work with Nina Hoss. Artists often talk about a muse who is important for their creativity. Can one describe your relationship in these terms?

CP: With a muse the part of the woman is too weak. She is not a muse. For that she is too independent.

DD: Since you developed the story in a conversation with Ms. Hoss, did you have her in mind for the part of Laura?

CP: I actually had intended to give the part to someone else and was also quite far in the process. But then I preferred observing how Nina Hoss would approach the part. This is more interesting than finding the perfect fit for the part.

DD: You often cast actors whom you already know. How important is it for you to collaborate with actors with whose acting you are familiar?

CP: I'd be happy to shoot with completely new actors. In this case, I had the idea not to cast the woman as a seductive femme fatale, as that's the case in *Postman*, but with a man as a seducer with a lot of physicality. This is why in the scene when they sleep with each other it is he who lies naked on the bed whereas she's dressed. I really liked this twist. It works because Benno Fürmann is one of the few German actors who effectively uses his body when acting.

DD: You are considered a representative of the so-called "Berlin School." How do you assess its influence on the German film industry?

CP: Given its bad reputation, this is no longer a compliment. But I am glad that these films exist and hope that the directors can continue making films. Anyone who wants to know in twenty years how we lived today will have to watch these films.

DD: Notwithstanding the criticism, one cannot deny its influence...

CP: I notice the influence when I teach seminars. When I started at the dffb [German Film and Television Academy] in 1988, there was no German cinema. Only comedies. I would have been happy to have something that could guide me. With its own perspective on Germany. Stories that come from this country. I would have been aided by this. Without Dominik Graf, I would have been lost.

DD: Now German cinema is no longer reduced to comedies. Realism has arrived—evidenced also by the box office numbers in the last few years.

CP: The "Berlin School" films are considerably more successful abroad than in Germany. Because they talk about this country. After all, what interests me about Danish cinema is its Danishness, and about French cinema its Frenchness. I want to see a French policier and not a French one that imitates an American one. Instead of trying to reenact 24 in Berlin, it is much more interesting to show our police with its linoleum floors and coffee cups. The civil service aspect [*Beamtentum*]. The low wages that in Munich doesn't suffice for police officers to live in Munich.

DD: Is this the reason why you are time and again drawn to the East with its apparently dead, almost extinct regions?

CP: No, rather because they are obsessed with America. These regions with their malls and highways look like America. An America without money. Pennsylvania. The industrial society that's as destroyed in America as it is here. In America, there are TV series such as [David Simon's] *The Wire* that is shot in Baltimore and reveals what remains when wage labor disappears. This decline transpired with brutal speed in Prignitz, where shipyards and the Singer sewing machine factory were destroyed in no time at all. What happens with love, with longing and dreams, when work has disappeared. One must tell stories about this.

DD: Is the region covered in what is perhaps also a cinematic melancholia?

CP: In *Yella*, they say that the women leave the towns and that there are no young women anymore. The women are the first fortune seekers. They all went into the West or to Leipzig and Berlin. If the young men follow them, then extinction is imminent. When I watch *The Wire*, I ask myself why its German counterpart isn't being shot in this region. All the contradictions, desperation, and unrealized dreams.

DD: Is something missing in Germany?

CP: I don't understand why we don't have this here. We have so much money, the richest TV stations in the world—the public ones. They waste it all on things that are so pointless.

DD: For example?

CP: Broadcasting rights for sports are just too expensive. Or that they make prime-time TV based on viewer shares rather than to experiment with long-term tenacity. The abbreviation of the good political shows. They cut down the production team for the WDR's documentary series, *Die Story*, which for years has practiced investigative journalism. I don't like this. For this shit I don't want to pay fees.

DD: What's your attitude toward the extremely expensive expansion of online offerings?

CP: When internet television arrives, the public stations will be closed down. No one will watch the *Volksmusik*-shit.[1] People between the ages of twenty and forty no longer watch TV. They instead create their own television program by ordering DVDs, downloading, streaming, or they go to the cinema—which would be the best decision. I no longer feel represented.

DD: Let's assume the public stations were to give you the funds to produce a series such as *The Wire* . . .

CP: We would need ten authors, seventy actors, who would not even be used to doing something with such an elaborate narrative structure. *The Wire* eliminates a clean distinction between primary and secondary characters. Here in Germany, only the lead receives focus, whereas the secondary roles are abused as caricatures or raped as stooges. In *The Wire*, each secondary character opens up the door to a new, complex cosmos. Perhaps it's necessary first to analyze what is going wrong here.

DD: The final question: life is a comic; what character would you be?

CP: It would have to be a character from Duckburg. Perhaps the servant of Grandmother Duck, Gus Goose.

---

1. Traditional folk music delivered in various television formats that has abided since the 1950s on German television.

"It's Risky Business"

Holger Kreitling / 2011

From "'Die Sache ist riskant.' Drei Regisseure, drei Filme, ein Kriminalfall: Christoph Hochhäusler, Dominik Graf und Christian Petzold über ihr Experiment 'Dreileben,' den deutschen Wald und die Selbstentleibung des Fernsehens" (It's Risky Business. Three Directors, Three Films, One Criminal Case: Christoph Hochhäusler, Dominik Graf, and Christian Petzold Discuss Their Experiment *Dreileben*, the German Forest, and the Self-Evacuation of Television), *Welt am Sonntag*, August 28, 2011. Reprinted by permission. Translated by Marco Abel and Jaimey Fisher.

Holger Kreitling: How did you decide on the Thuringia forest?

Christoph Hochhäusler: Originally we thought of the Spreewald [Spree Forest] because Dominik talked about jack-o-lanterns and werewolves. The word "Spreewald" evokes an imaginary space.

Dominik Graf: But one sees German actors move about in Spreewald boats all the time.

CH: We first contemplated what capacity this fictive location would have to have. Then we developed an imaginary map, first on a napkin. There was a mountain, a lot of forest, a long autobahn bridge, a hotel, a hospital, and police barracks. We sent out a location scout. To check out a freeway bridge, I then drove to Suhl. I liked it.

DG: The house we needed did not exist in Suhl; we found it in Schmalkalden.

CH: And we also shot in Oberhof.

Christian Petzold: Which is always confused with Oberstdorf. It was obvious that our stories would be in close proximity to one another. Thuringia has a rich mythology. Emperor Barbarossa awaits the resurrection in the mountains. In these stories crevices open, and something is uncovered. Or a boy follows a sheep into the mountain, returns one hundred years later, and thinks only three minutes have passed. I thought, "This is the perfect region, where something vertical supplements three horizontal stories." As soon as Dominik had left the location, the earth opened up.

HK: The crater of Schmalkalden that formed by a landslide in November 2010.

DG: That's when the vertical really made itself available. I received letters from all over asking what we had done.

CH: Someone said that what connects the three films is that the repressed returns. This has also something to do with the landscape.

DG: This province has incredible charm. There is emptiness; there are fallows and derelict buildings; the world of work is ruined. From my time in boarding school, I know how one can be bored in structurally weak regions.

CH: One of the policemen who played in my film told me that he earns additional income from breeding white doves that are released at weddings.

CP: In Suhl, you have the old right next to the new. Rotten latticework and the attempt at an H & M store next to each other. This is also how the region appeared to me in the soul.

DG: I also like the freeway bridge. I do not want to show the "poor people in the province." Where the GDR fallows are visible in all their horror, I sense beauty. It is like in the Bronx in the 1980s, where one could see open areas, as if a war had devastated the landscape.

CH: Something brightens up and reveals something about life.

DG: That's where the forces of resistance, the pain are visible to everyone.

CH: But it can also be tough. I asked a man from Suhl what his classmates are doing. He listed the last names, adding: "Drinks. Dead. Hartz IV."

DG: In a Woody Allen film [*Annie Hall*], there's a scene in which children rise and report what they will be in twenty years.

CH: Everyone looked away as the man spoke. Naked fear.

HK: What was it about the forest that interested you?

CP: The forests in Brandenburg are more like dried-out swamps. As a child, I was often in Thuringia. When I fell asleep in the car on the way home, the last images always were of a forest and a clearing. Back then there were the blue Hanser books about film directors. In the Fritz Lang book, the first pages showed Siegfried in the Säulenwald [column forest] from *Nibelungen*. I thought, "This is not an image you can make in France or Italy, even Peter Jackson cannot do this in New Zealand. This is a German image."

CH: I spent a lot of time in the forest and feel at home there. An open space, a strange zone that humans never managed to imitate. In the forest. I become calm; I quite miss it.

DG: No other devil's tale has occupied me as much as "A Heart of Stone" by Wilhelm Hauff. It takes place in the Black Forest, featuring the good glass-imp and the evil Dutch-Mike.

CP: That's a fantastic story. There's an East German film adaptation, but it is a bit disappointing.

DG: I always wanted to adapt it myself. But no one is interested. Oh well. I'll do it one of these days.

CP: When shooting up there in the Thuringia Forest, I remembered again the rhyme from "A Heart of Stone." "Treasure-man in forest old . . ."

DG: ". . . More than a hundred years, I'm told. You own this wood. If this be true, . . ."

CP: ". . . As Sunday's child I come to you." The forest traditionally plays an enormous role. Whenever something terrible happens in society it has to be outsourced in the forest—and at some time returns from there.

HK: Prior to this project you intensively debated about genre theory and film, and you even sharply disagreed with each other.[1] This project emerged out of this debate. Is *Dreileben* an implementation or the result of this debate?

CH: The connection is not quite that strong. We talked with each other and agreed that it would be great if we could work together. Because it is fun and productive. But we did not experimentally test theses.

DG: We exchanged film historical impressions.

CP: To direct is a solitary activity. You have a lot of people around you who pretend to be your best friends. But you are alone after all. I was always jealous of how the people of Italian neorealism, the Nouvelle Vague, and also New German Cinema talked to each other. This is stunted today.

DG: Completely. One even gets the impression that this is not desirable. Directors are supposed to be stylized into lone wolves so that they also feel the system's pressure alone and don't form human connections.

CH: I didn't have this experience. In connection with the magazine *Revolver*, which I copublish, we communicated a lot with directors such as Benjamin Heisenberg, Ulrich Köhler, Maren Ade—and with you two.

CP: Whenever we corresponded and talked I felt that I am smarter than if I were alone, as well as more intoxicated with inspiration.

DG: At the film academies there are group productions. In our case, there was a crazy competition. But in the end it was nice to have such a discourse in reality. We had a day in Oberhof when the three of us occupied the entire hotel. Each of us shot on a separate floor. To observe how the other says "action."

CP: One usually doesn't have a chance to observe this anywhere!

DG: One constantly asks oneself how someone else responds. What happens when a production manager declares, "Only ten more minutes." Will he freak out?

---

1. Refers to an email exchange in which Petzold, Christoph Hochhäusler, and Dominik Graf debated the Berlin School, film genres, and their role in historical and contemporary cinema. See "Key Resources" for citational information.

CP: I was totally nervous on that day. I taught myself how to act as a director on set, as I did not apprentice as an assistant. And I thought now someone will be there who will tell me that what I've been doing for twenty years is completely wrong.

HK: Is television the right medium for three stories like these?

DG: In principle, television is the best medium for such a project. The question only arises because TV ruins itself by robbing itself of its greatest potential and insisting on rigid formats and broadcasting slots. What we are doing now—with permission and desire—is almost a form of "old television," which also tries to animate public discourse.

CH: It's risky business. It's impossible to know whether people would like to watch all this in one evening. Most films made for TV try to avoid this risk by all means. They exhibit an aesthetics of avoidance. You can see it in the staging [*Dramaturgie*] of the material, in the looks that are being produced. We avoided this.

DG: In the past, I often fell asleep in front of the television. When waking up, there was either snow, as in [Tobe Hooper's] *Poltergeist*, or real late-night programming. The films were different. Stranger, wilder, crazier. Even back then Godard wasn't on at 8:15 p.m. [i.e., prime time/just after the evening news]. One had the feeling that television was getting larger the more it burrowed into the night. Christoph's film, *One Minute of Darkness*, has the breath of a night film. We were comparatively relatively tame. One could also start with this film.

CH: No, not really.

DG: The fixation on such formats kills such films. It'd be stupid to make from now on each prime-time film as experimentally as possible. It is necessary to broaden the entire program.

HK: You only saw the three films together at their premiere?

DG: We allowed ourselves to do this and thought afterwards: we did the right thing.

CP: It would have contradicted the spirit of the project if each of us had watched the films at home on DVD. It was really fantastic. Normally I can't bear premieres. Narcissistic mortification: I always run out. For the first time I perceived the audience as an attentive mass. It is the viewers who hold the films together, not the three of us with our concept.

DG: I've certainly also had quite different experiences at the Berlinale. I always sit in the front row so that I don't notice when a lot of people leave the cinema.

CH: At the Berlinale, they booed my first film. People got up and said, "Why are you doing this to us?"

DG: When in Christian's film the murderer appeared with the knife, my wife screamed, "Christian!"

HK: Director Caroline Link.

DG: She had such a scare.

CH: One has to protect oneself. She shouted, "Why do this!"

HK: In your email correspondence is a Wim Wenders quotation about [Thome's] *Red Sun*, stating that this film is not embarrassed to take place in Germany.

CP: I always liked this sentence. Wenders treated, for example, Wuppertal and the area along the border between East and West Germany similarly.

HK: How the freeway bridge is photographed is exciting.

CP: Bridges are artworks. In [Michael Cimino's] *The Deer Hunter*, there's a scene in which the men go hunting but one of them first has to go pee. In the background, you can see a wonderfully curved bridge.

CH: The guys from the freeway maintenance office said they had already had delegations from China. They were proud of their bridge.

DG: There were times when one tried to avoid letting Germany look like Germany. Everything was supposed to look American. Only after many years and parallel to your [the Berlin School directors'] rise did Germany become a location that I was able to define and show.

CH: With your television series *Der Fahnder*, you managed to approach the reality of West German pedestrian zones. I thought that would be impossible to photograph. All of these brown-colored bistros with Rotamint slot machines. You transformed this into something aesthetic.

DG: This also had to do with the neon light of the 1980s. It is really due to cinematographer Helge Weindler that I could even tolerate watching my own films. When one makes films here one is in conflict with the country. One doesn't do this in harmony; one doesn't have a sense of pride.

HK: In German television series, mountains and forests always look lovely.

CP: It's like with factory farming: the worse the fate of the chicken and pigs, the more impressive are the pictures on the packaging. The viewers are conceived from the point of view of audience ratings, which is why we have to endure such images. Christoph creates in his film an interesting place through looks; it's no longer mere background, but a habitat. In television, it is no longer possible with merely eighteen shooting days to develop a relationship to a location and to reflect on it.

CH: The more serially you work, the more the aesthetic is impacted by logistics. How things look often simply depends on how much time one has. I grew up in Munich. Mountains mean something to me. I always thought of it as a brutal, merciless landscape. I've never understood the mountain kitsch. Folk tales do not mirror this. It's similar with the forest.

HK: Have you tasted blood: would you like to repeat the *Dreileben* experiment?

CP: Yes. I do.

DG: I am proud to have participated in such a project. That's a good feeling. Of course, the next project would have to be different. We've now done the deconstructive approach. It must not get too "sticky." We now ideally shoot our films in close proximity and move from one set to the next. If one shooting day gets on your nerves then you can do mine.

CH: There are thought experiments: each of us shoots the same script. But we nevertheless have to make our own films.

CP: When we talk with each other, something comes out of it. But each of us takes our own, different impressions with them back home. That's how I imagine it. We pull together the energy to do a project. And then each of us realizes their own idea of this energy.

An Interview with Christian Petzold

Jaimey Fisher / 2011

From "An Interview with Christian Petzold," in Jaimey Fisher, *Christian Petzold* (University of Illinois Press, 2013), 147–67. © 2013 by the Board of Trustees of the University of Illinois. Used with permission of the University of Illinois Press.

Jaimey Fisher: Places and spaces, especially in small cities and towns, are consistently important in your films. Where did you grow up? Can you describe the region, the particular place, where you are from?

Christian Petzold: That has to do with my parents, who grew up during the Nazi period. At the end of World War II, they were children—actually, they were refugees, so children of migration. My father is from Saxony [in the former East Germany] and my mother is from what is now the Czech Republic. They met, then, as refugees in a small town in the southern Ruhr region near Dortmund and Dusseldorf [in far western West Germany]. So, we always lived in transit spaces [*Transitorte*], often in something like a bungalow. So, where I grew up was a bit like a "trailer park" [*said in English*].

There were so many buildings that had been destroyed in Germany during the war that there was a significant lack of houses and apartments. So, for the first couple of years, I was really a refugee child in the city where I grew up and also always a bit on the margins. Since that time, when I arrive in a new city, for example in Milan or Madrid, I always go for walks in places far away from the tourist sites; instead, I always end up at the trailer parks. I do not know what attracts me to such places. For me, those are the interesting spaces, always kinds of transitional spaces [*Durchgangsorte*]. I guess I do not have a true home [*Heimat*].

JF: What was the first film you can remember seeing in a movie theater? I ask because I always think that clarifies the time, the moment, in film history when one is growing up.

CP: That was an interesting moment. I was six or seven and in a small town where I went to the cinema with my friends and without our parents—that's probably why I can remember it. That is why cinema will never die out: it is a place without parents. We went to see [Wolfgang Reiterman's] *The Jungle Book* and there was a trailer beforehand for a film called *Liane, Jungle Goddess* [Eduard von Borsody]. Liane was rather like Tarzan, and there was a scene with her, this young woman probably twenty-one or twenty-two years old, very beautiful and with hardly any clothing on, and she was being roasted in a cage over an open fire by cannibals. She was screaming for help, and from that moment on, cinema has always been for me a sexual space. Godard wrote a text about *Liane* because, for him, this was finally an intriguing film from Germany. Later, Harun Farocki met the woman who played Liane, Marion Michael. Even though he is older than I, it was an important film for him, too, because suddenly, in the middle of all these terrible German movies full of literary adaptations and theatrical styles, suddenly there was something out of 1920s and 1930s German cinema—suddenly a cinema of bodies, the erotic, secrets, and forests. That's really something I can remember, this *Liane*.

JF: So, there were not any film societies, clubs, or anything similar for non-commercial or older films?

CP: Yes, once a week, there was a film evening. Then, when I was eighteen, I did mandatory civil service instead of military service in the army. I was in social work [at the German version of the YMCA] that also allowed me to work with film some—I organized a little film club for the young people there. According to the teacher there, I always had to organize a double program, so as to include a film for those who were not as educated. I never liked this kind of division between, for instance, a literary film and then a Bud Spencer film. I really never liked that at all, so I just mixed the program up, which was really fun. It was all on 16mm, and we had to do everything ourselves, pick it up at the train station, write the texts about it. That was really a great time of my life. And then, of course, I would also watch the films alone at night—I really saw an unbelievable number of films in that time and decided to pursue film then.

JF: You came to Berlin to study literature? Berlin was pretty different at that point than it is now. Could you describe the atmosphere then when you got to Berlin?

CP: Back then Berlin was simply *the* city, as it is now, I think, where one simply wanted to be. Besides Berlin there were maybe two or three other centers, maybe Munich, Cologne, Dusseldorf, and Hamburg. But the politicos, the leftists, and the anarchists all went to Berlin—in Berlin, there were no parents and there were subsidies for the city [*laughs*]. In Hamburg, etc., one already had to find a job, earn money, as the rents were quite high. I liked everything about Berlin. Berlin was the exact opposite of the place I grew up, the exact opposite—politically, but also in terms of the rhythm, the light, everything. And since my parents were refugees from East Germany, I knew they would never come to visit me in

Berlin. They would have had to pass through East Germany, so I was, in a certain sense, free.

JF: So, you began your literary studies in Berlin?

CP: Yes, but I really only went to the cinema. And all my writings at first were about the relationship of literature to cinema.

JF: So, you were always oriented in the direction of cinema?

CP: Yes, always in the direction of cinema, but it is also funny to think back and realize that the best times in my studies were not really when I was writing about the relationship of cinema to literature, but rather about structuralism—that and maybe Middle High German lyric poetry. So, what I liked about my literary studies was precisely where there was no cinema. I was not very convinced when they tried to introduce cinema into literary studies, where education [*Bildung*] tried to become popular.

JF: And then you transferred to the German Film and Television Academy in Berlin [dffb]?

CP: I wanted to finish my literary studies and then ended up applying to the dffb in 1987 but was rejected. I thought I would certainly be accepted, as I had already been an auditor with [Hartmut] Bitomsky, [Harun] Farocki, and [Dominik] Graf for like two years, and I really found it all great and was clear that this is what I wanted. And they rejected me, and I'm still indignant when I think about it [*laughs*].

JF: Of course, Fassbinder was rejected, too, no?

CP: Yes, and they told me that, something like, "Fassbinder was also rejected, and you'll make it too." But I said that's total nonsense! So, in 1988 I applied again, and in 1989 I started my studies. And my experience as I started studying there was a total shock because I had written many short stories beforehand and wanted to make feature films immediately, but then you are sitting there with seventeen, eighteen other people, young and all. One sits there and talks the whole day, watches films, and suddenly I did not understand how cinema works at all. Looking back, confusion and contemplation are great and all, but, at the time, it was a total crisis for me. It was similar to the crisis I had when I first heard the Sex Pistols and then heard the *Talking Heads: 77* album. With those two albums, I suddenly did not know what to do anymore. I did not do anything for a whole year. I just watched films with my friends at the editing table, watched Griffith and all of Stroheim. I would see three films a day, and so, I would guess, at least a thousand films in that year.

JF: Of course, you had already seen a lot when you were working at your civil service job, no?

CP: I knew about New Hollywood and the New Wave, found them great, but, with all the works from film history, I really watched very different films and began to think about actors. By the end of my studies there, I really was a failure because I had not produced anything. I made some short films, but some of the other students were already going to festivals and winning prizes, and so forth.

JF: I saw some of the films from this period, like *Ostwärts* [*Eastwards*], *Süden* [*South*], and *Weiber* [*Women*] [short films made during his dffb studies].

CP: Yes, exactly, I managed to make those kinds of films, but I really did not know what I should be doing, so I traveled and read literature, especially American literature, Anglo-American literature. I have to admit that that literature really influenced me the most. And then I began to read [Anton] Chekhov and [Georges] Simenon, and I thought, OK, let's try to make a feature film. I made a twenty- or twenty-five-minute film [*The Warm Money*] and then I had the courage to write a whole script. When I was done, I went to Harun [Farocki]. I always thought that he hated fiction and feature films, but he read it and he was really taken with it, and we talked about it for weeks and what could be changed in it. That was maybe the most important moment for me—I thought, yes, this is it. And so then I made *Pilots*, my first film, as my graduation film.

JF: And so you have worked with Harun Farocki from that time on. I have a few questions about your collaboration, but I would be happy to hear about it now, if you prefer.

CP: Yeah, it is kind of like when one is happily in love, and then someone asks, why are you in love, and it is uncannily difficult to say, one can only respond, I love her [*laughs*]. Yes, I was just at Harun's the day before yesterday, as I had a problem with a scene that we are supposed to shoot next week [for *Barbara*]. As I explained the problem to him, I just was not clear on what the scene is really about, what the suspense of the scene is supposed to be. I explained the problem, we smoked and had coffee, and even as I explained it, the problem solved itself. I could not have managed that with anybody else; he just says one or two things. Kleist calls it "on the gradual formation of thought in speaking" ["*Über die allmähliche Verfertigung der Gedanken beim Reden*"]. One should add to the Kleist quote that the space for articulation matters, too, the social and intellectual or emotional and mental space. And Harun, well, he is precisely such a space for me.

JF: How do you find Farocki's nonfiction films? For example, you have mentioned his film about Georg Glaser and how it relates to history, particularly how Glaser fell out of history.

CP: Yes, exactly. As I was working on *The State I Am In*, Harun gave me some writings of Glaser's, including some biographical material that is not in the film. I find his Glaser film fantastic—one really has to say that Harun really found something with it. With his films, Harun is searching for a certain type of place, sort of transit spaces [*Transitorte*], where something fundamental undergoes transformation. For example, how the working class is transformed in its representations of itself or how life itself is fundamentally transformed in a school. And sometimes I sit there as I might in front of a feature or fiction film, and I think cinema is not at its end, that there is still so much to uncover.

JF: You were enrolled at the dffb during the *Wende* [the fall of the Berlin Wall in 1989 and the reunification of Germany in 1990]. Did these events make a strong impression on you? I am thinking of your [short film] *Eastwards*, for example, and was wondering if there is a certain continuity in your work from this time, for example, *Yella* and *Jerichow* both unfold in the former East Germany.

CP: Yes, it came up again for me over ten years later.

JF: So, a certain belatedness [*Nachträglichkeit*] was in play?

CP: Exactly, I think that this belatedness is important. We had the *Wende* and then the Soviet Union collapsed—or rather, it was transformed into a neoliberal state [*laughs*], partially with oligarchies and such things. It was an absolute crime. And we saw all that. We saw, for instance, films from the Moscow Film School, which had been a totally subsidized space in the university and suddenly it received no more money. I saw two films from that school at that point, and they were fantastic, but they had not really found a language to express what had happened in that country, and I thought, that is what we also have to do. Then Peter Nestler also came for a seminar and said exactly the same thing to us: you have to take your cameras and have to look at what is happening. That's how *Ostwärts* came to be. Thomas [Arslan] also made a very, very beautiful film about how the Wall was dismantled. But mostly people shot things as if they were downloaded from the internet, the images that we all knew. And I myself could not manage it—I did not really find any images, at that point, for the *Wende*. I realize that I should have directed the camera at myself as well. I saw the same problem with September 11th in the US, when the very next day in Germany, there were exactly the pieces you would expect on King Kong in Manhattan, etc., as if they had already been written.

I think one really has to live with the confusion a while. And with the *Wende*, I was totally confused, as were my parents—they came from East Germany, and they really did not know what to think. This state of balance just was not maintained. And then I thought, this has always preoccupied me, so after *The State I Am In*, which was really a matter of working through the 1970s, I was able to finally address what happened: the transformation of a state-socialist system into a neoliberal system. In particular, I wanted to explore what happened to the people in the process of this transformation—and what kinds of films could be made about that.

JF: Did these events have a personal meaning because of your parents?

CP: My parents, in so far as they are refugees, were anti-Communists. I was of course a communist just to provoke my parents, but I did not really know what that is. Of course, I had read everything, Marx and everything, but right up to today, I do not know how to explain all that to my children. But for me the failure of East Germany was the failure of [all of] Germany, the utter failure, particularly as a counter-idea to the Nazis, as a leftist counter-idea. But one just cannot base socialism on a single country. One ends up with a nationalist socialism, as in North Korea, which, of course, is a complete disaster. For example, my wife is Turkish, and we were at a party three days after November 9, 1989, and there were some young people from the GDR there. And the first thing they said was, "There are so many foreigners here!" And I thought, uh-oh. I knew then that this isolation of the GDR allowed for no connection to, for no engagement with, others, and realized then that the former GDR would have a problem with racism.

JF: I would like to ask you a couple of questions about film genre, as I think it is worth noting that you frequently mention genre films, although it is clear that you do not find the consensus cinema of the 1990s very productive. You often mention genre films as an influence on your own films, for example [Edgar G. Ulmer's] *Detour* on *Cuba Libre*, *Near Dark* on *The State I Am In*, *The Driver* on *Wolfsburg*, *Carnival of Souls* on *Yella*, and [Bob Rafelson's] *The Postman Always Rings Twice* on *Jerichow*. What influence have such genre films had on you? Is it much different than in New German Cinema, for example, with Fassbinder, or than in the New Wave with Godard, who both worked with genre films from the US?

CP: I think the difference is that we are twenty years on. [These directors] took genre as a grammar, and they used that grammar to destroy genre and to unleash a new kind of energy—they quoted, destroyed, deconstructed genre, no? But as we began to make films, there was not any cinema anymore, no genre cinema at all. When you go to the cinema today, one does not see police films, they are all on television. One does not see melodrama, it is all on television now, in the afternoons. It is simply not there anymore. Maybe a few comedies, but in general it is mostly mythic adaptations, like comics. So, we had to approach it differently, it was more the case that I wanted to rediscover genre; I did not want to destroy it, therefore not *de*construct it, rather *re*construct it. I guess that is the way one can put it. It is a kind of archaeology. And therefore we, with the Berlin School and such, wanted to build it back up again.

A film that I find really excellent in this regard is [Peter Bogdanovich's] *The Last Picture Show*, as it achieves something in this direction. It is not a conservative or sentimental film; it is a historical film, yet the viewer is aware very precisely that it unfolds today. And it is a film about love, about the love of cinema, the love of images, the love of America, but, also simultaneously, the poisoning of all this. I really found that great. And with the last film, *Dreileben*, I showed all the actors

The Last Picture Show. They really are not familiar with films anymore—one can buy films everywhere, but no one really watches them. Godard said that, too. Everybody copies books, but no one reads them.

JF: So just a kind of consumption of the media.

CP: Yes, exactly. I do not think one needs to be familiar with that many films, sometimes thirty is enough. I do that with my shoots, I hold little film seminars for the actors. For example, before beginning the shoot [for *Barbara*], I just tried to find an image for the male leading role. A friend of mine, Alexander Horwath, wrote a piece about [John Ford's] *My Darling Clementine*, a film that really left a deep impression on me. The piece is about a scene with this image of Henry Fonda in a chair on a porch [opens a large binder to an image that shows Ford tipped back on his chair on a wide porch with a western landscape in the background]. He brought the scene into a balance, and the film is exactly like that: the town has not yet fully formed, America is not yet settled, everything is in the balance. And as long as there is this kind of balance, one can tell a story, one can make a film.

JF: So, it is what you have elsewhere termed an abeyance [*Schwebezustand*]?

CP: Yes, precisely. That's really the only interesting approach. Anyone who demands films that are not in such an abeyance, not in a crisis (as crisis is also an abeyance), anyone who would upend such a balance—they destroy cinema. The salespeople in Hollywood and at the TV stations here in Europe, they all demand the same stuff. They demand secure box-office receipts, and such an approach just leads to decline and collapse.

JF: But I find it really fascinating that you so often mention American genre films, like old westerns and horror films: this is something very unusual, even unique, among contemporary European auteurist directors.

CP: I always wondered about that as well. I thought all [directors] have to think in this way, because I worked in theater, and ancient Greek theater is, fundamentally, the beginning of democracy. In the *Oresteia*, one learns that it is no longer the gods who issue judgements, but rather the people. And the American western is the ancient drama of the modern, especially for America. How many court cases are there in westerns? In the saloon there are constantly hearings and negotiations: courts, lynch justice, and so forth, really just constantly in those works. And that is all fictional. These towns do not make any sense—there's a ranch there, but how could even eighty people live from it? Nothing is growing there at all. Such a community is really just an abstract idea. It is like a stage, and yet somehow there is always something new emerging there. There is always some new negotiation. And that, for me, is genre.

Film noir is also a genre. There the question is how can one, as an individual, live in a shitty and corrupt world, how can the individual go on.

JF: And these films contemplate the questions you mentioned about transformation and transition?

CP: Yes, they contemplate them. How can one manage it? Philip Marlowe is not a good man, but he is trying not to be a bad one. That is also a balance situation, and I find that intriguing. And New Hollywood understood that, not least in the crisis at the end of the Vietnam War. Like Robert Altman in *The Long Goodbye*, they took these figures and made them new.

JF: As in [Roman Polanski's] *Chinatown*?

CP: Yes, *Chinatown*, too. And they do not make fun of their genre models. That is something many European directors do, they make parodies of these genre films. I hate that like the plague. That's really the cheapest shot: the parodist says, I actually know more than this, I am just parodying. That really disgusts me. One sees with *Chinatown* or *The Long Goodbye* that they really love these films, that they have great respect for them.

JF: Do you know the thesis of Thomas Elsaesser in his book about New German Cinema? One of his theses was that New German Cinema lacked, and was searching for, an audience—it had critical success, but never really popular success or even interest. I wonder if the interest in genre for you is also partially this concern and this search.

CP: I do not really think so, because there's simply not an audience anymore for such films.

I experienced something once, at the beginning of the 1990s or at the end of the 1980s, when [Garry Marshall's] *Pretty Woman* was showing in Berlin. As students of the dffb, as film students, we could go into any cinema in the city for free, so for four years I went to see everything. That was a wonderful education, of course. One day, at 3:30 in the afternoon or something, I went to see *Pretty Woman* on the Kurfürstendamm [the former main commercial street of West Berlin] and there were all these secretaries [sic] in there, all these women who were watching Richard Gere, not Julia Roberts. And I was amazed: they were screaming "what a man!" He had been sitting in a bathtub for about two hours, and then he turned on the hot water again—with his big toe. One could see that Richard Gere had really sat in the bathtub for at least two hours, as they showed his skin in a close-up. And the women in the audience just screamed.

And then I realized: this is American cinema, that has a certain physicality [*Physis*]. And that is for me also genre. That they do not just rummage through material, but really discover something new in it. And what recurs all the time in these genre films is how men look at that particular historical moment. In *Pretty Woman*, Richard Gere is a neoliberal ass, he destroys companies or whatever, but he represents a new kind of body. Neoliberalism brings out a new kind of masculine body. That comes right out of F. Scott Fitzgerald, runs from the southern states directly to Richard Gere—and the German audiences see that and realize that they are seeing something new on the screen. I always realized that and thought: this is sexy, and this is dangerous. But we can only understand this newness when we tell the old stories and tales—*Pretty Women* is, after all, just Cinderella. And I find that all so interesting.

JF: Two things in particular are really interesting in what you just said. First, that often you depict such physicalities in your film and that you leave time for the viewer to perceive it. Second, that you often seek this corporeality with the actors, with Benno Fürmann, for example. It reminds me of what David Harvey, the theorist of, among other things, neoliberalism, and of what he has written about such corporeality. He describes the neoliberal body as a strategy of accumulation. That had me thinking of Yella as she crosses over the border, and it is clear that this, too, is a form of the body as accumulation strategy.

CP: Yes, precisely. But the actors really have to work that out—it is not just there already, they have to really develop it. We're starting to shoot [*Barbara*] next week, and, as I said, I offer a kind of seminar in a room where we watch films and read—but not psychological material. And then we go to the locations with the actors—we go walking where we are going to shoot. And that's the exact opposite of theater, go there and really look at the location. Then they see what there is, how it smells, how it tastes, and they do that themselves. I hate theater—I mean theater not as a form, but in film.

JF: I have some questions about individual films. Can you describe how you came to the political themes of *The State I Am In* after your three feature-length films for television [*Pilots*, *Cuba Libre*, and *The Sex Thief*], which are not, at least not as conspicuously, political.

CP: The RAF was dead, really no one was interested in them anymore. Then [Wolfgang] Grams was shot to death in Bad Kleinen, and I wondered: Where did he come from? Where have they been the whole time? What did they do the whole time? Then I started to write a screenplay about it. At the beginning, it was to be about a son of the terrorists, and the son was supposed to be me, with Harun, so to say, as my father. But then I thought that was too autobiographical, so I introduced a daughter instead, and it immediately became different. This history of domestic terrorism really permeated West Germany, in which the guilt of the fathers [generation] was supposed to be worked out. With the anti-Semitism, too, that was deep in there, it was all so complicated and complex, and then came [Chancellor] Helmut Kohl and said, we are not talking about it anymore.

So, I wrote the screenplay, and thought it was really pretty good, but then I only received government grants for it, not television support, and one really needs one third TV support. But they said no. They said, "The story is good, but why not just make it with bank robbers who have a child?" But I thought that was complete nonsense.

The funny thing is that I wrote the story in the US, with Harun, in Berkeley and Los Angeles. That really helped me, this distance from Germany, to be in the US, to have to drive around in a car. In Los Angeles, I went to the villa where Brecht had been [in exile], to the Feuchtwanger villa, so I really was in a land of exiles, which fit the script. Then I finally got a bit of money from a television station and could shoot it on a really small budget.

JF: And you have said Bigelow's *Near Dark* is important for the film, no?

CP: Yes, for the way in which the actors could find a metaphor—ghosts are one metaphor, but then that does not help so much with the physicality of the characters. I thought the vampire metaphor was actually pretty good: they drive all over the country, cannot really die, but also not really live, living in the dark, hanging around transit spaces, in bars, in campers, in trailer parks, etc. [as they do in *Near Dark*]. And I said, the vampire is also something German, was really invented in Germany. And then I thought, the Nazis have caves, Hitler in his bunker and everything, but where were the terrorists the whole time? They were everywhere in pictures, on wanted posters, etc., so not in a cave, but rather they were everywhere and nowhere, thus transparent.

Otherwise, I asked myself, "What are terrorists, really?" They are people who want to simplify a complex world. They do not want to wait, they do not want to work, they want the end and want it immediately. And so I thought they are people who want to abbreviate history, so they were thrown off track and end up next to or outside of history. No one needed them anymore.

JF: Many critics at the time said they found it regrettable that *Something to Remind Me* was made for television. And Michael Haneke, for instance, has emphasized that there are real differences, even a gap, between TV films and cinema films. What do you think about this distinction? Do you see TV films as essentially different than cinema films?

CP: When I was making *Something to Remind Me* and *Wolfsburg*, which was also financed by television, I just pushed the whole discussion away from me not to have to think about it. I made the film exactly as if it were for the cinema. But the consciousness that the film would at some point run during prime time and would then have a different "neighborhood" [*said in English*], that was clear to me and that, of course, changes some things. I knew, for instance, that one has fewer means with which to produce a film. For example, I did not have the money to buy the rights for the Burt Bacharach song ["What the World Needs Now is Love"]; otherwise, the film would actually have made it into theaters. The people at the television station and the producers, they would definitely have given the film a theatrical release. But that song alone would have cost, for the seven or eight minutes it plays, like $300,000.

JF: Yeah, and so with a budget of around $1.4 million, that would be impossible.

CP: Yes, exactly. It was dumb of me, pretty unclever of me, but maybe I did not want to be clever. I was so shocked by the success of *The State I Am In* that I did not know what to do. I wanted to make two films in two years, one right after the other, so retreat a little bit to television to have my quiet, rather like in a laboratory where you can experiment with different things. There is always the dictum that the second film decides one's career—after every big success, people say the next one will really tell. I wanted to hold myself out of it for a bit and so made two B-films.

JF: I wanted to ask about *Yella* and its relationship to *Carnival of Souls*, as it seems to play an important role in the conceptualization and realization of your film.

CP: Yes, the Herk Harvey was my point of departure. I always wanted to make something based on *Carnival of Souls*, but with unemployed workers. I had a project with Harun Farocki, who made a film in which the unemployed are being trained on how to present themselves. Nowadays, the worker is an individual and has to know how to present him- or herself; the whole world is a big casting call and audition. When I saw the film of Farocki's, I thought, these are just ghosts who have to act as if they are people, having to sell themselves as something else. In *Carnival of Souls*, she dies but does not even notice she is dead. At first I thought this was too much of a student idea, but then I made *Something to Remind Me* with Nina Hoss and then saw *Nothing Ventured*, and thought, that's it! Not someone who is a victim, but rather a perpetrator. She takes off from the East and wants to head West; her destination is simply neoliberalism. To get there, she wants and achieves a new body.

I did, however, forbid the actors from seeing *Carnival of Souls*, and I myself did not look at it again during production, but when I was done, I saw it, there is really so much from the film in *Yella*. It really stayed in my memory even though I did not resee it before shooting *Yella*—I still remembered almost every shot. It is really one of the most modern films that I know.

JF: I also wanted to ask about *Jerichow* and ethnicity in the film. With Ali, a Turkish-German who lives in the country in former East Germany, I immediately thought of Fassbinder.

CP: Yes, exactly, that's why he is named Ali in the film, and we watched *Merchant of Four Seasons* in preparation. My wife is Turkish, and migration stories are quite personal for us. I always thought that all these films in which Turks in Germany seem like victims are just not very convincing. It is racist as well to say that they are all nice people and just treated badly by society. I thought I would represent someone who did everything right, like so many immigrants who come to a country and do everything right: they are attentive and friendly, and yet no one likes them. The more they try to assimilate, the more they are excluded from society. And I find that tragic, and this immigrant a tragic figure. Ali could not be more German: he has bought himself a blonde wife, a Range Rover, and a house in the forest. And this German veteran, a complete failure, and this wife, who is totally in debt, they want to kill him. I found that just really brutal. On the other hand, Ali can be a total jerk: he is so masculine, so oriented to what other men think of him, that he handles his wife like a car. He says, "Go ahead, touch it, take it for a test drive." At the end, they are all totally lost. I like it in films when characters realize things too late, and then the moviegoers, and this late recognition, leave the cinema and go out into the world.

JF: With your contribution to the three-part *Dreileben*, you return, as you did with *The State I Am In* and *Ghosts*, to a plot featuring adolescent protagonists. What do you find interesting about this age in particular and how does your return to this constellation in *Dreileben: Beats Being Dead* fit into your work in general?

CP: There was a time in my life, between eighteen and twenty-two, when I was on the move all the time, in Italy and elsewhere, and in this time I discovered the cultural as well as the political underground. Now that I'm over fifty and take a bit of a retrospective look back to this time, I guess it also must have something to do with my parents' always being on the move, always fleeing, and never actually arriving anywhere. So, this condition of being on the move and seeking a place in the world—that really interested me in the terrorism story that became *The State I Am In*. Similarly, in *Dreileben*, it is a young woman who is also on the move, fleeing from Bosnia and working in a hotel, thus in search of something. On the other hand, in this same small town, there are the longtime inhabitants, the ones who have big houses, who work in the hospital, who are educating their children in the schools that have always been there. But then, in times of crisis like that depicted in the film, the social relations loosen up temporarily, and, all of a sudden, maybe a homeless person can be taken into the fold, or, as in [Pier Paolo] Pasolini's *Teorama*, someone who does not belong there suddenly shows up. Or, inversely, a rich person (as with the young medical student in *Dreileben*) ends up abruptly in some poor neighborhood. In horror films (like *Dreileben*, in its way), such things are worked through in the plots, like high school students visiting some place in the countryside.

In any case, if you think about how I took up such themes in *Ghosts*, it seems that, for me, it comes up every five years or so—every five years, I have to go back and analyze my youth, when I discovered so much.

JF: You have emphasized how, in *Barbara*, you set out to make the DDR colorful, something one notices immediately in the broad color palette of the film, in the vivid colors of its lovely 35mm photography. Why was this approach, one full of remarkable color, so important to a film about East Germany?

CP: It is related, I think, to things I saw when I still living in Cologne, where there was this group Filmclub 813, the name for which they got from Truffaut films. They would show musicals from East Germany, like [Joachim Hasler's] *Hot Summer* with Frank Schöbel, and, as I was remembering those films, I thought to myself: East Germany had to regard itself as colorful, too. The US had Technicolor, but they in the East had certain Agfa processes, where the reds are like those in Nicholas Ray's films or in Douglas Sirk's melodramas from the 1950s. Today, almost like propaganda, we tend to imagine that East Germany had no color at all, that it was all just gray—as if a sunflower that grows in the West somehow reaches up to the sun with much more brilliant color!

Since *Barbara* is not trying to make some kind of accusation, not some kind of propagandistic message from the West, the film tries to show what beliefs, what dreams, people had in this country. A country does not survive forty years unless there is some substance, some core to it, even if that substance was growing more attenuated at the end, its dreams more faded and empty. But it was a nation that had proudly proclaimed about itself: we, more than the West, offer peace, security, nourishment, and will never again turn to fascism. The romances of such a country, many influenced by Soviet literature, always took place after the summer, after the harvest, there was a certain kind of dancing and kissing—of course, that culture has its own conservative longing for the countryside, for manual labor, for hands and bodies.

And I thought, "We have to work into the film these kinds of dreams that the GDR had of itself. But we also have to show how this dream was, simultaneously, beginning to fade more and more." People were starting to say that we just don't believe these messages, these claims, anymore. Just as in New Hollywood films, when Robert Altman in *The Long Goodbye* uses CinemaScope and vivid colors to show that the society is decaying and rotten—that is the message, even when the images are so beautiful.

JF: A few final questions about certain continuities and recurrences in your cinema. Can you describe what you understand as a ghost or phantom? Why has it become such a central figure for your cinema, such that you base many of your films on it?

CP: I find that, fundamentally, the ghost is *the* figure of cinema. I thought that the ghost is not only about fear, but rather this falling out of time and place, not belonging anymore, that is, to be on the margins, to be unemployed, or even to be an unloved child—such people feel themselves to be ghosts. And cinema always tells the stories of people who do not belong anymore, but who want to belong once again. John Wayne in [John Ford's] *The Searchers* is also a ghost. The ghost wants to materialize itself; it wants feelings, skin, and that, for me, is a key theme. Isolation makes one ghostly, and the cinema goers are also ghosts, because they are there and they are not there. And it all feels like a dream.

JF: Of course, you are interested in this in our particular historical moment, how everything has been accelerated with neoliberalism's rapid turning of people into ghosts.

CP: Yes, absolutely. For example, when we watched *The Deer Hunter* [for the preparation for *Jerichow*], one sees how the local industry is dying out there, how the steel industry is vanishing, and therefore the male characters go to Vietnam. Not only because they have to, but also because they no longer know what to do with their masculine bodies anymore. And twenty years later, there are hardly any jobs anymore, they are all in Mexico or in China. They are ghosts in such cities, and I think that one has to make films about such ghosts.

JF: What does the car mean throughout your films? What do you find so fascinating about the automobile and mobility in general? Does the car have a special meaning in Germany that it does not possess elsewhere in Europe or in the US?

CP: When I was assistant director with Hartmut Bitomsky, I discovered his film about Wolfsburg [the *VW Komplex*]. I wondered why the automobile has not found a place in German cinema. Of course, there are road movies, but they could just as well be riding on horses, there is not really any difference. I wondered: what is specific to the automobile, especially when every second job in Germany is related to the car industry? Why is Germany an enormous Detroit, only more modern, and why are there no stories about it in Germany? What does the automobile change in our perceptions of the world? That's really my concern. Then I read [Paul] Virilio as well as [Georges] Simenon, and they wrote about the automobile and what it means, in particular what it means to fall into this kind of half-sleep while riding in the car. What is cruise control? What is a car radio? And then there is this entire mode of perception and corporeality when sitting in the car that does not have an adequate presence in cinema. And I thought that one should take the automobile seriously, so *Wolfsburg* was a reaction to this thought, a decision to make a film about cars. Of course, it was already somewhat that way in *The State I Am In* and even in *Pilots*, where the car is a space not only for movement but a philosophy of life [*Lebensphilosophie*]. The automobile forms individuality, subjectivity, me and the world, by isolating one, as with the hotel. My father, when he had problems at home, would go for a drive. This is the second aspect of the car: the family as it appears in the car, the stereotype of children in the backseat, woman in the passenger seat, and the man behind the steering wheel. What does it then mean for the child, in the backseat, to look at his or her parents but without being able to see their faces, and then to sense that they are in some sort of crisis. So, the car is really a social space, not simply a means of transportation.

JF: And, of course, this is linked to mobility in Germany, now, no?

CP: Germany is an unbelievably networked country. I know that American actors who like to shoot in Germany do not come here because they like German cinema but because they can drive 300 km per hour on the autobahn. Germany is really a nation of freeways, the idea of the freeway is deep in the country. The freeway, in fact, replaced German Romanticism. Caspar David Friedrich [the famous German Romantic painter, whose compositions Petzold seems to use in *The Sex Thief*, among others] would today paint the freeways. But then again it is changing even now. I notice that the car is starting to play a smaller role again—my children are not going to get driver's licenses. I think that Tarantino's *Death Proof* did not do very well because the myth of the car is dying out. When you see *Two-Lane Blacktop*, the car is fantastic, but one could not make that anymore. Today there are fifty magazines in Germany about computers, but only three about cars.

JF: You have criticized excessive exposition in films before. More often, you seem to try to convey things through the body of the actors, which is something one sees very clearly with Nina Hoss and Benno Fürmann. How do you realize this kind of physical reality? How does what you have called "bodily memory" function in your films?

CP: I think in many ways Nazism took our bodies away from us. 1968 saved us, but if you see cinema of the 1950s, it is clear how dominant dialogue is. People articulate everything, explain everything. On the one hand, one really has to work a lot with the actors so that they do not have a specific task but rather a serenity [*Gelassenheit*]. On the other hand, I think that film production in Germany has so little money, and so few days to shoot, that one simply has to get through it, so the directors just tell the actors how they should cross the street or get in a car.

JF: Yes, that reminds me how often hotels come up in your films. I do not know if you wanted to say something about the hotels in your films, but it reminded me of the difference between place and space that often unfolds in hotels.

CP: Yes, that has many connections. Hotels and cars, they are simply transit spaces in which people have an incredible desire to leave something behind. Two things come to mind: first, Andy Warhol, who found tape recorders fantastic not because you could record something but rather because you could erase something. There's a longing to go to the hotel because you can just push everything away from yourself. But, in this escape to the hotel, there is also an unbelievable loneliness and sadness. And therefore, this sort of space of absolute nothingness is filled also with these extremely lonely individuals. And that is what I like about hotels. The hotel is a space of longing but also, at the same time, a place that scares you. One sits there, the television is on, but one can also take out a pistol. How many suicides occur in hotel rooms?

JF: On the other side, there are very often houses, homes, in your films, and there is frequently a shot of the protagonist outside the house looking in, for example in *Jerichow* or *Yella*. And I find that this creates a strong tension between such transit spaces and these homes.

CP: Yes, that is correct. With houses, one thing always interested me. In Germany at least—I do not know if it is true in the US (!)—people build their houses like spaceships, like outposts on the moon, as if there is no social context at all. This is where we are building, and this is where we are living, that is our security and safety. But, of course, there is always a window there, and one looks out, and, outside, someone is going by, and they look in, and suddenly one is no longer alone in the world. People always fantasize about their vacations with romantic images of one house, a lake, five trees, and two children, and no one else in the world. Cinema becomes interesting when the second house is built: one wakes up one morning and, right across the way, someone else is building a house. Or in *The Great Gatsby*, people are living there, and then Gatsby builds a house across from them. And immediately there's pressure there. One has to come to terms with it, one has to become social, and that is where I put the camera.

JF: Many of your films concern work, which is a major theme in literature obviously, but not so much in cinema. And in almost every film of yours, work and/or workers play a central role, but a role that is in some way refunctioned—both the worker and the work.

CP: I think that, generally speaking, work does not really take place in cinema. People go to the cinema, after all, to avoid and seek some refuge from work. And yet cinema has not totally forgotten work, there is factory work and alienated work—especially on this latter count, there are bank robbers, craftspeople, people with real "skills" [*said in English*], for example, people who can break into cars. And I like that. I like to see in Walter Hill's *The Driver* how Ryan O'Neal drives—that is really his work, his labor. And in general, it is important that a film unfolds and plays out something that people can comprehend: of working, of kissing, of car-driving. And that the characters have really mastered or learned techniques and skills—I like that in films.

JF: You once said that the spaces in your films should have a kind of soul. What did you mean? What role do places and spaces have in your films?

CP: There is a book by Joel Sternfeld called *On This Site* [Petzold gave the German title, *Tatort*] that has beautiful images of houses and underneath each image there is a caption that says something like "This is where John Downey was shot" and "Here so and so was run over." And suddenly these spaces have a real aura.

When one goes through a German pedestrian zone or a German mall, one should have the feeling that there is somehow an idea, a ghost, a phantom in these places—maybe just the ghost of the architect or the developer. But something has to be at work behind the space. Tarantino manages to do that in the most unlikely places. In his *Jackie Brown*, there is this really disgusting shopping mall—as I find all these malls disgusting—but nonetheless, in the escalators and in the people that eat there, there is an idea, an idea of a way of life. So, spaces have to have soul, not just as background. And if they do not have something like [a soul], when the spaces are completely ugly and broken, then the kiss that the lovers have in such a space has to transform that space, has to enchant it. Yes, with magic. There's a poem by Eichendorff that I always find fantastic and that I liked even as a child: "A Song Is Sleeping in All Things" [*Schläft ein Lied in allen Dingen*]. That means that in all things, something is sleeping; one just has to be able to see it. I always say that to myself before I shoot. One really cannot forget that.

"I Wanted for the GDR to Have Colors"

Cristina Nord / 2012

From "'Ich wollte, dass die DDR Farben hat,'" *taz*, February 11, 2012. Reprinted by permission. Translated by Marco Abel and Jaimey Fisher.

Cristina Nord: Mr. Petzold, *Barbara* is about a doctor in East Germany who filed for permission to leave the GDR, as a result of which she was relocated to a provincial hospital. How did you think of this story?

Christian Petzold: It's been almost ten years since I first thought about it. I really liked a book by Hermann Broch, a novella called *Barbara*. It's about a communist resistance fighter who works in a hospital, falls in love with a doctor and he with her, but she has to move on and dies. The era that Broch describes was the end of the 1920s: SA troops already existed, the German justice and executive apparatus already had people hunting communists, murders occurred. But I was not able to imagine this milieu in terms of a film: I did not have any images for this in my head.

CN: How come, then, that you transposed this story into the GDR in 1980?

CP: In 2006, I got to know a doctor from Fürstenwalde who told me about applications to emigrate filed by his colleagues. The men were put into reeducation camps in order to humiliate them, afterwards they had to work as military doctors. The women were relocated to provincial hospitals, a kind of exile. That's when I remembered the "Barbara" story, not least also because I was always interested in the East; my parents are from there. My parents' most profound feeling was homesickness for the East.

CN: Your parents are from the area in Mecklenburg-Vorpommern where the film takes place?

CP: No, I would not have been able to do this: that would have been too personal. When I arrived at the film academy, I wanted for my very first film to take place at the locations of yearning of my youth, at the original locations, at the junction box, at the autobahn rest stop, at the autobahn bridge, in the park, the city library. But these locations had lost their magic as soon as I stood there with my camera. One cannot film sites of memory. And my parents' sites of memory are of course also mine because we frequently drove into the GDR. I know these locations by heart. As a young boy, I was also in GDR hospitals when I injured myself.

CN: A hospital is a location of heightened intensity because it is about matters of life and death. Television series about doctors such as *ER* time and again act this out. Were you intrigued by this?

CP: Of course. My children always watched the series *Doctor's Diary*, which I found pretty funny as well. I'm also familiar with *ER*, but the mother of all series about hospitals is *Hospital at the End of the City*, a Czechoslovak television series that was popular in the West as well. The Americans copied everything from it. Most of the time the stories are about arranging dates while cutting open abdominal walls. We did not want to do this. And unlike in Western hospitals, the GDR hospitals didn't have this pressure. There were libraries, reading groups, soccer teams, sailing clubs. It was much calmer. The nurses who advised us had tears in their eyes when recalling this era. One gets the feeling that one had time there to get healthy. Here it's more like a factory.

CN: My impression was that in *Barbara* you work quite sparingly with the props from the time and area.

CP: We are precise to the last detail. Every tiny object is correct, the X-rays are correct, the fabrics are correct. But we must not put the work we've done on display. For example, one doesn't see caravans of vintage cars, which I just can't stand. I want to have living spaces, which means that the objects have to have been touched. Kade Gruber, the set designer, and his crew finish building the sets two months prior to the start of shooting so that the actors can make the rooms and objects into their own. They really drank from this glass, this photo camera really contains film material, and they really drive the car alone.

CN: You shot during summer, as so often before. Why?

CP: Because I wanted for the GDR to have colors. I visited the GDR every year; I remember a colorful country. I really wanted to start shooting in the middle of August and finish by October because this period entails the colorfulness of the onsetting fall with its slight brown tones. And after I shot my previous film digitally, I decided to work again with Kodak and 35mm. The color palette is so human.

CN: At one time, Barbara walks into a forest in order to meet her lover from West Germany. In this sequence, Nina Hoss is wearing an incredible blue eye shadow. Is this not a bit too glamorous?

CP: No. When she drives to this guy she wants to look—as Nina puts it to herself—"as if I drive to a tango dance." Which is why we did not skimp with the makeup. If she had foregone her hairdo, makeup, and long eyelashes then, for this character, it would have been tantamount to being defeated by this system.

CN: With her elegance she defends herself against the imposition of the GDR system?

CP: Exactly. The assistant doctor played by Christina Hecke does not have any of this. She is a pretty woman, but she says: "All of this is Western shit, this bimbo crap." In the Protestant and Prussian East, one was opposed to luxury and waste, and Barbara fights against this—with Dunhill cigarettes and silk underwear . . .

CN: . . . which she gets from her West German lover. It's nothing new that in your films feelings and material advantages are imbricated with one another. There are no feelings that could not be valorized.

CP: Yes, but they are also allowed to be wasted! Barbara believes that in West Germany she will find deep and true and light feelings, that she can be wasteful there. For the East is too reasonable for her. Just like when [Wolf] Biermann sings, "Here order is big, just like with the seven dwarfs." Barbara wants to dance, she wants silk, sweat, wastefulness—for her, that's the West. And then her lover tells her, "When you are in the West you can sleep in. You will no longer have to work." She hears this sentence lying in the hotel bed; after a cut, she sits in a railcar and looks out the window. And in her face something is working, but we don't know what it is.

"Our Identity Defines Itself through Work"

Wenke Husmann / 2012

From "'Unsere Identität bestimmt sich über Arbeit,'" *Zeit Online*, April 26, 2012. Reprinted by permission. Translated by Marco Abel and Jaimey Fisher.

Wenke Husmann: The protagonist in your latest film, *Barbara*, is, according to our contemporary views, a very emancipated woman. But the film is set in the GDR of 1980. What was it that made the working life there so modern from the point of view of women today?

Christian Petzold: From early on, the GDR had daycare and preschools so women could work. As I recall them, they were very strong and adult in a different sort of way. In the townhouse communities in the West where I grew up, there were hardly any daycares or preschool spots. And the few that existed were expensive. As a result, women stayed at home, every now and again an Avon consultant rang the bell or someone organized a Tupperware party. And today? Politicians of the CDU/CSU discuss the so-called care allowance, which is once again reflective of the conservative attitude that families should receive financial support if they leave their children at home and the woman no longer goes to work.

WH: Why is the topic of work so important for you?

CP: We have a big problem. Industrial work has disappeared, in general more and more jobs disappear, and yet our identity defines itself through our work. At a party one asks, "What do you do?" when women answer, "I take care of the kids," they do not have an identity and instead belong to the large mass of mothers.

WH: Is this the reason why in the film Barbara's West German lover predicts her prospects: "Once you've come over, you'll be able to sleep late. I earn enough, you won't need to work."

CP: Strangely enough, after viewing the film everyone in the West said that the most important sentence is: "In this country"—i.e., in the GDR—"you can't be happy here." But the crucial sentence is the one you quoted. For with it, the West—which lures with pretty smells, fantastic tobacco, and silken hosiery, and from where it is not so far to Italy, to yearning and openness—suddenly becomes a townhouse community. Within just a few seconds. This affects Barbara like poison.

WH: You yourself grew up in the West as a child of a mother who had to quit the job she used to have in East Germany and became a housewife, and of a father who very much cared about his job. But he was eventually laid off and for a while was not able to find new employment.

CP: For three and a half years, he was unemployed.

WH: Is this the source for your critical attitude towards the Western model?

CP: Not only. Back then, I was still young—twelve or thirteen. But it is indeed remarkable: I grew up in a townhouse, and these houses are exceedingly functional. There is a large living room that one traverses from the front to the back on the way to the yard. Next to it is a kitchen with a service hatch and a guest toilet. A spiral staircase leads to the second floor. There is the bedroom of the parents and two small rooms for children, and there's a bathroom. That was our home, and that's how all townhouses looked like that I've seen. This house is living, eating, sleeping, and children. When my father lost his job, there was no room for him anymore. For three and a half years, he walked through the house not knowing where he should sit down. He eventually installed a small office in a small corner in the bedroom. It looked like a prison cell. The man was simply expected to be out of the house. Eventually, my father wondered if this system so directed at work is, in the end, just a horrible prison.

WH: Today, every company, every supermarket tries to motivate their employees and instill in them the feeling that one belongs together. Is it harmful when employers try to get their employees to identify with the company?

CP: People probably want this up to an extent because without it this terrible form of work is intolerable. They work at Beiersdorf of VW or Bayer and also call themselves accordingly: "Beiersdorfer," "VW-ler." They compulsorily identify with their employer, often as they do with a soccer club. Today's corporate policy believes that it's enough for offices to look good, that there's an espresso machine, that one can casually hang out, and that a new hedonistic colloquial tone holds sway. I think behind all this lies the employers' fear that a strong union may emerge once more that simply says: we are not going to go along with this shit.

WH: As a journalist, I do identify with my work a lot, and I assume you do too. And this feels good.

CP: We are a different case. We are not Schlecker.[1] We do intellectual work, are academics.

---

1. A sprawling chain of drugstores that carried cosmetics, health-care products, and household goods, among other everyday items. It went bankrupt in 2012 and closed its remaining retail stores.

WH: What does this change?

CP: We work in a field in which we are granted more freedoms because we also have to do research and think. We do not have to clock our time. But 80 percent of all people have a job that is not represented on television. There, detectives play the saxophone, live in lofts, and basically live like curators. We no longer have an image of the kind of work most people still experience: they go into factories, behind walls.

WH: In your film, there is a man who pursues his work with passion or at least great rigor. But of all people this is the Stasi officer. In addition, he is the only protagonist who has a social circle, friends and family.

CP: People who do the most terrible things don't do this because they are evil but because they want to do good deeds. That's what hurts. In conversations and while researching I realized that the GDR found itself constantly under fire. In the fifties, all skilled workers fled: they were poached by the West. The country suffered from bloodletting, and some thought: we trained people such as the well-educated Barbara, who just want to earn some money, who want to go to the West, to Cannes or Saint-Tropez, for our common good. If they want to leave, I am going to mess them up! For we have a country here, a community: we are responsible for one another! This is why I did not want for this Stasi officer to come out of nowhere, to be merely a script idea; I wanted for him to have friends and girlfriends and his own suffering. His wife with cancer paints, and the room in which she lies dying is nicely furnished. I believe it is important to show that the so-called evil or oppressors often act the way they do because they obviously believe they are the good guys.

WH: In *Barbara*, you have once again connected a love relationship with a working relationship. This, too, was not typical of West Germany. Even though we were literally ruled by work, we always tried to save love—at least in film—from the domain of work. What, then, is our problem?

CP: I, too, find this strange. Almost all couples that are walking down there on the street right now got to know each other in a working group or a seminar. But this is not depicted on TV or in the cinema. And this is because—especially in German cinema—work doesn't take place. Cinema always starts when work is over. Strangely enough, exceptions can be found in science fiction films, pirate films, or in westerns. In those films, people are working, but this is work in a fictional space, which isn't our everyday space, a space that is present to us. Yet the people who are shown are adults: they work and love. The title of a Godard book is *Liebe Arbeit Kino*. These three things relate to each other, and we have to resume this connection.

WH: Do you already have a topic to which you want to attend next? As a chronist of contemporary Germany, you always like to turn to current issues.

CP: Oh, cinema dreams itself in reality. I do not take a cover story from the *Spiegel* as the basis for my next script. If this happens it is too late for film. My next film takes place in Berlin shortly after the end of World War II, between May and November 1945.

WH: Will it feature again a female protagonist?

CP: Yes. And a man. It's about Auschwitz.

"What Lunatics There Were!"

Stefan Schirmer and Martin Machowecz / 2013

From "'Was es da an Irren gab!,'" *Die Zeit*, January 31, 2013. Reprinted by permission. Translated by Marco Abel and Jaimey Fisher.

Stefan Schirmer and Martin Machowecz: Mr. Petzold, you grew up in the West, but you are making films about daily life in the GDR. Do you frequently have to justify yourself to those who knew the GDR?

Christian Petzold: Sometimes. When recently I presented *Barbara* in cities such as Chemnitz, I knew: the people really pay close attention to what this West German has done with their history. For you cannot please everyone: not everything was bad in the GDR, yet everything was horrible! It was a rich life, but it was terrible! I especially always dread the eggplant debate.

Schirmer and Machowecz: The eggplant debate?

Petzold: In *Barbara*, there is a scene in which ratatouille is being cooked. I keep being accused of this: "We did not have any eggplants!" Yet I researched this very carefully. Even my parents, who are from the GDR, had an East German cookbook that included a recipe for ratatouille. And eggplants were available; for East Berlin I know this with certainty.

Schirmer and Machowecz: What is the problem: that everyone believes that their experiences are those of all GDR citizens?

Petzold: Yes. You have to understand that in this State not everyone ate the same or had the same experiences. A life is not a linear narrative, not even in the SED-country[1]—and most film narratives fail to understand this. A life consists of things that do not fit, of banal things, of boredom. There were people between Fürstenwalde and East Berlin who liked and ate eggplants.

Schirmer and Machowecz: Films without contradictions are pithier.

---

1. A country run by the East German Communist Party, the SED or Sozialistische Einheitspartei Deutschlands.

Petzold: That's the problem. Especially of these history film two-parters, the tunnel-Wall-Rommel[2] films. Sometimes I think the producers of such films hope that at some time there will be a Leitz-folder[3] that accurately is labeled: this here was the GDR; and this here was the FRG. [Uli Edel's] *The Baader Meinhof Complex* was basically a reenactment of photos that everyone knew; they restaged photos for cinema! That's why the story didn't come alive. I prefer to show bizarre, internally contradictory biographies.

Schirmer and Machowecz: Biographies such as those of your parents?

Petzold: Yes, my parents had neither a GDR nor a FRG biography. They were refugees. They came to the West in 1959. My mother is a Sudeten German, my father was from Saxony. Both never fully arrived in the West.

Schirmer and Machowecz: The era of ruptures, of the big revolutions, that was 1989–90. Are there good films about this?

Petzold: I can think of *Material* by Thomas Heise. A masterpiece. In fall 1989, Heise simply traveled with a camera through his own country. The Wall falls, and he looks behind the prison walls. The guards wonder whether they should now throw away their uniforms and simply leave. Then a prisoner arrives who, I'm not sure, is in prison because of blackmail or robbery, and he says, "Please don't forget us." He's afraid to be forgotten in prison. This is crazy. This desperation! The *Wende*: this was not merely Rotkäppchensekt[4] at Brandenburg Gate.

Schirmer and Machowecz: Did you also strike out?

Petzold: I was at the film academy in West Berlin. In a seminar, documentary filmmaker Peter Nestler told us: take a camera and go over there. So, I proceeded to film Bundesstraße [Highway] 2, which traverses Germany and for a long time was separated by the Wall. I simply made a documentary about the part that leaves East Berlin. One could see how in this time of crisis identities crumbled. What lunatics there were! I met a woman, the proprietor of a shack at the side of the road, who in all seriousness offered facial painting. She had a GDR swimmer as a customer who a year earlier won third place at the world championship. And now she had her face painted like a cat.

Schirmer and Machowecz: And your fellow students: what did they do?

Petzold: One, Thomas Arslan, walked along a section of the Wall where demolition work had already started. He filmed how Turkish workers chopped down

---

2. This refers to the spate of historical films focusing on recurring topics like the escape from East Germany ("tunnel"), the Berlin Wall, and the wartime and postwar media star, General Erwin Rommel, the so-called "Desert Fox."
3. A German stationary product that comprises a folder system signifying careful and neat order given to diverse materials.
4. This refers to a sparkling wine from East Germany that was particularly popular, also in the western parts of Germany, in the celebrations around 1989–90 and thereafter.

these lampposts, these asbestos posts. Welcome to wage labor of the West! They earned 6.30 DM per hour and essentially destroyed a world heritage.

Schirmer and Machowecz: A few years later, the first films about the peaceful revolution existed, such as [Frank Beyer's] *Nikolaikirche*. Did they impress you?

Petzold: Well, the message of these films often seemed more important than the script, according to the motto: "Well, we show the people here in Leipzig with their fears." And then a bunch of small stories are invented in simplistic fashion: the young hooligan, the wife of the pastor, the prostitute.

Schirmer and Machowecz: Did those films about the *Wende* simply come too early?

Petzold: Exactly. One was too close to the historical events. It had not yet sunk in, yet one already wanted to be part of history—with a film. I think this is wrong. I prefer to dream up things anew that are already past. But, of course, a film such as *Nikolaikirche* had its justification.

Schirmer and Machowecz: It was directed by Frank Beyer, who died in 2006 and who once was one of the most important GDR directors.

Petzold: Yes, and I very much liked this film. But my sense is that it's been possible to make really good films about the *Wende* era and the GDR only in the last two or three years. Now there is enough distance. Heise released *Material* three years ago. He was able to order and view his reels only now.

Schirmer and Machowecz: Why does Veronica Ferres play so often the lead role in TV films about the GDR?

Petzold: I once was asked whether I'd make a film with her. A mean-spirited question. Why not? They also put down John Wayne. One always picks someone whom one can demean. It is not Veronica Ferres that bothers me about these two-parters.

Schirmer and Machowecz: What, then, is it that bothers you?

Petzold: Before even watching them I know that I won't like them. I can tell from how they are being advertised. And that the talk show guests have already been picked to debate on *Anne Will*[5] right after the broadcast. In such films there's nothing left to discover. I hate films in which I have already been calculated and planned as a viewer.

Schirmer and Machowecz: There's hardly a film that's as well-known as [Florian Henckel von Donnersmarck's] *The Lives of Others*. Does it deserve its world fame?

Petzold: Why not? But it's not a film about the GDR. It's more of a Hitchcock film. The GDR is merely a studio. A studio for history that is not derived from the GDR itself.

---

5. A popular TV news talk show that succeeded *Sabine Christiansen* on the German public TV station ARD upon Christiansen's retirement in 2007.

Schirmer and Machowecz: You mean: a cliché?

Petzold: Well, I too liked what they tried to do: to represent the GDR as a West German dream. As a West German nightmare. And Ulrich Mühe plays brilliantly in what was perhaps the first big film that did not make fun of the GDR.

Schirmer and Machowecz: Is the GDR by now fodder for Hollywood?

Petzold: For a long time. One of the first big films about the GDR was *Torn Curtain* by Alfred Hitchcock with Paul Newman in the lead. Alas, Hitchcock wasn't allowed to shoot in the East. They shot it somewhere in England, and they did so amazingly realistically! What they reconstructed is often more real than the original. And also more original.

Schirmer and Machowecz: Your film *Barbara* is about a young GDR medical doctor who filed for permission to leave the GDR and then as punishment is moved from Berlin to a provincial hospital in Mecklenburg. When watching the film, one wonders how one finds such a hospital. One that still looks so much like the GDR!

Petzold: Through a website where people exchange information about "uncanny locations." A colleague of ours discovered there the old hospital of Kirchmöser, which is part of Brandenburg/Havel. Since the *Wende*, the place has been empty; one can purchase it for 1 euro. We rented it and renovated two floors.

Schirmer and Machowecz: Was it an uncanny place?

Petzold: Not at all. The people of Kirchmöser were nostalgic, for this used to be their hospital; many were born there. People came and cried because our shoot reminded them that Kirchmöser used to be a city. One that was alive! Not just a location with a Penny and Lidl supermarket. A place with a restaurant, a butcher, a café on the square. Now most of it is closed. What's left is an insurance branch office with a faded image of Boris Becker in the store window. And then a film team arrives, and suddenly there's once again life at the hospital. Suddenly such a location regains its dignity.

Schirmer and Machowecz: You once said that as a patient you would wish for a hospital like the one in *Barbara*.

CP: In any case, I'd prefer it to that in *ER*. For it has an entirely different aesthetic than the hospitals in US doctor TV series. For viewers there's an excess of hospitals on TV. Our TV has almost more detectives and doctors than real people! And then I arrive in Kirchmöser and see this completely different hospital architecture! These linoleum floors—fantastic!

Schirmer and Machowecz: Does the East provide the more interesting images?

Petzold: I think so. My colleague Dominik Graf once explained why the East was interesting for films: because they never tore down the city center. When you get to Halle you're confronted with the untouched downtown. The GDR did not have money to renovate. They simply built a large new city. Whereas in the West they demolished everything, in the East the beautiful stayed. That's what I like so much about Halle. Sure, it's been now painted with funds from the EU, and they added everywhere pretty wooden floors and a ceramic fireplace with a glass window. But one can still detect the old. Go to Leverkusen, Essen, Bochum. These cities were designed and divided from the perspective of a car. Live here, shop there, and work over there. And that's it.

Schirmer and Machowecz: For your films, you veritably revive the GDR. Why?

Petzold: I don't like backdrops; rather, I want that when a closet from the GDR is opened there are books from the GDR in it. I want for real locations to be palpable in how the actors play. The windows that they open are windows from the East. And the beverage they drink is bean coffee. And I don't do this because I'm a fetishist.

Schirmer and Machowecz: Why then?

Petzold: Because this era is not so long ago, yet it appears to us as if it's been hundreds of years. Every detail has to be right or else no one believes it. There's nothing sadder than the melancholia of a flea market. When one negotiates some price, it is really all about childhood, objects that once meant something. The actors are supposed to feel this melancholia.

Schirmer and Machowecz: You send the actors back in time.

Petzold: Take Nina Hoss. In *Barbara*, she plays someone from the opposition who had intended to leave this country. I wanted that even she would think of the locations in the film as beautiful. Each path she takes or rides with her bicycle has to be beautiful. It is more difficult to leave a place that you like. Life is never black or white. Put differently: there was the Stasi, but there were also eggplants.

Schirmer and Machowecz: Why do so many films show the GDR gray-on-gray? In *Barbara*, the country has strong colors.

Petzold: Frankly, I did not even think about this. Until our sound designer, who is from Meißen, said: "Wow, these are real colors, at long last!" That's when I noticed that this is correct. Here a country shows its potential and thereby makes it hard on the one who tries to flee. There is sensuousness and a coffee that someone brings you in the morning. That too was the GDR: a utopia. A dream of total care, anti-fascism, equality, a life far from greed. That the film appears so colorful is probably also due to the fact that capitalism is in a serious crisis: forty percent of Europe's youth is unemployed.[6] The ones who are watching how an older system is dying are less arrogant when they also mistrust their own system.

---

6. The number of unemployed cited here refers to the series of economic crises in the Euro-zone (including Germany) in 2011–13, partially as a result of the worldwide crises of 2008–9.

Schirmer and Machowecz: It is moving how grateful some people are to you for showing the GDR so colorful.

Petzold: I'm surprised by this. After all I am not the first. Think of Dominik Graf's *The Red Cockatoo*. In the first twenty minutes, you have bodies and park and music. This inspired me to film this lust for life. This existed as well, even in this stinking, petit bourgeois state.

Schirmer and Machowecz: In order to show in *Barbara* the West's love of life, you dug up a *Quelle*[7] catalogue from 1980. Where did you find it?

Petzold: On eBay, for 16 euro. On set, everyone wanted to flip through it. We even had to interrupt shooting. Do you know what in 1980 was still important in *Quelle*? Eating. A world of mountains of ground meat. This catalogue still catered toward the hunger and renunciations of the postwar era. It put on display: look what the West is capable of!

Schirmer and Machowecz: In the film, Barbara and another woman—two lovers of rich West German men—sit on a bed in the Interhotel and discuss whether the men will take them to West Germany.

Petzold: And shortly before, the film's death sentence was uttered. Her lover tells Barbara, herself a doctor: come with me to the West, where you can sleep in and will never have to work again. All East German viewers—all—immediately recognize: what a stupid sentence! Many in the West don't even notice it. They grew up with the idea that women would stay at home, whereas the men would go to work. The old BRD would never have produced an Angela Merkel. If a West German man had told her, "Come with me, over there you can sleep in"—she would've given him an earful!

Schirmer and Machowecz: A Merkel film: is this something still missing?

Petzold: As two-parter produced by teamWorx, as biopic? Angela Merkel's youth? Yikes: she'd hate this. And I would never want to do this.

Schirmer and Machowecz: Apparently the East has the more interesting stories. Think of your film *Jerichow*: a solider who served in Afghanistan returns. There's racism, deep province. So much comes together!

Petzold: There's some truth to this. Suddenly the East has to master at highest speed a development for which the West had a lot of time. That's how friction, losses, crises come about. For me it is as if I were to go on vacation in Antalya and am confronted by the behavior of these masses of these Russian tourists that remind me of how obnoxious we ourselves were in the 1960s on Mallorca. And when I look at the cheap greed in the East, or the unemployment there, then I'm seeing the 1970s West all over again.

---

7. Quelle was a popular mail order business with a thick and lavishly illustrated catalogue from the western part of Germany. It started in the 1920s and was restructured in bankruptcy in 2009.

Schirmer and Machowecz: Is this a gap in the market: the West film?

Petzold: *Dreileben* is a real West film.

Schirmer and Machowecz: But it takes place in Thuringia.

Petzold: But it's about people who do not come from there. For example, there's a doctor who allowed himself to be relocated there so that he could earn 30 percent more and become chief doctor. I wanted to depict this new parvenu class: upstarts like doctors, lawyers, tax accountants, and business consultants. A film about how Westerners go to colonize.

Schirmer and Machowecz: Is the East still unique?

Petzold: I insist on the differences. To be East German is an imprinting. It started with the humiliation of the GDR, prior to the fall of the Wall, for thirty years; and its inhabitants were humiliated as well. With *Quelle* catalogues, with fantastic cars, with "what kind of clunkers do you drive in the East?" The one who's always being humiliated does not forgive so easily. No wonder that it's still lasting.

Interview with Christian Petzold about *Phoenix*

Peter Osteried / 2014

From "Interview mit Christian Petzold über *Phoenix*," kritiken.de, August 26, 2014. Reprinted by permission. Translated by Marco Abel and Jaimey Fisher.

Peter Osteried: How did you learn about the novel by Hubert Monteilhet?

Christian Petzold: In the late 1970s, the film magazine *Filmkritik* ran a special issue on Hitchcock's *Vertigo*, which one couldn't see at the time. He had withdrawn five films from circulation, including *Rear Window*, so that he would later be able to score with a rerelease once he had no more success otherwise. That's why *Vertigo* was a mythic film, a legend. This *Filmkritik* issue included a real sequence in photos, and this charged up the film that one had not yet seen and was not able to see. And towards the back of the issue, there was a text by my coauthor, Harun Farocki, about women and literature and film who were mixed up. About men, who kill one woman and put another one in their place. The Pygmalion theme, etc. The text was fantastic. At the time, I fulfilled my civil service obligations and did not yet know Harun, but I always read the magazine, and this was an important text for me. When I got to know Harun, I asked him about this text, because it was the first that I associated with his name. And then he gave me this book by Hubert Monteilhet, which back then was no longer available either. It was an edition from the 1960s. I read it and thought, "French literature is full of stories about people who return from the hell of war or the Holocaust. These stories try to describe the return. That hardly exists in Germany. Maybe Wolfgang Borchert or Peter Lorre's *The Lost One*." But there's hardly any literature about homecoming. Nor is there much literature about survivors from the camps who are brought to new camps for displaced people but later on are not accepted back into society. And in the context of this novel, Harun and I spoke about this refusal to accept people back into society as a topic. Over the course of twenty years, we claimed that one cannot make a film based on this material, that it is too difficult. When I had shot *Barbara* and watched it with Harun, he said, "Now you have a couple of lovers with Ronald Zehrfeld and Nina Hoss who are so strong together that you can tackle this topic."

PO: Is the novel *Return from the Ashes* really a different story from the one of your film?

CP: Totally different. The novel was just the occasion. The basic plot is the same: a woman, who returns from Auschwitz with a severe facial injury, is not recognized by her husband. That she plays herself is also in the novel. It is a letter-diary novel. The woman, who returns from the camp, writes in the first person. She is part of the French bourgeoisie and is really rich. She also has a daughter who does not recognize her either. It's a bit of a pulp [*Kolportage*] novel. I was interested in the plot.

PO: "But I assure you, no one will. None of these people will ask," Johnny says. That's the key moment of the film. The people really do not want to know.

CP: What was great when we shot this scene in the basement and Ronald Zehrfeld says this so simply: we were all shocked. Suddenly we realized: that's exactly how it is. They are not being seen. No one is interested. In the past, I played on a soccer team with Harun. Wolfgang Neuss was also part of it until he could no longer play. He wrote a biography called *Ein faltenreiches Kind*. He talks about how he returns from the war to Berlin in May 1945 and that in there were over 1,000 applications to open up cabarets and clubs. One has to imagine that basically the entire city wanted to dance. It wanted to do away with fascism. On the one hand, this world that wanted to live again, and on the other hand, those who return and are not noticed by those who just want to dance. I felt this was one of the most horrifying impressions one could gain from Wolfgang Neuss's book.

PO: The secondary character Lene is also not able to cope with this. She says that she feels closer to the dead than to the living.

CP: I too believe that you shudder when you see only traces of lives in the form of photos and inherited objects, and this shudder does not pass without leaving its mark. Many people who worked for the Agency[1] were not able to endure this. Today everyone can listen to the Frankfurt Auschwitz trial testimonies and similar events on the internet. It deeply affected me to listen to all of these people trying to describe what they had experienced only to have language fail them, to have it simply collapse or stop. When imagining that a woman such as Lene dealt on a daily basis with witnesses, survivors, or the objects the dead left behind, I believe that she feels infected by death.

---

1. At the time, it was called the Jewish Agency for Palestine and would later be renamed the Jewish Agency for Israel, one of the largest Jewish nonprofit agencies in the world.

PO: It's an unusual love story that is being told, almost a ménage à trois with only two people. Or perhaps four? Nelly, the Nelly she plays, the Johnny who loves her, and the Johnny who lives in postwar Germany.

CP: That's correct. It was by accident that we eventually discovered that "Speak Low," the song that plays an important role in the film, was written by Kurt Weill for a musical that subsequently became [William A. Seiter's] *One Touch of Venus* with Ava Gardner. In order to be able to make it through shooting this difficult material without ending up being depressed for three or four months straight, I did research about Kurt Weill—just to have some fun in life. And I kept coming back to our film. Kurt Weill wrote the musical himself. It's about the Pygmalion theme: a fool wants to marry a woman and buys two wedding rings. He is supposed to meet her at a museum, but as he's ten minutes too early he tests the ring out on the statue of Venus. And then one sees how the stone hand contracts, and she becomes human. For she was under a curse, and when a man offers to marry her she is allowed to leave her stone dungeon and become human. She immediately falls in love with this fool, but she realizes after four or five months during which they are together that he is a fool, and she decides to become a statue again. She returns to the museum, steps on the pedestal, and while she's becoming stone she sings "Speak Low." The moment in which she became human is the only beautiful moment because it's a moment of love. And because you are asking about ménage à trois: sure, it's a ménage à trois, perhaps even a quadriga, because he, too, isn't the same anymore.

PO: Johnny detects in Esther a hint of his wife, but he is not able to recognize Nelly. Is this an unconscious decision of his character, not least also with regard to the guilt he carries with him?

CP: Well, everyone else recognizes her. The female proprietor but also her husband who flees the garden because he can't confront his guilt. At the train station everyone recognizes her as well. Only he doesn't. And she doesn't recognize herself. Because you only recognize yourself in the regard of the other. She could of course say to him, "Listen, Johnny, it's me. I had this surgery, but it's healed up." Spoken in a completely naturalistic way. But she would lose him that way. It's sort of like it when you fall in love and expect of the other to say, "I love you," but they don't. And then, when you then ask, "Do you actually love me?" the love is over, for with this question you are coercing the other. For it doesn't come on its own. Due to his guilt, Johnny doesn't recognize himself, or her, anymore, and that's what's brutal: she wants to become what she used to be so that he will recognize her and she gets a second chance. That's her pipe dream.

PO: When you wrote the script, did you know from the start how the film would end?

CP: The last line was "Nelly leaves." I like it as literature, but when we neared the end of the shooting I asked myself what these two words actually contain. Are we leaving with her—we, the narrators, the camera, the viewers? Or is she leaving us? After all, the two words contain both, so that in the end many questions remained unanswered. Until we understood that we cannot go with her. That which I suspected at the beginning—what these two words could mean—only really became clear to me at the end. But that's the purpose of shooting as well: to get a feeling for something and to comprehend it. Sometimes it's also the other way around.

PO: One wonders, too, whether the two might be able to continue, whether they could become again what they used to be.

CP: I am a huge fan of Douglas Sirk's films. One of the best aspects of his films is that at the moment when something is about to end this grandeur—what once used to be—reappears one more time. When at the moment of the eternal and miserable separation at the end we notice how deep the love between these people used to be. I think there's such an intensity in the looks that one feels how passionate this love, which at this moment ends forever, must have been. This is something I like about cinema: that termination is already part of the moment of appearance. Similar to how, when the people drive away with their loot after robbing a bank, we already know that they will be caught. But the moment was beautiful.

PO: I had exactly this feeling. That is the film's magic.

CP: That's interesting. You can theoretically write something like it into the script, but we did not really understand this until the end. Since we shot chronologically, it happened only at the last day of shooting. I have to say it was enlightening. We departed, each for themselves, and I think even the nonsmokers started smoking.

PO: How difficult was shooting, considering that you as well as the actors had to deal with a depressing topic?

CP: Often one hears from people shooting a comedy that the actual filming was horrible. And when you make a heavy film one hears how easygoing things were behind the camera. With this film, it was different still. We did not really shoot in Berlin but in Brandenburg, where we had a studio of sorts. We were in a kind of time bubble, and the countryside is quite nice there. When, after the end of a shooting day, one bicycles back to one's apartment, then one returns to reality, so that we were able to manage all of this fairly easily. Otherwise, it would have been rather horrible. We shot chronologically, which is always good because the actors as well as I myself and the others who are involved can get more easily into the story. We really filmed for eleven days in this basement. I think the film has a certain kind of airiness. I remember that my father said the summer of 1945 was the most beautiful one. Because it was hot, there was no police, no teachers, and no school; one was outside all day long, and the city was a playground. We tried to capture this in the film as well.

PO: Do you already have plans for the next film?

CP: After two historical films I'd like to do something in the present. I had talked a few times with the Bayerischen Rundfunk and Cornelia Ackers, whom I got to know two years ago, about *Polizeiruf*. I really wanted to make one because I really love Matthias Brandt—and I will start shooting in eight weeks. It will be a *Polizeiruf* that will consist of 50 percent interrogations. After that I have prepared a film I cowrote with Harun. It's an adaptation of Anna Seghers's *Transit*. It is one of our favorite books. It takes place in Marseille in 1940, so once again a historical film. This is why I am quite happy that in between I am shooting a *Polizeiruf*. Munich in 2014, in autumn, everything is muddy and real, so I don't need any costumes. I'm looking forward to it.

PO: With the Marseille location I assume the film will be more colorful, right? Germany postwar tristesse in *Phoenix* is quite oppressive.

CP: Yes, but when you drive out into the forest or to the lake then it is actually quite beautiful. A pretty country. I looked at so many photos, these Agfa color photos that existed since 1935. Even 1945 in the Tiergarten, when they cut down everything to have something to burn for heat, one can recognize what a beautiful country it is. I wanted to show this in the film as well. I told the cinematographer that I do not want any filters, no mud-tristesse. I wanted a really beautiful sky. I very much liked what Dominik Graf said about *Beloved Sisters*: the point is not what Schiller has to say to us today but what we have to say to Schiller. That's how one can approach historical materials. What do we have to communicate to history? We don't want to suck history dry but also give it something and narrate from our point of view. That's why I needed liveliness in form of wind, light, and sound.

"Uuuuuh, This Won't Only Be Pleasant"

Norbert Thomma and Christiane Peitz / 2014

From "'Uuuuuh, die Sache wird nicht nur angenehm,'" *Tagesspiegel*, September 23, 2014. Reprinted by permission. Translated by Marco Abel and Jaimey Fisher.

Norbert Thomma and Christiane Peitz: Mr. Petzold, all of your films take Germany as their topic. The RAF, the GDR, the postwar period. When was the first time that you realized with pleasure: Hey, I am German!

Christian Petzold: When West Germany beat England 3–1 at Wembley Stadium in 1972 during the European Championship. Netzer, Beckenbauer, Hoeneß, Grabowski. I could not believe that such beautiful soccer could come out of this grouchy country in which I grew up—incredible!

Thomma and Peitz: Do you have a specific Germany image in your head?

Petzold: There's none. When the French make an advertisement for Gauloises, it's quite easy. They show the copper roofs of Paris, a girl with a dress like Isabelle Adjani in [Jean Becker's] *One Deadly Summer*, a glass of red wine. . . . And Germany? Two men with beer bottles at a BBQ? Images of Germany have yet to be invented. In this regard, I'm in line with Jewish thought: the Messiah is yet to come.

Thomma and Peitz: And what's the sound of Germany?

Petzold: I was recently on a plane, and when we crossed through the clouds I thought: "Über den Wolken" ["Above the Clouds"] by Reinhard Mey is really a great song. Never before did someone sing lines such as "Irgendjemand kocht Kaffee/in der Luftaufsichtsbaracke" ["Someone is cooking coffee/in the aerial supervision barrack"]. What story does the song tell? That we Germans can breathe freely only above the clouds, not on earth, not on the "wet asphalt" of this song. It's the only good German folk song.

Thomma and Peitz: What are your three favorite Germany films?

Petzold: I love lists; I just don't like producing them myself. It's always guys who do this, as in Nick Hornby's novel, *High Fidelity*. But OK: *Alice in the Cities* by Wim Wenders, because when I was fourteen it was there that I saw for the first time how much world exists also in the cinema. It was shot in Wuppertal, and in the ice cream parlor Taormina, where I myself licked strawberry ice cream. Next is *Rocker* by Klaus Lemke. In our small town, there was the Haaner fair with a jaguar express, a fast carousel that drove through a cave. Cars sped by, girls screamed. There were tattooed guys, men with wide leather bands with rivets and Jim Morrison pants that emphasized the genitals. I saw *Rocker* and knew: this is the film from the cave. And Helmut Käutner's *Under the Bridges*. As the shitty Nazi system was crumbling, Käutner collects the rest of what was humane as if in a bomb shelter.

Thomma and Peitz: By now there are countless films about the Shoah. Now also yours.

Petzold: The room with Shoah films is much smaller than the room with lukewarm entertainment films with Walter Giller that take place in Italy. And there's hardly any film that is about those who return, which was the primary motive for me. Does literature exist about this? Heinrich Böll and Wolfgang Borchert's *Draußen vor der Tür* [*The Man Outside*], which was required reading in school during my time, but that's about it. We don't have films about homecoming; instead, we have *Heimatfilme*.[1] They look like electrical train worlds, with a reconstruction of the dream of harmonious happiness: there's a church, a market square, and the train always goes around in circles—it never escapes.

Thomma and Peitz: Your new film, *Phoenix*, is about survivors of the Nazi camps. When was the first time you had an idea about the Holocaust?

Petzold: When they showed Alain Resnais's *Night and Fog* in school. That's when the horror assumed an image for me. Later on, I learned that the West German delegation protested when the film was supposed to play at the Cannes Film Festival in 1956; they really took it out of competition.

Thomma and Peitz: What do you recall?

Petzold: The ribbing of the steel chair and the associations it triggered in me: tortures, executions, medical experiments. Resnais shows images of Auschwitz after war, the ruins, merely the traces. There's a long traveling shot across the area of the concentration camp, and we listen to a text by Paul Celan, something like: "Who will protect us when the perpetrators will return, will we be more alert . . ." The chair is a hairdresser's chair, perhaps completely harmless, but with these words it is pure horror.

Thomma and Peitz: Resnais also shows mountains of corpses.

---

1. The most popular film genre during the genre-heavy 1950s (although it likely started in the 1920s or 1930s and continues to today, the 1950s were considered its highpoint). They tend to be films that focus on small-town and rural life with conflicts frequently rendering those tradition-focused bastions against urban modernity.

Petzold: It's impossible to process those in their incomprehensible brutality. Back then I was eleven or twelve years old.

Thomma and Peitz: Christian Streich, soccer coach of SC Freiburg, told us that during school he was unprepared for such images, which overwhelmed him. He said that they completely disturbed him.

Petzold: That's right. It's impossible to process them. This is my experience to this day. As a soldier, Sam Fuller took part in the liberation of a concentration camp and filmed this with his 16mm camera, but he was never able to edit this material. Alfred Hitchcock, too, saw the corpses and was not able to make a film out of this.

Thomma and Peitz: Your parents left East for West Germany towards the end of the 1950s. You were born 1960 in West Germany. With what stories did you grow up?

Petzold: My parents did not talk much about this, neither about the GDR nor about National Socialism. The latter was a repressed topic, more for my mother because her father was a member of the *Waffen-SS*. My father must have experienced horrible things towards the end of the way, which deeply affected him. They also could not explain the Cold War to me. Their desire to go to the West was not an anti-communist reflex; they wanted to listen to American music, watch films with James Dean, wanted whitewall tires.

Thomma and Peitz: And yet your parents spent all vacations with you in the GDR.

Petzold: For me there was no North Sea, no Mallorca, just the East. Wolf Biermann wrote, "Here order is big—just like with the seven dwarfs." That's how I experienced the GDR: on Saturday, you eat plum cake underneath a tree, the official celebrations are obligatory, one lives in a bubble.

Thomma and Peitz: The West of that time was stuffy, too.

Petzold: But in a different way! I grew up in townhouse projects in North Rhine Westphalia. The secretary of transportation said that no citizen should live more than three minutes away from an autobahn exit, and that's how the region between Wuppertal and Dusseldorf looks.

Thomma and Peitz: Was there ever any consideration to return to the GDR?

Petzold: Yes, for my father. I was surprised by this. He was laid off in 1974, the consequence of the first oil crisis, and was unemployed for three and a half years. He realized: a townhouse has a living room a bedroom, two children's rooms—it is designed for men with a job, for the kitchen is the mother's realm. He no longer had a room for himself. He then left the house, took an alcoholic beverage with him, sat in his Citroen, and listened to classical music with closed eyes. A ghostly image. I understand well if people today feel humiliated at job centers, in a society in which everyone is supposed to find their identity through work. When someone asks you at a party, "What do you do?" you can hardly answer: I sit in my Citroen and listen to Beethoven. Notwithstanding all of the state's support one becomes a ghost, gets to the point of fading away. My father said, I will go back to the GDR. But then only the hours in the car became longer.

Thomma and Peitz: Soon we celebrate twenty-five years of the new Germany. Where were you on November 9, 1989?

Petzold: I was together with friends in Berlin-Wedding, near the Bornholmer Street. We heard the news on the radio and immediately went to the border crossing, watched how people crossed: that looked great. A few days later, I heard for the first time, "You all have too many foreigners." The next summer we road our bicycles to Königs Wusterhausen—my wife, Harun Farocki...

Thomma and Peitz: The filmmaker with whom you closely collaborate and have written all of your scripts.

Petzold: ... there was supposed to be a nice public outdoor swimming pool. Harun is half-Indian, my wife Turkish. When we arrived, they confronted us: what do you want here? We returned and thought: Uuuuuh, this won't only be pleasant.

Thomma and Peitz: Do you still see this today: East and West?

Petzold: Immediately. Not with every person, but the East went through an entirely different reconstruction. The GDR had no money to deconstruct the city centers; they let the historical core decay and built anew at the periphery—Halle-Neustadt. A nicely renovated center: that's how I recognize the East.

Thomma and Peitz: Do your children, eighteen and fourteen years old, still think in such categories?

Petzold: Oh, no. They move through Berlin without any East-West sense. Sometimes I show them where the Wall used to be, but those who didn't know it can barely notice the disappearance of the border.

Thomma and Peitz: What do you show visitors of Berlin?

Petzold: The longer I live in Berlin the more I need to have visitors from outside in order to perceive the city. It was only with Hanns Zischler's book *Berlin ist zu groß für Berlin* that I went back out to discover the city. This city doesn't know itself who it is, which you can tell from the debate about the Tempelhof Field. That's where I bike through the Hasenheide, a beautiful English park with valleys and the Rixdorfer Höhe, and then arrive at this airport that's flat like a pancake. Such an undefined part of the city is terrific. Simultaneously I'm in favor of a built, designed city. But after the fall of the Wall, Berlin was simply handed over to capitalism. Potsdamer Platz, Alexanderplatz, hardware stores at every corner, veritable eye sores, a desert around the main train station. The grandeur is missing.

Thomma and Peitz: In 1989, you studied at the dffb, the German Film and Television Academy, and made a small documentary film, *Ostwärts*, about the Bundesstraße [Highway] 2.

Petzold: Our teacher sent us out: "Kids, here are some cameras: go do something." The B2 connects Germany's South with the Northeast and passes through Berlin. One year after the fall of the Wall I started, at the Alexanderplatz, with one of the dffb's orange-colored busses. There was a drunken man in Burberry clothes, very expensively dressed, he waved to us and slurred: "Tassi!" We explained that we weren't a taxi, and he slurred: "Fooum'otel." We said, the Forum Hotel was right over there, but he didn't get it: "Drive me there," so we drove him a few meters. Traffic around the Alex is for a drunk person quite dangerous. It turned out that the man was a manager who purchased properties for funds and had on this day appropriated several prime properties—that's what he'd celebrated. He gave us 50 DM for our services.

Thomma and Peitz: You are an obsessive cinemagoer and . . .

Petzold: . . . because of the children, it has decreased. I still watch almost every day one film, but now much more on DVD. I have about 1,200 at home. When I go to the cinema, then preferably alone, precisely because others are there as well. Cinema is a location of collective loneliness.

Thomma and Peitz: The director Pepe Danquart likes to sit all the way in the front in order to be completely inside the film.

Petzold: Those who sit in the first row, according to Rolf Dieter Brinkman in his poem "Piloten" ["Pilots"], would like to fly away with the film. I don't want this. I prefer to sit in row ten, on the right side. There I have a bit of distance and can leave earlier, without bothering anyone. For me, cinema is: to see a silhouette of viewers' heads and behind it the screen.

Thomma and Peitz: The three best Berlin cinemas are . . . ?

Petzold: The FSK at the Oranienplatz. I walk there and watch whatever they are playing. That's the opposite of DVDs. I do not make a purchasing decision. Really important is the question of what you do afterward. You need a path afterwards that does the film good. That's why I like the Neue Off in Neukölln, as well as the Zoo Palast and the Delphi with their surroundings. The old Arsenal would be the best cinema in the city, but now it is at Potsdamer Platz, which is truly the end.

Thomma and Peitz: And the three best films of all time?

Petzold: I've seen *Vertigo* fifty times. Because the film approaches dreaming without fog, without flowering meadow in beautiful light. It shows obsession: you observe a perverse guy who tries to get an erection again. And the women are made up for this purpose. I've also hated the film at least twenty times. *Deer Hunter* by Michael Cimino is one of the great masterworks. And I also include the animated film *Spirited Away* by Hayao Miyazaki, which I once watched with my children when they were small: a girl moves with her parents and is being torn out of her life. The film doesn't show this, which is great. Bad films show at the beginning happiness, a wholesome world, that which the heroes lose. Good films show the lost person who suffers from the loss. At some point the parents transform into pigs. At that moment half the audience left—numerous children had to be carried out.

Thomma and Peitz: And yours?

Petzold: They are tough.

Thomma and Peitz: Mr. Petzold, you once said, "I am never lonely when I write." Your close friend and collaborator Harun Farocki died this summer of a heart attack, when he was seventy.

Petzold: I still have projects we did together. I'm currently shooting a *Polizeiruf*. Then I'll do *Transit* based on Anna Seghers, which we also still wrote together. So, I have distractions. I always ride my bicycle from Kreuzberg across the Modersohn bridge to him in Friedrichshain. Through the Knorrpromenade, where around the corner is a fan bar of Borussia Mönchengladbach; I watch soccer there. Next year I'll take a break. I have to think about how I'll go on without Harun. At this moment, I can't even imagine it.

To Truly See: Christian Petzold at the dffb

Volker Pantenburg and Michael Baute / 2015

From "Richtig sehen: Christian Petzold an der dffb," *Über Christian Petzold*, eds. Ilka Brombach and Tina Kaiser (Berlin: Vorwerk 8, 2018): 61–75. Reprinted by permission. Translated by Aylin Bademsoy.

The Beginnings

Actually, I didn't come to the film academy because I had the desire to produce. The wish to make pictures is actually a myth. I wasn't in the academy because there was a flood of images in me and because I had seen so many things. On the contrary: I hadn't seen anything. While watching films at the Institute for Theater Studies at the Free University in Berlin, I sensed something, but I hadn't yet opened my eyes. Ludger Blanke, whom I met together with other theater scholars at the Free University, entered the film academy in 1984—and, of course, we also took part whenever we could, because the dffb is a legend. I think it's the best institution that the FRG ever brought forth. Ludger always talked about what he was doing there. And I met his fellow students, among others Michel Freericks. Ludger also talked about the seminars of Harun Farocki, who in my view was a star because of *Filmkritik*, and I asked if I could join in. And that was exactly why I went to the film academy, because of such seminars. Not because I really wanted to hold a camera. First, I wanted to see films. To "truly see." When I started at the dffb I wrote thousands of little scenes. The diverse film drafts in my dffb record are all projects that I overzealously registered.

When I had seminars with Farocki and Hartmut Bitomsky, I already had three years of experience with production. First, I needed to look. In the first year at the dffb, you have to go to the film laboratory, cut, do sound, light, and camerawork. You have to do all that for six, seven weeks. Amazing! That's more than just learning how to brush your teeth; it is to feel an apparatus. But the two years after that I basically didn't feel like making a film at all. That we made films anyway was for us just to leave something behind, to have a memory trace. For me those weren't works but rather etudes. I had the feeling that I'd manage to write stories anyway. I didn't need an American script doctor for that. That was obviously also a mistake, for you do need it. But first the pendulum has to swing wide, to the other end.

dffb, 1988

I was in the cohort of '88. That was a great cohort, free of the "Feuerzangenbowle-mentality."[1] We hang between the cinema of the 1970s and the not yet existing cinema of the 1990s. That's why we battled farcical, belated conflicts, but at the same time we realized that these were farces, and we sensed that something had to change.

Usually, each cohort was divided into three. Automatically, there was Team Poetry, which stood for, in a disparaging sense, fog machines at the Wannsee. Second was Team American Cinema, a little bit in the direction of *steadicam*, they told stories of cocaine dealers, filmed into nostrils with endoscopic cameras, and lionized Alfred Vohrer as modern. I belonged to the third group: Team Avant-Garde-Destruction. Christian Frosch and Jan Ralske were also part of it. In our self-conception, we couldn't make films anymore, which is a disaster for people who just started at a film academy. But we didn't choose it; we just fell into it somehow. And especially the people in Farocki's seminars were mostly Avant-Garde-Destruction types; the others obviously went to the more practical seminars. There was a division: "nonfiction" versus "fiction." In the aftermath, one can see how ridiculous that was. It's also striking that it took a while until those who were in the seminar with me made films. Over-reflection can also lead to passivity.

Seminars: Harun Farocki

The seminars with Harun were always structured as follows. In the morning, we watched the film in the movie theater, then we walked up to the cutting room and sat around the editing table with 35mm copies of some German motion pictures that were easy to get hold of. That wasn't about being precise and working on the best copies from New York, like with other lecturers, but working with what was there in that moment. And then we went through them take by take; after

---

1. "Feuerzangenbowle" refers to the Christmas or New Year's party tradition of burning a block of sugar into an alcoholic beverage that is then communally shared. Here, Petzold means a freewheeling, nostalgic escapism.

each take there was a break, where we pondered: why does this take follow that one, what happened there, what kind of decision is that? There I felt for the first time that the closing of each scene is already narration and not only handcraft in the sense of "That's a bit boring, let's approach it from this side now." Everything has narrative exigency, each change of perspective. And then, after we worked through a whole roll until the afternoon, we went back to the movie theater with this roll and saw the whole projected film once more. And this had a surprising effect . . . Perhaps it's also what distinguishes Harun's films: that he disassembles the world, but without unraveling it, for a new myth emerges at the end. Basically, that's also what distinguished him from the "Red Decade," where people unravel the world and nothing was left: everything was lost, dead.

What Harun did was the most intense experience I had in a seminar: editing table, a copy, watching it projected in the movie theater first, then looking at each take one by one. Then to take the whole 35mm roll again—which took about eighteen minutes—to go back to the cinema and see it in context. That all sounds as if the myth or the secret of a film would be ruined. But, in fact, the precise opposite was the case. One dissolved something, and in the end it was even more mysterious than before. The first seminar was entitled: "How to See Films." No, the first one's title was: "The cameraman is a gravedigger at the bed of the film." Harun taught together with Axel Block. We saw *To Live and Die in L.A.*, which surprised me a lot. I thought I'd only see avant-garde films or arthouse cinema, but that was the exact opposite. *The Mackintosh Man* by John Huston, with Paul Newman, also quite surprised me, especially one scene. Paul Newman is kidnapped and hidden in a furnished basement apartment. An agent story. He showers and lies down on the sofa in his bathrobe. One of the kidnappers, the beautiful one, brings his breakfast. And he gestures to her to put the tray on his lap. Harun looked at this gesture nine or ten times at the cutting table. That's something I really like, he said, that in midst of an agent story an actor moves out of the agent story and presents his stardom with a gesture and hence eroticizes the scene and that, on the other hand, it becomes an espionage story again when the kidnapped comes back to the story—reenters the narrative—with the little means he has. That surprised me, because I thought Harun hated any kind of naturalist "method acting" or identification acting and was actually a Brechtian. I had read many texts by him that said German actors should cut out their facial musculature. And this was quite the opposite, which irritated me—greatly irritated me, indeed.

Harun really taught through his own enthusiasm—one always felt that Harun himself just discovered something in that very moment. And through us he could share this discovery with the group, and the group gave something back. His thoughts gradually elaborated, developed while speaking. That's why these seminars weren't theoretical at all. It always felt like everything you knew about a film already broke off through the concept of "take by take" and "discover, discover, discover," and after the discovery: enjoy. Not only the discovery, but also the film. The more you reflect on a film, the richer it looks back at you.

There was a scene at the very beginning of *To Live and Die in L.A.* The actor, who was later successful in a TV show [William Petersen], stands on a bridge and is about to bungee jump. But we don't know yet what he's about to do. Previously, he had given his buddy, who was going to be on duty for only one more week and then retire, a fishing rod. And now he is standing up there, the camera circling around and hovering above him, and you see that there is an abyss in front of him, where he'll be jumping down. That is all in one take. Then, Harun asked Axel how that was shot. Axel Block left (that was often the case with those two: they left, did some research mostly at the library, and came back with information). In this case, Block told us about a new light metal crane arm onto which you could mount a light 35mm Arri camera—Robby Muller I think was the cameraman—which then did this strange remote-controlled bow movement. Harun liked that a lot, not only because it was a technical novelty but also due to the very simple thought behind it: to show the effect before the cause. To show a man who stands at the edge of an abyss. One can read something in his face. You only get to know later what it was, but you get a sense of it already.

Or a sequence in *Rumble Fish* by Coppola. Mickey Rourke and Steve are both drunk and walking on a street of an industrial suburb. Steve says: "My God, why didn't we stay on the main road? Everything's so tight here, that's scary." And then the camera is above and moves on a rail system like a helicopter, and you can see them down there very small like in a gorge. One of the students criticized it for being a duplication. First the sentence, "I am scared, that's like a gorge," and then the image: aha! It's really like a gorge. That made Harun think. At lunch break, he said that he was not coming with us to the fucking cafeteria of the SFB [Sender Freies Berlin, a Western public radio and TV station nearby—eds.]. He went to the library instead. He always had a little mechanical typewriter with him, on which he wrote little texts, little Selznick memos. And then he came back and gave us these texts, run off of a matrix, like in elementary school. And in this little text he wrote, roughly: suggesting that an image of a gorge and someone saying, "It's like a gorge here," are one and the same presupposes that the sentence and image are identical, yet the difference is cinema.

I always felt like Harun didn't know these things previously either. He sensed something and put it into public view. Then, in his conversing with us, or in our conversing with him and with each other, he understood something that we sensed but didn't know yet. That is a seminar as it ought to be.

Seminars: Hartmut Bitomsky

The seminars of Hartmut Bitomsky were more pedagogical. He had a brilliant seminar, where I learned a lot. The seminar proceeded as he picked a scene from a film. We watched [Godard's] *Contempt* and [David Lynch's] *Blue Velvet*. And he said, "Now sketch out the floor plan of the apartment. Where is the kitchen, where is the bathroom?" Film strips down space, organizes space and time. It organizes them sometimes only because the conditions are restricting. And sometimes it organizes them in order to create suspense. And sometimes a film organizes space in a way that time lasts and sometimes so that time disappears. Once you register what's there, at this point you become a director. As a person makes films, they are confronted with reality, with true relations. And you have to think about: How do I film that, where do I put the camera? Where will this take happen and where will the next one be so that they can yield to a third take? There are given conditions: the architecture itself implements conditions of life. Space is categorized; a townhouse is different from a villa. That's what Harun Farocki and Hartmut Bitomsky perhaps wanted in their seminars: they wanted to drive us away from the interchangeability of the TV and cinema apartments and realisms of the German film at the time.

At the time I worked on films of Hartmut Bitomsky: *Das Kino un der Wind und die Photographie* and *Die UFA*. I also got involved in Harun's works. There you learned how to do research, how to look. For Harun I drove to all those commercial films, for *Ein Tag im Leben der Endverbraucher*. You notice that what you do at the seminar is actually production. And you can also make films of these production conditions, be an assistant or a researcher. But the way of talking about the cinema has already a lot in common with making films. Making cinema and TV films consists 99 percent of speaking. You speak with costume designers and makeup artists. And the way of speaking wasn't so much different from the one in the seminars. When you read Bitomsky's critique of [John Cassavetes's] *Love Streams*. . . . He saw it only once at the Berlinale and can recall things that today most people, who have a DVD of it in front of themselves, could not. I think not only what is remembered but also the act of remembering has to be written down as part of a text.

Seminars: Helmut Färber

Färber had obtained all these one-reelers from Munich for the film history seminars, on Griffith, for example. They were all expensively put on 35mm. We messed them up later, scratched them twice while working at the editing table.

After that we never received copies from Munich again. We had a production manager back then, his name was Müller, he came to the cinema and watched them with us. That's the case at all elite institutions. If you got through the filter of the vast number of applicants and were accepted, then you landed in the myth. And the relationship between the staff and the students is also a class relation. So Färber came with his Griffith films, and we watched them in the cinema. And then this Müller, who actually was some kind of production manager, came in. He watched these films for about thirty minutes, left, and told Färber that it was like Johann Peter Hebel's *Schatzkästlein des rheinischen Hausfreundes* [1811]. Färber was happy for three days about that. A single sentence summed up that cinema provided the USA what Hebel achieved with his texts here in Germany. They're information but also folklore. We talked about that for three days, and we all felt that there was a reconciliation with the working class. There were between five and ten students in the seminars of Färber, Farocki, Bitomsky. Not more, from the whole film academy, which always has about sixty students. The others couldn't see the point in attending: "We've been here for five years and have production resources, material, films, VW buses, lights. We have to make use of that, as we'll never have that again." That argumentation touched my core too, as there's a truth in it. But, on the other hand, I felt, "When I have the camera in my hands, I have absolutely no clue what to do with it." I thought rather, "I can make films later. First, I have to do something else, I have to ditch a lot of things, especially the academic stuff"—which I despise to this day. What I had at the Institute for Theater Studies at the Free University [FU]: to categorize films, to museumize them—I couldn't stand that, for they have to stay alive. I was basically an FU student, who worked his first two years on ripping the FU off his bones.

Films: *Ostwärts*

Ostwärts was developed during the seminar with Peter Nestler. He said, "Come, we drive out now and observe the East. Now, you all are here in Berlin, you have cameras and everything, production resources. And first of all, we have to observe. I'm interested in that myself." We drove towards Poland, then to the boat lift Niederfinow, and looked at Jewish cemeteries, which had been vandalized immediately after 1989. Nestler showed us all that. It thrilled me a lot. Once he said, "What we see here is post-communism. The *Treuhand* [trust agency] is here now.[2] The work environment here is being demolished at the moment. These people don't even know yet what they are in for. They won't have any jobs soon.

---

2. The controversial agency created in 1990 by the (soon-to-be-dissolved) East German government to sell East German state assets to private interests.

They will live in areas where there is no production. Those will all become dying cities." And we could see that.

Ostwärts consists of multiple blocks. The three interviews about people helplessly trying to make sense of the circumstances are central. This desperate situation of GDR society, which relied on industrial work and was suddenly confronted with ruins, and people wanted to breathe new life into them, only they didn't know how. And then people from the West who haven't dealt with production in a long time come and say, "We will do something here. We will offer computer classes and Face Art Royal." People from the East think that you can earn something with that. And people from the West think that this is some kind of new California. We liked that madness a lot. Yet there was always the moral question: Do I take these people seriously? Am I making fun of them? That became a problem for me when I showed the film. When I showed it for the submission, everyone laughed at the poor woman who painted people's faces. Then I thought to myself, "Nah, I won't drive to the East and make these people look like fools."

Projects: A Culture Magazine

Around 1990, Farocki, Bitomsky, and Michael Klier wanted to publish a culture magazine together with the dffb students. An editorial department from Bremen gave us the opportunity to produce a documentary TV show with diverse contributions. We had already started to produce some of the clips. I was doing research for Bitomsky. There are agencies for TV, just like there is AP or Reuters for the newspapers. In a headquarters located in the Hessischer Rundfunk, everything that was produced around the world was screened on hundreds of monitors, and TV channels could buy the material. I drove there and saw how a referee in Brazil was hanged on a crossbar by an outraged audience. That was obviously not bought despite it being sensational material; such a thing cannot be shown on TV. Bitomsky wanted to make a film about this room, the decisions of the editors, and how they choose.

The second contribution I worked on dealt with the portrayal of symbolic photos. When there is a news story on refugees in the [daily] newscast the *Tagesschau*, there's a picture in the background. Back then it was on the Blue Box, today it's on the Green Screen. How does that image change over the course of the years? I wanted to do that together with Harun. We had also already collected the clips. You could observe that at the beginning there was still a family looking as if they were about to open a Greek restaurant. Later, that turned into an undefinable mass in front of a toll gate. Hence, one could've done a social history of the FRG on the basis of these symbolic photos.

Films: *Abzüge*

The culture magazine came to nothing, but I made a film contribution for it, which I never finished: *Abzüge*. The remains are still somewhere in my office—a beta, half-cut version. It's a pity that it's unfinished because it was really beautiful footage. Bernd Löhr of my cohort did great camerawork. But then there was my final film project, *Pilots*, and I said to myself that I won't make any documentaries anymore.

Abzüge was a film on the laboratory of Foto Wegert in Lichtenrade. Millions of photographs that have been shot in Berlin are all developed there. They flash by on assembly lines and are packed in bags mechanically for each customer. There were eight students employed to sort out blurred or overexposed pictures. Those pictures were printed first but then dumped. The students were employed also by the police for detecting child pornography.

I interviewed these students, and they talked about the fast-track of the pictures. We hardly recognized anything there, while they recognized the course of history. The colors of Christmas, Easter, children's birthdays, company parties—they could see all this just by looking at the flash. And they told me that there was always a lot of sex, nudes. I asked them, "What about 1989, the fall of the Berlin Wall, how did the pictures change?" And they answered that at daytime you could see the chopping and the "Mauerspechte,"[3] but at night they also took nude photos of themselves: sex-selfies.

While I recorded the students there, the doors of the darkroom opened, and a blind man came out. He was working there in the darkroom as a profiler. At the time, [Jonathan Demme's] *The Silence of the Lambs* had just come out, which we also saw in Harun Farocki's seminar. Harun and I were thrilled, and we read the original draft by Thomas Harris, where a profiler appears for the first time. To me, the laboratory depicted the same: *The Silence of the Lambs* was in this Berlin lab. I wanted to add a comment to the film; I was actually pretty close to finishing it. Perhaps I should get the material out again. But to me it was clear that I cannot make documentaries.

Networking/Production

In the group that watched films with Harun, there was, of course, no commissioning producer. We didn't get anything out of these seminars that would help us in the job market. We weren't represented at festivals. The others traveled around,

---

3. Literally "wall woodpeckers," or those who hammered, chiseled, or otherwise acted to dismantle the Berlin Wall after it was opened in November 1989.

networked, and went to commissioning producers' meetings. We had nothing to show in this regard. Very different was, for example, Benedikt Neuenfels, who was also in my cohort. They made films like crazy and also found producers. To this day, I am friends with Benedikt Neuenfels, because I still believe that he might have been right. Meanwhile, we didn't have a network at all, and didn't know anyone.

My friendship with Benedikt began actually only after the dffb. In conversations with him, I noticed that he actually admired us, because they felt like they were just scratching the surface in order to operate a machinery that basically abused the film academy. That was where the machinery extracted its talents. In comparison, we were a little bit like a monastery cell. Perhaps it was something like a balance that came into being. After three, four years at the academy I started to make films. By then I felt like, "This is the right moment now. I understand how you can narrate something." I still remember we had seen Jean Eustache's *My Little Loves* in a seminar. The first five minutes are one of the most sensual openings of a film. I only grasped this in the seminar. The grandmother brings the boy a coffee, the window is there. . . . That, on the one hand, cinema reproduces reality fantastically and that, on the other hand, it is itself a reality: I could talk with the others of my cohort—Mark Schlichter, Benedikt Neuenfels, Conny Walter—about such things. But I can tell the following to all of you: One learns best at the editing table.

One learns everything when one sees the films on the editing table. Even acting direction. All other things have to be brought along already. Empathy, how you move at a shooting location within the set-economy . . . you can't learn these things in seminars. The problem with the film academy is that you have seventeen directors. And they have to collaborate. And later you don't have similar situations. There is never a set where a director visits the other. With *Dreileben* we tried that, Dominik [Graf], Christoph [Hochhäusler], and I. That was a wonderful experience and reminded all three of us of our times at the various film academies.

The variety of the films produced by my cohort was linked to the different films we saw. To me, Alexander Kluge was important; *Yesterday Girl*, which we saw in Harun's seminar. There, Harun's enthusiasm was less directed at the construction than at the woman. That led me to make *Das warme Geld*. I thought that there was no such cinema anymore. And I wanted to reestablish the connection to the early New German Cinema. Leos Carax's film *Mauvais Sang* was possibly the film that Wolfgang Schmidt took as a starting point for *Cannae*. And for Thomas Arslan, it was surely Philippe Garrel. One looks for a connection. And the second Nouvelle Vague was kind of a second laboratory. These are people who in part worked together for the *Cahiers*. For example, we saw André Téchiné's

Thieves, which made a big impression on me. Godard and François Truffaut were being rediscovered then. There's this quote by Helmut Färber: you have to make films in a way that in twenty years one can see how people lived, loved, and labored back then. And that you could see in these films; in Visconti's as well as Philippe Garrel's, or in Rossellini's *Anima nera* and *Europe 51* or *Fear*. In *Fear*, there's this 360-degree rotation around a family, where the rotation establishes the family but also determines it: The woman, the man, the kids. The man had come back from the war, and the woman isn't an academic anymore, just a mother. That's shown by the rotation. Before the woman realizes what happens to her, the movement of the camera says: "That's going to happen." There you see how the discovery of the 360-degree rotation must have occurred to Rossellini that day.

Films: *The Warm Money*

At the beginning, when I was still an auditor, Farocki sometimes made me look like a fool because I came from the university. Our friendship was established later as we played soccer together and went swimming in the open-air pools. I've always written stories and gave him the story of *The Warm Money*. He said he liked it, and there it began.

The films that all of us saw when we came to the academy, by Gerd Conradt and others, in whose tradition we automatically stood—and we liked to reside there—namely, to engage with the society, to examine it, and to build labs . . . I thought: that's over. In March 1990, there was the GDR's last Chamber election, where Helmut Kohl's puppet, [Lothar de] Mazière, was elected. It was clear to all of us that the GDR was going to be cleared—and with that a lot of other things.

During this time, 1989–90, Harun was the only one who immediately, from December 1989 until March 1990, drove with the seminar to East Berlin in order to meet people. Back then, there were these documentary film studios, Dok Leipzig and Dok Berlin. We met them all. They showed us their films, we showed them ours. That's how we saw the films of Jürgen Böttcher. All of us dealt with Germany. We didn't want to imitate films. But at that point it was already clear what had influenced us—just that we didn't know it yet. Angela Schanelec, for example, writes incredibly beautiful dialogue. *I Stayed in Berlin All Summer* and *My Sister's Good Fortune* are incredibly beautiful films. And then there was this film by Thomas Schultz, *Zwischen Gebäuden*, which impressed us a lot. But at the same time, some of us didn't have any ambitions, which I don't consider a bad thing at all. I didn't really understand myself at that time, but I knew that I was ambitious.

In regard to the notion "Berlin School," we actually didn't feel like the films were communicating with each other. People communicated, but not their films. That came ten years later, with the beginning of the 2000s, and was linked to the success some of us had with films and the fact that we were there at the same time. We noticed that others saw these films together, and that Christoph Hochhäusler in Munich, Ulrich Köhler in Hamburg, as well as some others oriented themselves towards these films. Something from our seminars went a long way.

The filmmaker who impressed me most was Dominik Graf. He taught in the summer of 1990 and made one film after the other. Harun did the same. I didn't want to have *one* project either that was all encompassing and then became an insane piece. Instead, I preferred to do one thing and then not something completely different but something close alongside. If I overlooked something or didn't have time for it, I'd say to myself, let's look at it now. Kind of a continuity. And that's also related a little bit to the films that we watched in the seminars. There were, after all, a lot of B-movies included, from people who produced nonstop. No matter if it's Rossellini or Godard or Garrel: they all worked all the time.

Interregnum

The most beautiful time is the interregnum. From 1988, when I began, until my graduation in 1994, there was only one interregnum at the dffb. The rectors at that time—Martin Wieben, Reinhard Hauff, Thomas Koebner—all came from very diverse fields: an editor, a director, an academic. But actually that's completely irrelevant. The place is basically ungovernable, in the best sense of the word. If anything, the academy would change the director, rather than the director changing the academy.

The *taz* asked Ludger, Thomas Arslan, and me for an interview on one of these yearly recurring themes: "Where is German film going?" or something like that. Christiane Peitz was the interviewer, and we said to her, "We are glad that we may fail here." In the *taz* that sounded like we all considered ourselves to be Helmut Berger, walked around in white jeans and thought we could live a Bohemian life with our scholarship (which back then was still available at the dffb) for five years. But what we meant was something else: we don't have to produce for a market, we can observe the market. That, however, sounded like we were bragging so much that after the interview we were asked to come to the administration office where the director said, "Are you insane? If the board of trustees, the sponsors, read that, we'll be finished." There I noticed for the first time that you had to be more careful with what you say. But actually there's some truth in what [Christoph] Schlingensief later called "Scheitern als Chance" ("Failure as a chance").

It's imprinted on my memory as follows: that for five years one could talk, watch, and drop into a lab—in a space surrounded by all the films one wants to see, but where one is also a little bit cut off from history. You wake up at seven o'clock in the morning, have breakfast, go to the academy, and sit there in a seminar for ten hours, watch films, and fathom something. Those were the happiest years.

The Cinema Is a Warehouse of Memory: A Conversation among Christian Petzold, Robert Fischer, and Jaimey Fisher

Robert Fischer and Jaimey Fisher / 2016

From *Senses of Cinema*, no. 84 (September 2017). Reprinted by permission.

Jaimey Fisher: I had a question about your collaboration with Harun Farocki, since this must be a transitional phase in your career in light of his death in 2014. You collaborated with Farocki on all your work through *Polizeiruf 110: Circles*, but I have not so much heard from you what he contributed to your films, which themes, for example. You've explained how you worked together, how exactly you collaborated, but not so much what his cinema has meant for you in general.

Christian Petzold: It's true, it's a good question, because I always tend to explain only how we worked together. But what is most important is how we would go places together and float things to each other, that is, we would go for long walks, miles upon miles, and look at architecture together and, at the same time, discussed stories.

Sometimes they were just galvanizing observations, for example, he would pose a question like "Which American novel takes up class struggle in the US?" Everyone immediately thinks of *Grapes of Wrath*, but Harun came up with James M. Cain's *The Postman Always Rings Twice*. He also thought that [Luchino] Visconti understood how the Cain novel engages homosexuality and racism as well, insights that Visconti then worked into his film *Obsession*. Harun believed that American B-movies work through these great themes by having them truly unfold between the people. Whereas on German television, even in prime time, we have commentators standing around with those advertisements on the collars of their shirts, for example during sport shows (Mercedes, champagne, or whatever). But the working through of real material is definitely there in the tradition of the US B-movies.

That kind of observation got us to thinking, and out of that we developed *Jerichow*. We had made *Yella* in this area in Wittenberge, and we were walking around once again, and you could see just how broken the working class was there, in this former railroad town, but now the unemployment is like 80 percent in the city—it's a ghost town. This had us thinking of *Deer Hunter*, also a film about the disappearance of an industry, the steel industry in Pittsburgh. What do you do with all the young men who used to work in it? You send them to war, just as has been the case for thousands of years: when there is no work, just send people to fight. And then you'll get a new economic miracle afterward. And Cimino tells us exactly this story, but without even mentioning unemployment, etc.

From these kinds of conversations, we would derive the scripts. I had a public conversation with Rosa von Praunheim at the film school in Potsdam, and he was saying Harun is so cold and you're so warm, as if we were like hot and cold water, red and blue on the faucet. I replied, "That's a totally wrong theory." It would seem to suggest that the documentary is cold and feature film warm. But in our work it was always so: I was the one who would want to create order, and he was the one who liked to play around with the romantic dialogue.

For *Wolfsburg*, for example, he wrote the first dialogue when the man forgets his wife in the living room. He turns the light off, and she complains. He doesn't have any empathy; he doesn't think of others. This is where the audience can get a sense of how he could leave a child lying, dying on the ground.

Robert Fischer: But the work method was that *you* wrote the scripts after your conversations and your walks and then gave it to him when the script was done, to read, and he offered advice on its overall shape, no?

CP: Yeah, that's true, but it certainly was work to finish the writing, and, to be honest, I would have been happy to give it to Harun to do. I usually started by writing the first seven, eight, nine scenes, maybe thirty to forty pages, and he would read them. And we would think about how it was then supposed to go, how the yarn could be spun further. I would write some more, and then he would say, now you have to throw the first seven scenes out, it just does not work.

After all, he is the master of ellipses—I really learned that from him. Cinema is what you leave out. But then I would still have the impression, when writing, that nobody is going to understand this or that; but what you simply omit, the audience will understand.

With *Polizeiruf*, too, the viewer would have to work more. For example, viewers might get: "Detective gets out of the car, right door, short dolly, rings, 'Come in!' door opens, through living room, down the stairs"—that kind of thing takes nine and a half minutes. If one were to leave that out then one has a lot more room to explore, has more to do. Of course, to shoot that kind of meaningless minutia is also a lot of work, at least for the cameraman.

JF: I wanted to ask you a bit about *Phoenix* and about *Barbara* as well. Can you say something about the decision to make this kind of historical film? And how you, in these films, work with genre—which, as you know, I think is a recurring key question with your work. But it seems to me that these historical dramas that you have recently made are simultaneously critiques of the sort of historical films that have recently been produced in Germany.

CP: I read a very beautiful sentence by Truffaut as he was criticizing Jean Renoir about how the historical film has to be produced in a studio. If the winds in such a film are from today, wrote Truffaut about Renoir's *The Golden Coach*, that simply does not work. Renoir had shown a carriage in it, and Truffaut said that just did not work: we have to create a completely artificial world for such films to be persuasive.

And I believed that for a good while, thinking that I could not make a historical drama because I simply cannot bear to be in the studio. But then I started to think maybe Renoir had been right, after all: that we, today, with our contemporary winds and in our contemporary sunlight, should think about the past from that perspective.

I agree with this: the question is not what the GDR in 1980 means to us, but rather what do we, the future, mean to the people in the GDR in 1980, who were living in a system in utter collapse. How are they keeping it together? I think that we, from the perspective of today, have to be humble. That's what interested me in this historical drama.

Phoenix had much more of a laboratory character, much more of the studio. With *Barbara*, the GDR still exists in many ways; you just have to drive five minutes from Berlin, and the GDR starts in certain ways. I remember something Hans [Fromm] said when we were there: we were back in Wittenberge, and we saw a street that had been repaved in the most expensive way, with new asphalt and bus stops with LED lighting, and then this street just ends. And Hans got out of the car and said: I want to have my solidarity tax back![1]

With *Phoenix*, the sort of fascism in Germany during the Nazi period does not exist anymore, so we really had to recreate it in the laboratory, so to say, in the studio.

JF: *Phoenix*'s reception in the US was much more positive than in Germany. Do you have a theory about this divide?

CP: Yeah, first, that really did bolster my confidence a bit. The Americans are OK with me, as are the French.

---

1. A reference to a tax paid by Germans to support the post-1990 absorption of the former East Germany into "new states" of the Federal Republic.

That was certainly harder in Germany. For me, the distance between pulp [*Kolportage*] and fascism is not so far apart. I think that Visconti had a similar insight when he staged the murder of Röhm, with Wagner's "The Ride of the Valkyries," etc., in *The Damned*. The gay, orgiastic group depicted in the film is then slaughtered by the SS people. It's an amazing scene.

And *The Damned* is also not loved in Germany—it is the hardest to locate of all of Visconti's films. Otherwise, Germans love his films. Fascism is pulp [*Kolportage*], and that is not looked upon positively here in Germany, as we have to have films [on fascism/Nazism] to which we can send our school classes. And *Phoenix* is just not appropriate for such a thing.

And there's something else that is relevant that we discussed on the second-to-last day of shooting. We thought that after Nelly sings, she goes out the door and into the light, and her longtime friends stay back. We discussed what the camera should do, whether it should go with her, because we, the audience, certainly want to go with her as she leaves.

But we thought, "No, we should stay," because we belong, indeed, to those who stayed. In *Phoenix*, in this way, we have, so to say, dismantled and destroyed our own culture. We do not allow the viewers to go with the remnants of the culture to Tel Aviv [as Nelly might—JF] and pretend we're going to be happy in a Kibbutz. And that was a big decision for us during the shoot on that second-to-last day. I think it is probably something that Germans did not want to hear, that they had to stay back.

JF: And, with *Phoenix*, I was also curious whether you worked with rubble films, the films made at and about this time, that is, shortly after the war.

CP: Only the one, [Wolfgang Staudte's] *The Murderers Are Among Us*, in part because, I have to admit, I'm just a Hildegard Knef fan. I really find it interesting what she ended up doing during the 1950s.

I like Staudte a lot, but even he makes an angel out of a survivor coming back from the camp. These camp inmates, after all, had been selected, killed, completely destroyed, their culture annihilated—and they have to come back [to Germany] to save us! I wondered if the postwar Germans had all gone crazy. And I thought that I'm not going to watch any more of this, I'm only going to read about it.

JF: To follow-up on Staudte's *The Murderers Are Among Us*, I think Fassbinder also worked with that film when he made *The Marriage of Maria Braun*. I thought of the Fassbinder film when I saw *Phoenix*, for instance, with the kitchen and the table as a particular space of conflict in this time.

CP: Well, I have seen a lot of films in my life and will continue to see a lot, simply because I like watching films. But with certain films I avoid seeing them around the time I am working on a project because I worry that they will become too close to the film I am making. For example, I notice now that in *Jerichow* there is plenty of the Tay Garnett film, which I did not even realize at the time. It is the same with the cellar scenes in *Phoenix* and the Fassbinder. But these are souvenir pictures [*Erinnerungsbilder*] of Fassbinder. That is what the cinema for: it is a warehouse of memory.

JF: There are references in both *Barbara* and *Phoenix* to Walter Benjamin. In *Phoenix*, for example, there is a picture on the Wall, the Klee picture "Angelus Novus."

CP: Yeah, and it cost me 900 euro! You are right, I absolutely wanted that picture in the film: it's the angel that is being pushed forward but that looks back at us. I think that's the historical drama, that we are driven forward but that we do look back. That's how the historical drama should be.

JF: It's that way in *Barbara*, too, I think, when Barbara looks back from the bike, against the wind.

CP: Yes, exactly, that is the same look back.

RF: Last night, we had here at the festival a world premiere of *Polizeiruf 110: Wolves*; if I'm counting correctly, that was the fourteenth long-form film, and the second *Polizeiruf* that you have made. The first was *Polizeiruf 110: Circles*, made one year ago, and another one, a third, will follow, as we heard yesterday.

Your last film for the cinema was *Phoenix* in 2014, but now two *Polizeirufe*, one after the other. The question would be, of course, what attracted you to contribute episodes to an ongoing television series?

CP: At first, I was approached by Cornelia Ackers, the producer of *Polizeiruf*, to see if I would have any interest in doing something in this direction. Harun was still alive at that time, and we worked together some on *Circles* before his death. At first, Harun said: we can't do something like that! He meant: an 8:15 p.m. detective show [*Tatort*], something like, "Let's drive over to Dr. Smith's now, the man interests me" [8:15 p.m. is prime time/just after the evening news]—we couldn't even begin to write such sentences. But then, three weeks after Cornelia Ackers had raised it, he said to me, "I've now watched a whole bunch of *Polizeirufe* and *Tatorte*, and they have been getting better." I asked him which he had seen, and he said this and that, but I don't want to name names!

RF: Please, go ahead and do!

CP: OK, Rostock was really great, well made, one with Edgar Selge not as detective, but as a Berliner at Alexanderplatz, we watched that one. And then we discovered Matthias Brandt, and we both found him great. So, we thought, let's give it a shot.

I wrote it all alone, because Harun was on a trip around the world with his art installation. He came back one week before the soccer World Cup final in 2014, and I read it aloud to him. Then we chatted about it during the half-time of the Germany-Argentina final, and he approved it. A week later he died.

It really was fun, this work on the *Polizeiruf*; I mentioned this yesterday, because one does not have the pressure of producing a major "artwork." With *Phoenix*, I had to travel all around the world for a whole year to premieres, to North America, etc., because this kind of artwork is a product belonging to the whole word.

But television is just an everyday B-movie, in the best sense of the expression, and that was just a lot of fun—from this Toronto and San Sebastian world [of major festivals] to some screening in a Berlin courtyard for the local press.

RF: How great was the freedom in your making it? And what were the parameters on which you had to build? Was the figure of Matthias Brandt the only one?

CP: We really had a lot of freedom. At the beginning, I thought, uh oh, there will be rules, and I'll have to fight for what I want to do, but the producers were loyal to the directors, at least in my case. With Brandt, yes, there are inspectors who have been investigating since World War II, and they have considerable influence on the scripts, they can demand rewrites, etc. I prepared for complaints like "no one is taking this sentence away from me!" But with Matthias Brandt and Barbara Auer—it was a true ensemble, with the greatest facility and concentration.

RF: With such a B-movie, with which aspects could you do exactly what you wanted—or perhaps what you always wanted to do—and how do such conditions influence the final form of the work? Did you just sit down with Hans Fromm and say, "OK, now we're going to make a *Polizeiruf*"?

CP: No, not really. We had been shooting 35mm the last few years, since we feel more at home in this analogue, celluloid world. *Phoenix* was also 35mm—it is just lovely material, it is so humane [*menschlich*] and has a certain place in the cultural history of the image. The Kodak color palette could be from Goya, I always say.

So, I have tended to avoid shooting in digital, but then we had a podium discussion of *Dreileben*, the three-part film I made with Graf and Christoph Hochhäusler, with whom I'm good friends. Christoph is always so pointed. I'm only that way when alone with a couple of others, but he can be that way in public. And when I said that about 35mm, how beautiful it is, with a Goya-like color palette, etc., he said, "You're so from yesterday"—that kind of comment about me in front of everybody!

It didn't offend me so much as brought me to thinking about, for example, how vinyl might also be a beautiful material for records, but is it what we need right now?

We realized that the *Polizeiruf* episode could not be shot in Super 16 or something like it. Those times are over, so we decided to do it in digital, and I thought: two cameras in an interrogation situation, that interests me, especially because

I regard that a key difference between film and theater. Of course, Justus von Dohnányi, Matthias Brandt, and Barbara Auer have all studied theater, as have almost all German actors. Many German films fail for this reason, I think: they are simply too theatrical in front of the camera.

So, I set out to explain to them what the difference is: above all it's the reverse shot, whether it is in an interrogation or in a love story. In theater, one speaks out over the fourth wall, to the audience, and that's why a lot of these horrible TV films have a kitchen with the range and dishwasher in the middle, an open kitchen as with the rich, so the actors can sit on one side of a kitchen island like a stage, with lines like, "Did you pick up the kids?" and "Yeah, and I saw the corpse."

And the reverse shot really is cinema, meaning that the cinema holds itself in the in-between spaces, that's where there is tension and pressure. And so I said to Hans [Fromm]: "Let's shoot with two cameras," and not just letting them run, but in the interrogations, of which we have a lot in *Circles*. We even used three of them, "Black Magic" they're called, small little black cameras like a cell phone, that was an interesting experience.

I discussed with the actors this notion of the reaction shot in the interrogation, and they were enthusiastic. I explained how the interrogation is like a seduction and raises questions about whether the shot should be over the shoulder or should be purely frontal, whether it observes or breaks the axis—those are all big discussions in both interrogation and love.

Indeed, that was the theme in *Circles*: the interrogation of the truth as well as the interrogation of love. Anyone who has suffered from jealousy, and that would be more people than there are voters for Brexit, knows that a jealous conversation sounds a great deal like a police detective doing an interrogation.

And a camera can do a great deal in such a situation. That's just fun for me. That kind of reaction shot is the foundation of television: the interrogation, the police detective, the love story—that is television [in Germany] at 8:15 p.m. [8:15 p.m. is prime time/just after the evening news].

That we have to invent again, we have to make our approach to the genre precise, pure, and clear—that was my thinking. Not invent the newest in crime and policing of it, be it serial killer, psychological profiler, all this nonsense from the new shows. I don't want this focus on the evil ones from outside; I want to focus on those coming from our own imaginations.

RF: The central image in *Circles* is the model train. The title *Circles* refers, among other things, also to the circles of the model train. But then, intriguingly, the character explains that it is not a circle, but rather that it goes in the underground and then comes back out in the open. It's the most petit bourgeois image that one could think up: that is, the 1950s Economic Miracle trains in postwar, that is Märklin [a toy train] and narrow-minded, also a dream, a dream of children, of young people, also a status symbol. How big was the model train in one's childhood? How rich were one's parents—there's a lot that plays into it. And one goes in the cellar, such trains are usually in the cellar. That interests you, no? To dig down into the German mentality in this *Polizeiruf*.

CP: Yes, I would only do things that interest me, I would never just make fun of something. Horst Seehofer in Beckmann,[2] he had a model train in the cellar, too, although not built to the end. One sees suddenly that he's fourteen, that is, how he was when he was fourteen: that the model train is also there in the desires and dreams of the adults. Many of them make a career out of being the guardians of a certain order. They build worlds, rather similar to how the Brexit voters imagine England: everything in this circle is completely harmonious, border closed, maybe once in a while a little bicycle accident, but then the society rises to the occasion, and Dohnányi explains the train always travels the same route, around and around, the same mountain, the same market square, and nothing changes. And that calms us, of course.

But then the new generation of model train builders that I know from Berlin: they break this circle, this stability, deliberately. They stage demonstrations, for example, women's demonstrations against sexual harassment in the workplace, right on the model train set. And they also build into the model tricks of the eye and mind, for example, that one train disappears and a new one appears.

And I liked that, the struggle of new generation against the older one. The Dohnányi character tries to escape these circles, tries to find the train that would take him out of the circle, and he notices at the end that the act he has committed closes the circle. I should have written that back then in the press materials!

RF: With *Wolves*, that's the first time that Harun Farocki did not work on the script at all, did not have any influence.

CP: With *Circles*, I wrote it all alone, and he just approved it. That was an important moment for me, since sometimes I really did write nonsense, and then would sit with him in his kitchen, and he would make an espresso—always overcooked, by the way, for twenty-five years in his stove-top espresso maker, the coffee was totally burned! And then the rubber seals not really put on so that the brown stuff would flow out of it onto the stove. Harun was also king of putting the coffee spoon in the sugar so it was all clumped up.

---

2. Horst Seehofer is an important right-wing German politician, at the time of the conversation the head of the conservative CSU party and governor of Bavaria. He had displayed his train set on the television show *Beckmann* shortly before the conversation. See "In Seehofers Eisenbahn-Keller," *Frankfurter Allgemeine Zeitung*, May 9, 2016, http://www.faz.net/aktuell/politik/inland/das-spielzimmer-des-csu-chefs-in-seehofers-eisenbahn-keller-14223321.html, accessed July 30, 2017.

And I sat there waiting for his reaction. "*Circles* is great," he said. He said, "Make sure you build the model train set carefully," and Hans [Fromm] really did a great job here in the Bavaria Studios with a special camera from Hamburg. We had these tiny figures on the model, so the special camera is cantilevered.

That was actually the first day of shooting of *Circles*: no actors, the team really getting its first chance to work together, we have the big train set—the boys really have, for the last time, control; Barbara Auer has not appeared yet. We had a model train expert—I did not understand a word he said, he was from Altötting, so he spoke in a Bavarian dialect. I just pretended by nodding. I have no idea what he was talking about and still do not know, but he built an incredible train set. He was so happy, he did not care if I understood him, I think. Of course, he would not allow me to leave while he worked on it.

So, it was the first day I was on at the Bavarian lot, a mythical lot, where it says everywhere "*Das Boot, Das Boot, Das Boot*" was shot here. Munich, if I may say it, is a bit stuck in time, as if they are still shooting *Das Boot*. All the cantinas were closed, and it reminded me of *Contempt* by Jean-Luc Godard: Cinecittà in Winter, with Brigitte Bardot and Michel Piccoli, but, of course, all in the Bavarian style. The actors came the next day. So, we had the team from Berlin, meeting the personnel from Munich. And you know how Berlin and Munich do not always get along perfectly, the people from Munich were a bit mouthy [*hatte eine Schnauze*], as were the Berliners. For example, when the Berliners flew down here, the Munich team picked us up with cappuccinos at the gate—in Berlin one would never do such a thing. We were shamed by how nice they were to us, and within five minutes we were all friends.

RF: There are so many surprises in *Wolves*. In that film, we have someone who has been mocked as a child due to his cleft palate. How did you research this? Did you anticipate any kind of protest from the disability community? Especially since you have people running around with masks, depictions of murder, and, in the end, putting a bullet in his head.

CP: Well, when I started elementary school at six years old, my best friend was Peter Lauchs from Haan, whom I still know well. And he had a severe cleft palate, which was later surgically repaired. When we were kids, it was never a problem for me, I don't think children really contemplate that kind of thing. His parents owned a large factory, and they had a lovely house in Haan, the town where I am from. There were big rooms upstairs, with all the family photos of this traditional Haan industrialist family, with a genealogy or family tree. And the photos with Peter, they were always covered over in some fashion, often with the lower half of his face covered so that one could only see his eyes. He suffered incredibly, as he explained to me much later. He somehow just didn't belong.

I do not think that just because someone shows someone with a disability who becomes a murderer that all people with disabilities will feel accused. Here, similarly, with the Turkish fascists, the Gray Wolves as I call them, that does not mean that I am accusing Erdogan or something.

Sometimes a small insult causes lasting consequences. What was that, in Wim Wenders's *The American Friend* at the beginning: just one time, Bruno Ganz won't shake Dennis Hopper's hand, and that means that Dennis Hopper wants to kill Bruno Ganz. There are people who are wounded by such trivial things.

If you hear what Dr. Biesinger in *Wolves* recounts, that he had to sing a song whenever the others were bored because he had hissed all the "s" sounds, and they fell over laughing. And he sang nonetheless, even if they laughed, because the laughter was more important to him than his own pride, that it would bring him closer to happiness, even though it also made him unhappy—this kind of thing just destroys people. And he emigrates to Denver to start his life—it's the people who leave who return with double the vindictiveness, or with double the longing. Often it is the sons who leave to find themselves who return as the prodigal sons asking their fathers why, why?

Running away does not help. That is the terrible experience that he has trying to flee. So he can, for the first time, speak and understand life with Barbara Auer—understand that it was all pointless. He couldn't realize his longing. Now that I understand that, he thinks, it is too late—and this, I think, also is one of the fundamental topics of film, that it is always too late.

RF: The connecting element of this trilogy for *Polizeiruf* is the love story, the love duel, and the growing closer of these two wounded figures, Barbara Auer and Matthias Brandt. That is the foundation, but then there are many additional elements to this foundation. One could also say that's the actual story, and then there are the peripheral stories.

In *Wolves*, the case that Matthias Brandt is handling is initiated at the beginning, but that does not end up being the core of the story. And there, instead, you rely on genre cinema, on *giallo* elements, also in the staging as well as in the color palette, in classic *giallo* scenes and sequences, especially at the end.

And one thing that puzzled me, particularly for a Sunday evening detective show: there's a masked killer, as in an Edgar Wallace film.[3] Dr. Biesinger is standing there at the end, the Dario Argento light disappears, then we find ourselves in the cold light of the present (although that does come up in Argento, too). And

---

3. Genre films, usually somewhat campy crime thrillers, that were based on the work of the British author Edgar Wallace (1875–1932). The most important were made between 1959 and 1972, and many were produced by the Berlin-based production company Rialto Films. Many did, indeed, offer a masked criminal, as Robert Fischer suggests.

the guy pulls the mask off in this genre mode, like a monk with a whip or a blue hand suddenly pulling the mask from his head. They are really audacious things for an 8:15 p.m. detective show [8:15 p.m. is prime time/just after the evening news]. What was the idea, and what was your goal with such things?

CP: He actually pulls the mask off fifteen minutes earlier. But, in any case, I think you are right. It was only yesterday that I first saw the color-corrected copy, done by Hans [Fromm] and his team, and I also thought that this green light is a Dario Argento touch. But the great thing is that when this bright neon light of the laboratory comes on, it usually renders the people under it extremely ugly. But here they become, for the first time, beautiful. I like that: that laboratory light is supposed to see the truth, to uncover what is beneath and make it visible. Then, through the dialogue and through their bodies, we see that they are of a regular body temperature, are full human beings. That pleased me.

I also have to say that I find that both Barbara Auer and Matthias Brandt really are beautiful people, in a cinematographic sense. There's a mistake that is often made that one has to recognize or one is doomed to repeat it: we watched *Creature from the Black Lagoon* by Jack Arnold, and I had the sense that we had to stage a dance, a kind of erotic dance, between Barbara Auer and Sebastian Hülk as the creature.

RF: Yes, it's the classic confrontation, *The Beauty and the Beast*, the innocent and the monster . . .

CP: Yes, exactly, and I did that from the point-of-view of the monster as he circles around Barbara Auer, just as in *Black Lagoon*, but then I realized that was wrong. I had to narrate it from the view of Barbara Auer: it was her delirium, after all. We ended up shooting a lot of garbage, but then by editing we saw the truth—thus under the laboratory light of editing, so to say, we could see more clearly.

RF: You did do a theater piece at the Deutsche[s] Theater [in Berlin], *The Lonely Way* [*Der einsame Weg*] by Arthur Schnitzler, in 2012 with Nina Hoss and Ulrich Matthes—was it difficult for you to do?

CP: No, no. That was a time—well, I came home, and my family said to me, theater? When are you going to do a music CD? I should have taken more of a break; it is very stressful making films. One has to take breaks, I think. Not to lounge in the spa or anything, but to read, to go for walks, and not to always be thinking of using every minute.

And I went from the shooting of *Jerichow* direct to the theater to direct that production. Nina [Hoss, who is in a theater ensemble in Berlin] had always said to me that I rehearsed just as they do in the theater, but they have more time. They really work on eliminating the clichés of the body and movement, as I like to. And I was envious about theater and its long rehearsals as she described it. So, I took a really difficult play and worked with them and really learned a great deal. I also learned a lot if I ever want to make a comedy, namely, in the cafeteria of a theater you learn all about the art of intrigues. They are so smart, these theater actors.

JF: Did you also offer those seminars that you put together before films for the theater actors?

CP: Yeah, and I showed them some films. For example, I showed them *Love Streams* by John Cassavetes. In that film, Cassavetes plays a writer who has burnout, and that fits perfectly the burned-out cultural zombies in the play by Schnitzler. He has money and success, but he is also drinking all the time and womanizing. Then suddenly, he has to take care of a child, so he goes to Vegas with the kid. He takes off with some woman and leaves the kid alone in the hotel room for three days. The child is only six, and he doesn't know how to get food or something to drink—he could have ordered something, but he ends up totally starving. And then the character that Cassavetes is playing realizes that he is totally at the end. It is such a great and sad film. *Love Streams*, the love flows. Gena Rowlands plays his sister, and what a great, incestuous relationship that is, one that cannot be requited, of course.

I showed that to the actors. And then I showed them Amando de Ossorio's *Return of the Evil Dead*, which is one of my favorite films. In a little village in northern Spain, some Templars, from the order of medieval knights, are buried in a mausoleum in an old stone fortress, but then, at full moon, they climb out and get on their ghost horses. The villagers have to sacrifice a virgin to them, whose blood they suck so that they can live another week. So, I showed that scene to the actors to drive them, for the six weeks, totally crazy.

The scene has so much intelligence in it. They, of course, undress the young woman, as these kinds of films made their money in train station theaters [*Bahnhofkinos*], with beautiful women, models, showing their breasts, etc. They attack her body with whips and drink the blood from her breasts—and this idea, naturally, is a sick idea rooted somewhere in Catholic iconography. But it was still Franco fascism at that time, and one has the sense that the old dictator was sucking the blood out of the country's young people. That these people were nourishing themselves on the maimed body of the future mother. It's really an interesting film.

So, this kind of thing we discussed, because the three authors in Schnitzler are sucking the blood out of young people, as a lot of older artists do, a lot of older artists and a lot of people in general.

JF: And you tend to do these seminars even before the rehearsals start?

CP: Yes, for *Wolves*, around the tenth of September when it was pretty warm, we had two days in Berlin, then watched some things and discussed some. Usually, we read the script through again, but it is just a table read so I can hear the voices again, and then we watch films and listen to music. We go for walks and look at photos from the settings that Hans and I have already scouted, explaining why we choose them, how they relate to one another, etc.

Then, four days before the shoot starts, we rent a coach, and I'm in front with the microphone like a tour guide for Munich who has absolutely no idea, and we drive around to the settings with the actors, where they will be acting. And then they have a couple of days alone, so they have some time with the material—and, as they contemplate their characters, they now have a sense of the spaces in which they will be acting, something real.

And then on the day of shooting, I say that we should not wake up the actors before 8 a.m., because, on TV, they very often look as if they have been woken up at 4 a.m. And the makeup looks terrible, especially now with the HD TVs. Anyway, then we meet around 8:15 a.m. or 8:30 a.m. on the set—at that point, it is just the assistant director, the actors, and myself as director. In costume, but not yet in makeup. And then we rehearse what we plan to do that day, so we really have some time. Hans [Fromm] comes at 10 a.m. or 9:30 a.m. to watch the final rehearsals and think about the lighting, and we start to discuss how we will film what we just saw, where the camera will be, etc. We make a plan for it, and then, after all that, we shoot pretty quickly.

The thing is that it means that we do not shoot until after 12 noon. If a producer comes by at 11 a.m. and sees that nothing has been shot yet, they get suicidal tendencies.

RF: Because it is, indeed, getting so late, I would ask at this point for any audience questions.

Audience Member: When one sees you in person, here at "Filmmakers Live" or at a press conference, you're extremely funny, but often the films are very serious. I was wondering if you ever considered making a comedy. For example, what Maren Ade has recently managed, with melancholy and humor [with her 2016 *Toni Erdmann*].

CP: Well, let me first say I am very happy about Maren Ade's *Toni Erdmann*, which represents a kind of film that I just cannot manage—I like it a lot. I have to say that at press conferences or here, I worry that I'm completely boring. In any case, I would like to make a comedy. I was sitting around with friends, and we could come up with only fifteen or so good comedies. I have two favorites: *Bringing Up Baby* by Howard Hawks and the remake by Peter Bogdanovich, *What's Up, Doc?* I would be absolutely delighted to be able to make such films.

I find that *Toni Erdmann* is not a comedy; I cried quite often in the film. Maybe it's close to a sentimental tragedy. If I made a comedy, I would love something like *Väter der Klamotte* and Hanns Dieter Hüsch,[4] this kind of Hal Roach approach. And I can still watch Laurel and Hardy for hours, for example, in *Big Business* in which they sell Christmas Trees door to door in the summer in Los Angeles—there is a knockdown, drag-out battle with someone who doesn't want to buy one, with a complete destruction of his house, it is so wonderfully anarchic.

That's what I have in mind. But one can't do that alone: it takes studios, it takes ten or twelve writers, five actors who have worked together for years, as in an ensemble. I just do not have those kinds of production conditions; one is more alone than one thinks. I cannot write that kind of thing alone. To create a "writers' room," I would have to rent a loft, employ three people. It would be like a welfare job creation program [ABM], and I'm sure nothing very funny would come out of it.

AM: I wanted to go back to this question about Truffaut and Renoir, and the comparison between Truffaut and Renoir. How do you see that relationship?

CP: For Truffaut, Renoir is the great director. But he criticizes one small detail, as sons often do, saying, "You're the best father in the world, but you can't have white wall tires," or "You can't have an Opel." And I think Renoir is the director for historical films: he can make a film in a studio, but you have the feeling that the films have been made today. He avoids the actors speaking too theatrically and the costumes being too heavy, because even in the Middle Ages, one could move in a fleet-footed way, speak funny dialects, have a sense that they are living now and for today. They didn't stand there theatrically declaiming this or that. This kind of vivaciousness, this kind of physicality—that's what I have in mind when I think of historical things.

The shadows of the past live between us today, and that is what I try to film, not to act as if we are in the eighteenth century. That is what I find really great with Dominik Graf's *Beloved Sisters*: it is sensuous, the water, the being cold, the three fantastic actors. Ronald Zehrfeld at the end giving a slap—it's a modern slap that he gives. It is not any kind of theater, it's cinema—the cinema is a real kind of active looking.

AM: You often have fantastical elements in your films, can you discuss that? How do you think about such elements and their plausibility?

CP: Yes, it's true, I have some fantastical elements in my films, but I always aim to have everything make sense. For example, in *Wolves*, even though while watching you might think it is all supernatural, by the end it all makes logical

---

4. Comedy series from the 1910s and 1920s, primarily of single-reelers, tending to physical comedy. Hüsch (1925–2005) was a cabaret performer who later did voice-over commentary for them when they were rebroadcast on German television, especially in the 1960s and 1970s, when Petzold was a child growing up in West Germany.

sense, without any kind of magic. I have this on-going discussion with Christoph [Hochhäusler]: what is more important, the plot or the atmosphere? And I find that the plot has to be in order. I love American and Australian detective literature because it all has to make rational sense, and, if it all makes sense, then you can do what you want. If you just let yourself work, just with feelings and with atmosphere, then I think it's too easy. I, as author, have to work with the laws of plausibility, just as the police detective represents certain laws. It gets interesting when that law is broken, but the law has to be established first.

"A Space in Which We Are at Home": Interview with Christian Petzold

Ilka Brombach / 2017

From "'Ein Raum, in dem wir heimisch sind': Interview mit Christian Petzold," *Über Christian Petzold*, eds. Ilka Brombach and Tina Kaiser (Berlin: Vorwerk 8, 2018), 19–60. Reprinted by permission. Translated by Marco Abel and Jaimey Fisher.

Ilka Brombach: You were born in Hilden in 1960 and then grew up in Haan. What were your parents like? What did you experience in your time in school? Where did your interest in literature and film come from?

Christian Petzold: If I start now with the memories of my youth, school.... My mother died in October [2017], she had an accident.

During the shoot for *Transit*, I often asked myself: why was *Transit*, the novel by Anna Seghers, the favorite book of Harun and me? I got it at the end of the 1980s from Harun, who knew it, in turn, from Ingemo Engström. He said he read the book once every year. It was similar with me. I have already read it about twenty times. *Transit* is similar to the novels of Georges Simenon. Everything seems really clear. The story is clear, the plot is somehow clear, and yet you can't really explain how it's really about something else, something like being adrift, thus, whether there is something like a home [*Heimat*] security, being protected—without all that being about ethnic belonging and race. The novel itself creates a kind home for its narrative subject who is completely homeless, one could even say without an identity. But in the moment of his narration, he creates for us, and for him the lonely narrator, a space in which we are at home. That is the task of art, I think.

When my brother and I buried my mother, we discussed how our parents were never at home here, exactly like us. They were also refugees. My mother is from the Sudetenland, my father from Saxony. They were separated from their families much too young, thus much too early alone, already at fifteen or sixteen. My father worked in a mine, my mother was in a transit camp and then landed in the Rhineland, where she did an apprenticeship as a chemical laboratory technician. And the feeling that one is not really at home. To try to build a world to which one belongs, through a savings book, a townhouse, three kids, but nonetheless to know that you lost something that is not attainable: that is what she communicated to us children. Things that were obvious for many people—like the voluntary fire department, the Malteser Hilfsdienst,[1] the wine festival, the PTA meetings—were not obvious for my parents. They felt like guests: tolerated but not rooted.

Harun had a different experience of flight from the one I had. He was actually born in the Sudetenland (he wanted to form an Association of Filmmakers from the Sudetenland to get subsidies). *Transit* is a book that bound us closely together. We read to each other from it. Although the novel is almost autobiographical, Anna Seghers's language is really beautiful, the relationships strained but nonetheless lovely, not angry. She affirms the great Greek myths, literature, Herman Melville. This literature offers her a home. When I shot the film, I made out of its first-person narrator a third-person narrator to try to show how you can make a home for yourself by storytelling.

In small towns, you develop an essentially more intensive relationship to the things that you are interested in. There is not much on offer, no internet, no good bus connections to the city. Back then, when I was in high school, a friend and I started reading *The Clown* and then Nietzsche, which the director of the town library recommended to us. One noticed suddenly in school that you are distinguishing yourself from others by reading. At some point, a young philosopher from Milan appeared, he was working at the Pizzeria Vesuvio: Raffaele Scelsi, now the executive editor at Feltrinelli. He's out with his guitar in Schiller park and played and read—as if philosophy and music had something to do with each other. He played Víctor Jara, the Che Guevara song, and he taught us a different form of philosophy, Marxism, seeking revolution.

Everything that we did, we did very intensely. As I started to read, within six months I knew all the order numbers of the Suhrkamp books[2] as if they were the box scores. I spent all of my holidays and long weekends at my uncle's in Celle. He had one of the biggest record stores in Lower Saxony. I worked there because my father was unemployed, and we didn't have any money at home. I had to pay for everything myself, for clothes, too. There I was able to learn within three weeks

---

1. A large Catholic relief agency, active primarily in Germany. It employs approximately 35,000, has over 50,000 volunteers, and has over a million members or registered supporters.
2. Suhrkamp is a prestige publisher in Germany specializing in theory and fine literature that had a standardized look and order system (thus "order numbers").

the order numbers of Ariola, Elektrola, and Deutsche Grammophon; I could recite the Bielefelder Katalog without ever in my life having touched a piano key.

With this, too, there is an interest for certain people. One learned that Böll took in Solzhenitsyn, that Wolf Biermann could stay at Willi Hoss's. It was a network in Germany: texts, images, music, people that had a certain correspondence with each other. Escape to the feeling of not being alone in this craziness of a sleepy town between Wuppertal and Dusseldorf. We drove to see Hanns Dieter Hüsch, Franz Josef Degenhardt, and Wolf Biermann, to the Ruhr festival in Recklinghausen, to Moers and to Dusseldorf to go to the theater. I read *The Aesthetic of Resistance* with Harun. A little bit like the boys at the beginning of the book, that's how we were. The workers from Wedding who meet for the art that they love that, on the one hand, the rich, the bourgeoisie, and the aristocracy have produced but, on the other, that the workers nonetheless rate highly. These workers meet to show that this art is also theirs, even though it has been taken from them.

IB: In 1981, you went to Berlin and studied theater and German studies at the Free University.

CP: We were a clique: Thomas, Nikolai, Lutz, and myself. Each of us had our specialty. Lutz was a huge fan of jazz rock, could play the bass parts of bands like Kraan. Thomas was a designer, with him it was all about art and photography, with Nikolai philosophy and literature. Myself, I discovered film, through the Hitchcock book by Truffaut. A young guy who came into the class, Harald Hohberger, brought the book with him. I borrowed it, and that was really the initial spark. I suddenly understood some things. The central thesis for Hitchcock is that society suddenly, overnight, can exclude somebody and they cannot get back in. Sometimes, as in *The 39 Steps*, love is stronger [than this mechanism]. Truffaut's interview with Hitchcock is the book of a son who is querying a father (a figure I was certainly searching for) and the book of a man who can report his own fears such that they become art—something I find fantastic about Hitchcock. At the same time, it was a book that got my juices flowing. I knew the films only from TV because there was no more cinema in my town.

IB: Besides German Studies, you studied film studies at the Institute for Theater Studies at the Free University of Berlin.

CP: My friend Ludger Blanke was already accepted by the dffb in 1985. In 1987, he took me as an auditor to a Harun Farocki seminar. When I sensed the intensity there, it was clear to me that I had to go there. It was also that there were only eight people around an editing table instead of a hundred sitting in front of a television in the Institute for Theater Studies. And the equipment—that was actually great [at the Free University—eds.]. They had new VHS players. Before you just didn't have access to the films, you just had to wait until they played at the Arsenal. And then all of a sudden there was VHS, and the films were all copied from television.

I was happy as an auditor for the seminars at the dffb. I was accepted in 1988 after applying for a second time, at a time when I was already close friends with Harun. And when I got there, it was about techniques for creating film copies, about camera techniques, about holding a camera. I noticed that the practical aspects didn't interest me much. All these stories about how Spielberg made a film at six, Tom Tykwer at seven, that wasn't the case for me at all. I read, and, for me, cinema and literature belong together. I only really wanted to look at films and see the world. I had no desire to go to festivals and to show what I can do.

IB: You made eight films at the dffb. And worked on various ones, also six as assistant. So, you didn't only watch films?

CP: No, but it is also a case that one did the seminars and had to make a seminar film. Most I didn't even finish—I was afraid that one would notice what a fake I was. If you don't finish something, then there's still some promise in there. I had a feeling I didn't even know what I was about. But around me there were all kinds of activities, my colleagues who already knew what they wanted and just took off with the cameras.

The first film was *Ich arbeite alles ab . . . Ehrenwort*. That was a seminar film that six of us made, an exercise in synchronizing. Then came *Weiber*. The film takes place in the spaces of my youth and told the story of my brother, who wrote a love letter to Natassja Kinski. But that didn't work, the material protected itself from my melancholy, against sentimentality. I had to go another way. In *Süden*, I took a Super 8 camera and a little Nagra recorder. I wanted to travel through Turkey with my wife and make a film about how everyone always wants to go to the south. I also had a twenty-line text, called "Süden," from Ernst Bloch's *Traces*. It is about a friend who says that the south is paradise, with the siesta, the midday sun, a glass of wine, simply to sit there. And Bloch replies that is the death-like dream that someone who is exhausted has—when you're there, you'll go crazy. I wanted to shoot that. One goes there, listens to the entertainment, looks at the hotels, and sees that there's nothing, no infrastructure. I had the books that I brought to the south, they are there and sunbathing, fluttering in the wind. Harun was very enthusiastic about this film, the fluttering books he found really beautiful. They probably had something to do with the short film he made, *Die Worte des Vorsitzenden*, in which weapons are made out of books. We then had this joke: with him weapons are made out the books, and with me, after the attack, they take a vacation.

After I came back from the trip, things went better. From that moment on, I started to write scripts. Before then, I wanted to make films that were not based on a script. Associations, images, music. At some point, I just didn't have the desire to make this kind of avant-garde crap. And Harun, I did not expect this—it was he who really encouraged me. He said that he was also of the opinion that the great avant-garde, except for a few things by Maya Deren, emerged within the mainstream: Hitchcock and Bresson, Buñuel or also Robert Wiene's *The Hands of Orlac*.

IB: Did you write the script for *Das warme Geld*?

CP: Yes, that was the first script on which I worked with Harun. He found that good, the money is warm when it comes out of the machine, and it is winter, the women are freezing, because the money is like warm bread out of the oven. With this film, I learned everything. I had never been an assistant director, so I had no idea how to work with actors. Manuela Brandenstein, who played the main role, was a very good actor for dubbing and had a great way of speaking. She plays the street smart one who always steals, and Martina Maurer was a bit the innocent. The shoot was a lot of fun for me. The film had very little success because it was the wrong length. One made a film up to fifteen minutes or more than forty-five minutes, but nothing in between. Otherwise, there was no festival that would show it. I didn't trust myself and chose this length deliberately so that no one would see it. Harun criticized that a lot. He asked why I didn't use the scenes that I had cut out. I still remember that he liked the dance scene with the man that I later took out. It unfolds in a bar, in the background "Greek Wine" is playing—I should have included the whole thing in the film.

Then, the commissioning producer from *Kleines Fernsehspiel*,[3] Annedore von Donop, saw it and asked if I had anything else like that. I gave her the script to *Pilots*, for which I had received a subsidy. Then she called, and I had my first contact to this fast-paced branch, going out to dinner, meeting in Einstein [an upscale, Viennese-style café in Berlin—eds]. I was happy to not have to pay for my own Schnitzel but couldn't deal with the praise for the script. Then she wanted me to change something related to the pregnancy, about which she was right. So, I worked on it some more with Harun. That with the representative from Puma sport shoes in *Pilots* is something Harun and I had encountered in our research. A Puma rep explained how he couldn't sell anything in the former GDR because the people there had no money and that, economically, it was going down the drain. Harun figured we should ask a sales rep about an area, then we'd get an idea what was going on.

Can you read me the title of the films that I was supposed to have made?

---

3. "Das kleine Fernsehspiel" is an important, ongoing series of TV films made for the public TV station ZDF that has launched or affirmed the careers of many influential art-cinema directors, including Fassbinder, Kluge, Agnès Varda, and Jim Jarmusch.

IB: *Mission.*

CP: That is a Super 8 film that I made with my friend in Haan. It was ten minutes long, the monologue by Captain Willard from *Apocalypse Now*. First, we laid down the soundtrack and then shot in the small town, as if the small town was Vietnam. Complete crap, but a lot of fun, a parody.

IB: *Glanz und Elend des Hochbegabten* [*Glamour and Misery of the Highly Talented*].

CP: That was a seminar film, from the seminar of Clemens Klopfenstein, that I didn't finish. It was a good title. The film shows me, as I woke up on the day that the DDR dissolved itself. Boring.

IB: *Ostwärts, Abzüge.*

CP: *Ostwärts* is from the Peter Nestler-Seminar. *Abzüge*: because I didn't have any success with *Pilots* at first, I didn't edit the film immediately. I was at festivals, had to prepare *Cuba Libre*, and didn't finish *Abzüge*. The big photo lab back then in Berlin was Wegert, and you could drop your film off there. Two days later you got your prints. It is still around, only digital now. The film was developed down in Lichterfelde on an assembly line [*Fotostraße*]. The photos rushed right by. Students who worked there sat there and looked at them and took out-of-focus photos out, also child pornography. They did the police's groundwork. *Abzüge* was a portrait of these students. I wanted to know what they saw in November 1989 and the time right after. That was really interesting. That explained how the pictures changed over the course of the year. At Christmas, you always had Christmas trees, at Easter certain colors that one quickly recognizes. They didn't see individual pictures, rather streaks, but on the basis of the colors, one could identify, for example, child pornography. They see skin color rush by, saw the blue sky because it was summer, in September when the people developed their summer holiday photos. But in 1989 there were irregularities. First, one had images of the Wall and the area around it. There was a different light, the light of the neon streetlamps of the GDR. Two months later, one saw the people naked on the Wall, showing their penises, their breasts, their sex acts as selfie. They were saying that it belonged to them once again, the Wall.

I didn't finish the film because I didn't have the rights to the photos. But the material is still there. Maybe I'll make a twenty-minute documentary out of the two hours of material.

That was all the films. If you count all the minutes together from six years at the dffb, you would not even get to a feature-length film. That is tough to hear.

IB: There are the dffb films on which you worked, above all as an assistant with Hartmut Bitomsky and Harun Farocki, with *Das Kino und der Wind und die Photografie; Kino, Flächen, Bunker; Die Ufa; Hans Scharoun—Eine imaginäre Architektur; Kamera und Wirklichkeit, Rumänien 1989;* and *Ein Tag im Leben der Endverbraucher.*

CP: Yes, I learned a lot with my two Hitchcocks. I was at Jacob [Coffee] in Bremen in the archive and looked at the 35mm rolls, the advertising films for *Ein Tag im Leben der Endverbraucher*. Harun thought, after he saw the stuff, that you could make a social history of West Germany, from the coffee table from 1950 until today, at the beginning with roses and Meißner porcelain, and then in the 1970s everything became Ikea-like, there's crockery rather than porcelain. Those were the thoughts we had. But, for it, I looked at the stuff for days, stayed in 35 DM hotels, froze, ate badly. I learned something there.

IB: Do you research your own films in this way?

CP: Yes, but I don't like any films that are over-researched. It is really hard work to do research, and one has the desire to see it reflected in the feature film. But that is a big mistake. With me, it is like this: I look at the material, and I read a lot about it. Then I sleep and try to remember. From this sleep I write a script. If the research is research worthy of a dream, then it is cinema, I think. But when you do the research and want to translate that research directly into fiction—I don't want that. As Harun was making *Nothing Ventured*, I was reading a book by Kathrin Röggla about finance guys who come face to face with death in airport hotels of Frankfurt, and that reminded me of *Carnival of Souls*. Harun and I thought about bodies. Why were the civil servants at the windows of the city banks so milquetoast [*spießig*]? There had to be something civil-servicey about them, or else you would not trust them with your money. But, suddenly, in the advertisements for the new Braun Sixtant 6000, they run around on trains and shave. Then comes a woman who looks great and strokes the cheek of the man and looks at him, giving a thumbs up that he looks good. And the man is happy. And now we suddenly trust these people with our money. People who shave on the train, who wear Armani suits, and who let themselves be stroked on the cheek by models. Which means, more or less, you can follow me like a prostitute. Harun thought there would be an explosion when such bodies and money come together. In that time, we wrote *Yella*, and two years after that there was the huge financial crisis. Somehow you could sense that. This is our research. We can, of course, research like sociologists, read texts. But then you have to begin dreaming them. I don't know how else to describe it.

IB: How did you perceive 1989?

CP: Let me think about it. After one year at the film academy, the Wall fell. I was already at the end of my twenties, but still had no clue, no origin that was secure, including in a philosophical sense.

My friend Ludger [Blanke] made a film, *Reporter*, in which one could see how they were already closing entire factories in Brandenburg. A little later, then, when I was shooting in Wittenberge, I saw how the people had been duped. The workers from the East German train company there had to be hired by the West

German train company, the Deutsche Bahn. But Deutsche Bahn was already on the way to privatization and going public and, of course, didn't want to take on thousands of East-German rail workers. So, they made them an offer: we don't have jobs for you here, but you can go to the West, to Minden, and work there, guaranteed, for the rest of your lives. Or you stay here, and we pay you 10,000 DM. Eighty percent of the people took the money. And there were BMWs everywhere that some West German assholes had sold them with broken cylinder head gaskets. The people were suffering, there was nothing left. You should have seen it.

The big theme for Harun and me was work. Without work, we don't have an identity. If someone takes our work, we are nothing, we become ghosts. If you're at a party, you're asked what you do. And when you don't answer, then your interlocutor thinks you just inherited some money. But that alone is not a reason to fall in love with someone. When you say I inherited two million, I don't need to work anymore, then you'll get, if you're lucky, the WAG who dropped Bastian Schweinsteiger. But if you say, "I work here at the Institute for Acoustics, and we're working on how to reduce flight noise"—then people are interested. Or if someone says, "We're renovating old Junker castles on the Havel," that person, as a worker, also has something to talk about. Someone with money has nothing to say. Storytelling that comes from work has an erotics, an identity—that is the theme that emerged when the Wall fell in 1989. The people in East Germany inhabited a society where your work was your identity. There was a duty to work in East Germany. With us in the West, the lousy unions had already sacrificed the unemployed. And suddenly people took their work away. That means they didn't have any identity in this country anymore. They don't even know today who they are, and that was our subject. 1989 started that.

IB: *Ostwärts, The Warm Money, Pilots, Cuba Libre, The Sex Thief*—with these late student films and the first TV movies of yours, it's always about money and work. When one looks at them, one has the impression that you worked out here, content-wise and formally, the foundation for your later work?

CP: You could say that, as well as about the ways in which I work. I threw things overboard, a certain way of overthinking. I learned through the work with the actors, with the editor Bettina Böhler, and with Harun. I began to work dialogically.

IB: And how did you develop such a dialogical method of work?

CP: With *Pilots*, I had for the first time the conditions that one could describe as film industrial. There was a script, a producer, catering, travel, logistics. With money, there was a budget so I couldn't overspend. Labor law. I was confronted with all that. On the first day, I said to the actors that we could do the scene in this way or that way. We had met shortly before, and I noticed that it was a catastrophe to offer actors alternatives, but I didn't know why. That was great, meant freedom, one trying out a thousand things, a bit like by Straub. Then Eleonore Weisgerber came to me and said you can never do that. Actors are not models. If you make a film with actors, you can't say to them you can be someone totally different. Otherwise, they get outside themselves and are gone.

Afterwards, I spoke a great deal with the two actors, Nadeshda Brennicke and Eleonore Weisgerber, about the characters. I explained their back stories and noticed that the actors liked it when I gave them material without telling them how to act. I also explained a great deal about myself, about my mother who was an Avon cosmetics sales rep, about the women who are always on the move with their work clothes and who have to sell something, who always have to look put together, because they are reps for cosmetics. But evenings they are in business hotels where 98 percent of the guests are men.

Eleonore Weisgerber told me that no one had ever prepared her for a role like this, and I thought that I just had to share with the actors what I see as my ideal research. I began then to spend a whole week with the actors before shooting, including with *The Sex Thief* and *The State I Am In*. We listened to music, saw films, indulged a bit in memories and stories. The actors spend this time together.

In the rehearsal week, an ensemble-body forms, and then the shooting is actually a time when the ship's crew is at work.

IB: When we get to your first four or five films, then it seems that the themes and motives are similar. For example, it always concerns money that the characters have not earned through work, but rather through theft and robbery. Why?

CP: There are films in which robbery is not a kind of work, and there are films in which robbery is a kind of work.

Harun said back then that work does not appear in cinema. That's true. We were surprised when in Paul Schrader's *Blue Collar* that was really work no one can see, with unions, work lockers, etc. But, otherwise, the world of work does not appear. *Workers Leaving the Factory* is the first film that was shot, and so cinema begins when the workers leave the factory:[4] in the evening, out on Main Street, etc. In cinema, there are images of reproduction, not production. That was our thought, a lovely thought. But how do you sneak in the work, that which is excluded, that is, the dialectical thought, back into cinema? It's the work of seduction. A woman tries to conquer somebody. She uses, learns, literature. Or the safe-cracking films that there are in the history of cinema. Gangsters who think deeply about the steel and the drill technologies. The specialists who meet to prepare a bank robbery. And then ask afterward: how can we best invest the money?

---

4. Petzold is referring here to the Lumiere Brothers' film *Workers Leaving the Lumière Factory*, although it is perhaps also worth noting that Harun Farocki made a nonfiction film that uses the Lumiere Brothers' film as a point of departure. Farocki's film is entitled *Workers Leaving the Factory*.

Cinema tells the story of labor continuously without going in the factory. Therefore, there is no film of mine in which there is not some crime. Cinema needs crime because it doesn't show work.

IB: Another question to your early films. There are many echoes of other films, for example, of Wim Wenders, no?

CP: I have never quoted or consciously restaged scenes. But I am sometimes shocked after the fact that there are considerable similarities, but that is simply the way it is. I have seen many films, especially between sixteen and twenty-five years old. Also, the books that I read at the time, even if I have not fully understood them, influenced me a great deal. And a lot of it pops up when I'm writing. I have a pretty expressionistic writing style, I think. That comes from the fact that I read early on Franz Jung, Heinrich Hauser, and Georges Simenon, and I really liked their language, their quick short sentences.

I saw *Alice in the Cities* by Wenders back when I was fifteen or sixteen—the film ran on a Sunday afternoon on TV. Afterward, I went and bought *Tago Mago*, the LP by CAN. I still have it.

Alice in the Cities plays in part in Wuppertal and on the Rhine, in places that I know. I thought about how Wenders looked at my reality and enchanted it, that's why I went to the cinema. I want that it is enchanted, all this unbearable ugly crap here. The enchantment that is within things that we don't typically perceive, that's exactly what cinema can rediscover. A little bit like Eichendorff in "*Schläft ein Lied in allen Dingen*." Wenders has, I think, this Romanticism. And that really impressed me, I'm sure that reappears in my own work. Harun was not a Romantic at all, but I was Romantic, I think.

IB: Being without a home is one of the basic themes of Wenders. The two men in *Kings of the Road* are stranded in their childhood home on the Rhine, in an empty house they do not want to set up or furnish.

CP: Yeah, but the films have not held up in my memory. Wenders, who is a great writer, wrote a text against Italian westerns. He said that the western is a ballad of loss, of dwelling on the moment in which civilization is founded and certain people don't belong anymore. The Italian western is, compared to that, no western, but rather a nerdy event for students. That really left an impression on me, and after that I saw many westerns. But Wenders always tells masculine stories. Every film by him is a man's film. It simply doesn't work the way the man in *Paris, Texas* comes out of the desert, and his wife is beautifully illuminated. I think Natassja Kinski is a great actor, but she is here only a projection. That wasn't for me—my own masculinity bores me, any kind of self-love doesn't interest me.

IB: *The State I Am In* diverges from the films that you had made up until that point. It is no longer so much about the present but rather about a chapter of German history, the RAF.

CP: I think that with this film I took my leave of Romanticism. Before, they were Romantic films about women and about longing. The desires of women are different than mine, and that was interesting for me. They talk with one another, with a different sensuousness. I can't really put myself entirely within that. I can listen to them, be empathetic, but I cannot be identifying with them.

1993, Bad Kleinen.[5] I was still a student at the film school. I thought that can't be true, I went to Harun's that evening and said: at the train station, there are ghosts from the past sitting around. They run through this train station into a city of which I had never heard. In the eastern part of our republic. And these ghostly events arise from the 1970s, from my youth. The German hatred back then was already ghostly for us. But now here come the ghosts again. And then I thought: Truffaut, Hitchcock, the son, the father—I as a teenager, the ghosts. Then I got the idea that ghosts have children. In a seminar, we had watched *Near Dark* by Kathryn Bigelow. That fit together. They drive around with the car, as vampires cannot stop anywhere, but they want to participate in normal life. And there was blood, the sensuousness.

Out of all this stuff, I wrote an exposé for which I then received a script subsidy. I used that to write the script together with Harun. After shooting *The Sex Thief*, I went to Berkeley, that's where we completed it. Then I received no money for three years, was unemployed for three years. In that time, I wrote *Wolfsburg* and *Ghosts* to keep busy. I had 1.5 million DM and governmental subsidies for film, but not one cent from television. They said that the RAF will not interest anyone anymore.

On the contrary, I thought, it was time, in a now unified Germany, after sixteen years of the government of Helmut Kohl, with its black financial accounts, to really think about where we are living and where we came from.[6] The cinema no longer seems the place for it. On the other hand, that is a big question for the cinema. When I watch *Stromboli* by Rossellini ... husband and wife stand at the fence of a refugee camp, how completely reality is narrated there, and at the same time Rossellini realizes this fantastic sort of cinema, that corresponded to the imagination I had.

IB: *The State I Am In* tells the story of former RAF members, and at the same time it is a film about a family. In that time, between 1996 and 2000, your own children were born. Did that experience play a role?

---

5. This is shorthand for a major event in the early history of unified Germany. In June 1993, the GSG-9 (police tactical unit) discovered former RAF terrorists who had been living underground. In an exchange of gunfire near the Bad Kleinen train station, a GSG-9 officer, Michael Newrzella, and a RAF associate, Wolfgang Grams, were killed.
6. Petzold refers here to the donor scandal that marked the conclusion of Kohl's chancellorship and that helped end it.

CP: Yes. This is the way it is: family dynamics, dinner, table, education, all that is politics, micro-politics. That was interesting to me and was related to the fact that my wife and I tried to have a child even before the birth of our daughter. I sensed that it was necessary for me to get out of my narcissistic search for myself. Therefore, I really wanted to have children. With a desire to have children, I also started making films. The dialogical work method I used to rehearse, think through, and edit the films has a lot to do with the dialogical situation within families. Families strike me like a modern political cell. Without a longing for hierarchical order, with the father at the head of the table. Modern cells—how can they survive in this era, how does the family change?

IB: To have the RAF and family stories referring to another also allows you to show different dynamics?

CP: Yes, that is necessary to tell a story about the RAF. The RAF is an impatient organization that wants to improve the world. This macro-politics of world improvement intersects the micropolitics of the family, which means patience, to be able to wait, to hold on, to repress things. When these two come together, then it gets really interesting. And I have to admit that I really liked the performances of Barbara Auer and Richy Müller. The film does not represent them as jerky 68'er oppressors who turn reactionary, as people who want to take it all back, exculpation, making us feel sorry for them. They learn through their daughter that they have missed something. Through their daughter they talk about things like love, trust, loyalty. I liked that. Actually, they are on the way to something very modern. Certainly, the state wants to shoot them and to take their daughter into custody. Nonetheless, they have a utopian perspective, I think. Ghosts of the past and, on the other hand, ahead of their time, with the Volvo, a bit like the Greens. Greens on the run.

IB: Is *The State I Am In* then a film about not only the RAF but also people from the leftist milieu and what became of them?

CP: I was at a reading of Gerd Koenen's *Das rote Jahrzehnt* [*The Red Decade*] and thought to myself: you all invested so much intellectual energy and power for ten years to break through the fascist crust, all linked up with the discourse of Marxism, Hegelianism, and the 1920s, all rediscovered the literature of Franz Jung, Erich Mühsam, all looked at the Soviet republics. I find it incredible what they achieved. But they also, in those ten years, pushed their thinking far from every sensuousness, every bit of freshness, every beauty—that is just brutal. I was shocked how these people who did so many Marxist courses in the 1970s couldn't tell you, when I asked fifteen years later, anything about how surplus value works. That is like the Latin I learned: it had no grounding.

The two of them in *The State I Am In*, the two who drive around, are among those who did not forget everything. But they are now reduced to their family, they have to bring their daughter through it, and that is the sacrifice they are making. Because to treat the daughter like a sister and to go on alone, basically, their journey into death. Without their daughter, they will die because their daughter means life.

That was a great moment when the parents sit in the front seat, the mother and father are driving, and the daughter screams behind them for her life: "I love you, I don't love him, I love you." That was great, and it wasn't even in the script that way.

IB: As you were waiting to shoot *The State I Am In*, you wrote the scripts for *Wolfsburg* and *Ghosts*? Also for *Something to Remind Me*?

CP: Yeah, I wrote the script for *Wolfsburg* and the treatment for *Ghosts*. *Something to Remind Me* came later.

Wolfsburg really pleased me because it was a really clear plot and because I wanted to do another story about cars after *The State I Am In*. I was with Hartmut Bitomsky for his Scharoun film in *Wolfsburg*, and it occurred to me at that time. Wolfsburg is the city of Germans. I am from near the city of Leverkusen, and it's exactly that way there—for example, both have soccer clubs in the first league that are sponsored [by large corporations—eds.] and aren't funded from their own proceeds.

Harun read a short story on a flight back from America. It was really simple: a man meets a woman, she sleeps with him, the next morning he wakes up and is getting dressed. When she wakes up, he says, "Listen, you think that I just wanted to go" (this is all in a hotel room). "That's not right, quite the opposite, I'll go get breakfast and then we'll get married. That might sound stupid, but you are the woman of my life, and that was the best time I've ever had." Then she says, "Stop, no, that won't work. I can't stay with you. I will leave you, we can't see each other again. I have a sister who was murdered. The perpetrator is in prison, and he will someday be released, and if I get married, fall in love, have children, then the death of my sister is final. That has to be avenged, and I have to sacrifice something—I have to deny myself happiness." And goes. This was the story that I told to the ZDF, and they said, yes, you can make it. And then Harun and I wrote *Something to Remind Me* within ten days. A few things about the work world did flow into it, especially about attorneys.

IB: During this time, did you study genres like revenge films, TV crime thrillers, and horror films?

CP: I would never quote them, that would be boring. I also wouldn't crack open a genre because they do not exist anymore. Because, today, the people who see films do not recognize the grammar of the genre anymore. You can't rely on the audience anymore. But I believe that I was educated in the melodrama of Douglas Sirk, in the films of Robert Siodmak, the black series, and Fritz Lang—those are cinematographic educations.

But the theme for me are people who drop or fall out. The vengeful woman in *Something to Remind Me* has dropped out, the single-mother in *Wolfsburg* has dropped out. There's the boss who wants to tango with her because she's pretty, and he has power. Otherwise, he'd never have the confidence to talk to someone this pretty. He's her superior, and he can make her life hell. Because she has a child, she can be hurt. And these people who drop or fall out are those who want to get back to the living—that is the theme. They take for themselves what's available, in a criminal manner. Because the social context itself is criminal. I find it criminal when people who work in a preschool earn 11 euro an hour. The wage structure in Germany is a social crime.

IB: The fury with which your films worked ten years ago is only becoming clear now, socially speaking.

CP: Yeah, the fury is there, and the fury is also holding the society together. But the people who are furious are mostly too meek. I read back then these doctor stories, "A Night in June," by William Carlos Williams: "Let the successful carry off their blue ribbons; I have known the unsuccessful, far better persons than their more lucky brothers."[7]

IB: *Ghosts*—the film is different from your other films. It's not about suspense, not about crime. The film is more a kind of station drama, narrated over twenty-four hours, a certain moment in the life of a teenage girl. And it comprises two places in the heart of Berlin, the Potsdamer Platz and the Tiergarten. How did the film come into being?

CP: That was a bit as I described above. I had written a short story, and Harun read it. That's how every script starts. Sometimes the short story doesn't really contribute much, then it's thrown out and forgotten. Sometimes, as in this case, it becomes the script.

A girl works in a bakery, a woman comes in and orders bread, and she is fully confused. She goes away and stands in front of the window looking back into the bakery. Then the girl gets off, her boyfriend picks her up, they drive around, her boyfriend sleeps with her. The next day she's tired out, as she hardly slept, is sad, because her boyfriend is a jerk. She is back in the bakery, stands behind the counter, the woman comes back in and the girl asks: was there something wrong with the bread, as she had bought a whole loaf the day before? "No," the woman answers. "I have a very dumb request—can I see your shoulder blade?" The girl asks, "Why? Naturally, you can't see that." "But I would like to know whether you're the one who has a birthmark in the form of a rose on your shoulder." And the girl says, "That doesn't concern you at all." To which the woman begins

---

7. This quote is actually from *The Autobiography of William Carlos Williams* (New York: New Directions, 1951), 358.

to cry and says that she has to know. The girl just wants the woman to leave, but she doesn't, and then the baker comes out and throws her out. After work, the girl notices the woman is following her. She goes home and looks in the mirror, and you see that she has this rose.

Harun thought that it was a good story. I wanted to narrate, in a very distant fashion, the deep melodramatic and Late Romantic subject there in the material. The deep longing of the characters: for origins, a middle, a center, identity. Where do I come from? Who am I actually? What kind of city is Berlin, really? The Tiergarten, the Potsdamer Platz, the center, who are we really? All the politicians are yelling for the center and identity and the German museum, but nothing is really learned, nothing grasped. That was the subject.

The relative lack of success for the film really took it out of me, I have to say. I had planned a French part with Isabelle Adjani that we didn't end up shooting, so we had to work around it. The figure of the woman did not really have to be a French woman, that might have simplified the whole matter. And we didn't cast any stars in it. Maybe a film that takes up a lack of a center has to have a star in it and an identity in order to engage with a lack of identity. Oh well, regardless, the scene with the casting is still my favorite scene in my work.

IB: Yeah, the casting scene is the most beautiful of *Ghosts*.

CP: The brutal thing is that we had to shoot the scene twice. The first time the scene was different, perhaps even stronger, but maybe not. It was incredibly well played, lasted ten minutes. It was incredible what Julia and Sabine did, and also Benno, we were all exhausted afterward and knew that it was great. We shot with several cameras, and as we looked at the whole thing afterwards, there were two problems. The whole time we could hear the heartbeats of the women. That was so loud because they so identified with what they were doing that the mic could pick up their hearts. We could've digitalized that out, but then there was also something not great with the background of the image, it "pumped" the whole time, and even now we still don't know what that was. The producers thought that we couldn't leave it that way, and I said, no, don't make us shoot it again, please don't. The insurance reviewed the material, for otherwise I would not have had any money to reshoot. Then I had to ask Julia Hummer to do the scene again. She broke down because she thought she was not good enough. I had to explain all that with the pumping and the insurance. And then we tagged on the reshoot to the end of the shooting days we had planned. With the second take, there is more defiance, more fury. As we shot it the first time, I thought the two will break down completely.

IB: In *Ghosts*, the locations have a special meaning. The party space in which the two women dance becomes a kind of red color-space. The Tiergarten that is next to the Potsdamer Platz is a kind of thicket. In your other films as well, the houses are on the edge of the forest, not next to a street.

CP: That has something to do with how the physical has been lost in the cinema of Germany. The physical for me is not only the houses but also the wind, the leaves, the forest, the transition from one aggregate state to another, the dampness, the cold. All of that is part of the enchantment [*Verzauberung*]. It has a lot to do with Antonioni's work, which I really, really like to watch. I found it great in *Blow-up* that an Italian nobleman who lived his whole life aristocratically, who built houses on Sardinia with Monica Vitti, went to London and understood the Beat generation [*sic*]. He can film concerts, trees, parks because he sees the city. That is a cinema that can perceive the world.

It was similar for me with *Ghosts*. Look at it: the freeway, Berlin, one drives into it like a real city. The city doesn't know what it is. One drives out to Müggelsee, there's a villa, a former industrialist's villa. Ruins of the industrial society, and a film producer moves in. Places of the industrial society become places of the leisure society. And in this world unfolds a very simple story, a tale of the Brothers Grimm.

IB: *Yella* is another ghost story. You worked here again with Nina Hoss, who received a lot of recognition for her dramatic achievement as Yella.

CP: When shooting *Something to Remind Me*, I hardly knew Nina. There she performs herself, as a projection for the male gaze. She deceives the man, steals his laptop, and takes from the other one his life.

For *Wolfsburg*, I had at first another idea for casting the main character. With the dark wig, as a single mother, Nina comes across as if she were born in the false world. She has something aristocratic about her, and the role is a proletarian role.

IB: Jean Renoir cast his actors against their social origins.

CP: *My Life and My Films* by Renoir is another of the really great books, translated by Frieda Grafe.

Yella is another projection story. The blonde woman lives in the east with a man who loves her a ton but runs his small, middle-class business into the ground. And she is a queen and dreams herself somewhere else: I want to leave, I want to go there where the new, sexy pictures of capitalism are. And, of course, it's a star who feels that way. She's a minor goddess; Marlene Dietrich or Romy Schneider could have played that role. And I thought, "Nina has to play this."

Nina comes from a theater family, from another world, but somehow makes the impression to belong nowhere in particular, no matter what the social origin. There it was important that she played it. Also because of her way of performing. Because the character in *Carnival of Souls* is a woman who is not from this world and has already crossed into the realm of the dead, because she doesn't any have real life anyway. And Nina's way of performing really pleased me. She only has for very short moments something quotidian about her, very short moments that are great. She drinks a cup of coffee.

IB: A smile.

CP: In the break, on the balcony, as the others listen to Mozart, she has to laugh, for it is fun for her. Finally, she thinks, the man that I, as a queen, wanted on my side. Not this doofus, played wonderfully by Hinnerk Schönemann, whom she transforms in her dream into this wonderful man who smells fantastic and who listens to music barefoot in his suite.

Jerichow was not planned for Nina Hoss at first. The figure of Laura is really the town hussy [*Ortsschlampe*], who falls in with a Turk, who sells her body for money—a hussy but a sad one in debt who has screwed up her life.

After *Yella*, I drove back from Hof with Nina. I had an old Mercedes at that point, and she sat in the passenger seat. While we were chatting, I told her about *Jerichow*, and while I was explaining it, we heard a string quartet by Beethoven and were quiet for a moment, and then Bresson came into my mind. He had cast Anne Wiazemsky, daughter of a diplomat, from an upper-class family. He asked her to walk like a peasant and put wooden shoes on her. So, I asked Nina—say, do you want to play it, with cowboy boots and all? She loved that idea. She played the character with an embittered mien because that is, after all, also a fallen queen.

With me, the characters all get a backstory that doesn't get into the film. This character had opened a fitness club until it became clear that McFit[8] was coming with its much cheaper prices, so bankruptcy followed, with lots of debt. She met the Turk who said, "Listen, you can drive around here with a Range Rover, you live in absolute luxury, but you have to tolerate—although you are, in your blonde heart of hearts, a racist—that I would like to sleep with you every night. So, you belong to me." And she sells herself and that leads to the fact that she would like to murder him.

IB: Alasdair King characterizes *Jerichow* in his essay on it as a *Heimatfilm*-noir.

CP: The notion is correct. Franz Jung wrote in his book at the beginning of the 1920s a lot about class struggle in the US, about the Pinkerton detective, the employers, the mine owners, the bloody clues that they left behind as they destroyed the working class and its unions. Woody Guthrie tells this story a lot in his songs. As I read the book—Harun had given it to me for my birthday—I asked myself: where does the class struggle come up in US cinema or, rather, how is it hidden? Because of McCarthy and the blacklist, the subject could hardly be taken up, but nonetheless it did come up. Harun thought that *The Postman Always*

---

8. McFit is a German-based chain of budget "fitness studios," that is, gyms across Europe.

Rings Twice by James Cain is the book of class struggle. So, we came up with the idea of writing *Jerichow*. That's why that's right: a *Heimatfilm*-noir.

IB: *Jerichow* plays in the Prignitz. The region is, in your work, an impoverished, barren anti-homeland.

CP: The people are trying to be American there, drive pickups, wear flannel shirts and jeans, they all seem as if they are from Hornbach, the home improvement story, all home improvement people.

IB: In 2009, you made *Dreileben* with Dominik Graf and Christoph Hochhäusler.

CP: That was a real pleasure. We needed maybe half a year more for preparation, to adjust. We could have done it so you couldn't see afterward who made which film. That would have been fun, in retrospect. But that wasn't up for discussion. I still find the films all so good, in their autonomy. But only together could we create that *Twin Peaks* atmosphere that marked Thuringia. Maybe we had a bit of fear before. There is never a situation, when you're a director, to observe another director on set. Only as an assistant. But, funnily enough, when we were shooting and were on the sets of the others, it was actually lovely. I found it great to see how Dominik and Christoph work. I felt great curiosity. That was like with three carpenters who meet and ask, "What did you do with the wood?" We learned that if you love the object—if you love cinema—then feelings of competition don't play any role at all. I would love to work with the two of them again.

IB: *Beats Being Dead*, your film in the trilogy, takes up the theme of growing up, as in *The State I Am In* and *Ghosts*.

CP: As I was in the US with Harun, I read that in earlier doctor novels the doctors always fell in love with the nurses who looked so good in their uniforms. But this motif had disappeared, and, in the newer doctor serials, the doctors marry among themselves instead of the office assistants. What happened there, we wondered. Then Harun found out that the rents in New York had gotten so high that a doctor and a nurse could never afford an apartment. Everyone has to stay within their class to maintain their living standards. From that, we had an idea for a film.

The protagonist meets someone, a refugee girl, from the lowest socioeconomic group, a bit like [Coppola's] *Youth without Youth*. At the same time, he's on the way to an upper-class life and has to choose the girl from the upper class. Through this he kills the other girl. He feels the pain and guilt, and then the film ends.

IB: *Barbara*. From the three chapters of German history that [your] cinema takes up, East Germany history is one of them. In *Yella* and *Jerichow*, they appear indirectly, as a trace in the present. Why did you want to make a historical film at that point?

CP: I planned to make three historical films, which I named, "About love in the time of systems in decline." About moments in history about which one wonders: how can one survive privately?

I had become familiar with *The Enchantment*, a novel by Hermann Broch, a long time ago through a friend, back at the end of the 1970s. I always found his novella *Barbara* great. And as I was in Stuttgart with Nina to shoot *Something to Remind Me*, I saw the Insel edition of *Barbara*. I bought it and gave it to Nina as a gift, because on the cover there was a painting that looked just like her. She was already Barbara.

Then I met a doctor from the GDR, who told me what happened to doctors who applied for exit visas. Men had to become military doctors, women were sent to the provinces.

I worked for two weeks with Harun on the script, at Scharmützelsee. That went really quickly.

IB: When did you have the idea to make historical films?

CP: After *Jerichow*. I didn't know when and in which order I would shoot them. But that the films would be based on *Transit*, *Return from the Ashes*, and *Barbara* was clear. One of the three would play in the disappearing East Germany, another in the disappearing Nazism, and the third in a disappearing civil society. With *Barbara*, it was clear Nina would do it. The character from *Der fremde Freund* by Christoph Hein is also a female doctor who has a relationship with a man who wants to go to the West and later dies. Bodies pulled back into themselves, mistrustful conversations. Family bubble around the grill where one can be open, but outside an oppressive atmosphere. That's how I perceived East Germany.

It was a pleasure to research the film. I could ask my mother, who came from there. I saw that the GDR was a country of oppression that also had wonderful summers and longing, "You forgot the color film." And *The Lives of Others* got on my nerves a bit, that it was the only image of East Germany. I didn't want everything to be gray. I found great photos at my mother's, slides from summer vacation, that radiated like Technicolor. That's how it had to look.

IB: *Barbara* is also different from some films that show East Germany as very colorful, like [Leander Haußmann's] *Sun Alley*. For you, it's not only about color but also about beauty?

CP: When systems decline and are about to disappear—as with a flea market when the things that belong in the trash are put out once more, shortly before they land in the garbage—they show their grandeur one more time, show what was beautiful in them. And East Germany in decline shows once again the justification for its existence, what its dream was. Namely, that people work, that they love their work passionately, and that, through work, identity is produced. Not through money, money plays no roll at all. The money that one got from the West had no exchange value, is merely a symbol. Everything else—food—plays a much bigger role. The eggplant is worth more than 10,000 DM. I wanted to show what kind of life these people who came out of exile, out of the camps, also from the camps of Stalinism back to East Germany, what these peopled dreamed—that once again a breath of fresh air goes through the history. Before it became clear that the apparatchiks made it into nothing. That the beauty that was shining in this summer when Barbara wants to leave the system, that this beauty is there once more. I want that it appears more important than the supposed freedom that the West offers when the lover says, "You don't need to work, I'll earn enough for us both." That is all that West Germany is for her in this moment, a reactionary beauty, while East Germany destroyed its revolutionary beauty.

IB: The film's end is, however, staged quite ambiguously.

CP: I explained to the actors how I saw it going further, before we shot the end. I didn't say when the camera would stop recording, just that it was clear that she would stay. She might get one or two years of prison, but the man loves her. Then she comes out, and they work together. And then 1989 comes, and they unfortunately have to separate, the whole thing falls apart, their love blowing up in their faces.

IB: But she stays as well because she wants to save the girl, to stand up for someone.

CP: Exactly. Nina said that if she had such a position in East Berlin at the Charité hospital, she must have denounced people as well. She would have cleared an old guilt. I found that not bad at all.

IB: *Phoenix* came right after *Barbara*.

CP: While I was editing *Barbara*, I was contemplating what I should do next. Then Harun saw *Barbara* on the editing table shortly before it was to be released, and he said that I should work more with the couple Ronald and Nina, that they are really good, and that I could make *Phoenix* with them. Then I wrote the script, got the money, and had good things happen during the shoot.

From the first day on, I knew that I was doing colportage. Of course, *Return from the Ashes* is a pulp [*Kolportage*] novel. Cosmetic surgery, face surgery. I had to laugh—back then there was a program in the Marmorhaus, the cinema on the Kurfürstendamm. Twelve films for twelve DM. Sometimes I liked to go because it was trash, gangster films or comedies, and once there was *Emmanuelle 6* [Bruno Zincone], an erotic film. I watched it because I had seen [Just Jaeckin's] *Emmanuelle 1* with my uncle. That occurred to me, somehow I like that, that is also cinema. And the dumb assholes think that one has to stage Nazism without colportage.

IB: In films about the Holocaust, directors like to play classical music, with a lot of violins, in the background.

CP: Yeah, against that you have what Rossellini did in *Rome, Open City*, to show the lesbian and the prostitute who worked with the fascists, a real affront. In general, to think fascism and sexuality together. The conviction that the German officers never raped anyone has really been deeply implanted.

I knew I was working on a somewhat mined topic. And this knowledge didn't leave us during the whole shoot. *Phoenix* is, indeed, a story about Nazism, guilt, and repression—and, at the same time, a colportage, a story of men and women. About directors, their muses, women whom they create, a Pygmalion and Galatea story.

It was very stressful to shoot in this ambivalence; the actors always had to maintain this balance. Such a thing can really tip over, into comedy or fake sentimentality. Against that, I wanted to maintain the balance. I wanted that those who returned, the survivors, had the desire to turn back time, to annul everything, to plug up this nihilistic hole. And at the same time, to show that that is impossible.

IB: The film allows the Nelly character to implement the dream of return because the cinema can fulfill dreams and realize such a resurrection? I thought of *Ponette* by Jacques Doillon. The film fulfills the impossible wish of the girl to see her dead mother again. The scene plays in the cemetery and is quite trashy.

CP: The scene in which you see the hand of the mother? That is lovely, a great film.

IB: I don't know if you can compare that . . .

CP: One can, indeed, compare it. As I wrote the script, I thought about how Primo Levi and Jean Améry, to survive in Auschwitz, fled into parallel worlds. Jean Améry reconstructed Proust's *In Search of Lost Time* in his head. He went through all eight volumes. And Primo Levi did similarly, fled into the memories of his childhood as well as into the natural sciences, into the periodic table. I imagined that Nelly is in Auschwitz and imagined to herself that she returned to her husband, to work herself back into her life. There are parallels to *Yella*, also because Nelly and Yella are similar names. The dream of a woman, who otherwise can't handle the unimaginable. That was the basic thought. She is actually dead, and at the end she goes and leaves us behind. We are the ones left behind. She goes as if it's a Jacob's ladder, faraway. I didn't say it that way to the actors during the shoot, maybe I should have. It's a difficult balance.

IB: *Phoenix* reminded me of the films of Pedro Almodóvar that also often play with trivial culture.

CP: Exactly. In Germany, no one really liked *Phoenix*. But in the US, in Toronto, France, England, it was a big success. There are countries, I thought, in which the cinema plays a big role in self-understanding, where they get their identities from cinema. We don't have that, we don't trust the cinema because it was the propaganda department of Ufa, brought to you by Goebbels.

IB: After *Phoenix*, you made *Wolves* and *Circles*. Were you commissioned to do the *Polizeirufe* or were they done on your own initiative?

CP: After *Phoenix*, I wanted to make a couple of B-films, to breathe a bit.

During the Berlin Film Festival in 2012, Cornelia Ackers, the commissioning producer of Bavarian TV, asked me if I had any interest in making a *Polizeiruf*. Through my friendship with Dominik Graf, my heart beats a bit in that direction. After he got his degree from film school in Munich, Dominik directed thirteen episodes of *Der Fahnder*. That is comparable to Robert Altman's work on *Bonanza*. There, he, if you will, had a second education and learned the film grammar that had been destroyed in the film schools.

I always love it when Dominik would talk about it, and I thought to myself that would be interesting: ninety minutes, a given framework with a limited budget, characters that are already written, and a context of television. Before me, the news, and after me, Anne Will or Günther Jauch.[9] That means that I don't have to build an architectural artwork from the ground up but rather fill in a vacant lot between buildings. Then I can decide: either for the retro-baroque of neoliberal Berlin and make a film that, like many of these films from 8:15 p.m. [i.e., prime time/just after the evening news], only acts as if it's a film. Or to be more humble and more creative.

After I got the call from Ackers, I looked at various *Polizeiruf* episodes. I was familiar with the figure of Hanns von Meuffels that Matthias Brandt plays from episodes by Dominik and that from Jan Bonny with the fantastic title *Death Makes Angels Out of Us All*. As I watched additional episodes, I thought that really is a whole world. Inwardly, I had taken my leave of police stations because, in the last ten years, I had nothing to do with police, crime, Germany. I only saw people who are vegan and who live in lofts, play the saxophone. And that annoyed me a bit. Police work was for me still filter coffee, trench coat, worn-down shoe soles. That was still for me George Smiley, John Le Carré. That was still freezing, darkness, marriages that are destroyed. The police don't have a nine-to-five job, don't participate in social life, are on the edge of society. And their loneliness that I found in the old figures with Eric Ode or by Derrick, but above all in the US films like Don Siegel's *Madigan*—there I saw the Matthias Brandt character. Then I wrote, very quickly, with this character in my head.

Harun had been for many years constantly traveling. When you are an artist—and Harun became an artist—you have to constantly travel with your work. As if the work only counts if the artist is also there. I don't even know with how many different time zones and jet lags he dealt. I think that the many trips were primarily responsible for his early death. After *Phoenix*, I was alone. I was exhausted

---

9. Hosts of popular TV news talk shows.

and had the feeling that I needed to change my work methods, my storytelling perspective. For years, I had made films that were experimental designs, labors of love. And *Phoenix* was probably the hardest labor of love. Not for nothing was the short story by Alexander Kluge, "Ein Liebesversuch," really important for me.

So, now I had this model train story. Here, there are individual parts around in the room, behind you the train station of Kehl, all my life I've loved model trains. I wanted to tell a story about a person who builds models. The character is played by Justus von Dohnányi. About someone who lives a false life, who's imprisoned in a social prison and who frees himself through his models. At some point, he loses the boundary between the model landscape and reality, goes into his model landscape, and kills there. But this death is bloody, stinks, and hurts. At the end, he's had this experience and turns himself in. That is basically the story.

I met with Cornelia Ackers, the first time with Matthias Brandt. Matthias is a careful person. That is unusual for actors. The first meeting between director and actor is always a scary encounter because it's a kind of date and one can do a lot wrong. I liked as he listened, looked, probed, and I had the feeling that the figure of Hanns von Meuffels had a lot of this actor in it. Of course, I also knew that he is the son of Willy Brandt, knew his approach. I don't really believe that someone can perform entirely differently than he or she actually is.

It was a Saturday, we sat in the literature café in the Fasanenstrasse. I said that I had to go at 3:30 p.m. to watch soccer. I noticed a flash of the eyes, then everything went quickly: Werder, Gladbach, Günter Netzer,[10] favorite book, 1970s. We liked one another immediately, I think, at least from my side.

[Hanns von Meuffels] is a character from a novel. Or like a novel author who collects the stories of others and processes them, but who himself lives through no stories of his own. I found that worked as a metaphor for the detective very well. Then it occurred to me: perhaps Barbara Auer, who is one of best actors that I know. And I thought that she is also someone who is in her early fifties, a film and tv actress. The characters that she has played are her biography, such that she also had no life of her own. I thought that she is pretty but also tough. I thought to put them together in the first scene in a car and to let them struggle, to let them discover love, before they are fearful. So came the second character.

So, there were two stories, that with Justus von Dohnányi and that with Barbara Auer and Matthias Brandt. That they once more in their lives stand at this crossroads, have this opportunity once more—perhaps they've dreamt of it, but they are simultaneously enormously afraid of it.

---

10. The first three elements of the list reference important parts of 1970s soccer culture. Netzer was a star attacking midfielder of Mönchengladbach, the team that Petzold supports.

I had twenty-three shooting days. Through my experience over the thirteen films and with Iris Jung, the assistant director with whom I've worked for fifteen years, I was able to work very efficiently. I never seek locations by, for instance, driving all around looking for a pretty house, a parking lot, to find something beautiful. I work with everything in one neighborhood. Maybe that arises from the fact that I drive very little when I'm seeking motifs; instead, I am on the move on foot or on a bike. I seek a main motif and then go around and look where I can shoot the other things and change the script to accord with it. I would rather not lose so much energy through moving. If you have only twenty-three shooting days, it's already over when you have to move around the area with sixty or seventy people and nineteen trucks. Then there's just too much work for logistics, and everyone is moaning about it. For that reason, I'd rather build up an area from which we can then drive to our guerilla attacks. That has worked pretty well. We even won a prize as best production.

I start at 9 a.m. and finish by 5 p.m. A number of friends—for example, Dominik—hate that, but I am as a I am.

IB: A breaker of norms?

CP: Exactly, not a strike breaker, but a norm breaker. It was a lovely shoot, and I learned a lot through the collaboration with the actors, with Barbara and Matthias. There's a feeling of being adult, of calm, reflection. At the rehearsals, we watched *Le petit Lieutenant* by Xavier Beaujolais together. The observations by Barbara and Matthias and their commentary showed much of their life experience. I thought that I would like to make a series or a trilogy with them. As *Circles* was well received, I could, indeed, make a second *Polizeiruf*.

IB: *Wolves*.

CP: I wrote a story about werewolves at some point. Sometimes I do that like this: Saturday, Gladbach lost, it is a horribly long Saturday, I'm alone at home, so I sit down and write a little story to distract myself. It was a little short story, but then I revised it. The good thing was that I had two characters, those from Barbara Auer and Matthias Brandt, who are already there, who have biographies. I had a feeling that these figures were looking at me, and I imagined what they would do in certain situations.

Yesterday, I read the Truffaut-Hitchcock book one more time, the new edition in which Fischer Verlag extended the afterword. The afterword is based on a text from Truffaut that he wrote after the death of Hitchcock about Hitchcock's last year alive. In it, Truffaut describes how Hitchcock would explain to his interlocutor precisely the next film he planned to make. I do that, too: I explain the film from the first image on, which colors I will have, all the details. By checking whether I can tell the story and how someone listens, I see whether it works. As I explained, what I was imagining to Matthias and Barbara, I had the feeling that

that was effective with the wolves. As we shot *Wolves* in the Bavarian Forest, we were all in a hotel, and there the story for the third part occurred to me, which we just shot.

It is also a love story that I do not want to show directly: for example, detectives in pajamas, a female detective who gets out of the bed of a male detective, who is half-naked and goes to shower, and he makes them breakfast—I don't want that at all. Therefore, in the first part I told the story of how they get to know each other, how they did not want to get to know each other, but the feelings are strong. And in the second part, they become a couple, although it is after the end of this part. In the third part, they are apart again. That is also part of a crime film, that the act is already over.

IB: How did you become interested in wolves and wolf mythology?

CP: There is in Germany a revival of wolves: as Nazis, as wolves protected by the Green Party, as wolves attacked by hunters, as wolves hated by farmers, myths and fairy tales of "The Wolf and the Seven Little Kids," werewolves. That all seemed a bit absurd to me. I had the feeling that it is actually a media story. We pretend that we don't all shop in the same malls at H&M or at Peek & Cloppenburg, don't all use the same social networks that have rendered the whole world indifferent, this horrible exchange value making everything the same. With the wolves, something from much earlier emerges. But somehow you have the feeling that there is only one wolf that they shoot, that there's only one Nazi with a wolf tattoo. The Gray Wolves[11] at the beginning of the 1980s were something like a deep state in Germany, the horrible fascist agents and murderers. But for me, those were all retro images. I found that I could not present the theme at 8:15 p.m. [i.e., prime time/just after the evening news] and have Anne Will speak afterward about wolves, but rather I had to show that this is all a lot of nonsense. Please do not act as if we live in a jungle here. That was my thought, and I think that that was one turn too many, a bit too clever of me.

IB: Once more to *Circles*. You said that for you it had to do with maintaining the framework of a TV detective drama, to take seriously its world and characters. Is that true, too, of the milieu that *Circles* takes up: a business-owning family, a mansion?

CP: The artificial worlds that cinema creates, such as the suburban mansion or, in the case of television, the pharmacy- or doctor series in which all German actors act, are purely constructed worlds. Behind the walls of this, upper-middle-class—as in the houses of the nobility earlier in the literature—intrigues

---

11. A series of organizations that started as offshoots of a Turkish extreme right-wing organization, the Gray Wolves now comprise in their entirety a large, extreme right-wing organization in Germany.

and passions play out that only the police see. Therefore, everyone wants to be a police officer or a gangster, because they get to go in. The gangster enters this world, steals the jewelry, and is shot dead. The detective can pose questions: what were you doing, where were you? He has the power and, at the same time, satisfies our curiosity, like tabloids. Instead, today, there is a kind of realism. Some screen writers have to rework every theme that appears in the newspaper for a *Tatort* or *Polizeiruf*, be it Nazis, child abuse, computers, virtual reality. Instead of that, what interested me was this world in Munich-Grünwald. The rich build themselves fortresses because they have the feeling that it isn't right that they have so much money.

IB: When did you return to your plan to film Seghers's *Transit*?

CP: Originally, I wanted to start to write the screenplay for *Transit* after *Phoenix*, and had even sent a treatment to Harun. He wrote me a week before he died that that was great, but that I shouldn't have so many people die at the beginning—the story starts with a roundup—otherwise I'd have to build to thousands of people dying at the end. As Harun died, I didn't want to work on it anymore. *Transit* was our favorite book. I couldn't even open the notes that we'd worked on together.

Somewhat later, I wondered why I didn't have any desire to do *Transit*. I didn't have any desire to make another historical film. That was the reason. And then an idea occurred to me: *Transit* plays in 1940–41 in Marseille, but I shoot it today and, indeed, as yesterday. I have people from 1941 run around in today's Marseille, they look like today, wear Adidas, but they talk like back then, stating, for example, that tomorrow they have to get on the ship because the Nazis are already in Paris.

IB: So, you let the time levels oscillate?

CP: Exactly, and I wanted to shoot that analog. We shot at the MuCem, a museum right on the Mediterranean. That is Marseille, a city open to the Mediterranean, and at the same time there is a fort that closes off the Mediterranean. A place of freedom and breadth, in which power, in the Foucauldian sense, at the same time establishes the opposite. Wherever there is sexuality, there is repression. Wherever there is the opening of borders, borders are drawn. Such was the thought.

A friend who helped Dominik Graf with his film *Beloved Sisters* gave me a quote. With it, Adorno introduced the Hegel lectures in Frankfurt. To the shamelessness of the question of what Hegel means to us today, one can answer only in the following way: what do we mean to Hegel? Adorno starts with that. I liked that—sounds a bit conservative, but what is meant: history is not only something from which we learn, from which we serve ourselves, that can form us. We also have to justify our contemporary present to history. People who gave their lives in 1871, 1848,[12] and 1918 in the November revolution—what do we say when we stand before them? When those exiled in 1940–41 in Sanary, near Marseille, swore that something like this would never happen again, what can we tell them today? That was the political thought.

---

12. With 1871 and 1848, Petzold is referring to revolutionary moments in French and then broader European history. In 1871, the Paris Commune was formed and then dismantled by the French national army with great loss of life, while 1848 saw uprisings across Europe pursuing concessions on bourgeois rights from the powers that were.

"Escape Is the Normal Condition"

Christiane Peitz / 2018

From "Flucht ist der Normalzustand," *Tagesspiegel*, February 16, 2018. Reprinted by permission. Translated by Marco Abel and Jaimey Fisher.

Christiane Peitz: Mr. Petzold, how did you encounter Anna Seghers and her novel *Transit*?

Christian Petzold: In the 1970s, I discovered her story "The Dead Girls' Outing" ["Der Ausflug der toten Mädchen"]. At the time, I was a big fan of Wolfgang Neuss; his record with Wolf Biermann is about the history of German lyrics, and after the line "Ist unser Volk der Reimerchen seit Gottfried Benn im Eimerchen?" ["Is our people of rhymesters done for?"], Neuss makes fun of Anna Seghers. That's why I thought that Seghers must be horrible. But then I read the story, not least due to the terrific title. An incredible story. Shortly thereafter I got to know Harun Farocki....

Peitz: ... with whom you cowrote for many years your scripts ...

Petzold: ... he gave me the novel. At the time, I read almost exclusively American literature and could not believe what I read: that's like Charles Willeford, Jim Thompson, or Hemmingway! A first-person narrator who says, I'm going to tell you a story, as if at the bar or harbor—the story of German emigrants in Marseille plays in a harbor city. *Transit* connects to all the stories Harun and I had previously told in our films.

Peitz: Stories about lost people?

Petzold: About people who are looking for home [Heimat] and whose sadness is the result of their belief that they have a home. At the end of John Huston's *Asphalt Jungle*, Sterling Hayden, who is bleeding and dying, walks on a horse pasture, and the viewer learns that he used to live on a ranch as a child. The banks have destroyed the farms. This is a real loss of home. In Anna Seghers this doesn't exist. The origin is at best a theme, when the narrator remembers how his mother used to sign a song for him. But he cannot go back there.

Peitz: How come you keep making films about homeless, about the invisible, from *The State I Am In* to *Ghosts* to *Phoenix*?

Petzold: Perhaps it has to do with the fact that both Farocki and I are children of refugees. Invisible identities are the basis of cinema. They are still in the process of becoming, transparent, fleeting, still looking for themselves. Cinema itself is a transit space. Otherwise, it turns into *Lindenstraße*.[1]

Peitz: *Heimat* is a much-discussed topic these days. You say it doesn't exist?

Petzold: Escape is the normal condition. That's what *Transit* is about. The novel reveals: all ideologies that claim a stable identity or place [of belonging] exist are false. Our small town that we have to defend: this always leads to problems. [Martin McDonagh's] *Three Billboards Outside Ebbing, Missouri* ends with a protagonist driving with a sawed-off shotgun and contemplates revenge. *Transit* in an incredibly consoling book—about the space of transit where the real stories and identities are located. A space that otherwise is precisely not a narrative space. We do not listen to the refugees.

Peitz: You mean today's refugees?

Petzold: Once or twice a week, I play badminton in a court at Columbiadamm right across from Tempelhof airport, where for two years 3,000 refugees were housed. We do not get to know their stories; I did not even see them. We render these people invisible by virtue of the fact that we do not perceive them. Today's refugees were an important trigger for *Transit*. We had started writing the script earlier, as a historical film, even though after *Phoenix* I was no longer in the mood for making another costume drama. To rebuild a past world requires a lot of strength—having to deal with men with their twirled mustaches and the advertising slogans, "cash for antiques," having to rent these old cars. I didn't want this anymore. In any case, every film is in the present. It isn't the job of art to be like the past but, rather, to image one's own perception.

Peitz: What does this mean in relation to *Transit*?

Petzold: We both had the sense that something was off. Then Harun unexpectedly died in July 2014. At first, I needed time. I shot a *Polizeiruf* and traveled with my son to America, where I continued to write. But the desert was so hot that my computer hard drive burnt. The data could not be recovered, and I had no backup. The people at the computer shop thought I needed to go to the ER, but the opposite was the case: I was relieved.

Peitz: Because you could start anew?

Petzold: I suddenly knew that I did not want to adapt a novel but instead wanted to discover why I'm reading it. Is it for biographical reasons: my

---

1. Long-running (1985–2020) and very popular German soap opera that foregrounded daily life and troubles on a street in Munich (Lindenstraße).

Sudeten-German mother, my grandmother who was raped, the Beneš decrees,[2] the SS past of my grandfather? It is about what is not told in Germany. Harun and I thought a lot about Hoyerswerda, Mölln,[3] and the figure of the refugee. I imagined it literally: A man in southern France in front of the embassy today. He says, "You have to help me, the Nazis are trying to get me." It didn't seem strange to me. You just have to substitute "fascists" for "Nazis" because the former captures right-wing radicalism in Europe better.

Peitz: You locate the novel in contemporary Marseille without "updating" it. Because you want to make a different historical cinema. What do you mean?

Petzold: That which is non-pedagogical. On TV, Maria Furtwängler has to discuss on a talk show *Die Flucht* as its heroine after its screening. Not her experience as an actress but as if she herself had been on the run. No one would have ever gotten the idea to ask Robert De Niro to ask how it is to live as a Vietnam vet after *The Deer Hunter*. Such a conception of film and acting kills me. Cinema is much more resistive! It's always been a place where the state, propaganda, is not able to prevail. In John Ford films, thousands of Native Americans are killed, and yet one never has the feeling that his films are racist. Because a sense of guilt always resonates, the suffering of the victims, the complexity of the story.

Peitz: You say that we do not hear the stories of the refugees. Is your film one of these?

Petzold: All films try to tell their story. Cinema has more to do with oral history than we want to realize. I always had wanted to work with voice-over, even if voice-over has gotten a bad reputation. I now did it, with Mattias Brandt's voice.

Peitz: A Petzold film with voice-over? And with new actors: Paula Beer, Franz Rogowski. How come?

Petzold: Paula Beer also claims that this film is different from my others. I think previously I made laboratory films: I constructed a situation and observed what is happening with the characters. With empathy, but I did not want to show this too strongly. In *Barbara*, I already allowed for some measure of consolation, but this too was an experimental setup. GDR 1980, here the woman who wants to go to the West, there Ronald Zehrfeld who stays and tries to do good. Art is construction, composition, but with *Transit* I felt for the first time that it is not a laboratory, the narratives overlap and take on a life of their own, just like in Chekhov's plays. And they say: no, we won't board the ship, we remain here, in this transit space.

---

2. This refers to the decrees of the president and the ordinances of the Slovak National Council (SNR) concerning the status of ethnic Germans, Hungarians, and others in postwar Czechoslovakia and represented Czechoslovakia's legal framework for the expulsion of Germans from the country after World War II.

3. Sites of major attacks on refugees and asylum seekers in the 1990s. The attacks resulted in major bodily harm and even death, including three girls killed by arson in Mölln in 1992.

Peitz: In the novel, Marie [Paula Beer] is a mysterious woman of whom one can't quite get a hold. All the men want to save her. Kind of a stereotypical image of women.

Petzold: Charm, beauty, grace derive from intelligence. Since I started making films I've been asking myself: Why is my protagonist once again a woman? What relationship do I have to her? I'm not shooting in a bathrobe, we work together: victimizer-victim structures have no place there. *Transit* is a novel by a woman, with a man as a first-person narrator and two categories of women. The one with whom the hero has sex, and Marie, the disembodied with the Christian name, the holy. Paula Beer thought it was strange that a female author would describe a female character in this way. She did not want to be an apparition, she wanted a body, a story. Thanks to Paula Beer the character escaped the cliché.

Peitz: And Franz Rogowski?

Petzold: He's a trained dancer, has a rhythm, a great physicality and empathy, which feeds off life experience. He too is incredibly smart—and graceful. He doesn't look for his text but for his situation. All actors in *Transit* are characterized by the fact that they do not try to showcase themselves but seek to explore situations. This way of acting unfortunately exists in Germany all too rarely.

Peitz: You signed the letter that triggered a debate about the Berlinale and Dieter Kosslick.[4] A good debate?

Petzold: When the uproar all started, I was in Paris. It's always good not to be in Germany when things are turning particularly German. Our appeal was personified and turned into a settling of scores with Kosslick, even though he had nothing to do with the matter.

Peitz: The letter states that the festival should be programmatically rejuvenated and streamlined. This is not supposed to be criticism?

Petzold: The financing of the Berlinale significantly depends on ticket sales, on the variety of films. This means the federal government would have to provide more funds so that the festival can become more independent.

Peitz: And few people are supposed to attend?

Petzold: No, that's not what I mean. My impression is that the individual festival sections are not clearly distinct and curated. A section such as the Panorama sometimes strikes me like the unending offerings of Netflix. Also: I am deeply troubled by the fact that the Berlinale, intended as it is for local audiences as

---

4. With longtime festival director Dieter Kosslick's contract running out in 2019, there was a heated debate in 2017–19 about the direction of the Berlin film festival, the marquee festival in Germany and one of the "Big Three" A-level film festivals in Europe (with Cannes and Venice). The debate included an open letter in April 2017, signed by seventy-nine prominent filmmakers (including Petzold), encouraging a new direction for the festival. Many filmmakers like Petzold were critical of what they considered the overly commercial direction of the festival under Kosslick.

well, subtitles many films not in German, but only in English. Berlin isn't just an Easyjet hub and international but also a community. This doesn't have anything to do with homeland ministry [*Heimatministerium*] but with an understanding of the city.⁵ A city, a central location, Potsdamer Platz, which is brought to life year after year by the Berlinale.

---

5. Petzold's comments here resonate with some of the 2017–19 debate about the festival and with issues around local and national cultures in the age of globalization and neoliberalism. With the reference to Easyjet, Petzold is underscoring how Berlin is a major discount airline destination and one of the biggest tourist destinations in Europe, especially for young people (one year surpassing Rome), but, of course, it is far from clear what that would and should mean for culture in Berlin or Germany. At the same time that he is critical of some of these globalizing trends, Petzold is also, by referencing a "Heimatministerium," distancing himself from any simplistic fetishization of German heritage.

"The Cigarette Was a Respite in Life"

Carolin Ströbele / 2018

From "'Die Zigarette war eine Lebenspause,'" *Zeit Online*, December 15, 2018. Reprinted by permission. Translated by Marco Abel and Jaimey Fisher.

Carolin Ströbele: Mr. Petzold, your new *Polizeiruf* is called *Tatorte*—did you come up with this joke?

Christian Petzold: Yes. I always wanted to make a *Polizeiruf* called *Tatort*. Or vice versa. Just to confuse the viewers.[1]

CS: Did the ARD approve this without objections?

CP: Originally, the title was *Warum hast du mir nicht gesagt, dass du zwei Beine hast?* [*Why Didn't You Tell Me You Have Two Legs?*]. This was so long that the *Hörzu*[2] surely would not have been able to squeeze it in its program box. As a result, there were no discussions.

CS: You have a reputation as a great inventor of protagonists in German cinema. Was it not a problem for you to make a film about Hanns von Meuffels [Matthias Brandt],[3] a previously existing character from serialized television?

---

1. Petzold is making a joke about the title of his *Polizeiruf 110* episode: "Tatort" is the German word for "crime scene"; "Tatorte" is its plural. As explained in our introduction, *Tatort* [*Crime Scene*], which originated on West-German TV, is German television's longest-running drama, and *Polizeiruf 110* [*Police Call 911*], originating on East-German TV, is its longest-running competitor. The former more so than the latter has a unique, unequaled status in the German cultural landscape. Its episodes, always broadcast on Sunday during prime time at 8:15 p.m., are invariably part of Germans' "water cooler" conversations the next morning. Petzold, in other words, is being playful here in that he acknowledges that *Tatort*'s status is culturally higher than *Polizeiruf 110*, perhaps somewhat analogous to how, in the age of classic Hollywood, A pictures were seen as superior to B movies. Yet to keep with this (somewhat imperfect) analogy, Petzold may be implying that in the context of *Polizeiruf 110*, he was able to make a superior "Tatort"—in the form of the pluralized *Tatorte*—in the same way that over time many B movies have been valued as superior to the erstwhile A pictures.
2. A German magazine that offers extensive TV listings and coverage.
3. An ongoing detective character in *Polizeiruf 110*, played by Matthias Brandt, the son of former German chancellor Willy Brandt.

CP: No, I found it easier. I wrote the script for my first *Polizeiruf: Circles* in three weeks. It was great fun to invent something within an existing structure. When you make a film for the cinema, it has to stand on its own, in the world, at festivals. When you make a television film, there's the *Tagesschau* before it and *Anne Will* afterwards. One is part of a community and has to fill a construction gap. It is much harder to invent a new character from scratch. Meuffels is part of a great tradition of Georges Simenon characters: men who walk across train tracks in wet trench coats with turned-up collars, enter a bar, and drink wine. One doesn't know whether they are lonely or alone. Meuffels has this aura as well.

CS: A frequent complaint is that German TV has so few multifaceted female protagonists. But I think there is an equal lack of multifaceted male protagonists.

CP: In American cinema, the mature, exhausted male is a great character: Humphrey Bogart, Edward G. Robinson. The actors in film noir aren't machos but people with a lot of life experience. This is missing in German fiction: the experienced man.

CS: You invented Meuffels's colleague and, eventually lover, Constanze Hermann [Barbara Auer].

CP: Constanze, too, is a character who walks across train tracks in a trench coat. Both are damaged people—but we do not know why. At first, they hate each other because they recognize themselves in the other. The love they begin to feel for each other scares them because it could result in loss of control.

CS: So, in fact you did not write a crime story for Sunday evening television but a love story?

CP: Yes, from the beginning I wanted to tell a love story in stages: to fall in love, to promise one another, to separate again.

CS: In this third and final case, Constanze has left Hanns von Meuffels. And he is simply heartbroken, lovesick.

CP: He can't go on; he can't do his job any longer either. Sometimes he hides his pain; at other times he just doesn't care anymore. Sometimes he's entirely lacking in humor, at others he is once again incredibly funny. At the very moment when he loses his grip on his life, he shows once more what a fantastic person he is.

Together with my brothers I just liquidated my parents' house. We threw everything in a dumpster, every porcelain vase, because everything seemed ugly to us. Then people arrived and retrieved things from the dumpster and took them with them. A few of these things I subsequently saw on neighbors' windowsills. And when they stood there, by themselves, I thought: really not bad. When you lose things, they briefly reveal once more their grandeur, their beauty, their original magic. This is more or less how I had imagined the situation for Meuffels's last case.

CS: There's a great scene in which Meuffels comes home: Constanze is moving boxes are everywhere, and then he—the great aesthete—grabs this incredibly ugly laundry basket and intends to start ironing. Until he realizes that she has taken the iron with her.

CP: Abandoned, he wants to pretend that everything is how it was before. I am alone; I prepare a TV dinner; I do the ironing myself and listen to music while doing so; I love this. In the past it was called a bachelor lifestyle. When my wife and kids are gone, it makes its appearance in my life as well. In those moments I, too, like to iron and relish in being alone. But Meuffels is just fooling himself. He is not coping well at all. He is actually quite happy that Constanze has taken the iron: because then he has a good reason to call her. They also immediately manage to make conversation. Constanze laughs; they talk about work. But when he is back in his apartment for a second time, with a new iron, he can't go on. He doesn't even manage to read the manual. It was important to me to show this degree of exhaustion.

CS: *Tatorte* is also very much about communication or, more precisely, the absence thereof. When Meuffels and Constanze got to know each other, they did not talk much; a lot happened via looks and music to which they listened. Now Meuffels has a young female colleague [Maryam Zaree] who is over-motivated, and the conversations they have while driving don't work at all.

CP: Meuffels has no interest at all in other people anymore. He has isolated himself, is about to quit internally and externally. And now a young woman is assigned to assist him, who tells him, "My entire life I just wanted to sit next to you, you are my role model." But the role model is exhausted and can only disappoint his new student, for everything is dead inside him. This gnaws on him and simultaneously gives him a bad conscience.

I had the same experience as a film student. The professors that I thought were so great had been in their academic jobs for twenty years, and secretly one thought, "Why can't you be like back in the day?"

CS: I very much like that you resurrect the cigarette as a lubricant for communication.

CP: I myself was a smoker for a long time. Now I'm just puffing on e-cigarettes: this is the Methadone for smokers. In the past smoking was completely normal in film. When Yves Montand smoked a cigarette, exhaling was an inner monologue. When someone went outside and lit a cigarette and the smoke rose up, one was able to visualize thoughts that way. A cigarette can't do this anymore. A crazy health policy has banned it from interior spaces, from social life, and thus also from film. Unfortunately, we have not found a replacement yet.

CS: What about smoking do you miss?

CP: In the past, we had smoking breaks stipulated by union contracts. Smoking was a reason to step out of the flow of work and necessities. The cigarette in hand meant: I am not going to participate anymore. The cigarette was a break, a respite in life. Today one regards smokers as people who have lost control over themselves: as poor pigs, sub-proletariat. Why not sacrifice two, three years of one's life if one improves the rest of your life a bit? But such a thought is completely frowned upon today.

CS: Many cultural technologies can no longer be filmed—to phone someone, to listen to LPs. In serial narratives, directors escape into some retro-look or into fantasy time levels.

CP: These fantasy worlds, which are created in the TV writers' rooms, don't appeal to me of late. I think English miniseries such as *Bodyguard* and *River* are fantastic, for they draw on what is there. The educational crisis is fatal, cities look fucked-up, real-estate pigs destroyed everything. It's in that world that we have to find stories. We have to take stories from it and then launch them back at it. We have to enchant ourselves so that we can bear living here.

Lives in Transit: An Interview with Christian Petzold

Richard Porton / 2019

From *Cineaste* 44, no. 2 (Spring 2019): 17–21. Reprinted by permission.

Richard Porton: I've read that Anna Seghers's *Transit* was one of your frequent collaborator Harun Farocki's favorite novels. Did you discuss the script with Farocki before he died?

Christian Petzold: Harun Farocki has been dead four years and sometimes I go to his grave in a Berlin cemetery—where Seghers, Bertolt Brecht, and many other famous people are buried—and talk to him like Henry Fonda in *Young Mr. Lincoln* talked to Ann Rutledge in John Ford's graveyard scene.

Anna Seghers was a communist who spent most of her life in the German Democratic Republic. She was not at all respected in West Germany where I grew up and we in fact made fun of her.

RP: Was she considered a Stalinist writer?

CP: Yes, and her language and use of metaphors were considered old-fashioned. But we weren't really familiar with her work.

Once, at the end of the 1980s, Harun and I were driving in a BMW to a football match (we played on the same team) and I made some bad, ironical jokes about Anna Seghers. He stopped the car and starting yelling at me: "What, are you crazy? She's one of the world's greatest writers." And he gave me *Transit* to read, as well as a collection of stories entitled *Dead Girls' Outing*. It was fantastic. The title story was only a few pages, but they were fantastic pages. When you're twenty-five or so and you discover a composer or writer you're captivated by, you want to hear or read everything by that person. When I saw two of Fritz Lang's films, I wanted to see all of them. So, all that summer, Harun and I read everything Anna Seghers published. And we considered *Transit* our book—because it was a novel about people searching for their identity, not their national identity but an identity that transcends national boundaries.

RP: Given the European refugee crisis, did it seem appropriate to film *Transit* at this time?

CP: The timing is more of a coincidence because in 2005 Harun and I discussed adapting *Transit*. At that time, the subject of refugees wasn't as topical. We were wary, though, because of Hitchcock's dictum that only bad novels make good movies. He's right because, for the most part, when "good literature" is made into films, people go to the cinema and compare the images to what's on the printed page.

RP: Literature is often the basis for what the *Cahiers* critics disparagingly termed "the tradition of quality."

CP: I hate the tradition of quality! So, previously, I made films derived from "cheaper" sources. *Jerichow*, for example, has a relationship to *The Postman Always Rings Twice*. The characters in those films are also in transit, stuck between two places.

RP: And, since *Transit* is a sort of thriller, it shares some affinities with Hitchcock.

CP: Yes, and after *Phoenix*, I didn't want to make another period film. I'll tell you a story that explains why I wanted to avoid period films. In *Phoenix*, we had to find a street that resembled Berlin devastated by bombs in 1945. You can find such streets in Poland, which suffered bombing attacks during World War II and were also scarred during the communist era. So, when we were driving through Poland and scouting for locations in a Mercedes, we found a street and started taking photos. We looked up and saw that the people staring at us through windows were afraid. They might have been thinking, "We're poor people in this ruined neighborhood and the capitalists are coming to steal our houses." They probably thought we were going to seize their property and build a shopping center.

I joked, "Germany destroyed Poland in 1939 and now we're coming back again to destroy it once more." It became a moral crisis for Harun and the whole crew. Harun said, "I want to make a documentary on this subject." I replied that I didn't want to be part of any such project. But, for him, it would have made a fantastic documentary on how German representatives of art cinema returned to terrorize Poland again. So, for this reason, I didn't want to make a period film again.

After Harun's death, I threw away the notes on *Transit* and began to focus on more contemporary material. I first had an idea revolving around architecture and then rescreened Robert Altman's *The Long Goodbye*, one of my favorite movies. It's based on a novel by Raymond Chandler that, although it was published in the fifties, takes place during the 1940s. Chandler was a European and in this book you can feel the European crisis because it's about a crisis of loyalty and a desire for loyalty. You can feel the nihilism in the book. In Altman's film, Philip Marlowe, the detective, drives a forties car and shares the same forties morality.

But he's not surrounded by refugees from Hollywood but by the New Hollywood of the seventies, something that Robert Altman feared. The studio system was in crisis and Altman made a film that dealt with both contemporary Hollywood and the Hollywood of the forties. It was not a joke that Philip Marlowe drove a 1940s car in Altman's film. It opened up possibilities.

RP: So, did this sort of "opening up" inspire you to blur the boundaries between past and present in *Transit*? You've often referenced Walter Benjamin's "Theses on the Philosophy of History," an essay that deals with the infiltration of the present by the ghosts of the past.

CP: When a schoolteacher takes a class to the cinema to see a period film, the past becomes like a museum. Then the students have homework assignments based on this film.

On the other hand, there's a great saying that was uttered by Theodor Adorno, the German philosopher. In 1963, he started his lectures on Hegel in Frankfurt with this sentence: "To the brazenness of the question—'What does Hegel mean to us today?'—we can only answer: 'What are we to Hegel?'" This is the same sort of question that occurred to me while thinking about the historical situation of 1942. I didn't want to regard it as a museum. When you think of those who escaped Germany like Mann, it's true that, while some were privileged, they were also suffused with fear. Some, like Benjamin, committed suicide. After the survivors of this situation came back to Germany in the late forties, they wrote our constitution—and their experiences are imprinted in this constitution.

There's a sentence in this constitution that guarantees asylum to anyone fleeing political, sexual, or religious oppression. But the government destroyed this idea from the time the first refugees began to enter Germany in 1991. So, again, we have a transit situation.

RP: And it's interesting that you decided to include voice-over in the film from the perspective of a minor character instead of Georg, the protagonist.

CP: Yes, that's because I have a problem with voice-over in movies. Sometimes I love it, though. A few weeks ago, I saw Claude Miller's *Deadly Circuit*. It's about a detective played by Michel Serrault and also stars Isabelle Adjani. In this film, voice-over works, because it's about a detective who has lost his desire and feels empty. He's following Isabelle Adjani and convinces himself that she's his daughter, even though that's impossible. Although voice-over can be a literary device, the movie is independent from this.

Anna Seghers's novel of course includes first-person narration, but I chose to write the voice-over from the perspective of a detached man, a bartender telling his life story. It's not literature; it's oral history. All the refugees have to tell him their stories because they're lonely. All of these stories recount what the refugees have lost and miss. For me, this was not a voice-over that substituted words for images. He's a witness, but a very bad witness because he's an unreliable narrator. He claims, for example, that the film's central couple kiss, even though they don't.

RP: At one point, the narrator alludes to a film that sounds like Romero's *Dawn of the Dead*.

CP: Yes, I love *Dawn of the Dead*, especially because the zombies end up at a shopping mall! And at one point, when they need to bury someone, I love how they bury him in the gardening section. It's like a modern version of *Robinson Crusoe*.

RP: What, then, is the relationship of *Dawn of the Dead* to *Transit*'s narrative?

CP: Because it's difficult for contemporary audiences to know what the refugees in 1942 were experiencing, I felt I had to use *Dawn of the Dead* to make the connection. [*Laughs*] The whole crew was laughing because I had only written these lines about ten minutes before the shoot.

RP: Of course, many of your films are in dialogue with other films—e.g., *Jerichow* with *The Postman Always Rings Twice*, *Phoenix* with *Vertigo*. Maybe *Transit* is in dialogue with [Michael Curtiz's] *Casablanca*?

CP: Yes, I told the previous interviewers that Anna Seghers was aware of *Casablanca* because she sent *Transit* to Warner Bros. and they told her that they're also working on a movie about refugees, a love story, that also takes place in a port. I'm pretty sure they used *Transit*'s narrative construction as inspiration for *Casablanca*'s ending, where the hero doesn't go off with the heroine.

RP: But she wasn't given credit for this.

CP: No, but Hollywood later made a film based on her novel *The Seventh Cross* [Fred Zinnemann] with Spencer Tracy. After World War II, when the Nazis were defeated, she wanted to stay in the West. She loved Mexico and Los Angeles. When she went to West Berlin, all of her communist friends said she had to go to the East. She became a bureaucrat in the writers' union. If you read her later novels, they're full of ambivalence toward East Germany. And they weren't well received in the German Democratic Republic. But they are great books.

RP: Although you have mentioned that Seghers was not respected in West Germany, the American paperback edition of *Transit* includes an afterword by the West German novelist Heinrich Böll. So, he obviously liked it.

CP: Yes, the East Germans wanted to publish his and Günter Grass's novels, but they didn't have the money for the rights. So, Böll made arrangements for this and helped publish Anna Seghers's novels in the West. It was a kind of exchange between Luchterhand Literaturverlag, who published Grass in the West, and Aufbau-Verlag, who published Seghers in the GDR.

RP: I've read that your rehearsals with actors involve extensive rehearsals and meetings with the actors that are almost like seminars. What were your meetings with the actors like before the *Transit* shoot?

CP: Although we had a table reading, it was very cold—colder than cold. Most of our preparation involved watching movies. We watched one of Louis Malle's films; we also screened Jean Renoir's *A Day in the Country*. It's also about the experience of letting someone go. During the shoot, we constructed a cinema on the roof of the hotel where we were staying. We had to wait until dark, but every other night I taught the seminar. The subject of the seminar was New Hollywood. I didn't want to show these young actors any films related to their roles. I wanted to show them films illustrating depictions of rooms, colors, and atmosphere. The first film we saw was *The Graduate*.

Then I pointed out that Mike Nichols was born in 1931 in Berlin. He was the grandson of Gustav Landauer, the German anarchist killed by the Freikorps, the predecessors of the Nazis, in 1919. Nichols escaped the Nazi pogroms in 1939 and came to the United States. Although he started out directing plays, he came to Hollywood when there was a crisis within cinema because of television. He made two fantastic films—*Who's Afraid of Virginia Woolf?* and *The Graduate*—which featured a totally new structure and editing style. For me, it was a pleasure to see these movies again with these young people. Now they're really avid cinephiles. Paula Beer has seen all of Hitchcock's films and knows everything about them. It's good for the actors to know that they're not just showing up to read their lines. They're part of the history of cinema.

RP: *Transit* is the first film you've made in a while without Nina Hoss.

CP: Yes, we've made six movies together. But we decided to take a break for a while.

RP: You don't think she could have played Paula Beer's role?

CP: No, I don't think so. The young girl that Paula Beer plays is a writer's muse. She's not an adult; she's a girl on the way to becoming an adult. In this movie, she finally makes decisions as an adult. But, to me, Nina is already a fully formed adult. I need Nina for stories where the situation is reversed, where she's losing her adulthood.

RP: Why did you model the protagonist of *Transit* on the writer Georg K. Glaser?

CP: The other important book for Harun and myself was Georg Glaser's autobiography. He was a communist and took the same route from Germany to France, even though he never went to Marseille. Because he was a Communist Party member, a network of communists hid him. He wasn't as completely alone as the Georg in *Transit*.

RP: Did he die in West Germany?

CP: No, in Paris. He was an artisanal metalworker and Harun made a documentary about him, *Georg K. Glaser—Writer and Smith*. In the documentary, he constantly hits the metal with his hammer. After the first hit, Harun asks him,

"Do you think about your hits?" And he responded, "There's a tiger in a tree and, when a sheep comes by, the tiger jumps seven meters into the vein of the sheep. Then the tiger says to himself, 'I'm very, very good.'" Then Harun starts laughing. It's a fantastic movie!

RP: In previous interviews, you've said that you wouldn't want to, say, make a film about the contemporary refugee crisis in Calais.

CP: Yes, because I'd think, "What is my position?" The Germans in Marseille in 1942 are my people. I went to Calais and saw where the North African refugees are housed—they call it "the jungle." I could film "the jungle" or film the oppression, but I wouldn't be able to find a story. I'd have to turn the camera on myself and film how I reacted. I could have done that but chose not to.

RP: You'd prefer to have more critical distance from this subject? Or make a documentary?

CP: You know, I'm now a member of the Academy [of Motion Picture Arts and Sciences] that gives out the Oscars. Because of all of these shitty documentaries they're sending me, my English is getting better. The documentaries they've sent me are very stylish, full of heavy music and montage sequences. There are all of these reenactments that feature people who have been trained to act in front of the camera. I'm glad there are directors like Frederick Wiseman who don't use that approach. The other directors know what they want to tell us, even before they've switched on the camera. This sort of thing I don't like. On the other hand, the Quincy Jones documentary isn't so bad. He's a fantastic guy.

RP: Of course, Errol Morris was largely responsible for this preoccupation with reenactments in documentaries.

CP: He's considered a master for these young documentarians. This is true in Germany as well. We always have two brothers like Cain and Abel: Frederick Wiseman and Errol Morris. [*Laughs*] You have to make a choice.

RP: Of course, Harun Farocki, like Chris Marker, was somewhat different than either of those directors because Farocki and Marker made essay films.

CP: Yes, Chris Marker's films are fantastic. *Sans Soleil* was a very important influence for the voice-over in *Transit*. I showed this film to the actors, and it was especially important for my friend Matthias Brandt, who plays the bartender. The voice-over is in the form of letters that don't recount that the narrator has seen something in Japan but has written that he's seen it. This was a departure point for us in *Transit*. And Georg is a witness. He's like a policeman in old movies by Don Siegel. These guys don't have private lives but feed on the passions and misfortunes of others.

RP: He assumes someone else's identity, which is a very Hitchcockian device.

CP: That's right.

RP: And just as you assume that the book that Marcel is writing in *In Search of Lost Time* is in fact the book you are reading, one assumes that the manuscript that Georg takes from Weidel resembles *Transit*.

CP: Yes, that's right. We used Proust's book as an inspiration while shooting *Phoenix*. Primo Levi and Jean Améry were in the same section of Auschwitz/Birkenau. They were working in the medical section under Mengele. They knew each other but didn't recognize each other after the war because survivors never recognize each other. Survival is a difficult fate. Primo Levi survived because he was enveloped in a tunnel of science; all he thought about was chemistry. Jean Améry was in a tunnel preoccupied with Proust. It's a book about remembering, and Améry used it as a survival mechanism.

RP: *Phoenix* is also a film about the process of remembrance.

CP: Yes, it's a film about memory and Nina Hoss read Proust during the shoot.

RP: I recently saw Nina Hoss in Thomas Ostermeier's play *Returning to Reims* when it traveled to St. Ann's Warehouse in Brooklyn.

CP: Yes, I met with them when the play was produced in Paris. I once worked with Nina on a play and it was fine; I enjoyed the rehearsals. But at the end I said to Nina, and she was a little perturbed, "I have to admit that I think that cinema is the superior art form."

RP: Well, the thing is—when a play is bad, it's really bad.

CP: Yes, and when a film is bad, it's not quite as bad.

RP: Is Driss, the North African child in Transit, your way of referencing the contemporary migrant crisis?

CP: Yes, that's right. The idea was that the first time Georg opened the door, the film refers to the past and the second time the reference is to our time. The idea was to use the door as a bridge between the eras. I usually don't like shooting with children because their parents are always in the background. I don't like how the children are directed to respond by being given sweets. They destroy their character with this process. But this young guy, Lilien, had a German mother and his father is from Mozambique. The parents live in Paris and are friends of our coproducer. They sent me a video where he's playing soccer, which is of course an important part of the movie.

He was just great because he wasn't interested in movie-making and wanted to go back to Paris. But he loved Franz Rogowski. Lilien doesn't have any siblings and Franz was like a brother to him.

RP: What's interesting about your films is that they often have a relationship to genre cinema and what is termed art cinema. Are you concerned with bridging the gap between these two categories?

CP: I don't like these categories. When Harun went from the cinema to creating installations for galleries, it was a chance for him to reinvent himself. But I said to him, "All of those techniques they're using in galleries now correspond to what you invented in the cinema during the sixties." It's not an ideal situation because people come and go without seeing the entire installation. We talked about Errol Morris and Frederick Wiseman.

But, for Harun, there was no longer any money available from film producers or television. I was so aggressively against museums and art cinema that I think I "infected" him. He said that the most effective art films are made within the mainstream. So, we made lists of films like Hitchcock's *Spellbound*, which used Dalí's designs, or *The Ring*, which was influenced by [Maya Deren's] *Meshes of the Afternoon*. Films don't need audiences of millions, but we agreed: they should be viewed by a community.

"I Write in a Condition of Complete Mental Derangement"

Andreas Busche / 2020

From "'Ich schreibe im Zustand völliger Umnachtung,'" *Tagesspiegel*, February 23, 2020. Reprinted by permission. Translated by Marco Abel and Jaimey Fisher.

Andreas Busche: Mr. Petzold, your last films each had political subtexts. Why did you choose for *Undine* a fairy tale as a template?

Christian Petzold: There are no unpolitical films. Even when having recourse to the elementary registers of German Romanticism, I cannot avoid politics. The characters live in a world that capitalism has disenchanted, one in which feelings have been commodified—that are then disposed of by returning them to Amazon. Maybe the ghosts can reenchant the world.

AB: Coming from you, this sounds rather pathos-laden.

CP: Please don't misunderstand this as a retro idea. German cinema has retreated into a historically reconstructed world. One wears historical costumes and thereby seeks escape from reality. But it doesn't work that way. We have to find magic in the very places that surround us.

AB: From today's point of view, mythological female characters are always problematic: Medea, Lysistrata, Phaidra—and Undine. Perhaps also because they emerged from male lore. To what degree are they ready for a modern update?

CP: I first became aware of this in 2001 when shooting *Something to Remind Me*. I had revisited Agnès Varda's *Cléo from 5 to 7*. And suddenly I saw something that I had never realized so clearly: Cléo is an object for the men with whom she surrounds herself. But, during these ninety minutes, something that was a male projection transforms into an active subject. And this transition, when the muses step out of the water and declare, "I won't play this game any longer," is what is of interest to me in cinema.

AB: Undine is a water nymph who receives her soul only in connection with a man whose infidelity she punishes with death. What excited you about this myth?

CP: Water ghosts are of course familiar from children's fairy tales. But I really discovered this myth only in Ingeborg Bachmann's *Undine geht*, in which the mythical being says, "I am a subject and you men are monsters! I no longer want to live of your desires."

AB: Your films have always featured self-determined women. To what do you pay attention as script writer and director when telling a story from a female point of view?

CP: Who is looking, and who is telling? Take the first eight minutes of *Undine*: we see a couple in a café, and we understand from the dialogue that he is in the process of leaving her. We observe them, as it's shot from an objective point of view: shot, reverse shot. The young woman says, "If you leave me, I have to kill you." When she leaves, she turns around one final time and regards her boyfriend from afar. In this moment, we see him from her subjective point of view, and at this moment it becomes clear that the film will be about her and advance through her actions. Through the end the film assumes her perspective. The question of the look is not an academic one, but also a moral one. One has to keep confronting this, for otherwise one quickly unlearns this.

AB: You made a "ghost trilogy," and the refugees in *Transit* are walking ghosts as well. Where does this penchant for beings that are neither alive nor quite dead come from?

CP: I think that almost all characters in the cinema are from the in-between world: people who are looking for a place where they can make a home. Ghosts of the cinema, who are stuck in in-between spaces, have really influenced me the most. Cinema shows people who want to become human.

AB: And how does one film a water spirit who has the presence of a real woman?

CP: In my film, Undine is already human. The danger is rather that she has to return to the water. Water pursues her: aquaria explode, faucets are running, her new friend Christoph, an industrial diver, takes her to a dive. The myth claws her back. For this you need intelligent actors such as Paula Beer and Franz Rogowski: working with them was beautiful and transparent. In such a scenario, male projections are quickly repelled. I don't do a traditional casting; rather, we meet to talk. One quickly notices whether there's a common sensibility.

AB: What is left, in essence, of a love story if one sheds the external experiences such as terror, dictatorships, or exile and instead focuses on it as an archetype?

CP: The point is to wrest love away from the given circumstances. Or can love even survive such circumstances? Undine is being loved by Christoph for the first time for her own sake, and this is also the first time that this happens in any of my films. My films are always about systems of oppression from which the characters try to save themselves with the help of love. Undine, however, is still being held back by the curse of the myth, which makes her into a freedom fighter.

AB: Undine is a city historian with a doctorate. One can also see your films as history films: what does *Undine* tell us about Berlin of the 2010s?

CP: My starting point were the models of Berlin's center that I accidentally discovered in the city government's office for urban development. One of these models was from the period shortly after the fall of the Wall. It was supposed to show people what the city government was planning to do with unified Berlin. Another model was from the GDR, with which the GDR had wanted to celebrate itself in the 1980s. When you walk through the city today and compare the city's reality with the visions from back, you recognize the danger that Berlin is facing.

AB: What is happening with Berlin right now?

CP: You just have to picture that Berlin is a drained swamp—the doing of Friedrich the Great so that the deserters would not be able to hide there. And when you drain a swamp and build up the city like today's Berlin, then elementary spirits are going to look for a new place to inhabit. This was the basic idea for *Undine*.

AB: In Berlin, history is either reenacted or disappears from the cityscape.

CP: I worked with a city planner on my script. At one time Undine says about the Humboldt Forum: we have a museum in the form of an aristocratic castle [*Herrscherschloss*] of the eighteenth century. In modern architecture, the principle of "form follows function" was always operative, but here the opposite happened. This means, in turn: in Berlin, progress is no longer possible, and we're moving in a retro-loop.

AB: Is the underwater world in which Christoph works a real location in Berlin?

CP: Industrial divers border myth and real world. They look like a mix of Jules Verne and *2001*. The underwater world is a fairy-tale world—the sounds, the slowness, the gliding, the green light. Two sorts of images always fascinate me: classical compositions à la Hitchcock or shots underwater, whether in James Bond films or in [Richard Fleischer's] *20,000 Leagues Under the Sea*.

AB: Would you call *Undine* an underwater film?

CP: I like to believe that we can feel the beauty of underwater movements in Paula Beer's and Franz Rogowski's performance. We shot these scenes right at the start, as a result of which the water element unconsciously permeated the entire shoot—all the way into the choreography and physicality of the two. There is a scene in Undine's apartment, in which Christoph asks her to give her lecture just for him. And while she's moving through the room and talks, she appears to swim around him. Suddenly both are back under water.

AB: You once said that when writing moments of blurriness are important. But your films appear so precisely researched and exact. Is this where your creative process kicks in?

CP: Roberto Rossellini always spent time thinking in bed, between wakefulness and dreaming. For me as a Protestant, a nap in the afternoon is really a lifesaver: two hours in between, and instead of counting sheep I imagine my film. And afterwards I never have to research it again. It is entirely possible that everything is wrong again; I have built in so many mistakes into my films. I write my scripts in a condition of complete mental derangement.

"As If We Were Dreaming It": Christian Petzold's *Undine*

James Lattimer / 2020

From *CinemaScope*, no. 83 (June 2020): 27–32. Reprinted by permission.

CinemaScope: How are you doing in these strange times? I heard you had the coronavirus.

Christian Petzold: Back in March, I was with Paula Beer in Paris to do press for the French release of *Undine*. It was a three-day trip, and our interpreter must have had it, as he collapsed during one of the interviews. The pandemic had just reached Paris and there was something about that extraordinary situation that I liked. I didn't feel bad at all. I remember we were sitting in a restaurant one evening and they suddenly turned down the music and turned on TV so that everyone could hear Macron's speech.

I looked at everything around me, the city of Paris becoming so still, its cafés shutting down, and I started thinking about the photos that Nina Hoss and I had looked at when preparing *Phoenix*, of Hitler's troops marching into Paris where not a single French person is out on the street. We all know the Leni Riefenstahl images, the staged images of crowds, of Hitler enjoying the direct contact with all the people, the women wanting to touch him . . . and yet in Paris, there's no one. The city showed him that if he arrived there, they would make him into a specter. Anyway, we flew back and three days later Paula and I both started getting symptoms. The illness isn't pleasant—it's pretty tough actually—but I didn't end up in hospital.

CinemaScope: After three films set in the past, *Undine* is a return to the present, but a present that functions differently than it did in, say, *Jerichow*. Why did you decide to leave the past behind, and was it important for you to take a different path after three films dedicated to such weighty historical themes? I also read that *Undine* is supposed to be the first part of a trilogy.

Petzold: This idea of thinking of films in trilogies was something that Harun Farocki and I came up with. I always liked it when Billy Wilder made two or three noir films back-to-back, or Roberto Rossellini grouped his own films into series. For cinema to become a work of art shown in museums or screened at festivals always implies individual films generating attention, with each one having to be something entirely authentic or particular. The serial qualities of B-movies, Hollywood films, neorealist works, the Nouvelle Vague, or Romanian cinema equally form part of cinema.

So back then, it must have been the start of the 2000s, Harun and I thought we would also think in trilogies, so that every time we had a film, the next one would have to be related to it and the following one too, before we'd head off somewhere else.

Barbara, *Phoenix*, and *Transit* were all about National Socialism or dictatorships, and I remember writing how much it annoyed me that such films were always conceived around the idea that love could somehow exist outside of society. I was interested in the relationship between love, society, and economy. Shooting *Transit* was great fun, while *Phoenix* and *Barbara* were a huge amount of work, because reconstructing a period is very different to engaging with what's already there. And for *Transit*, which was already in the present, I'd found these two young actors, Paula Beer and Franz Rogowski, and felt they could come with me to the new trilogy.

Here in Germany, we historically never had a proper society—we didn't win any revolution, we were made up of lots of small city states—but we do have Romanticism, myths, and the spirits of the elements. Elemental stories play a big role in German mythology, whereby beings emerge from the mountains, water, or fire. When I read *Undine geht* by Ingeborg Bachmann, followed by the original text by Friedrich de la Motte Fouqué, I had the impression that the story of Undine was one such myth. Afterwards, it was like a case of selective memory: I kept seeing Undine everywhere, water fairies, spirits, and so on, a trail of different stories running through German culture. And then I thought about what these myths still mean in our society today. Where do they play a role? Why do we understand them immediately without having to read them? Are they passed on to us via the songs of our parents, are they anchored in our childhood, or do we carry them around with us genetically? Are they important for our desires, dreams, and identities? And then I thought that this first myth, that of Undine, would have to be set in Berlin, which has no myths of its own.

The next film is about fire and is set in Mecklenburg-Vorpommern, on the northern coast of Germany. It's about two weeks in the life of a group of young people trying to love one another before being surrounded by a forest fire. It's the story of two men and the story of a man who is frightened of women. And a poem by Heinrich Heine called *Der Asra* plays a role; the title is taken from it.

CinemaScope: The film is set in the present, but the past still constantly makes its presence felt, whether in the figure of Undine or the history of Berlin, which still shapes this hypermodern city. And those two elements of the film come together in the scene where Undine gives Christoph a preview of her presentation on the Berlin City Palace (soon to house the Humboldt Forum). Where did your interest in Berlin city history come from, and what attracted you to the Berlin City Palace in particular? It almost feels emblematic for the film's conception of time as a whole, wherein past and present are entirely indivisible.

Petzold: Harun had an exhibition at the Hamburger Bahnhof, and one of the people at dinner afterwards was a historian specializing in the history of Berlin. We were standing outside smoking and looking at the skyline, and he suddenly started explaining to us how Berlin was planned in the nineteenth century, the concept of the central boulevards, how James Hobrecht developed a specific system for dealing with sewage to prevent cholera, which had killed thousands in Berlin, including Hegel. It felt amazing to me to suddenly understand the city in which I'd been living for decades. He explained how World War I basically destroyed modernism, but that people like Bruno Taut were still able to build housing estates in that style afterwards, and how National Socialism then destroyed modernism for good. He told us all this, and I was really excited by it.

Three days later, I went for a walk with my friend Christoph Hochhäusler; back then we were preparing to do *Dreileben* together with Dominik Graf. We would sometimes go for walks and tell each other the stories we had in mind, as they were supposed to intersect. So, we were walking and Christoph asked me if I knew the exhibition of different models of Berlin at the Märkisches Museum, and I said I didn't, so we went there. I saw the same presentation there as in the film, which was also given by a city historian. There was an exhibition of photos taken from Zeppelins that showed the city before the bombing and afterwards, as well as the reconstruction process and some more modern images. You could see how the city was destroyed and grew back; it had something physical to it. No one in Berlin comes from Berlin; we all come from somewhere else. The city is sort of a social laboratory: it lets us in and allows us to create our own networks and conceptions, but we don't really take care of it, we don't even know it so well. Now I suddenly began to see and understand the city I'd been living in for decades as a place with its own sense of autonomy and meaning.

I thought that I'd like to have Paula Beer explain all this to cinema audiences. So, I called the city historian and he then wrote the text for the film. I also asked him to write something about the Berlin City Palace, because it was actually added to the model the day I was there, as construction was starting. And I realized that the palace is actually Berlin itself, in the form of modern Berlin city policy. We tear down East Germany and then build a restoration of something from the monarchist era, but incorporate our own modern conceptions into it, including a shopping mall. And that's how Berlin ends up looking like shit.

It's also terrible to think how we were actually gifted an entire country in 1989—in the case of Berlin, an entire city. Everything belonged to the people, but everything was sold and privatized within the space of fifteen years, and now we can no longer afford rent. All of this plays out in the model too.

CinemaScope: Nearly all the important events in German history of the twentieth and twenty-first centuries appear in your films: whether World War II, a divided Germany, the German Autumn, the *Gastarbeiter* recruitment agreements, or German unification.

Petzold: That's true!

CinemaScope: And your films are as much about the way in which these events are represented as they are about the events themselves. The way in which you represent them is by no means restricted to simple realism, as is often the case. Can you talk a bit about your view of history and how you incorporate it into your films?

Petzold: I think you always need to look at yourself from the outside, from somewhere else. I grew up in a small, sleepy town between Leverkusen, Wuppertal, and Dusseldorf, and you have the feeling there that it's a place without history: it's as if it's always been there and will always stay the same. It's a bit like small-town America, where it feels like people have been getting in their SUVs, driving to Walmart, and buying stuff for a hundred years now, and it's going to be like that forever. It was primarily American cinema that got me asking myself whether everything wasn't just a dream. The first film where I felt that was *Halloween*; I was sixteen. The whole American world we know from TV series suddenly came across to me like a dream: the autumn leaves, the gliding camera, quite apart from the fantastical serial-killer plot. It was the way John Carpenter filmed the town and the people there, who feel a burden weighing down on them, like a nightmare, so that they themselves end up wandering around like ghosts. When I left the cinema and walked through my own town, I thought that it would also need to be filmed in the same way, as it has something ghostly about it too.

That's how *The Postman Always Rings Twice* or *Carnival of Souls* ended up turning up in my work: they are an American prototype for what I do, Americans looking at their own country with a spectral gaze. That's where it comes from, this way of looking at Germany via American cinema and finding a different way of seeing it as a result. I always imagined that you'd have to film Germany as if we were dreaming it.

When I write scripts based on existing material, like *Transit* or *Phoenix*, which are both novels, or *Undine*, I don't go back and reread. I try to remember the book and usually do so in bed, for an hour each afternoon. Sometimes I fall asleep, often even, and then I dream a bit and put everything into place there before starting to write again. I don't want to do conventional research; that's why I don't like watching films where it says "based on true events" at the beginning. Those films are seldom any good. That's because there's always a so-called reality and truth, which you carry out research on and then transfer to the screen. But cinema isn't about transferring or translating anything: cinema is a dream, it has to be a bit surreal.

CinemaScope: *Undine* doesn't just refer to history, but also to film history. That's nothing new, but I find it interesting just how many references to your own films are contained within this new one. Did you intend for *Undine* to function like a look back at your filmography? And can you talk about the process of incorporating film-historical references into your films, whether references to your own work or in general?

Petzold: Sometimes when you're out in the world, you see an image. You have the feeling that it's an image: it's not just there, but, rather, it recalls some image that you've already seen, even if you can't remember exactly where from. That often happens to me when I'm shooting. I choose a particular angle or decide with my cinematographer Hans Fromm to do an over-the-shoulder shot at one point, a wide shot at another. I often only realize what I'm referencing years later. I sometimes think there's just a single shot you have to find; different directors working in different places find it independently of one another, but the results correspond.

Cinema shows people who want, dream, or desire something; we show the objects of those feelings far less. I've always been interested in those looking for something, those in despair, those who desire—that's what cinema characters are. What they actually desire doesn't play such a big role. And there is always a point of view for this desiring gaze and the portrait of the person who desires. That makes up two shots that are edited together.

When I studied under Harun Farocki, that's all we did. We saw that in films that aren't good, with shots set up in such a way that the naked body of a woman was shown for hours, but the person looking at her for just a second. But the films that got us excited were always about the one who desires. And that's how references come about. All the many, many films that I've seen and talked about come to mind and they help me then. In *Transit*, when he's at the window and she comes to him, then he is the one who desires. She comes down but then passes by him on the way to the other window, whereupon she is the one doing the desiring. And that shifts back and forth, and it's a dance, and that only became clear to me in that scene.

In relation to my own films, I think in trilogies, which means that when I move from one film to the next, they're not so very different, even if I'm jumping from

East Germany in 1980 to Marseille in 1942. I'd like to be some sort of Howard Hawks, who can turn his hand to crime thrillers, comedies, historical epics, or whatever, but I'm more like Hitchcock, who nearly always did the same thing, but with a small change each time. His films were always based on similar configurations. For example, Nina Hoss is an object in *Barbara*: the men look at her through the window and describe her, one finds her desirable, the other finds her dreadful, a criminal. And she's both of those things. She's desirable, and for the East German state, she's a criminal. This woman's entire struggle is to have an identity that isn't determined for her by men. And all the basic stories in my films come down to the same thing: I've watched all the stories I've seen in the cinema to see where the objects, who are mainly women, begin to resist. The moment where the woman says, "I'm no longer going to go along with this, I don't want to." And that attempt at self-determination is in all the films, and sometimes they manage to achieve it, although they often have to pay a heavy price for doing so. That's essentially the underlying motif. It's in the next film too, I just realized.

CinemaScope: There are also elements in *Undine* I've never seen before in your work. I was thinking about the underwater images and that shot of Undine floating upwards toward the sun in particular. Can you talk a bit about your collaboration with Hans Fromm and how it's developed over the years? I rewatched *The State I Am In* recently, and visually it's very, very far from *Undine*.

Petzold: I watched it again at the retrospective at Lincoln Center, also with a degree of melancholy, because that was my first film for the big screen. I discovered things in it that I've continued to do and others that have become completely different in the meantime. Germany was still shown in a very realistic manner, and that was the intention. And this idea that Germany is a dream, or a dream within a dream, came over the course of the films and became really strong in *Undine*.

For *Undine*, I said to Hans that we should shoot things differently this time around. We watched some underwater films and did a storyboard for the very first time, as you can't just film underwater without having a particular conception of what you're doing. It had to be a place of work, where work was being carried out, but also a world of myth, an enchanted world alongside the real one. I watched the scene in [Charles Laughton's] *The Night of the Hunter* where Robert Mitchum drowns Shelley Winters and she's sitting in the car underwater and her hair drifts along with the current. We gradually developed a visual language, and then Hans met with a graphic artist to do the storyboarding. She created the picture of a girl floating on the surface of the water, which we later revised so that she could be seen from below floating upwards. But the tank we were using was only five meters deep, so we added the additional depth with CGI, zooming in and filling in the rest of the image via computer, which then made everything look even more dreamlike. If CGI is used economically, it can be really amazing. If it isn't used economically, at some point you just get a headache.

CinemaScope: Another important collaborator we've mentioned a couple of times is Harun Farocki, who died six years ago. As far as I know, *Undine* is the first film of yours he wasn't involved in at all. What was it like working on the script without him, and can you talk about your process a little bit? He's usually credited as "script consultant" or "script assistant."

Petzold: We spoke about *Undine* too! We really spent a lot of time together. From 1990 onwards, we saw each other two or three times a week. We started crediting him in that role so that he'd get paid, which he was always happy about—not because he was greedy for money, but because it meant it was a proper professional relationship. But we worked as follows: I'd write something and send it to him. Two days later, I'd go to his house; I'd always go to him, he'd never come here. We'd sit in the corner of his kitchen and go over his notes on what I'd written, and then we'd go for a walk. We'd think about all manner of different things while walking, what we liked or what we'd seen at the cinema. And then he'd show me the latest cut of one of his documentaries. All in all, it was just an ongoing conversation, which is why it was difficult to figure out the precise term to describe his role, because he would say that I was ultimately doing the writing.

He'd visit me on set and was shocked; he said he wouldn't be capable of doing something like that. He came to the *Phoenix* shoot and took photos everywhere, of Nina Hoss and Ronald Zehrfeld, and said it was really crazy seeing it all. He was wearing a white suit and had just got back from Vietnam with a present for Nina, the Vietnamese poster for *Barbara* where they'd inverted the image along with the writing, so that Barbara was riding her bike in the opposite direction, which looked totally different to all of us.

We were shooting the scene where Nina and Ronald walk down the street past the studio where they used to make music together and the door suddenly opens and he has to kiss her so that the musicians coming out don't recognize them. In doing so, he forgets his hat and goes to collect it after the kiss. There are many decisions that need to be made here, as she's being kissed by the man she loves, but he's only kissing her so as not to be recognized. For him, the kiss has nothing to do with passion; for her, it's everything. What do we film here—do we film the man picking up his hat, or the woman who's been kissed? Harun came up to me and said that it would be great to see just how deeply this kiss has affected her. I said that we should let Nina do her work, that she knows that already. He asked whether I should tell her that, and I replied that that would immediately kill the moment and that we would just go ahead and shoot it. He was really excited. So, Ronald kissed Nina and turned away and the camera stayed with Nina, who tottered on her feet for a second, as if she were having circulation problems. And Harun exhaled sharply and was thrilled.

CinemaScope: One final question: we've been talking again and again about films from the past, but I'd be interested to know what contemporary ones you're really into. And how has it been for you watching films at this time?

Petzold: The Safdie brothers are amazing! *Uncut Gems* is really great; it contains one of the most beautiful scenes about addiction I've ever seen. It's at the end, when he's trapped, the gangsters who want their money back between the two security doors, the basketball game is on, and millions of dollars are at stake. He's running around and explaining that what's happening to him is wonderful, the most important thing in the world. And the gangsters he's locked in see that he has an intensity in his life that they themselves lack and shoot him because they're jealous. The gangster becomes a petit bourgeois who shoots someone for doing better than he is. The film is wonderful for that scene alone.

Right now, I would even watch the evening news in the cinema! I can't stand it anymore, all this streaming bullshit, it's not the same. One of the beautiful things about being in the cinema is the solitude. The strange thing about watching TV is that you get together and watch with other people, like when football is on. But in the cinema, you see so many people who go there alone and like going there alone. I always used to like it in old American films when people on the run would go to the cinema. The police come and look and all those criminals are just sitting there, it's a beautiful sight. The cinema is simply the place you can go to alone, and I really miss that. Going out for an evening and maybe even seeing a film that isn't so fantastic, but sitting there in the dark nonetheless.

Key Resources

Books and Journal Dossiers

Abel, Marco. *The Counter-Cinema of the Berlin School*. Rochester: Camden House, 2013.
Abel, Marco, and Jaimey Fisher, eds. "Christian Petzold: A Dossier." *Senses of Cinema*, no. 84 (September 2017).
Brombach, Ilka, and Tina Kaiser, eds. *Über Christian Petzold*. Berlin: Verlag Vorwerk 8, 2018.
Cook, Roger F., Lutz Koepnick, Kristin Kopp, and Brad Prager, eds. *Berlin School Glossary: An ABC of the New Wave in German Cinema*. Bristol, UK: Intellect, 2013.
Fisher, Jaimey. *Christian Petzold*. Urbana Champagne: University of Illinois Press, 2013.
Landry, Olivia. *Movement and Performance in Berlin School Cinema*. Bloomington: Indiana University Press, 2019.
Prager, Brad. *Phoenix*. Rochester: Camden House, 2019.
Prager, Brad. *Yella*. Munich: edition text + kritik, 2021.

Articles and Chapters

Abel, Marco. "Christian Petzold: *Heimat*-Building as Utopia." In Marco Abel, *The Counter-Cinema of the Berlin School*. Rochester: Camden House, 2013
Abel, Marco. "Imaging Germany: The (Political) Cinema of Christian Petzold." In Jaimey Fisher and Brad Prager, eds., *The Collapse of the Conventional: German Film and its Politics at the Turn of the New Century*. Detroit: Wayne State University Press, 2010.
Bardan, Alice. "Europe, Spectrality and 'Post-Mortem Cinema': The Haunting of History in Christian Petzold's *Transit* (2018) and Aki Kaurismäki's *Le Havre* (2011)." *Northern Lights*, no. 18 (2020): 115–29.
Fisher, Jaimey. "Ghosts at an Early Age: Youth, Labor, and the Intensified Body in the Work of Christian Petzold and the Dardennes." In Marco Abel and Jaimey Fisher, eds., *The Berlin School and Its Global Contexts: A Transnational Art Cinema*. Detroit: Wayne State University Press, 2018.
Fisher, Jaimey. "Globalization as Uneven Geographical Development: The 'Creative' Destruction of Place and Fantasy in Christian Petzold's Ghost Trilogy." *Seminar* 47, no. 4 (September 2011): 447–64.
Hosek, Jennifer Ruth. "Towards a European Postmigrant Aesthetics: Christian Petzold's *Transit* (2018), *Phoenix* (2014), and *Jerichow* (2008)." *Transit* 13, no. 1 (2021): 52–70.

King, Alasdair. "The Province Always Rings Twice: Christian Petzold's Heimatfilm noir *Jerichow*." *Transit* 6, no. 1 (2010): 1–22.

Landry, Olivia. "The Beauty and Violence of *Horror-Vacui*: Waiting in Christian Petzold's *Tranit* (2018)." *German Quarterly* 93, no. 1 (Winter 2020): 90–105.

Osborne, Dora. "Too Soon and Too Late: The Problem of Archive Work in Christian Petzold's *Phoenix*." *New German Critique* 47, no. 1 (139) (February 2020): 173–95.

Prümm, Karl. "Der Geisterfotograf." *Augenblick: Konstanzer Hefte zur Medienwissenschaft*, no. 47 (September 2010): 52–77.

Interviews

LaGambina, Gregg. "Films Without Borders: An Interview with Christian Petzold." *Los Angeles Review of Books*, May 6, 2019.

Leweke, Anke. "French Cancan in the DDR: An Exchange with Christian Petzold." In Rajendra Roy and Anke Leweke, eds. *The Berlin School: Films from the Berliner Schule*. New York: Museum of Modern Art, 2013.

Stiegler, Bernd, and Alexander Zons. "'Das Kino ist die Zukunft, aber es schaut immer zurück. Ein Gespräch mit Christian Petzold." *Augenblick: Konstanzer Hefte zur Medienwissenschaft*, nos. 75/76 (2019): 5–124.

DVD Audio Commentary

The State I Am In, Christian Petzold.

Index

Aalto, Alvar, 49
Abzüge (unfinished Petzold film), 176, 201
Ackers, Cornelia, 162, 185, 217
Adjani, Isabelle, 163, 210, 234
Adorno, Theodor, 29, 221, 234
Aesthetic of Resistance, The (Weiss), 198
Akin, Fatih, xv, 55
Alice in the Cities (Wenders), 23, 93, 163, 205
Almodóvar, Pedro, 79, 216
Altman, Robert, 134, 139, 217, 233, 234
American Psycho (Harron), 106
Améry, Jean, 216, 238
Andersen, Hans Christian, 38
Angkor Wat, 63
Antonioni, Michelangelo, 25, 48, 70, 73, 211
Aoyama, Shinji, 62
Apartment, The (Wilder), 64
Apocalypse Now (Coppola), 83, 201
ARD (broadcaster), xiv, xv, 7, 7n, 153n5, 228
Ariola (record label), 198
Arri cameras, 172
Arslan, Thomas, ix, 9, 19, 28, 131, 152, 177, 179
Asphalt Jungle (Huston), 101, 223
Asra, Der (Heine), 246
Auer, Barbara, 186, 187, 189, 190, 191, 207, 218, 219, 229
Augé, Marc, 94
Auschwitz, 55, 150, 159, 164, 216, 238

Aust, Stefan, 13
Autorenfilm (auteur cinema), 23, 30, 93, 111
Autorenkino (auteur cinema), 23, 76
Avon (cosmetics), 4, 147, 204

Baader, Andreas, 13, 15, 22
Baader Meinhof Complex, The (Edel), 152
Baader-Meinhof-Komplex, Der (Aust), 13
Bach, Johann Sebastian, 29, 94
Bachmann, Ingeborg, 241, 245
Bacon, Francis, 83
Bad Kleinen (train station), 135, 206, 206n5
Bálazs, Béla, 63
Balibar, Étienne, xi, 104
Balzac, Honoré de, 29
Barthes, Roland, 29, 76
Baute, Michael, 28
Bavarian TV, 217
Bazin, André, 84
Beats Being Dead (Petzold), 138, 213
Beckenbauer, Franz, 163
Beer, Paula, xii, 225, 226, 236, 241, 242, 244, 245, 246
Beethoven, Ludwig van, 166, 212
belatedness (*Nachträglichkeit*), xiii, xvi, 131
Beloved Sisters (Graf), 162, 221
Beneš decrees, 225
Benjamin, Walter, xi, 83, 185, 234
Benn, Gottfried, 223

Berger, Helmut, 179
Berlin, Germany, 4, 55, 56, 57, 59, 84, 128, 129, 166, 167, 210, 211, 227, 227n5, 242, 246, 247
Berlin City Palace, 246
Berlin Is in Germany (Stöhr), 68
Berlin Republic, 19, 20
Berlin School, ix, xiv, 77, 99, 119, 123n1, 125, 132, 179
Berlin Wall (the Wall), xii, xiii, 3, 73, 86, 108, 131, 149, 152, 157, 166, 167, 176, 201, 202, 203, 242
Berlinale/Berlin Film Festival, 27, 50, 54, 55, 62, 91, 93, 124, 173, 217, 226, 227
Beyer, Frank, 153
Bielefelder Katalog, 198
Bierce, Ambrose, 89, 94
Biermann, Wolf, 146, 165, 198, 223
Bigelow, Kathryn, xi, 12, 136, 206
Bitomsky, Hartmut, ix, x, xii, xiii, 4, 6, 7, 18, 28, 41, 44, 45, 75, 129, 140, 169, 173, 174, 175, 201, 208
Blanke, Ludger, 28, 169, 198, 202
Bloch, Ernst, 199
Blow-up (Antonioni), 25, 62, 211
Blue Collar (Shrader), 204
Blue Gardenia, The (Lang), 88
Blumfeld (band), 35
Bodyguard (TV show), 231
Bogart, Humphrey, 229
Böhler, Bettina, 48, 52, 203
Bohm, Marquard, 9
Böll, Heinrich, 164, 198, 235
Bonanza (TV show), 217
Bonny, Jan, 217
Borchert, Wolfgang, 158, 164
Bornholmer Street (Berlin), 166
Böttcher, Jürgen, 178
Brandenburg, Germany, 93, 122, 154, 161, 202
Brandenstein, Mauela, 200

Brandt, Matthias, xii, 162, 185, 186, 187, 190, 191, 217, 218, 219, 225, 228, 228n3, 237
Brandt, Willy, 218, 228n3
Breathless (Godard), 99
Brecht, Bertolt, 83, 136, 171, 232; Brechtian aesthetic, xiii
Breloer, Heinrich, 11
Brennicke, Nadeshda, 8, 9, 204
Bresson, Robert, 60, 74, 200, 212
Bridges, Jeff, 9
Brinkmann, Rolf Dieter, ix, 4, 55, 74
Broch, Hermann, 144, 214
Brooklyn, New York, 238
Brothers Grimm, 56, 61, 211
Buñuel, Juan, 15

Cahiers (magazine), 30, 177, 233
Cain, James M., 118, 181, 213
Calais, France, 237
CAN (band), 93, 205
Cannae (Schmidt), 177
Cannes Film Festival, 55, 149, 164, 226n4
Cantet, Laurent, 63
Carax, Leos, 177
Carnival of Souls (Harvey), xi, 72, 89, 132, 137, 202, 211, 247
Carpenter, John, x, 82, 247
Casablanca (Curtiz), xi, 235
Cash, Johnny, 7
Cassavetes, John, 5, 72, 173, 192
Celan, Paul, 164
Celle, Germany, 197
CGI, 249, 250
Chabrol, Claude, 8, 30, 44, 112
Chandler, Raymond, 233
Chaplin, Charles, 90
Charité (hospital), 215
Chekhov, Anton, 80, 130, 225
Christiansen, Sabine, 20, 115, 153n5
Christl, Lisy, 52
cigarettes, in film and life, 5, 114, 146, 230

Cimino, Michael, x, 9, 125, 167, 182
cinéma direct, 39
cinema of consensus, 76
Circles (Petzold), 181, 185, 187, 188, 189, 217, 219, 220, 229
Cleo from 5 to 7 (Varda), 240
Clown, The (Böll), 197
Conrad, Joseph, 13
Conradt, Gerdt, 178
Cop, A (Melville), 5
Coppola, Francis Ford, 30, 83, 172, 213
Cronenberg, David, 55
Cuba Libre (Petzold), xi, 5, 79, 83, 85, 88, 132, 135, 201, 203

Dalí, Salvador, 239
dance, 67, 145, 146, 159, 191, 200, 210, 226, 248
Dancer in the Dark (von Trier), 18
Daney, Serge, 29
Danquart, Pepe, 167
Dark Water (Salles), 90
Dawn of the Dead (Romero), 235
Day in the Country, A (Renoir), 236
de Chirico, Giorgio, xi, 70
de Mazière, Lothar, 178
De Niro, Robert, 225
Dead Girls' Outing, The (Seghers), 223, 232
Deadly Circuit (Miller), 234
Dean, James, 165
Death Proof (Tarantino), 108, 141
Deer Hunter, The (Cimino), 125, 140, 167, 182, 225
Degenhardt, Franz Josef, 198
Deine besten Jahre (Graf), 28
Deleuze, Gilles, xi, 24, 26, 76, 83, 86
Denis, Claire, 63
Deren, Maya, 200, 239
Derrida, Jacques, 64
Detour (Ulmer), xi, 132
Deutsche Bahn (train company), 203

Deutsche Grammophon (record label), 198
dffb (Deutsche Film- und Fernsehakademie Berlin), ix, x, xiii, xiv, 3, 6, 8, 19, 19n5, 28, 45, 74, 75, 88, 99, 119, 129, 130, 131, 134, 166, 167, 169, 170, 175, 177, 179, 198, 199, 201
Diederichsen, Diedrich, 100
Dietrich, Marlene, 211
Dillon, Matt, 30
Dogme 95 (filmmaking movement), 39
Doillon, Jacques, 216
Dok Berlin (film studio), 178
Dok Leipzig (film studio), 178
Draußen vor der Tür (Borchert), 164
Dreileben (Graf, Hochhäusler, and Petzold), xiv, 123, 125, 132, 138, 157, 177, 186, 213, 246
Driver, The (Hill), 41, 50, 132, 142
Dunaway, Faye, 44
Duras, Marguerite, 56
Dusseldorf, Germany, 4, 5, 7, 25, 108, 127, 128, 165, 198, 247
Duvall, Robert, 83
Dylan, Bob, 97

Eastwood, Clint, 9
eggplants: in *Barbara*, 151, 155; in former East Germany, 215
Ehlers, Martin, 52
Eichendorff, Joseph Freiherr von, 143, 205
Eichinger, Bernd, 99, 100
Ein Liebesversuch (Kluge), 218
Ein Tag im Leben des Endverbrauchers (Farocki), 75
Elektrola (record label), 198
Elsaesser, Thomas, 134
Emmerich, Roland, 55
Enchantment, The (Broch), 214
Enke, Werner, 10
Enström, Ingemo, 196

ER (TV series), 145, 154
Europe 51 (Rossellini), 178
Evans, Walker, 101

Fahnder, Der (TV series), 215, 217
Fall (band), 100
Färber, Helmut, 31, 31n2, 59, 114, 173, 174, 178
Färberböck, Max, 40
Farocki, Harun, ix, x, xii, xiii, xvi, 5, 6, 7, 8, 10, 15, 18, 21, 44, 46, 48, 60, 65, 71, 75, 78, 90, 94, 96, 104, 109, 118, 128, 129, 130, 137, 158, 166, 168, 169, 170, 173, 174, 175, 176, 178, 181, 188, 198, 201, 204, 223, 224, 232, 237, 245, 248, 250
Fasanenstrasse (Berlin road), 218
Fassbinder, Rainer Werner, xiii, xv, 25, 32, 44, 74, 82, 129, 132, 137, 184, 185, 200n3
Fear (Rossellini), 29, 178
Feltrinelli, Giangiacomo, 197
Ferres, Veronica, 153
Field, Syd, 18
Fieser, Kerl, 106
Figgis, Mike, 77
Filmkritik (magazine), 6, 31, 31n2, 33, 44, 158, 169
First Name: Carmen (Godard), 30
Fischer, Joschka, 20, 34n1
Fitzgerald, F. Scott, 135
Flaubert, Gustave, 60
Flucht, Die (TV show), 225
Fonda, Henry, 67, 133, 232
Ford, John, 7, 23, 67, 88, 89, 133, 139, 225, 232
Fouqué, Friedrich de la Motte, 245
400 Blows (Truffaut), 65
France, xii, 22, 59, 61, 97, 99, 116, 122, 216, 225, 236
Free University Berlin, ix, 31n1
Freericks, Michel, 28, 169
fremde Freund, Der (Hein), 214
French New Wave (Nouvelle Vague), 99

Freud, Sigmund, 87
Friedkin, William, 28
Friedrich, Caspar David, 141
Friedrich the Great, 108, 242
Fromm, Erich, 28
Fromm, Hans, xii, 52, 82, 107, 183, 186, 187, 189, 191, 193, 248, 249
Frosch, Christian, 74, 170
FSK (cinema), 167
Fürmann, Benno, xii, 40, 41, 42, 44, 49, 58, 112, 113, 119, 135, 141
Fürstenwalde, Germany, 108, 144, 151
Furtwängler, Maria, 225

Gangs of New York (Scorsese), 100
Gansel, Denis, 54
Gardner, Ava, 160
Garrel, Philippe, 177, 178, 179
Gastarbeiter (guest workers), 247
Gere, Richard, 134, 135
German Autumn, 26, 247
Germany in Autumn (Fassbinder, Kluge, Schlöndorff et al.), 25
Ghosts (Petzold), 37, 55, 56, 59, 61, 62, 63, 64, 67, 70, 71, 72, 77, 84, 85, 87, 88, 138, 206, 208, 209, 210, 211, 213, 224
Ghost trilogy (Petzold), 87, 88, 241, 253
Giller, Walter, 164
Gish, Lillian, 63
Glamour and Misery of the Highly Talented (Petzold), 201
Glaser, Georg K., 21, 88, 130, 236
Go for It, Baby (Spils), 10
Godard, Jean-Luc, ix, xiii, 32, 69, 72, 75, 82, 88, 99, 113, 124, 128, 132, 133, 149, 173, 178, 179, 189
Goetz, Rainald, 25, 47, 67
Goldt, Max, 6
Good Bye, Lenin (Becker), 68
Grabowski, Jürgen, 163
Graduate, The (Nichols), 236

Graf, Dominik, xiv, 28, 42, 54, 71, 76, 77, 113, 116, 119, 121, 123, 129, 154, 156, 162, 177, 179, 186, 194, 213, 217, 221, 246
Grafe, Frieda, 31, 39, 211
Grams, Wolfgang, 135, 206
Gray Wolves, 190, 220, 220n11
Great Gatsby, The (Fitzgerald), 100, 142
Griffith, D. W., 63, 129, 173, 174
Grisebach, Valeska, ix, 98
Gruber, Kade, 52, 145
Grudge, The (Shimizu), 89
GSG-9 (police unit), 206
Guevara, Che, 197
Gunther, Anette, 52
Guthrie, Woody, 212

Halloween (Carpenter), 82, 247
Hamburger Bahnhof (museum), 246
Handke, Peter, 31
Hands of Orlac, The (Wiene), 200
Hans Scharoun—Eine imaginäre Architektur (Bitomsky), 7, 45, 201
Harris, Thomas, 176
Harron, Mary, 106
Hartz, Peter, 41
Hauff, Reinhard, 179
Hauser, Heinrich, 205
Hawks, Howard, 193, 249
Hayden, Sterling, 72, 101, 223
Heaven (Tykwer), 37
Hebel, Johann Peter, 174
Hegel, G. W. F., 207, 221, 234, 246
Heimat (home), 127, 196, 223, 224, 253
Heimatfilme (genre), 164, 212, 213, 254
Heimatministerium (homeland ministry), 227, 227n5
Hein, Christoph, 214
Heine, Heinrich, 246
Hellman, Monte, 50
Hermann, Constanze (TV character), 229, 230

Herrenbrück, Heino, 52
Herzog, Eddi, 3
Herzog, Roman, 79
Hessischer Rundfunk (broadcasting corporation), 175
Heuschreckendebatte (locust debate), 104n4
High Fidelity (Hornby), 163
Highsmith, Patricia, 47
Hill, Walter, 41, 50, 142
History Lessons (Straub and Huillet), 14
Hitchcock, Alfred, x, xi, 8, 18, 26, 28, 38, 44, 71, 73, 76, 79, 82, 95, 100, 153, 154, 158, 165, 198, 200, 202, 206, 219, 233, 236, 237, 239, 242, 249
Hitler, Adolf, xiii, 4, 21, 136, 244
Hobrecht, James, 246
Hochhäusler, Christoph, vi, ix, xiv, 46, 47, 48, 49, 50, 51, 52, 53, 54, 78, 81, 121, 123, 177, 186, 195, 213, 246
Hoeneß, Uli, 163
Hoffmann, E. T. A., 89, 94
Hohberger, Harald, 198
Holocaust, xii, 158, 164, 215
Homer, 79
Honecker, Erich, 88
Hopper, Dennis, 17, 190
Hopper, Edward, 82, 83, 85
Hornby, Nick, 163
Hörzu (magazine), 228
Hoss, Nina, xi, 35, 37, 38, 40, 41, 43, 44, 72, 87, 91, 92, 93, 94, 95, 97, 101, 102, 112, 113, 117, 118, 137, 141, 145, 155, 159, 191, 211, 212, 214, 215, 236, 238, 244, 249, 250
Hoss, Willi, 198
Hot Summer (Hasler), 139
Hoyerswerda, Germany, 225
Huillet, Danièle, ix, 14
Humboldt Forum (museum), 242, 246
Hummer, Julia, xii, 17, 37, 56, 58, 62, 63, 65, 70, 86, 210

Husbands (Cassavetes), 5
Hüsch, Hanns Dieter, 35, 194, 194n4, 198
Huston, John, 101, 171, 223

I Stayed in Berlin All Summer (Schanelec), 178
Ich arbeite alles ab . . . Ehrenwort (Petzold), 199
In Search of Lost Time (Proust), 216, 238
In the Mood for Love (Kar-Wai), 18
Indian Tomb, The (May), 63
Insider, The (Mann), 18

Jackie Brown (Tarantino), 143
James, Jesse, 90
James Bond (film series), 242
Jara, Víctor, 197
Jauch, Günter, 217
Jaws (Spielberg), 93
Jennings, Waylon, 7
Jerichow (Petzold), xi, 107, 109, 112, 114, 115, 117, 118, 131, 132, 137, 140, 142, 156, 184, 191, 212, 213, 214, 233, 235, 244, 253, 254
Johnson, Dennis, 47
Johnson, Uwe, 76
Jones, Quincy, 237
Jung, Franz, 21, 95, 205, 207, 212
Jürgens, Udo, 7
Ju-On (Shimizu), 89

Kamera und Wirklichkeit, Rumänien 1989 (Farocki), 201
Karmakar, Romuald, 18, 27
Käutner, Helmut, x, 38, 164
Kings of the Road (Wenders), 23, 205
Kino, Flächen, Bunker (Bitomsky), 201
Kino und der Wind und die Photografie, Das (Bitomsky), 173, 201
Kinski, Nastassja, 4
Kirch, Leo, 102, 116
Kirchmöser, Germany, 154

Klein, Naomi, 91
"kleine Fernsehspiel, Das" (TV film series), xv, 200, 200n3
Kleist, Heinrich von, 37, 130
Klier, Michael, 175
Kluge, Alexander, 17, 18, 19, 25, 29, 177, 200n3, 218
Koebner, Thomas, 179
Koenen, Gerd, 207
Kohl, Helmut, 25, 135, 178, 206
Köhler, Horst, 79
Köhler, Ulrich, ix, 54, 123, 179
Kolportage (pulp novel), 159, 184, 215
Königs Wusterhausen, Germany, 166
Körner von Gustorf, Florian, 34, 106
Kosslick, Dieter, 55, 226
Kraan (band), 198
Kracauer, Siegfried, 62
Kraftwerk (band), 35
Kristofferson, Kris, 7
Kubrick, Stanley, 95
Kurfürstendamm (Berlin avenue), 134, 215

Lang, Fritz, 32, 73, 88, 122, 208, 232
Last Picture Show, The (Bogdanovich), 132, 133
Le Carré, John, 217
Lemke, Klaus, 10, 59, 164
Lemmon, Jack, 64
Levi, Primo, 216, 238
Liane, Jungle Goddess (von Borsody), 128
Lincoln Center, 249
Lindenstraße (TV series), 224
Link, Caroline, 124
Lives of Others, The (von Donnersmarck), xiii, 153
Loden, Barbara, 66, 95
Löhr, Bernd, 176
Long Goodbye, The (Altman), 134, 139, 233

INDEX 261

Longing (Grisebach), 98
Lorre, Peter, 158
Lost One, The (Lorre), 158
Love Streams (Cassavetes), 173, 192
Lower Saxony, 197
Luchterhand Literaturverlag (publisher), 235
Lumet, Sidney, xi, 12
Lysistrata (Greek character), 240

MacLaine, Shirley, 64
Macron, Emmanuel, 244
Madigan (Siegel), 217
Malle, Louis, 236
Malteser Hilfsdienst (relief agency), 197
Manila (Karmakar), 118
Mann, Thomas, 76
Manta—Der Film (Timm), 9
Manz, Linda, 17
Map of the Heart, A (Graf), 42
Marker, Chris, 237
Märkisches Museum, 246
Märklin model railways, 5, 104, 104n3, 187
Marlowe, Philip, 134, 233, 234
Marmorhaus (cinema), 215
Marnie (Hitchcock), xi, 95
Marseille, France, 162, 221, 222, 223, 225, 236, 237, 249
Marx, Karl, 31, 87, 132, 197, 207
Material (Heise), 152, 153
Mauvais Sang (Carax), 177
McFit (fitness studio chain), 212, 212n8
Mecklenburg-Vorpommern (German state), 144, 154, 245
Medea (Greek character), 240
Meinhoff, Ulrike, 68
Meißen, Germany, 155
Melville, Herman, 197
Melville, Jean-Pierre, 5, 97
Mengele, Josef, 238

Mercedes, 43, 107, 115, 181, 212, 233
Merkel, Angela, xiii, 156
Meshes of the Afternoon (Deren), 239
Metz, Christian, 76
Mexico, 140, 235
Mey, Reinhard, 163
Michael, Marion, 128
Miller, Claude, 234
Minnelli, Liza, 63
Minnelli, Vincente, 39
Mitchum, Robert, 249
Modern Times (Chaplin), 90, 91
Moers, Germany, 198
Mölln, Germany, 225
Montand, Yves, 230
Monteilhet, Hubert, 158
Morandi, Giorgio, 52
Morris, Errol, 237, 239
Morrison, Van, 94, 102
Moseley, Hoke, 5
Mouchette (Bresson), 60
Mozambique, 238
Mozart, Wolfgang Amadeus, 94, 97, 212
MuCem (museum), 221
Mücke, Andreas, 52, 62
Müggelsee (Berlin lake), 211
Mühe, Ulrich, 154
Mühsam, Erich, 207
Müller, Heiner, xiii, 100
Müller, Richy, 13, 16, 207
Müntefering, Franz, 104
Murnau, F. W., x, 56, 64, 73, 89
Mutter (band), 34, 106
My Darling Clementine (Ford), 67, 133
My Life and My Films (Renoir), 211
My Sister's Good Fortune (Schanelec), 178

Nachträglichkeit (belatedness), 131
Native Americans, 225
Nau, Peter, 53, 81

Nazis, xii, 41, 43, 44, 89, 132, 136, 141, 216, 220, 221, 225, 235, 236
Near Dark (Bigelow), xi, 12, 136, 206
Nelson, Willie, 7
neorealism, 73, 123, 245
Nestler, Peter, 131, 152, 174, 201
Netflix, 226
Netzer, Günter, 163, 218
Neuenfels, Benedikt, 177
Neues Off (cinema), 167
Neukölln (Berlin district), 167
Neuss, Wolfgang, 159, 223
New German Cinema, 29, 54, 132, 134
New Hollywood, 51, 54, 129, 134, 139, 234, 236
New Wave, 26, 74, 99, 129, 132, 253. See also Nouvelle Vague
New York, 100, 102, 170, 209, 213, 254
Newman, Paul, 38, 154, 171
Newrzella, Michael, 206
Nichols, Mike, 236
Niederfinow boat lift, 174
Nietzsche, Friedrich, 197
Night and Fog (Resnais), 164
Night of the Hunter, The (Laughton), 249
Nikolaikirche (Beyer), 153
No Pawing, Darling (Spils), 10
No Place to Go (Roehler), 18
Nosferatu (Murnau), 56, 64, 89
Nothing Ventured (Farocki), 90, 94, 96, 137, 202
Nouvelle Vague, 10, 78, 123, 177, 245
Nouvelle Vague Allemande, 99
Novak, Kim, 38

On this Site (Sternfeld), 142
One Deadly Summer (Becker), 163
One Touch of Venus (Seiter), 160
O'Neal, Ryan, 50, 142
Oresteia (Aeschylus), 133
Ostermeier, Thomas, 238

Ostwärts (Petzold), 130–31, 166, 174–75, 201, 203
Out of the Blue (Hopper), 17
Ozu, Yazujiro, 82

Paris, France, 27, 36, 56, 59, 78, 88, 98
Paris, Texas (Wenders), 205
Pasolini, Pier Paolo, 76, 138
Pavese, Cesare, 57
Peitz, Christiane, 163, 164, 165, 166, 167, 168, 179, 223, 224, 225, 226, 227
People on Sunday (Wilder), 60
Perfume: The Story of a Murderer (Tykwer), 100
Pethke, Stefan, 28
Phaidra (Greek character), 240
Phantom (Murnau), 89
Phoenix (Petzold), xi, xiii, 158, 159, 160, 161, 162, 164, 183, 184, 185, 186, 215, 216, 217, 218, 221, 225, 233, 235, 238, 244, 245, 247, 250
Phoenix, River, 12
physicality, 36, 50, 67, 87, 113, 119, 134, 135, 136, 194, 211, 226, 242
Pilots (Petzold), 4, 5, 6, 8, 9, 10, 18, 78, 85, 130, 135, 140, 176, 200, 201, 203
Pippig, Sven, 37
Poland, 174, 233
Polizeiruf 110 (TV series), xv, 162, 181, 182, 185, 186, 188, 190, 217, 219, 221, 224, 228, 229
Pollack, Sydney, 44
Ponette (Doillon), 216
Postman Always Rings Twice, The (Cain), xi, 118, 132, 181, 212, 233, 235, 247
Potsdamer Platz (Berlin public square), 62, 63, 70, 71, 166, 167, 209, 210, 211, 227
Pretty Woman (Marshall), 117, 134, 135
Princess and the Warrior, The (Tykwer), 98

Prignitz (German district), 105, 108, 109, 119, 213
Proust, Marcel, 216, 238

Quelle (business and catalog), 156, 156n7, 157

Raab, Stefan, 45
RAF (Red Army Faction), 11, 13, 20, 22, 23, 25, 26, 30, 31, 47, 52, 58, 68, 78, 135, 163, 205, 206, 207
Ralske, Jan, 74, 170
Ray, Nicholas, 74, 78, 139
Recklinghausen, Germany, 198
Recoing, Aurélien, 63
Red Cockatoo, The (Graf), 156
Red Sun (Thome), 9, 23, 125
Redford, Robert, 44
Reichsautobahn (Bitomsky), 7
Renoir, Jean, 91, 94, 183, 194, 211, 236
Rentschler, Eric, 76
Resnais, Alain, 164
Return from the Ashes (Monteilheit), 158, 159, 214, 215
Returning to Reims (play), 238
reunification of Germany, x, xiii, xv, 78, 85, 88, 89, 95, 131, 206, 242, 247. *See also* unification of Germany
Rhine (river), 6, 12, 205
Richter, Gerhard, xi, 24, 83
Ring, The (Verbinski), 90
River (TV show), 231
Rivette, Jacques, 52
Robbe-Grillet, Alain, 57
Robinson, Edward G., 229
Robinson Crusoe (Defoe), 113, 118, 235
Rocker (Lemke), 10, 164
Roeg, Nicholas, 77
Roehler, Oskar, 18, 54
Röggla, Kathrin, 202
Rogowski, Franz, xii, 225, 226, 238, 241, 242, 245

Rohmer, Eric, 59
Romanticism, German, 89, 94, 104, 106, 141, 205, 206
Rome Open City (Rossellini), 216
Romero, George, 83, 235
Rommel, Erwin (General), 152
Rosetta (Dardenne brothers), 55, 114
Rossellini, Roberto, 29, 32, 178, 179, 206, 216, 243, 245
rote Jahrzehnt, Das (Koenen), 207
Rotkäppchensekt (sparkling wine), 152
Rourke, Mickey, 30, 172
Ruhr (German district), 108, 127
Ruhr Festival, 198
Rumble Fish (Coppola), 30, 172
Running on Empty (Lumet), xi, 12

Safdie brothers, 251
Saxony, 18, 127, 152, 196
Scarface (De Palma), 103
Scelsi, Raffaele, 197
Schanelec, Angela, ix, 19, 28, 178
Scharmützelsee (Brandenburg lake), 214
Schatzkästlein des rheinischen Hausfreundes (Hebel), 174
Schlecker (drugstore chain), 148
Schlichter, Mark, 177
Schlingensief, Christoph, 179
Schlöndorff, Volker, 11, 25, 76, 143, 205
Schmid, Hans-Christian, 54
Schmidt, Harald, 63
Schmidt, Helmut, 26
Schmidt, Wolfgang, 177
Schneider, Helge, 45
Schneider, Romy, 211
Schneider, Utz Jürgen, 11, 11n1
Schönemann, Hinnerk, 91, 103, 105, 106, 108, 212
Schultz, Thomas, 178
Schwebezustand (abeyance), xii, 48, 133
Scorsese, Martin, 100

264 INDEX

SED (Sozialistische Einheitspartei Deutschlands), 151, 151n1
Seeßlen, Georg, 92
Seghers, Anna, 162, 168, 196, 197, 221, 223, 232, 234, 235
Serreault, Michel, 234
Seventh Cross, The (Zinnemann), 235
Sex Thief, The (Petzold), 17, 18, 51, 79, 83, 85, 86, 135, 141, 203, 204, 206
Shrader, Paul, 204
Siegel, Don, 51, 217, 237
Silence of the Lambs, The (Demme), 176
Simenon, Georges, 17, 56, 80, 130, 140, 196, 205, 229
Siodmak, Robert, 208
Sirk, Douglas, 25, 79, 139, 161, 208
68-ers, xiii
Smiley, George, 217
Smith, Mark E., 100
smoking, 161, 230, 246
Something to Remind Me (Petzold), 27, 32, 34, 35, 36, 37, 38, 40, 42, 45, 48, 79, 85, 88, 91, 93, 108, 136, 137, 208, 209, 214, 240
Sommer, Elke, 4
Sophie Scholl—The Final Days (Rothemund), 68
Sözer, Hilmi, 112, 118
"Speak Low" (song), 160
Spellbound (Hitchcock), 239
Spielberg, Steven, 199
Spils, May, 10
Spirited Away (Miyazaki), 167
SS (Nazi organization), 165, 184, 225
Stalker (Tarkovsky), 201
Stammheim (prison), 13, 13n2, 24, 25, 52
State I Am In, The (Petzold), xi, 11, 13, 14, 15, 16, 18, 19, 20, 21, 22, 23, 24, 25, 30, 31, 32, 34, 35, 37, 45, 47, 58, 64, 68, 78, 79
Stewart, James, 36, 38
Straub, Jean-Marie, ix, 14, 32, 75, 204
Striesow, Devid, xv, 91, 94, 103

Stromboli (Rossellini), 206
Stuttgart, Germany, 13, 36, 39, 214
Süden (Petzold), 74, 130, 199
Sudetenland, 90, 152, 196, 197, 225
Suhrkamp (publisher), 197, 197n2
Sun Alley (Haußmann), 214

Tabu (Murnau), 73
Tagesschau (TV program), 26, 175, 229
Tago Mago (CAN LP), 205
Talking Heads (band), 26, 74, 129
Tatort (TV series), xv, 35, 35n3, 36, 142, 185, 221, 228, 230
Taut, Bruno, 246
teamWorx (production company), 36, 156
Téchiné, André, 177, 178
Teorema (Pasolini), 138
Thieves (Téchiné), 177, 178
39 Steps (Hitchcock), xi, 18, 198
Thomas, Ross, 71
Thome, Rudolf, 9, 10, 14, 23, 125
Thompson, Jim, 223
Three Billboards Outside Ebbing, Missouri (McDonagh), 224
Three Days of the Condor (Pollack), 44
Thunderbolt and Lightfoot (Cimino), 9
Tiergarten (Berlin park), 56, 62, 63, 84, 162, 209, 210
Time Out (Cantet), 63
Timoteo, Sabine, 66, 70
To Live and Die in L.A. (Friedkin), 28, 171, 172
Torn Curtain (Hitchcock), xi, 38, 154
Tracy, Spencer, 235
Transit (Petzold), xi, xii, xiii, 35, 162, 168, 196, 197, 214, 221, 223, 224, 225, 232, 233, 234, 235, 236, 237, 238, 241, 245, 247, 248
Transit (Seghers), 162, 168, 196, 197, 214, 221, 223, 224, 226, 232, 234, 235, 247

transit spaces (*Transitorte*), 78, 80, 81, 87, 127, 131, 136, 141, 142
Treuhand (agency), 93, 174
Trouble Every Day (Denis), 63
Truffaut, François, 28, 32, 59, 65, 70, 71, 73, 74, 82, 83, 99, 116, 139, 178, 183, 194, 198, 206, 219
Turn Down the Music (Arslan), 9
20,000 Leagues Under the Sea (Fleischer), 242
Twin Peaks (Lynch), 213
2001 (Kubrick), 242
Two-Lane Blacktop (Hellman), 50, 108, 141
Tykwer, Tom, 27, 37, 73, 98, 99, 100, 199

Uncut Gems (Safdie brothers), 251
UFA, Die (Bitomsky), 7, 63, 75, 173, 201, 216
Und tschüss! (TV series), 50
Under the Bridges (Käutner), 38, 98, 164
Undine (Petzold), 240, 241, 242, 244, 245, 246, 247, 248, 249, 250
Undine geht (Bachmann), 241, 245
unification of Germany, x, xiii, xv, 85, 88, 89, 95, 131, 247

Verne, Jules, 242
Vertigo (Hitchcock), xi, 28, 38, 44, 158, 167, 235
Vietnam, 134, 140, 201, 225, 250
Virilio, Paul, 140
Vitti, Monica, 211
Vogts, Hans-Hubert, 6, 6n3
Vohrer, Alfred, 170
Volksmusik (folk music), 120
von Dohnányi, Justus, 187, 188, 218
von Donop, Annedore, 200
von Hofmannsthal, Hugo, 89
von Meuffels, Hanns (TV character), 217, 218, 228, 229, 230

von Trier, Lars, 18, 43
von Stroheim, Erich, 84, 129
VW-Komplex, Der (Bitomsky), 45, 140

Waffen-SS (Nazi branch), 165
Walter, Conny, 177
Wanda (Loden), 60, 66, 95
Warm Money, The (Petzold), 7, 8, 10, 130, 177, 178, 200, 203
Wegert (photography processing lab), 176, 201
Weiber (Petzold), 3, 4, 74, 130, 199
Weill, Kurt, 160
Weindler, Helge, 125
Weingartner, Hans, 54
Weisgerber, Elenore, xii, 8, 9, 204
Wende (1989–90), 131, 152, 153, 154
Wenders, Wim, 20, 33, 74, 93, 99, 125, 163, 190, 205
Westermann, Antje, 41
Who's Afraid of Virginia Woolf? (Nichols), 236
Wiazemsky, Anne, 212
Wieben, Martin, 179
Wiene, Robert, 20
Wild Child, The (Truffaut), 70, 116
Wilder, Billy, 60, 64, 124, 245
Will, Anne, 153, 217, 220, 229
Willeford, Charles, 5, 6, 223
Winchester 73 (Mann), 36
Winterbottom, Michael, 55
Winters, Shelley, 249
Wiseman, Frederick, 237, 239
Wizard of Oz, The (Fleming), 101
"Wolf and the Seven Little Kids, The" (fairy tale), 220
Wolfsburg (Petzold), xv, 37, 40, 41, 42, 43, 44, 45, 46, 48, 49, 50, 52, 55, 58, 62, 71, 83, 88, 115, 136, 140, 182, 206, 208, 209, 211
Wolfsburg, Germany, 37, 41, 43, 44, 45, 49, 55, 140, 208

Wolves (Petzold), 185, 188, 189, 190, 192, 194, 217, 219, 220
Woman with the Red Boots, The (Buñuel), 15
work, theme of, 5, 7, 8, 18, 25, 29, 30, 42, 45, 50, 51, 53, 55, 58, 67, 69, 71, 77, 79, 87, 88, 90, 91, 95, 97, 101, 103, 104, 105, 109, 110, 113, 118, 119, 122, 131, 136, 137, 138, 142, 143, 144, 146, 147, 148, 149, 152, 155, 156, 166, 174, 175, 182, 188, 196, 198, 201, 202, 203, 204, 205, 208, 209, 210, 212, 214, 215, 216, 230, 236, 238, 242, 249
Workers Leaving the Factory (Farocki), 204, 204n4
Workers Leaving the Lumière Factory (Lumière brothers), 204n4
Worte des Vorsitzenden, Die (Farocki), 199
writers' room, 194, 231
Wrong Move, The (Wenders), 31

Wuppertal, Germany, 35, 73, 108, 115, 125, 164, 165, 198, 205
World War II, 6, 127, 150, 186, 225, 233, 235, 247

Yella (Petzold), xi, 85, 86, 87, 88, 89, 90, 91, 92, 93, 94, 95, 96, 97, 98, 101, 102, 106, 108, 112, 115, 118, 119, 131, 132, 135, 137, 142, 182, 202, 211, 212, 213, 216, 253
Yesterday Girl (Kluge), 177
Young Mr. Lincoln (Fonda), 232
Youth without Youth (Coppola), 213

Zaree, Maryam, 230
ZDF (broadcaster), xiv, xv, 7, 34, 40, 103, 200, 208
Zehrfeld, Ronald, 159, 194, 225, 250
Zischler, Hanns, 166
Zoo Palast (cinema), 167
Zwischen Gebäuden (Schultz), 178

About the Editors

Marco Abel is Willa Cather Professor of English and Film Studies at the University of Nebraska. The author of *The Counter-Cinema of the Berlin School*, he has published numerous essays on films by and interviews with filmmakers from this contemporary German film movement. Together with Jaimey Fisher, he has also coedited for *Senses of Cinema* a dossier on Petzold's work.

Aylin Bademsoy is a PhD candidate in the German Department at the University of California, Davis. Her dissertation project is a comparative study of genocide in literature and film, focusing on antisemitism and anti-Armenian ressentiments in early twentieth-century Turkish, Austrian, and German works, as well as their contemporary reverberations.

Jaimey Fisher, professor of German and cinema and digital media at University of California, Davis, is author of *The German Ways of War: The Affective Geographies and Generic Transformations of German Combat Films*, *Treme*, *Christian Petzold*, and *Disciplining German: Youth, Reeducation, and Reconstruction after the Second World War*. He has also been coeditor of, among others, *The Berlin School and Its Global Contexts: A Transnational Art Cinema* (with Marco Abel) and *Critical Theory: Current State and Future Prospects*.